Jumping Computation

Jumping Computation: Updating Automata and Grammars for Discontinuous Information Processing is primarily a theoretically oriented treatment of jumping automata and grammars, covering all essential theoretical topics concerning them, including their power, properties, and transformations. From a practical viewpoint, it describes various concepts, methods, algorithms, techniques, case studies and applications based upon these automata and grammars.

In today's computerized world, the scientific development and study of computation, referred to as the theory of computation, plays a crucial role. One important branch, language theory, investigates how to define and study languages and their models, which formalize algorithms according to which their computation is executed. These language-defining models are classified into two basic categories: automata, which define languages by recognizing their words, and grammars, which generate them. Introduced many decades ago, these rules reflect classical sequential computation. However, today's computational methods frequently process information in a fundamentally different way, frequently "jumping" over large portions of the information as a whole. This book adapts classical models to formalize and study this kind of computation properly. Simply put, during their language-defining process, these adapted versions, called jumping automata and grammars, jump across the words they work on.

The book selects important models and summarizes key results about them in a compact and uniform way. It relates each model to a particular form of modern computation, such as sequential, semi-parallel and totally parallel computation. It explains how the model in question properly reflects and formalizes the corresponding form of computation, thus allowing us to obtain a systematized body of mathematically precise knowledge concerning the jumping computation. The book pays special attention to power, closure properties, and transformations and also describes many algorithms that modify jumping grammars and automata so they satisfy some prescribed properties without changing the defined language. The book will be of great interest to anyone researching the theory of computation across the fields of computer science, mathematics, engineering, logic and linguistics.

Alexander Meduna is a theoretical computer scientist and expert on the theory of computation who was born in the Czech Republic. He is a full professor of Computer Science at the Brno University of Technology. Formerly, he taught theoretical computer science at various American, Asian and European universities, including the University of Missouri, where he spent a decade teaching advanced topics of formal language theory and Kyoto Sangyo University, where he spent several months teaching these topics, too. Concerning the subject of this book, he is the author of over 90 papers and several books, listed at: http://www.fit.vutbr.cz/~meduna/work.

Zbyněk Křivka is both a theoretically and pragmatically oriented computer scientist. Being a former PhD student of Alexander Meduna and, currently, his colleague at the Brno University of Technology, he has published several journal papers with strong focus on jumping models. His PhD thesis, which also deals with formal languages, has been published as a book.

Jumping Computation

Updating Automata and Grammars for Discontinuous Information Processing

Alexander Meduna and Zbyněk Křivka

CRC Press
Taylor & Francis Group
Boca Raton London New York

CRC Press is an imprint of the
Taylor & Francis Group, an **informa** business

Designed cover image: Shutterstock

First edition published 2024
by CRC Press
2385 NW Executive Center Drive, Suite 320, Boca Raton FL 33431

and by CRC Press
4 Park Square, Milton Park, Abingdon, Oxon, OX14 4RN

CRC Press is an imprint of Taylor & Francis Group, LLC

ISBN: 978-0-367-62093-6 (hbk)
ISBN: 978-0-367-63479-7 (pbk)
ISBN: 978-1-003-10791-0 (ebk)

DOI: 10.1201/9781003107910

Typeset in TeXGyreTermesX-Regular
by KnowledgeWorks Global Ltd.

Publisher's note: This book has been prepared from camera-ready copy provided by the authors.

To my students. AM
To Veronika. ZK

Contents

Part III Jumping Grammars

Part IV Conclusion

Preface

Living and working in today's enormously computerized world, most people use computers on a daily basis. Many of them make use of various artificial languages, such as high-level programming languages, in which they encode algorithms according to which computers process their data. In addition, apart from computation originated by humans in this way, many computer programs are created by machines, too. Indeed, the world is overflown with various clever machines, such as smart phones, which use their own languages in which they encode algorithms and, subsequently, perform computation based upon their users' requests. It thus comes as no surprise that the scientific study of computation, referred to as the *theory of computation*, fulfills a more important role today than ever before.

Writing computer programs in various languages gives rise to a constant struggle of proper formalization of languages in the theory of computation. Taking great advantage of mathematics as a systematized body of unshakable knowledge obtained by precise and infallible reasoning, this theory has developed *formal language theory* as one of its crucially important parts. Formal language theory investigates how to define and study languages in a rigorous and general way. From a mathematical viewpoint, this theory simply defines languages as sets of sequences of symbols. This straightforward definition is so general that it encompasses almost all languages as they are commonly understood. As a matter of fact, even natural languages are included in this definition. Of course, all artificial languages introduced within various scientific disciplines represent languages formalized in this way as well. Perhaps most obviously, this simple definition takes in all computer-related languages, ranging from machine codes through assembly languages up to high-level programming languages, such as all C-based languages.

The formalization of languages, most of which are infinite, necessitates the introduction of language-defining formal models. Traditionally, these *language models* are based upon finitely many rules by which they sequentially rewrite sequences of symbols, called words. They are classified into two basic categories—generating and accepting models. Generating models or, briefly, *grammars* define strings of their languages by generating them from special start symbols. On the other hand, accepting models or, briefly, *automata* define strings of their language by a rewriting process that starts from these strings and ends in a special set of strings, usually called final configurations.

Introduced many decades ago, original versions of automata and grammars reflect the classical way of computation, continuously working with a single piece of information from left to right according to algorithms designed for this purpose. Accordingly, the classical automata and grammars worked on words, which represented the information being processed, in a strictly left-to-right way as well. Modern methods, however, frequently process information in a fundamentally different way. For example, they process various parts of information frequently occurring far away from each other. As a result, the computational process based upon these methods constantly *jumps* over large portions of the information as a whole. As is obvious, classical automata and grammars inadequately and insufficiently formalize this modern way of computation, referred to as *jumping computation* throughout this book. To formalize and study it properly, the present book adapts these classical models so they work on words non-continuously just like the execution of jumping computation, which they formalize (Brandon Mull's well-known quote paraphrases a necessity of this update accurately: *when jumping is the sole option, you jump and try to make it work*). Simply put, during their language-defining process, these adapted versions, referred to as *jumping automata and grammars*, jump across the words they work on. During a single language-defining step, they modify a portion of the current word at a position, then jump over a portion of the word in either direction, and continue this process from there. Working in this way, they formalize and reflect today's jumping computation adequately and elegantly.

To give an insight into jumping automata, let us first recall the well-known notion of a classical finite automaton, M, which consists of an input tape, a read head, and a finite state control. The input tape is divided into squares. Each square contains one symbol of an input word. The symbol under the read head, a, is the current input symbol. The finite control is represented by a finite set of states together with a control relation, which is usually specified as a set of computational rules. M operates on words by making a sequence of moves. Each move is made according to a computational rule that describes how the current state is changed and whether the current input symbol is read. If the symbol is read, the read head is shifted precisely one square to the right. M has one state defined as the start state and some states designated as final states. Let a word w be written on the input tape. If M can perform a sequence of moves, made in the left-to-right way sketched above, so that starting from the start state, it reads the entire w on the tape and ends up in a final state, then M accepts w. In essence, a *jumping finite automaton* J works just like a classical finite automaton, except it does not read the input string from left to right. Instead, after reading a symbol, J jumps over a portion of the tape in either direction and continue making jumps from there. Once an occurrence of a symbol is read on the tape, it cannot be re-read again later during the computation of J. If J can perform a sequence of jumps so it begins from the start state, reads all the symbols of w on the tape, and enters a final state, then J accepts w.

To give an insight into jumping grammars, let us recall the notion of a classical *grammar* G, which represents a language-generating model based upon an alphabet of symbols and a finite set of rules. The alphabet of symbols is divided into two disjoint subalphabets—the alphabet of terminal symbols and the alphabet of nonterminal symbols. Each rule represents a pair of the form (x, y), where x and y are strings over the alphabet of G. Customarily, (x, y) is written as $x \rightarrow y$, where x and y are referred to as the left-hand side and the right-hand side of $x \rightarrow y$. Starting from a special start nonterminal symbol, G repeatedly rewrites strings according to its rules until it obtains a sentence—that is, a string that solely consists of terminal symbols; the set of all sentences represents the language generated by the grammar. In greater detail, G rewrites a string z according to $x \rightarrow y$ so it (1) selects an occurrence of x in z, (2) erases it, and (3) inserts y precisely at the position of this erasure. More formally, let $z = uxv$, where u and v are strings. By using $x \rightarrow y$, G rewrites uxv to uyv. The notion of a *jumping grammar* is conceptualized just like that of a classical grammar; however, it rewrites strings in a slightly different way. Consider G, described above, as a jumping grammar. Let z and $x \rightarrow y$ have the same meaning as above. When G rewrites a string z according to $x \rightarrow y$, it performs (1) and (2) as described above, but during (3), G can jump over a portion of the rewritten string in either direction and insert y there. More formally, by using $x \rightarrow y$, G rewrites ucv to udv, where u, v, w, c, d are strings such that either (i) $c = xw$ and $d = wy$ or (ii) $c = wx$ and $d = yw$. Otherwise, it coincides with the standard notion of a grammar.

To illustrate the essential difference between the classical and jumping versions of automata and grammars described above in a simple and straightforward manner, consider the infinite language L consisting of all binary strings containing the same number of 0s and 1s. Of course, L may fulfill a useful role in any scientific investigation that formalizes the subject of its study in binary. For instance, imagine a linguistic study that denotes any consonant and any vowel by 1 and 0, respectively, to schematize the words containing the same number of consonants and vowels by using L. In English, *subroutine* would be schematized to 1011001010, which is in L while *routine* would correspond to 1001010, which is out of L. Clearly, these schemes may be of some use when, for example, this study compares several languages in terms of the number of consonants and vowels occurring in their words. To take another scientific area, a social investigation might use L in terms of gender binary in such a way that 0 and 1 represent a male and a female, respectively. In this way, L actually represents all possible sequences of people with the same number of masculine and feminine persons, which might turn out as a topic under discussion during this investigation. Nevertheless, any scientific use of L necessitates its rigorous definition by a suitable automaton or grammar in the first place. Unfortunately, no classical finite automaton, which represents an utterly finitary model without any potentially infinite memory, accepts L. Indeed, reading strings in a strictly left-to-right way, no classical finite automaton can compare the number of 0s against the number of 1s, thus failing to accept L. On the other hand, a jumping finite automaton can accept L by repeatedly performing a two-jump computation during which it reads one occurrence of 0 and one occurrence of 1. If it eventually empties the input tape in this way, it accepts; otherwise, it rejects. Similarly, a jumping grammar can generate L by using only three rules—$S \rightarrow 0A$, $A \rightarrow 1S$, and $S \rightarrow \varepsilon$, where S and A are nonterminals, and ε denotes the empty string. Compare to this trivial jumping grammar, all the classical grammars for L are more complicated and clumsy as the reader can easily verify. Consequently, as just illustrated, under some circumstances, jumping versions of automata and grammars have important advantages over their classical counterparts, so their concepts and properties deserve a careful investigation.

Jumping automata and grammars, together referred to as *jumping language models*, represent the principal *subject* of the present book, whose main *focus* is on their concepts, properties and application-related perspectives in practice. The book selects crucially important models and summarizes key results about them in a compact and uniform way. It always relates each of the selected models to a particular way of modern computation, such as sequential and parallel computation. The text explains how the model in question properly reflects and formalizes the corresponding way of computation, thus allowing us to obtain a systematized body of mathematically precise knowledge concerning the jumping computation.

Concerning the properties of jumping automata and grammars, the book pays special attention to their power, closure properties, and transformations. Obviously, the power of these modern versions of language models represents perhaps the most important information about them, so the book always determines the family of languages that these versions define. The text also describes many algorithms that modify jumping grammars and automata so they satisfy some prescribed properties without changing the defined language. Algorithms of this kind fulfill an important role in practice because many language processors strictly require that the prescribed properties be satisfied. These properties also frequently simplify proofs demonstrating results about the models. Of course, the same languages can be defined by different models, and every computation-related investigation or application naturally selects the most appropriate models for them under given circumstances. Therefore, whenever discussing different types of equally powerful jumping language models, the book studies their mutual transformations, too. More specifically, given a language model of one type, the text carefully explains how to turn it to another model so both the original system and the model produced by this conversion define the same language.

Organization and Coverage

The text is divided into four parts, each of which consists of several chapters. Every part starts with an abstract that summarizes its chapters. Altogether, the book contains 10 chapters, each of which opens its discussion with a brief explanation of jumping computation in general while paying special attention to the subject of the chapter in question.

Part I, consisting of Chapters 1 and 2, reviews important mathematical concepts so that the entire text of the book is completely self-contained. Chapter 1 reviews rudimentary concepts from discrete mathematics. Chapter 2 introduces the fundamental notions of formal language theory. Part I can be only skimmed with respect to the notation and definitions used later in the book.

Part II, consisting of Chapters 3 and 4, gives the fundamentals of jumping automata. First, it gives an extensive and thorough coverage of jumping one-head finite automata (Chapter 3), after which it covers their multi-head versions (Chapter 4).

Part III consists of Chapters 5 through 7, and it covers jumping grammars as crucially important grammatical counterparts to jumping automata. Chapter 5 studies the jumping generation of language by classical grammars, which work in a strictly sequential way. Then, Chapter 6 discusses the same topic in terms of semi-parallel grammars. Finally, Chapter 7 explores the jumping generation of language by pure sequential and parallel grammars, which have only terminals.

Part IV, consisting of Chapters 8, 9, and 10, closes this book. First, Chapter 8 sketches how to formalize discontinuous computation by some alternative models, whose behavior differs from that based upon the jumping principle. Chapter 9 presents selected applications of jumping automata and grammars. Naturally, it concentrates its attention on the use in practice, but it also covers their applications in theoretical computer science. Finally, Chapter 10 sums up the entire text and makes many bibliographical notes for the serious reader.

As a whole, the entire text is intentionally written so that it allows the flexibility needed to study only some selected topics. Perhaps most importantly, each chapter of Parts II and III, which represent the heart of the book, always begins with a succinct explanation of jumping computation in general while paying particular attention to the subject of the chapter; as a result, the reader is freed from the necessity of studying other chapters of the book. To put it simply and plainly, the reader can read every chapter completely independently of the rest of the book.

As far as the writing style is concerned, the book introduces all formalisms with enough rigor to make all results quite clear and valid because this book primarily represents a theoretically oriented treatment. Before every complicated mathematical passage, the text explains its basic idea intuitively so that even the most complex parts of the book are relatively easy to grasp. If a parenthesized reference follows a statement heading, then the present book only sketches or even omits its proof, but the reference specifies where a fully rigorous version of the proof is to be found; for instance, a proof of Theorem 2.2 (Păun et al. [1998]) is omitted in this book, but Păun et al. [1998] proves this theorem rigorously.

From a practical standpoint, it is worth pointing out that the book proves most of the results in the chapters listed above effectively—that is, within proofs demonstrating them, it also gives algorithms that describe how to achieve these results. Perhaps most importantly, the book often presents conversions between equally powerful models as algorithms, whose correctness is then rigorously verified. In this way, apart from their theoretical value, the text actually explains how to implement and use them in practice. Several worked-out examples illustrate this use.

Figures

The text includes several figures, many of which diagram relationships between language families. In these diagrams, the following conventions are used. Let **X** and

Y be two language families. A double line between them means $\mathbf{X} = \mathbf{Y}$. A dash-dotted line between **X** and **Y** says that **X** and **Y** are incomparable—that is, $\mathbf{X} \not\subseteq \mathbf{Y}$, $\mathbf{Y} \not\subseteq \mathbf{X}$, and $\mathbf{Y} \cap \mathbf{X} \neq \emptyset$. If there is a solid arrow leading from **Y** to **X**, then $\mathbf{Y} \subset \mathbf{X}$, and if this arrow is dashed, then $\mathbf{Y} \subseteq \mathbf{X}$ with $\mathbf{Y} \subset \mathbf{X}$ representing an open problem. To illustrate these conventions, consider this figure

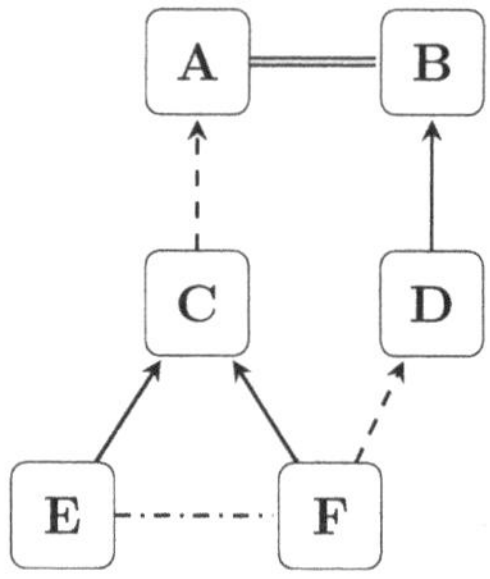

where **A**, **B**, **C**, **D**, **E**, and **F** are language families. The diagrammatic conventions given above imply that **E** and **F** are incomparable, $\mathbf{A} = \mathbf{B}$, $\mathbf{C} \subseteq \mathbf{A}$, $\mathbf{D} \subset \mathbf{B}$, $\mathbf{F} \subset \mathbf{C}$, $\mathbf{F} \subseteq \mathbf{D}$, $\mathbf{E} \subset \mathbf{C}$, which imply $\mathbf{D} \subset \mathbf{A}$, $\mathbf{E} \subset \mathbf{A}$, $\mathbf{E} \subset \mathbf{B}$, and $\mathbf{C} \subseteq \mathbf{B}$. By no means, however, these diagramatic family relationships are covered exhaustively in any way. For instance, in the figure above, the relationship between **D** and **E** is simply left out without claiming their comparability or incomparability.

Use

Primarily, from an utterly general standpoint, this book is helpful to everybody who takes advantage of modern computational technologies working in a jumping way to some extent. Perhaps most significantly, all scientists who make these technologies, ranging from pure mathematicians through computational linguists up to computer engineers, might find jumping automata and grammars, covered in this book, useful for their work.

The text allows the flexibility needed to study only some selected topics independently of the rest of the entire text. More precisely, Part I should be always skimmed with respect to the notation and definitions used later in the book; but apart from this, every other chapter can be read utterly independently of the other chapters.

Secondarily, the entire book can be used as a text for a one-term course about jumping grammars and automata at an upper-level graduate or introductory post-graduate level. As already pointed out, the text allows the flexibility needed to make a shorter course, which concentrates in depth on some selected topics. A sample schedule of a course like this might be one of the following:

- The essentials of jumping computational models: Chapters 1, 2, 3, 5, 8, and 9.
- Jumping automata: Chapters 1, 2, 3, 4, 8, and automaton-related applications in Chapter 9.
- Jumping grammars: Chapters 1, 2, 5, 6, 7, 8, and grammar-related applications in Chapter 9.

Nevertheless, in the authors' opinion, a full one-term graduate-level course covering the book in its entirety is the most appropriate way of using it as a textbook.

Finally, at any educational level, the serious student may find this book helpful as an accompanying text for any discussion related to formal languages and their models.

Support

For the sake of brevity, the text makes use of many mathematical symbols, including the symbolic denotation of several language families. Therefore, the end matter of this book contains some supporting material that should help the reader with a quick orientation in the text. This material includes the index to key language families and the subject index.

For the support on the Web, visit

`http://www.fit.vutbr.cz/~meduna/books/jc/`

Here, one will find further backup materials related to this book, such as suggestions for further reading as well as errata as we learn of them. We will also frequently update this website with information about new publications related to jumping computation and its models.

Acknowledgments

We wish to acknowledge our indebtedness to several people for their assistance in various aspects of this book. The text is partially based upon the dissertations by Radim Kocman and Jiří Kučera, Alexander Meduna's former PhD students, who provided them to us. Martin Tomko made a significant portion of Chapter 8 for us, and he brought our attention to a number of studies related to that chapter. The painful task of creating the figures, tables, and indices was largely performed in an excellent fashion by Dominik Nejedlý. Many more students, friends, and colleagues—too many to name them all—have contributed a good deal to the production of this book, both by setting us thinking about questions concerning its subject and by helping us to see the answers. We are also grateful to Acquiring Editor, Elliott Morsia and Editorial Assistant, Talitha Duncan-Todd at CRC Press for their encouragement and patience when we failed to meet deadline after deadline. To all of the above, we render our thanks.

In addition, this work was supported by two grants—namely, Brno University of Technology grants FIT-S-20-6293 and FIT-S-23-8209.

Brno, Czech Republic
June 2023

Alexander Meduna
Zbyněk Křivka

Part I
Introduction

In this two-chapter introductory part, we first review the mathematical notions, concepts, and techniques used throughout this textbook in order to express all the upcoming material clearly and precisely. Then, we introduce formal languages and rewriting systems that define them. We distinguish two principal approaches to this definition—the language generation and the language acceptation.

To make this book self-contained, Chapter 1 reviews the principal ideas and notions underlying some mathematical areas needed to follow the rest of this book. These areas include logic, set theory, discrete mathematics, and graph theory. Chapter 2 outlines the theory of formal languages and their models. That is, it introduces rewriting systems and demonstrates how to use them as language-defining models. It categorizes these models into two essential classes—automata, which accept languages, and grammars, which generate them. Apart from the classical well-known versions of these models, such as finite automata and context-free grammars, the chapter also covers less-known language models, such as Watson–Crick finite automata and state grammars, which are used later in the text as well.

Chapter 1
Mathematical Background

This chapter reviews rudimentary concepts from logic (Section 1.1), set theory (Section 1.2), discrete mathematics (Section 1.3), and graph theory (Section 1.4). For readers familiar with these concepts, this chapter can be treated as a reference for notation and definitions.

1.1 Logic

Next, we review the basics of elementary logic. We pay special attention to the fundamental proof techniques used in this book.

In general, a *formal mathematical system* S consists of basic *symbols*, *formation rules*, *axioms*, and *inference rules*. Basic symbols, such as constants and operators, form components of *statements*, which are composed according to formation rules. Axioms are primitive statements, whose validity is accepted without justification. By inference rules, some statements infer other statements. A *proof* of a statement s in S consists of a sequence of statements $s_1, \ldots, s_i, \ldots, s_n$ such that $s = s_n$, and each s_i is either an axiom of S or a statement inferred by some of the statements $s_1, \ldots, s_{i-1}$ according to the inference rules; s proved in this way represents a *theorem* of S.

Logical connectives join statements to create more complicated statements. The most common logical connectives are *not*, *and*, *or*, *implies*, and *if and only if*. In this list, *not* is unary while the other connectives are binary. That is, if s is a statement, then *not* s is a statement as well. Similarly, if s_1 and s_2 are statements, then s_1 *and* s_2, s_1 *or* s_2, s_1 *implies* s_2, and s_1 *if and only if* s_2 are statements, too. We often write $\neg$, $\wedge$, and $\vee$ instead of *not*, *and*, and *or*, respectively. In Figure 1.1, the *truth table* presents the rules governing the *truth* or *falsity* concerning statements connected by the binary connectives. Regarding the unary connective $\neg$, if s is true, then $\neg s$ is false, and if s is false, then $\neg s$ is true.

Convention 1.1 Throughout this book, truth and falsity are denoted by **1** and **0**, respectively.

s_1	s_2	$s_1 \wedge s_2$	$s_1 \vee s_2$	s_1 *implies* s_2	s_1 *if and only if* s_2
0	**0**	**0**	**0**	**1**	**1**
0	**1**	**0**	**1**	**1**	**0**
1	**0**	**0**	**1**	**0**	**0**
1	**1**	**1**	**1**	**1**	**1**

Fig. 1.1 Truth table.

By this table, s_1 *and* s_2 is true if both statements are true; otherwise, s_1 *and* s_2 is false. Analogically, we can interpret the other rules governing the truth or falsity of a statement containing the other connectives from this table. A statement of equivalence, which has the form s_1 *if and only if* s_2, sometimes abbreviated to s_1 *iff* s_2, plays a crucial role in this book. A proof that such a statement is true usually consists of two parts. The *only-if part* demonstrates that s_1 *implies* s_2 is true, while the *if part* proves that s_2 *implies* s_1 is true.

Example 1.1 There exists a useful way of representing ordinary *infix arithmetic expressions* without using parentheses. This notation is referred to as *Polish notation*, which has two fundamental forms—*postfix* and *prefix notation*. The former is defined recursively as follows.

Let Ω be a set of binary operators, and let Σ be a set of operands.

(1) Every $a \in \Sigma$ is a postfix representation of a.
(2) Let AoB be an infix expression, where $o \in \Omega$, and A, B are infix expressions. Then, CDo is the postfix representation of AoB, where C and D are the postfix representations of A and B, respectively.
(3) Let C be the postfix representation of an infix expression A. Then, C is the postfix representation of (A).

Consider the infix logical expression $(\mathbf{1} \vee \mathbf{0}) \wedge \mathbf{0}$. The postfix expressions for $\mathbf{1}$ and $\mathbf{0}$ are $\mathbf{1}$ and $\mathbf{0}$, respectively. The postfix expression for $\mathbf{1} \vee \mathbf{0}$ is $\mathbf{10}\vee$, so the postfix expression for $(\mathbf{1} \vee \mathbf{0})$ is $\mathbf{10}\vee$, too. Thus the postfix expression for $(\mathbf{1} \vee \mathbf{0}) \wedge \mathbf{0}$ is $\mathbf{10} \vee \mathbf{0}\wedge$.

Prefix notation is defined analogically except that in the second part of the definition, o is placed in front of AB; the details are left as an exercise.

There exist many logic laws useful to demonstrate that an implication is true. Specifically, the *contrapositive law* says $(s_1$ *implies* $s_2)$ *if and only if* $((\neg s_2)$ *implies* $(\neg s_1))$, so we can prove s_1 *implies* s_2 by demonstrating that $(\neg s_2)$ *implies* $(\neg s_1)$ holds true. We also often use a *proof by contradiction* based upon the law saying $((\neg s_2) \wedge s_1)$ *implies* $\mathbf{0}$ is true. Less formally, if from the assumption that s_2 is false and s_1 is true we obtain a false statement, s_1 *implies* s_2 is true. A *proof by induction* demonstrates that a statement s_i is true for all integers $i \geq b$, where b is a non-negative integer. In general, a proof of this kind is made in this way:

Basis. Prove that s_b is true.

Induction Hypothesis. Suppose that there exists an integer n such that $n \geq b$ and s_m is true for all $b \leq m \leq n$.

Induction Step. Prove that s_{n+1} is true under the assumption that the inductive hypothesis holds.

A proof by contradiction and a proof by induction are illustrated in the beginning of the next section (see Example 1.2).

1.2 Sets and Languages

This section reviews basic concepts of set theory. Most importantly, it defines languages as sets whose elements are finite sequences of symbols. Many language operations are covered, too.

In what follows, we suppose that there are certain *elements* taken from some pre-specified *universe*. A *set* Σ is a collection of elements taken from this universe. To express that an element a is a *member* of Σ, we write $a \in \Sigma$. On the other hand, if a is not in Σ, we write $a \notin \Sigma$. We automatically assume that these utterly rudimental notions exist, but they are left undefined, so they are considered as *naive notions* of set theory.

If Σ has a finite number of members, then Σ is a *finite set*; otherwise, Σ is an *infinite set*. The finite set that has no member is the *empty set*, denoted by $\emptyset$. The *cardinality* of a finite set, Σ, denoted by $\text{card}(\Sigma)$, is the number of Σ's members; note that $\text{card}(\emptyset) = 0$.

Convention 1.2 Throughout this book, $\mathbb{N}$ denotes the set of *natural numbers*—that is, $\mathbb{N} = \{1, 2, \ldots\}$, and ${}_0\mathbb{N} = \{0\} \cup \mathbb{N}$.

Example 1.2 The purpose of this example is two-fold. First, we give examples of sets. Second, as pointed out in the conclusion of the previous section, we illustrate how to make proofs by contradiction and by induction.

Let P be the set of all primes (a natural number n, $n \geq 2$, is prime if its only positive divisors are 1 and n).

A proof by contradiction. By contradiction, we next prove that P is infinite. That is, for the sake of contradiction, assume that P is finite. Set $k = \text{card}(P)$. Thus, P contains k numbers, $p_1, p_2, \ldots, p_k$. Set $n = p_1 p_2 \cdots p_k + 1$. Observe that n is not divisible by any p_i, $1 \leq i \leq k$. As a result, either n is a new prime or n equals a product of new primes. In either case, there exists a prime out of P, which contradicts the assumption that P contains all primes. Thus, P is infinite. Another proof by contradiction is given in Example 1.5.

A proof by induction. As already stated, by induction, we prove that a statement s_i holds for all $i \geq b$, where $b \in \mathbb{N}$. To illustrate, consider $i^2 \mid i \in \mathbb{N}$, and let s_i state

$$1 + 3 + 5 + \cdots + 2i - 1 = i^2$$

for all $i \in \mathbb{N}$; in other words, s_i says that the sum of the first i odd integers is a perfect square. An inductive proof of this statement follows next.

Basis. As $1 = 1^2$, s_1 is true.

Induction Hypothesis. Assume that s_m is true for all $1 \leq m \leq n$, where n is a natural number.

Induction Step. Consider $s_{n+1} = 1 + 3 + 5 + ... + (2n - 1) + (2(n + 1) - 1) = (n + 1)^2$. By the inductive hypothesis, $s_n = 1 + 3 + 5 + ... + (2n - 1) = n^2$. Hence, $1 + 3 + 5 + ... + (2n - 1) + (2(n + 1) - 1) = n^2 + 2n + 1 = (n + 1)^2$. Consequently, s_{n+1} holds, and the inductive proof is completed.

A finite set, Σ, is customarily specified by listing its members; that is, $\Sigma = \{a_1, a_2, \ldots, a_n\}$ where a_1 through a_n are all members of Σ; as a special case, we have $\{\} = \emptyset$. An infinite set, Ω, is usually specified by a property, p, so that Ω contains all elements satisfying p; in symbols, this specification has the general format $\Omega = \{a \mid p(a)\}$. Sets whose members are other sets are usually called families of sets rather than sets of sets.

Let Σ and Ω be two sets. Σ is a *subset* of Ω, symbolically written as $\Sigma \subseteq \Omega$, if each member of Σ also belongs to Ω. Σ is a *proper subset* of Ω, written as $\Sigma \subset \Omega$, if $\Sigma \subseteq \Omega$ and Ω contains an element that is not in Σ. To express that A is not included in B, write $A \nsubseteq B$. If $\Sigma \subseteq \Omega$ and $\Omega \subseteq \Sigma$, Σ *equals* Ω, denoted by $\Sigma = \Omega$. The *power set* of Σ, denoted by power(Σ), is the set of all subsets of Σ.

For two sets, Σ and Ω, their *union*, *intersection*, and *difference* are denoted by $\Sigma \cup \Omega$, $\Sigma \cap \Omega$, and $\Sigma - \Omega$, respectively, and defined as $\Sigma \cup \Omega = \{a \mid a \in \Sigma \text{ or } a \in \Omega\}$, $\Sigma \cap \Omega = \{a \mid a \in \Sigma \text{ and } a \in \Omega\}$, and $\Sigma - \Omega = \{a \mid a \in \Sigma \text{ and } a \notin \Omega\}$. If Σ is a set over a universe U, the *complement* of Σ is denoted by $\sim\Sigma$ and defined as $\sim\Sigma = U - \Sigma$. The operations of union, intersection, and complement are related by *De Morgan's laws* stating that $\sim(\sim\Sigma \cup \sim\Omega) = \Sigma \cap \Omega$ and $\sim(\sim\Sigma \cap \sim\Omega) = \Sigma \cup \Omega$, for any two sets Σ and Ω. If $\Sigma \cap \Omega = \emptyset$, Σ and Ω are *disjoint*. More generally, n sets $\Sigma_1, \Sigma_2, \ldots, \Sigma_n$, where $n \geq 2$, are *pairwise disjoint* if $\Sigma_i \cap \Sigma_j = \emptyset$ for all $1 \leq i, j \leq n$ such that $i \neq j$.

A *sequence* is a list of elements from some universe. A sequence is *finite* if it consists of finitely many elements; otherwise, it is *infinite*. The *length* of a finite sequence x, denoted by $|x|$, is the number of elements in x. The *empty sequence*, denoted by ε, is the sequence consisting of no element; that is, $|\varepsilon| = 0$. For brevity, finite sequences are specified by listing their elements throughout. For instance, $(0, 1, 0, 0)$ is shortened to 0100; notice that $|0100| = 4$.

Languages

Just like set theory has its naive notions, so does formal language theory. Indeed, it automatically assumes that there exists a pre-specified infinite set, referred to as a *universal alphabet*, whose members are called *symbols*. An *alphabet* Σ is any finite nonempty subset of this universal alphabet. Any nonempty subset of Σ

is a *subalphabet* of Σ. A finite sequence of symbols from Σ is a *string* over Σ; specifically, ε is referred to as the *empty string*—that is, the string consisting of zero symbols. By Σ^*, we denote the set of all strings over Σ; $\Sigma^+ = \Sigma^* - \{\varepsilon\}$. Let $x \in \Sigma^*$. Like for any sequence, $|x|$ denotes the length of x—that is, the number of symbols in x. For any $a \in \Sigma$, $\text{occur}(x, a)$ denotes the number of occurrences of as in x, so $\text{occur}(x, a)$ always satisfies $0 \leq \text{occur}(x, a) \leq |x|$. Let $A \subseteq \Sigma$, set $\text{occur}(x, A) = \sum_{a \in A} \text{occur}(x, a)$. Furthermore, if $x \neq \varepsilon$, $\text{symbol}(x, i)$ denotes the ith symbol in x, where $1 \leq i \leq |x|$. Any subset $L \subseteq \Sigma^*$ is a *formal language* or, briefly, a *language* over Σ. Set $\text{symbol}(L, i) = \{a | a = \text{symbol}(x, i), x \in L - \{\varepsilon\}, 1 \leq i \leq |x|\}$. Any subset of L is a *sublanguage* of L. If L represents a finite set of strings, L is a *finite language*; otherwise, L is an *infinite language*. For instance, Σ^*, which is called the *universal language* over Σ, is an infinite language while $\emptyset$ and $\{\varepsilon\}$ are finite; noteworthy, $\emptyset \neq \{\varepsilon\}$ as $\text{card}(\emptyset) = 0 \neq \text{card}(\{\varepsilon\}) = 1$. Sets whose members are languages are called *families of languages*.

Example 1.3 The English alphabet, consisting of its 26 letters, illustrates the definition of an alphabet as stated above except that we refer to its members as symbols in this book. Our definition of a language includes all common artificial and natural languages. For instance, programming languages represent formal languages in terms of this definition, and so do English, Navaho, and Japanese. Any family of natural languages—including Indo-European, Sino-Tibetan, Niger-Congo, Afro-Asiatic, and Japonic families of languages—is a language family according to the definition above.

Convention 1.3 In strings, for brevity, we simply juxtapose the symbols and omit the parentheses and all separating commas. That is, we write $a_1 a_2 \cdots a_n$ instead of $(a_1, a_2, \ldots, a_n)$.

Let **FIN** and **INFIN** denote the families of finite and infinite languages, respectively. Let **ALL** denote the family of all languages; in other words, $\mathbf{ALL} = \mathbf{FIN} \cup \mathbf{INFIN}$.

Let $x, y \in \Sigma^*$ be two strings over an alphabet Σ, and let $L, K \subseteq \Sigma^*$ be two languages over Σ. As languages are defined as sets, all set operations apply to them. Specifically, $L \cup K$, $L \cap K$, and $L - K$ denote the union, intersection, and difference of languages L and K, respectively. Perhaps most importantly, the concatenation of x with y, denoted by xy, is the string obtained by appending y to x. Notice that for every $w \in \Sigma^*$, $w\varepsilon = \varepsilon w = w$. The concatenation of L and K, denoted by LK, is defined as $LK = \{xy \mid x \in L, y \in K\}$.

Apart from binary operations, we also make some unary operations with strings and languages. Let $x \in \Sigma^*$ and $L \subseteq \Sigma^*$. The *complement* of L is denoted by $\sim L$ and defined as $\sim L = \Sigma^* - L$. The *reversal of* x, denoted by $\text{reversal}(x)$, is x written in the reverse order, and the *reversal of* L, $\text{reversal}(L)$, is defined as $\text{reversal}(L) = \{\text{reversal}(x) \mid x \in L\}$. For all $i \geq 0$, the *ith power of* x, denoted by x^i, is recursively defined as (1) $x^0 = \varepsilon$, and (2) $x^i = xx^{i-1}$, for $i \geq 1$. Observe that this definition is based on the *recursive definitional method*. To demonstrate the recursive aspect, consider, for instance, the ith power of x with $i = 3$. By the second part of the definition, $x^3 = xx^2$. By applying the second part to x^2 again, $x^2 = xx^1$. By another application of this part to x^1, $x^1 = xx^0$. By the first part of this definition, $x^0 = \varepsilon$. Thus, $x^1 = xx^0 = x\varepsilon = x$. Hence, $x^2 = xx^1 = xx$. Finally, $x^3 = xx^2 = xxx$. By using this recursive method, we frequently introduce new notions, including the *ith power of L*, L^i, which is defined as (1) $L^0 = \varepsilon$ and (2) $L^i = LL^{i1}$, for $i \geq 1$. The *closure of L*, L^*, is defined as $L^* = L^0 \cup L^1 \cup L^2 \cup \cdots$, and the *positive closure of L*, L^+, is defined as $L^+ = L^1 \cup L^2 \cup \cdots$. Notice that $L^+ = LL^* = L^*L$, and $L^* = L^+ \cup \{\varepsilon\}$. Let $w, x, y, z \in \Sigma^*$. If $xz = y$, then x is a *prefix* of y; if in addition, $x \notin \{\varepsilon, y\}$, x is a *proper prefix* of y. By prefixes(y), we denote the set of all prefixes of y. Set prefixes$(L) = \{x \mid x \in$ prefixes(y) for some $y \in L\}$. For $i = 0, \ldots, |y|$, prefix(y, i) denotes y's prefix of length i; notice that prefix$(y, 0) = \varepsilon$ and prefix$(y, |y|) = y$. If $zx = y$, x is a *suffix* of y; if in addition, $x \notin \{\varepsilon, y\}$, x is a *proper suffix* of y. By suffixes(y), we denote the set of all suffixes of y. Set suffixes$(L) = \{x \mid x \in$ suffixes(y) for some $y \in L\}$. For $i = 0, \ldots, |y|$, suffix(y, i) denotes y's suffix of length i. If $wxz = y$, x is a *substring* of y; if in addition, $x \notin \{\varepsilon, y\}$, x is a *proper substring* of y. By substrings(y), we denote the set of all substrings of y. Observe that for all $v \in \Sigma^*$, prefixes$(v) \subseteq$ substrings(v), suffixes$(v) \subseteq$ substrings(v), and $\{\varepsilon, v\} \subseteq$ prefixes$(v) \cap$ suffixes$(v) \cap$ substrings(v). Set symbols$(y) = \{a \mid a \in$ substrings$(y), |a| = 1\}$. Furthermore, set substrings$(L) = \{x \mid x \in$ substrings(y) for some $y \in L\}$ and symbols$(L) = \{a \mid a \in$ symbols(y) for some $y \in L\}$.

Let $w \in \Sigma^*$ with $\Sigma = \{a_1, \ldots, a_n\}$. We define *Parikh vector* or *Parikh image* of w by $\psi_\Sigma(w) = (\text{occur}(w, a_1), \text{occur}(w, a_2), \ldots, \text{occur}(w, a_n))$. A set of vectors is called *semilinear* if it can be represented as a union of a finite number of sets of the form $\{v_0 + \sum_{i=1}^{m} \alpha_i v_i \mid \alpha_i \in \mathbb{N}, 1 \leq i \leq m\}$, where v_i for $0 \leq i \leq m$ is an n-dimensional vector. A language $L \subseteq \Sigma^*$ is called *semilinear* if the set $\psi_\Sigma(L) = \{\psi_\Sigma(w) \mid w \in L\}$ is a semilinear set. A language family is *semilinear* if all its languages are semilinear.

The *shuffle* operation, denoted by $\sqcup\!\sqcup$, is defined by $u \sqcup\!\sqcup v = \{x_1y_1x_2y_2 \cdots x_ny_n \mid u = x_1x_2 \cdots x_n, v = y_1y_2 \cdots y_n, x_i, y_i \in \Sigma^*, 1 \leq i \leq n, n \geq 1\}$, where $u, v \in \Sigma^*$. Furthermore, for languages L_1 and L_2 over Σ, set $L_1 \sqcup\!\sqcup L_2 = \bigcup_{u \in L_1, v \in L_2} (u \sqcup\!\sqcup v)$.

For a string w over an alphabet Σ, the set perm(w) of all *permutations* of w is inductively defined as follows: (1) perm$(\varepsilon) = \{\varepsilon\}$ and, for every $a \in \Sigma$ and $u \in \Sigma^*$, perm$(au) = \{a\} \sqcup\!\sqcup$ perm(u). For a language L over alphabet Σ, perm$(L) = \bigcup_{w \in L}$ perm(w). If $L =$ perm(L), we say L is *permutation closed*.

Let Δ be a subalphabet of Σ. The *string projection* of y is the string resulting from y by removing all symbols from $\Sigma - \Delta$; formally defined as

$$\pi_\Delta(y) = \begin{cases} \varepsilon & \text{if } y = \varepsilon; \\ \pi_\Delta(x) & \text{if } y = xa \text{ and } a \notin \Delta; \\ \pi_\Delta(x)a & \text{if } y = xa \text{ and } a \in \Delta. \end{cases}$$

The *projection of a language* L is given by $\pi_\Delta(L) = \{\pi_\Delta(y) \mid y \in L\}$.

Assume o is an n-ary operation over languages, $n \geq 1$. A language family $\mathcal{L}$ is *closed* under operation o if $o(L_1, L_2, \ldots, L_n) \in \mathcal{L}$, where $L_1, L_2, \ldots, L_n \in \mathcal{L}$.

Example 1.4 Consider the alphabet $\{0, 1\}$. For instance, ε, 1, and 010 are strings over $\{0, 1\}$. Notice that $|\varepsilon| = 0$, $|1| = 1$, $|010| = 3$. The concatenation of 1 and 010 is 1010.

The third power of 1010 equals 101010101010. Observe that reversal(1010) = 0101. We have prefixes(1010) = $\{\varepsilon, 1, 10, 101, 1010\}$, where 1, 10, and 101 are proper prefixes of 1010, while ε and 1010 are not. We have suffixes(1010) = $\{\varepsilon$, 0, 10, 010, 1010$\}$, substrings(1010) = $\{\varepsilon, 0, 1, 01, 10, 010, 101, 1010\}$, symbols(1010) = $\{0, 1\}$, and $\pi_{\{0\}}(1010) = 00$.

Set $K = \{0, 01\}$ and $L = \{1, 01\}$. Observe that $L \cup K$, $L \cap K$, and $L - K$ are equal to $\{0, 1, 01\}$, $\{01\}$, and $\{1\}$, respectively. The concatenation of K and L is $KL = \{01, 001, 011, 0101\}$. For L, $\sim L = \Sigma^* - L$, so $\sim L$ contains all strings in $\{0, 1\}^*$ but 1 and 01. Furthermore, reversal(L) = $\{1, 10\}$ and $L^2 = \{11, 101, 011, 0101\}$. Next, L^* contains all strings from Σ^* such that every 0 is followed by at least one 1. To illustrate, the strings in L^* that consist of four or fewer symbols are ε, 1, 01, 11, 011, 101, 111, 0101, 0111, 1011, 1101, and 1111.

Since $\varepsilon \notin L$, $L^+ = L^* - \{\varepsilon\}$. Notice that prefixes($L$) = $\{\varepsilon, 1, 0, 01\}$, suffixes($L$) = $\{\varepsilon, 1, 01\}$, substrings(L) = $\{\varepsilon, 0, 1, 01\}$, and symbols($L$) = $\{0, 1\}$.

Next, $\psi_\Sigma(001) = (2, 1)$, perm(001) = $\{001, 010, 100\}$, and perm(L) = $\{1, 01, 10\}$.

1.3 Relations and Translations

For two objects, a and b, (a, b) denotes the *ordered pair* consisting of a and b in this order. Let A and B be two sets. The *Cartesian product* of A and B, $A \times B$, is defined as $A \times B = \{(a, b) \mid a \in A \text{ and } b \in B\}$. For some $n \geq 0$, A^n denotes the n-fold Cartesian product of set A. A *binary relation* or, briefly, a *relation*, ρ, from A to B is any subset of $A \times B$; that is, $\rho \subseteq A \times B$. If ρ represents a finite set, then it is a *finite relation*; otherwise, it is an *infinite relation*. The *domain* of ρ, denoted by domain(ρ), and the *range* of ρ, denoted by range(ρ), are defined as domain(ρ) = $\{a \mid (a, b) \in \rho$ for some $b \in B\}$ and range(ρ) = $\{b \mid (a, b) \in \rho$ for some $a \in A\}$. If $A = B$, then ρ is a *relation on* A. A relation σ is a *subrelation* of ρ if $\sigma \subseteq \rho$. The *inverse of* ρ, denoted by inverse(ρ), is defined as inverse(ρ) = $\{(b, a) \mid (a, b) \in \rho\}$. Let $\chi \subseteq B \times C$ be a relation, where C is a set; the *composition of* ρ *with* χ is denoted by $\chi \circ \rho$ and defined as $\chi \circ \rho = \{(a, c) \mid (a, b) \in \rho, (b, c) \in \chi\}$. A *function from A to B* is a relation ϕ from A to B such that for every $a \in A$, card($\{b \mid b \in B$ and $(a, b) \in \phi\}$) ≤ 1. If domain(ϕ) = A, ϕ is *total*. If we want to emphasize that ϕ may not satisfy domain(ϕ) = A, we say that ϕ is *partial*.

Furthermore, we say that a function ϕ is

- an *injection*, if for every $b \in B$, card($\{a \mid a \in A$ and $(a, b) \in \phi\}$) ≤ 1;
- a *surjection*, if for every $b \in B$, card($\{a \mid a \in A$ and $(a, b) \in \phi\}$) ≥ 1;
- a *bijection*, if ϕ is a total function that is both a surjection and an injection.

As relations and functions are defined as sets, the set operations apply to them, too. For instance, if $\phi \subseteq A \times B$ is a function, its complement, $\sim \phi$, is defined as $(A \times B) - \phi$.

Convention 1.4 Let $\rho \subseteq A \times B$ be a relation. To express that $(a, b) \in \rho$, we usually write $a\rho b$. If ρ represents a function, we often write $\rho(a) = b$ instead of $a\rho b$. If $\rho(a) = b$, b is the *value* of ρ for *argument* a.

If there is a bijection from an infinite set Ψ to an infinite set Ξ, then Ψ and Ξ have the *same cardinality*. An infinite set, Ω, is *countable* or, synonymously, *enumerable*, if Ω and $\mathbb{N}$ have the same cardinality; otherwise, it is *uncountable* (according to Convention 1.2, $\mathbb{N}$ is the set of natural numbers).

Example 1.5 Consider the set of all even natural numbers, $\mathbb{E}$. Define the bijection $\phi(i) = 2i$, for all $i \in \mathbb{N}$. Observe that ϕ represents a bijection from $\mathbb{N}$ to $\mathbb{E}$, so they have the same cardinality. Thus, $\mathbb{E}$ is countable.

Consider the set ς of all functions mapping $\mathbb{N}$ to $\{\mathbf{1}, \mathbf{0}\}$. By contradiction, we prove that ς is uncountable. Suppose that ς is countable. Thus, there is a bijection from ς to $\mathbb{N}$. Let ${}_if$ be the function mapped to the ith positive integer, for all $i \geq 1$. Consider the total function g from $\mathbb{N}$ to $\{\mathbf{1}, \mathbf{0}\}$ defined as $g(j) = \mathbf{0}$ if and only if ${}_jf(j) = \mathbf{1}$, for all $i \geq 1$, so $g(j) = \mathbf{1}$ if and only if ${}_jf(j) = \mathbf{0}$. As ς contains g, $g = {}_kf$ for some $k \geq 1$. Specifically, $g(k) = {}_kf(k)$. However, $g(k) = \mathbf{0}$ if and only if ${}_kf(k) = \mathbf{1}$, so $g(k) \neq {}_kf(k)$, which contradicts $g(k) = {}_kf(k)$. Thus, ς is uncountable.

The proof technique by which we have demonstrated that ς is uncountable is customarily called *diagonalization*. To see why, imagine an infinite table with ${}_1f, {}_2f, \ldots$ listed down the rows and $1, 2, \ldots$ listed across the columns (see Figure 1.2). Each entry contains either $\mathbf{0}$ or $\mathbf{1}$. Specifically, the entry in row ${}_if$ and column j contains $\mathbf{1}$ if and only if ${}_if(j) = \mathbf{1}$, so this entry contains $\mathbf{0}$ if and only if ${}_if(j) = \mathbf{0}$. A contradiction occurs at the diagonal entry in row ${}_kf$ and column k because $g(k) = \mathbf{0}$ if and only if ${}_kf(k) = \mathbf{1}$, and $g(k) = {}_kf(k)$; in other words, this diagonal entry contains $\mathbf{0}$ if and only if it contains $\mathbf{1}$, which is impossible. We make use of this proof technique several times in this book.

	1	2	$\cdots$	k	$\cdots$
${}_1f$	**0**	**1**	$\cdots$	**0**	$\cdots$
${}_1f$	**1**	**1**	$\cdots$	**1**	$\cdots$
$\vdots$	$\vdots$	$\vdots$	$\ddots$	$\vdots$	
$g = {}_kf$	**0**	**0**	$\cdots$	**0** iff **1**	$\cdots$
$\vdots$	$\vdots$	$\vdots$		$\vdots$	$\ddots$

Fig. 1.2 Diagonalization.

Let A be a set, ρ be a relation on A, and $a, b \in A$. For $k \geq 0$, the *k-fold product* of ρ, ρ^k, is recursively defined as (1) $a\rho^0 b$ iff $a = b$, and (2) $a\rho^k b$ iff there exists $c \in A$ such that $a\rho c$ and $c\rho^{k-1}b$, for $k \geq 1$. If for all $a, b \in A$, $a\rho b$ implies $b\rho a$, then ρ is *symmetric*. The *transitive closure* of ρ, ρ^+, is defined as $a\rho^+ b$ if and only if $a\rho^k b$ for some $k \geq 1$, and the *reflexive and transitive closure* of ρ, ρ^*, is defined as $a\rho^* b$ if and only if $a\rho^k b$ for some $k \geq 0$.

Let T and U be two alphabets, $K \subseteq T^*$, and $L \subseteq U^*$. A relation τ from T^* to U^* with domain(τ) = K and range(τ) = L is a *translation* from K to L. Let σ be a translation from T^* to U^* such that σ is a total function from T^* to power(U^*) satisfying $\sigma(uv) = \sigma(u)\sigma(v)$ for every $u, v \in T^*$; then, σ is a *substitution* from T^* to U^*. A total function φ from T^* to U^* such that $\varphi(uv) = \varphi(u)\varphi(v)$ for every $u, v \in T^*$ is a *homomorphism* from T^* to U^*; if $\varphi(a) \neq \varepsilon$ for all $a \in T$, φ is said to be an *ε-free homomorphism*. It is worth noting that a homomorphism from T^* to U^* does not necessarily represent an injection from T^* to U^* as illustrated in Example 1.6.

Let T, U, σ and φ have the same meaning as above. Observe that σ from T^* to power(U^*) can be completely and properly specified by defining $\sigma(a)$ for every individual symbol $a \in T$. Indeed, since $\sigma(\varepsilon) = \{\varepsilon\}$ and $\sigma(a_1a_2 \cdots a_n) = \sigma(a_1)\sigma(a_2) \cdots \sigma(a_n)$, where $a_i \in T$, $1 \leq i \leq n$, for some $n \geq 1$, we can straightforwardly obtain $\sigma(w)$ for all $w \in T^*$. As any homomorphism is obviously a special case of a substitution, we can specify φ analogously. In this elegant way, using this natural *extension*, we always introduce every new notion of a substitution and a homomorphism throughout this book. In the next example, which illustrates this kind of introduction, we make it in a tabular way (see Figure 1.3).

Example 1.6 Let Δ denote the English alphabet. The *Morse code*, denoted by μ, can be seen as a homomorphism from Δ^* to $\{., -\}^*$ (see Figure 1.3). For instance,

$$\mu(\text{SOS}) = \ldots{-}{-}{-}\ldots$$

Notice that μ is not an injection; for instance, $\mu(\text{SOS}) = \mu(\text{IJS})$.

Letter	μ	Letter	μ	Letter	μ
A	.–	*J*	.–––	*S*	...
B	–...	*K*	–.–	*T*	–
C	–.–.	*L*	.–..	*U*	..–
D	–..	*M*	––	*V*	...–
E	.	*N*	–.	*W*	.––
F	..–.	*O*	–––	*X*	–..–
G	––.	*P*	.––.	*Y*	–.––
H	....	*Q*	––.–	*Z*	––..
I	..	*R*	.–.		

Fig. 1.3 Morse code.

We now slightly modify μ to μ' defined as $\mu'(a) = \mu(a)\#$ for every $a \in \Delta$, where # is an extra delimiting symbol out of Δ. Observe that μ' from Δ^* to $\{., -, \#\}^*$ is an injection. For instance, $\mu(A) = \mu(ET)$ but $\mu'(A) \neq \mu'(ET)$.

We conclude this section by the next example, which demonstrates how to represent non-negative integers by strings in a very simple way. More specifically, it introduces the function unary, which represents all non-negative integers by strings consisting of as. Later in this book, especially in Part III, we frequently make use of unary.

Example 1.7 Let a be a symbol. To represent non-negative integers by strings over $\{a\}$, define the total function unary from ${}_0\mathbb{N}$ to $\{a\}^*$ as $\text{unary}(i) = a^i$, for all $i \geq 0$. For instance, $\text{unary}(0) = \varepsilon$, $\text{unary}(2) = aa$, and $\text{unary}(1000000) = a^{1000000}$.

1.4 Graphs

Let A be a set. A *directed graph* or, briefly, a *graph* is a pair $G = (A, \rho)$, where ρ is a relation on A. Members of A are called *nodes*, and ordered pairs in ρ are called *edges*. If $(a, b) \in \rho$, then edge (a, b) *leaves* a and *enters* b. Let $a \in A$; then, the *in-degree* of a and the *out-degree* of a are $\text{card}(\{b \mid (b, a) \in \rho\})$ and $\text{card}(\{c \mid (a, c) \in \rho\})$. A sequence of nodes, $(a_0, a_1, \ldots, a_n)$, where $n \geq 1$, is a *path of length n* from a_0 to a_n if $(a_{i-1}, a_i) \in \rho$ for all $1 \leq i \leq n$; if, in addition, $a_0 = a_n$, then $(a_0, a_1, \ldots, a_n)$ is a *cycle of length n*. In this book, we frequently label the edges of G with some attached information. Pictorially, we represent $G = (A, \rho)$ by drawing each edge $(a, b) \in \rho$ as an arrow from a to b, possibly along with its label, as illustrated in the next example.

Example 1.8 Consider a program p and its *call graph* $G = (P, \rho)$, where P represents the set of subprograms in p, and $(x, y) \in \rho$ iff subprogram x calls subprogram y. Specifically, let $P = \{a, b, c, d\}$, and $\rho = \{(a, b), (a, c), (b, d), (c, d)\}$, which says that a calls b and c, b calls d, and c calls d as well (see Figure 1.4). The in-degree of a is 0, and its out-degree is 2. Notice that (a, b, d) is a path of length 2 in G. G contains no cycle because none of its paths starts and ends in the same node.

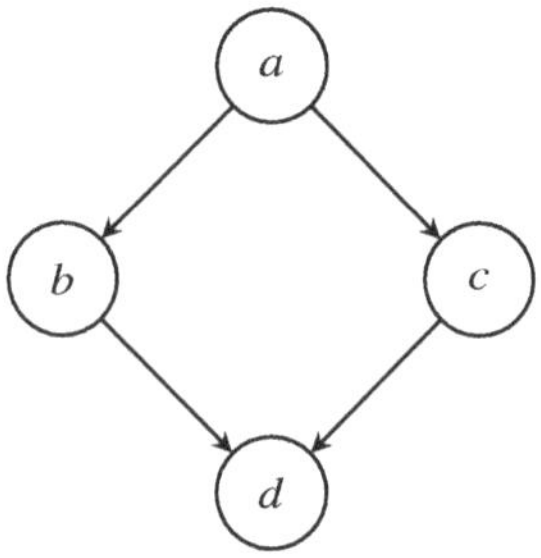

Fig. 1.4 Graph of G.

Suppose we use G to study the value of a global variable during the four calls. Specifically, we want to express that this value is zero when call (a, b) occurs; otherwise, it is one. We express this by labeling the edges of G in the way given in Figure 1.5.

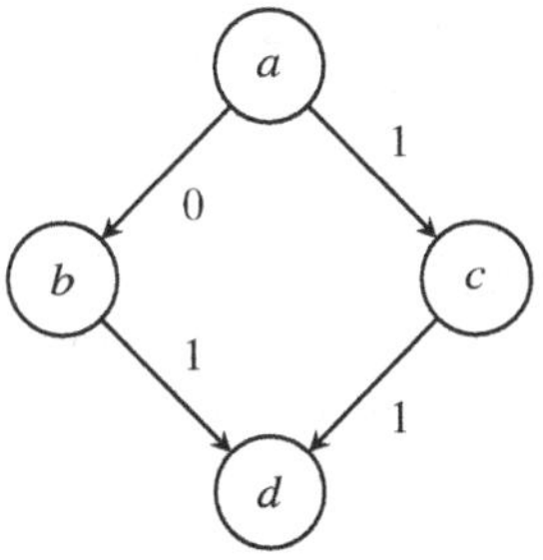

Fig. 1.5 Labeled graph of G.

Let $G = (A, \rho)$ be a graph. G is an *acyclic graph* if it contains no cycle. If $(a_0, a_1, \ldots, a_n)$ is a path in G, then a_0 is an *ancestor* of a_n and a_n is a *descendant* of a_0; if in addition, $n = 1$, then a_0 is a *direct ancestor* of a_n and a_n a *direct descendant* of a_0. A *tree* is an acyclic graph $T = (A, \rho)$ such that (1) A contains a specified node called the *root* of T and denoted by $\mathrm{root}(T)$, and (2) for every $a \in A - \{\mathrm{root}(T)\}$, a is a descendant of $\mathrm{root}(T)$ and the in-degree of a is one. If $a \in A$ is a node whose out-degree is 0, a is a *leaf*; otherwise, it is an *interior node*. In this book, a tree T is always considered as an *ordered tree* in which each interior node $a \in A$ has all its direct descendants, b_1 through b_n, where $n \geq 1$, ordered from left to right so that b_1 is the leftmost direct descendant of a and b_n is the rightmost direct descendant of a. At this point, a is the *parent* of its *children* b_1 through b_n, and all these nodes together with the edges connecting them, (a, b_1) through (a, b_n), are called a *parent-children portion* of T. The *frontier* of T, denoted by $\mathrm{frontier}(T)$, is the sequence of T's leaves ordered from left to right. The *depth* of T, $\mathrm{depth}(T)$, is the length of the longest path in T. A tree $S = (B, \nu)$ is a *subtree* of T if $\emptyset \subset B \subseteq A$, $\nu \subseteq \rho \cap (B \times B)$, and in T, no node in $A - B$ is a descendant of a node in B; S is an *elementary subtree* of T if $\mathrm{depth}(S) = 1$.

Like any graph, a tree T can be described as a two-dimensional structure. To simplify this description, however, we draw a tree T with its root on the top and with all edges directed down. Each parent has its children drawn from the left to the right according to its ordering. Drawing T in this way, we always omit all arrowheads.

Apart from this two-dimensional representation, however, it is frequently convenient to specify T by a one-dimensional representation, denoted by $\mathrm{odr}(T)$, in which each subtree of T is represented by the expression appearing inside a balanced pair of $\langle$ and $\rangle$ with the node which is the root of that subtree appearing immediately to the left of $\langle$. More precisely, $\mathrm{odr}(T)$ is defined by the following recursive rules:

(1) If T consists of a single node a, then $\mathrm{odr}(T) = a$.
(2) Let (a, b_1) through (a, b_n), where $n \geq 1$, be the parent-children portion of T, $\mathrm{root}(T) = a$, and T_k be the subtree rooted at b_k, $1 \leq k \leq n$, then $\mathrm{odr}(T) = a\langle \mathrm{odr}(T_1)\, \mathrm{odr}(T_2) \cdots \mathrm{odr}(T_n)\rangle$.

The next example illustrates both the one-dimensional odr-representation and the two-dimensional pictorial representation of a tree. For brevity, we prefer the former throughout the rest of this book.

Example 1.9 Graph G discussed in Example 1.8 is acyclic. However, it is not a tree because the in-degree of node d is two. By removing the edge (b, d), we obtain a tree $T = (P, v)$, where $P = \{a, b, c, d\}$ and $v = \{(a, b), (a, c), (c, d)\}$. Nodes a and c are interior nodes while b and d are leaves. The root of T is a. We define b and c as the first child of a and the second child of a, respectively. A parent-children portion of T is, for instance, (a, b) and (a, c). Notice that frontier$(T) = bd$, and depth$(T) = 2$. Following (1) and (2) above, we obtain the one-dimensional representation of T as odr$(T) = a\langle bc\langle d\rangle\rangle$. Its subtrees are $a\langle bc\langle d\rangle\rangle$, $c\langle d\rangle$, b, and d. In Figure 1.6, we pictorially describe $a\langle bc\langle d\rangle\rangle$ and $c\langle d\rangle$.

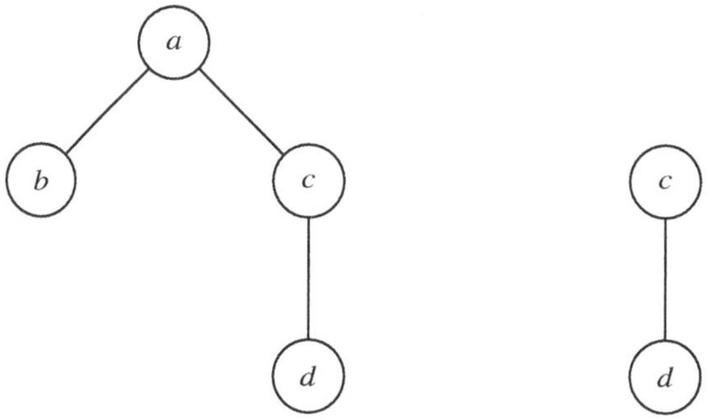

Fig. 1.6 A tree and a subtree.

Chapter 2
Automata and Grammars

Indisputably, the notion of a *procedure* is central to computation and, consequently, computer science as a whole. We surely agree that it consists of finitely many instructions, each of which can be executed mechanically in a fixed amount of time. When running, it reads input data, executes its instructions, and produces output data. Nevertheless, apart from understanding this notion intuitively, we need its formalization in order to obtain a systematized body of mathematically precise knowledge concerning it. Therefore, the *theory of computation* has developed an important field, called *formal language theory*, which formalizes the notion of a procedure by a large variety of *language models*. Despite their diversity, all the models are uniformly underlain by *rewriting systems*, which are based upon finitely many rules according to which they rewrite strings. They all can be classified into two basic categories—automata and grammars.

Automata define strings of their language by rewriting processes that start from these strings and end in prescribed special sets of strings, usually called start and final configurations. They formalize procedures that have only two outputs—"yes" and "no." The output "yes" represents a resulting affirmative response to the input, expressed by stating that the input is accepted. The output "no" means a negative response to the input, which is said to be rejected. *Grammars* are language-generating counterparts to the automata. Instead of accepting strings, they define strings of their languages by generating them from a special start string. Consequently, as opposed to automata, they formalize procedures that produce out data without any input.

Section 2.1 introduces rewriting systems in general and explains how to use them as language models. Section 2.2 define classical types of automata—finite and pushdown automata—while Section 2.3 covers a broad variety of grammars.

2.1 Language Models of Computation

As already pointed out, computer science customarily formalizes computation by languages defined by their models in order to explore it in a strictly mathematical way.

Despite a broad variety of these models introduced over the history of this science, almost all of them are based on the same mathematical notion of a rewriting system. In this section, we first introduce this notion quite generally. Then, we explain how to use this model as a base of two fundamental types of language models—automata and grammars.

Definition 2.1 A *rewriting system* is a pair, $M = (\Sigma, R)$, where Σ is an alphabet, and R is a finite relation on Σ^*. Σ is called the *total alphabet of* M or, simply, the *alphabet of* M. A member of R is called a *rule of* M, and accordingly, R is referred to as the *set of rules* of M.

Convention 2.1 For any rewriting system $M = (\Sigma, R)$, each rule $(x, y) \in R$ is written as $x \rightarrow y$ throughout this book. For $x \rightarrow y \in R$, x and y represent the *left-hand side of* $x \rightarrow y$ and the *right-hand side of* $x \rightarrow y$, respectively.

For brevity, we sometimes denote a rule $x \rightarrow y$ with a unique label h as $h : x \rightarrow y$, and instead of $h : x \rightarrow y \in R$, we simply write $h \in R$.

To give a straightforward insight into rewriting systems, we next illustrate them by two linguistical examples.

Example 2.1 Let Δ denote the alphabet of English small letters (this alphabet is used in all examples of this section). In the present example, we introduce a rewriting system M that translates every digital string to the string in which every digit is converted to its corresponding English name followed by #; for instance, 010 is translated to *zero#one#zero#*.

First, we define the homomorphism h from $\{0, 1, \ldots, 9\}$ to Δ^* as

$$\begin{aligned} h(0) &= zero, & h(5) &= five,\\ h(1) &= one, & h(6) &= six,\\ h(2) &= two, & h(7) &= seven,\\ h(3) &= three, & h(8) &= eight,\\ h(4) &= four, & h(9) &= nine. \end{aligned}$$

Intuitively speaking, h translates every member of $\{0, 1, \ldots, 9\}$ to its corresponding English name; for instance, $h(9) = nine$. Based upon h, we define $M = (\Sigma, R)$ with $\Sigma = \{0, 1, \ldots, 9\} \cup \Delta \cup \{\#\}$ and $R = \{i \rightarrow h(i)\# \mid i \in \{0, 1, \ldots, 9\}\}$. Consider h and R. Define the translation $T(M)$ from $\{0, 1, \ldots, 9\}^*$ to $(\Delta \cup \{\#\})^*$ as

$$T(M) = \{(s_1 \cdots s_n, t_1 \cdots t_n) \mid \text{for all } 1 \leq j \leq n,\ (s_j, t_j) \in R,\ n \geq 0\}$$

Notice that $T(M)$ contains

$$(\varepsilon, \varepsilon), (0, zero\#), (1, one\#), \ldots, (9, nine\#), (00, zero\#zero\#), (01, zero\#one\#), \ldots$$

For instance, since $(911, nine\#one\#one\#) \in T(M)$, 911 is translated to string *nine#one#one#*. Thus, M performs the desired translation.

Example 2.2 This example strongly resembles a simple morphological study (in linguistics, *morphology* studies the structure of words). Indeed, it discusses restructuring strings consisting of English letters, including strings that do not represent any English words, such as $xxuy$. More precisely, we introduce a rewriting system M that

(i) starts from nonempty strings consisting of small English letters delimited by angle brackets,
(ii) orders the letters lexicographically, and
(iii) eliminates the angle brackets.

For instance, M changes $\langle xxuy\rangle$ to $uxxy$.

Let Δ have the same meaning as in Example 2.1—that is, Δ denotes the alphabet of English lowercases. Let $<$ denote the standardly defined lexical order over Δ—that is,

$$a < b < c < \ldots < y < z$$

We define $M = (\Sigma, R)$ with $\Sigma = \Delta \cup \{\langle, \rangle, 1, 2, 3\}$ and R containing the following rules:

1. $\langle \rightarrow 12$, $12 \rightarrow 3$;
2. $2\alpha \rightarrow \alpha 2$ and $\alpha 2 \rightarrow 2\alpha$ for all $\alpha \in \Delta$;
3. $\beta 2\alpha \rightarrow \alpha 2\beta$ for all $\alpha, \beta \in \Delta$ such that $\alpha < \beta$;
4. $3\alpha\beta \rightarrow \alpha 3\beta$ for all $\alpha, \beta \in \Delta$ such that $\alpha < \beta$ or $\alpha = \beta$;
5. $3\alpha\rangle \rightarrow \alpha$ for all $\alpha \in \Delta$.

Define the translation o over Δ^* by this equivalence

$$(u, v) \in o \text{ if and only if } u = wxz,\ v = wyz, \text{ and } x \rightarrow y \in R, \text{ where } u, v, w, x, y, z \in \Delta^*$$

Based on o, define the translation $T(M)$ from $\{\langle\}\Delta^+\{\rangle\}$ to Δ^+ as

$$(\langle x\rangle, y) \in T(M) \text{ if and only if } (\langle x\rangle, y) \in o^*$$

where $x, y \in \Delta^+$ and as usual, o^* is the transitive and reflexive closure of o (see Section 1.3).

Considering M defined in this way, observe that $(\langle s\rangle, t) \in T(M)$ if and only if t is a permutation of s such that t has its letters lexicographically ordered according to $<$. For instance, $T(M)$ contains $(\langle order\rangle, deorr)$ because

$$
\begin{array}{lll}
(\langle order\rangle & , 12order\rangle) \in o & \text{because } \langle \rightarrow 12 \in R; \\
(12order\rangle & , 1o2rder\rangle) \in o & \text{because } 2o \rightarrow o2 \in R; \\
(1o2rder\rangle & , 1or2der\rangle) \in o & \text{because } 2r \rightarrow r2 \in R; \\
(1or2der\rangle & , 1od2rer\rangle) \in o & \text{because } r2d \rightarrow d2r \in R; \\
(1od2rer\rangle & , 1odr2er\rangle) \in o & \text{because } 2r \rightarrow r2 \in R; \\
(1odr2er\rangle & , 1ode2rr\rangle) \in o & \text{because } r2e \rightarrow e2r \in R; \\
(1ode2rr\rangle & , 1od2err\rangle) \in o & \text{because } e2 \rightarrow 2e \in R; \\
(1od2err\rangle & , 1o2derr\rangle) \in o & \text{because } d2 \rightarrow 2d \in R; \\
(1o2derr\rangle & , 1d2oerr\rangle) \in o & \text{because } o2d \rightarrow d2o \in R; \\
(1d2oerr\rangle & , 1do2err\rangle) \in o & \text{because } 2o \rightarrow o2 \in R; \\
(1do2err\rangle & , 1de2orr\rangle) \in o & \text{because } o2e \rightarrow e2o \in R; \\
(1de2orr\rangle & , 1d2eorr\rangle) \in o & \text{because } e2 \rightarrow 2e \in R; \\
(1d2eorr\rangle & , 12deorr\rangle) \in o & \text{because } d2 \rightarrow 2d \in R; \\
(12deorr\rangle & , 3deorr\rangle) \in o & \text{because } 12 \rightarrow 3 \in R; \\
(3deorr\rangle & , d3eorr\rangle) \in o & \text{because } 3de \rightarrow d3e \in R; \\
(d3eorr\rangle & , de3orr\rangle) \in o & \text{because } 3eo \rightarrow e3o \in R; \\
(de3orr\rangle & , deo3rr\rangle) \in o & \text{because } 3or \rightarrow o3r \in R; \\
(deo3rr\rangle & , deor3r\rangle) \in o & \text{because } 3rr \rightarrow r3r \in R; \\
(deor3r\rangle & , deorr) \in o & \text{because } 3r\rangle \rightarrow r \in R.
\end{array}
$$

Considering the pairs from o given above, we see that $(\langle order\rangle, deorr) \in o^*$, so $(\langle order\rangle, deorr) \in T(M)$.

Language Models

In this section, we return to the key subject of this chapter, which consists in using rewriting systems as language-defining models.

Given a rewriting system $M = (\Sigma, R)$ and a subalphabet $\Delta \subseteq \Sigma$, we introduce a rewriting relation $\Rightarrow$ over Σ^*. Then, based upon its transitive and reflexive closure $\Rightarrow^*$, we define the language of M over Δ. In fact, M can define its language in two different ways: either M generates its language or M accepts it as stated next. Let $L_{\mathcal{S}} \subseteq \Sigma^*$ and $L_{\mathcal{F}} \subseteq \Sigma^*$ be a *start language* and a *final language*, respectively. Let π_Δ be a string projection as defined in Section 1.2.

1. The *language generated by M* is defined as the set of all strings $\pi_\Delta(y)$ satisfying $x \Rightarrow^* y$ in M, where $x \in L_{\mathcal{S}}$ and $y \in L_{\mathcal{F}}$. M used in this way is generally referred to as a *language-generating rewriting system* or, briefly and preferably, a *grammar*.
2. The *language accepted by M* is defined as the set of all strings $\pi_\Delta(x)$ satisfying $x \Rightarrow^* y$ in M, where $x \in L_{\mathcal{S}}$ and $y \in L_{\mathcal{F}}$. M used in this way is referred to as a *language-accepting rewriting system* or, briefly, an *automaton*.

To give an intuitive insight into this definition, $\pi_\Delta(y)$ simply eliminates all symbols from $\Sigma - \Delta$ in any string $y \in \Sigma^*$.

Furthermore, observe that $x \Rightarrow^* y$, in effect, represents a step-by-step process that M makes according to its rules. If this process starts with $x \in L_{\mathcal{S}}$ and ends with $y \in L_{\mathcal{F}}$, M defines a string from its language. If this is the case, used as a grammar, M generates $\pi_\Delta(y)$, and used as an automaton, M accepts $\pi_\Delta(x)$.

The language defined by M is denoted by $L(M)$, but of course, we always have to explicitly state whether M is considered as a grammar or as an automaton.

Based upon this basic definition, we introduce most notions of grammars and automata later in the text. Whenever some of their parts, such as start and final languages, are automatically understood and, therefore, any confusion is ruled out, we omit them in order to keep this text as readable as possible.

Since the rewriting relation usually depends on a specific rule from R, we sometimes express which exact rule is used in a rewriting step.

Convention 2.2 To explicitly express that $r \in R$ is used in a rewriting step $x \Rightarrow y$ in M, we write $x \Rightarrow y\ [r]$.

Example 2.3 Let Δ denote the alphabet of English lowercases. Let L be the language consisting of all even-length palindromes over Δ (a *palindrome* is a string that is the same whether written forward or backward). For instance, aa and $noon$ belong to L, but b and $oops$ do not.

We define the rewriting system. Let $M = (\Sigma, R)$ be the rewriting system with $\Sigma = \Delta \cup \{\#\}$ and $R = \{\# \rightarrow a\#a \mid a \in \Delta\} \cup \{\# \rightarrow \varepsilon\}$.

First, we use M to generate L. We introduce the rewriting relation $\Rightarrow_{gen}$ over Σ^* so that for every $u, v \in \Sigma^*$, $u \Rightarrow_{gen} v$ if and only if $u = wxz$, $v = wyz$, and $x \rightarrow y \in R$. As usual, $\Rightarrow_{gen}^*$ denotes the transitive and reflexive closure of $\Rightarrow_{gen}$. For language-generating rewriting system, consider $L_{\mathcal{S}} = \{\#\}$ and $L_{\mathcal{F}} = \Delta^*$. We denote the language generated by M as $L(M)_{gen}$ and define it as

$$L(M)_{gen} = \{st \mid \# \Rightarrow_{gen}^* st, s, t \in \Delta^*\}$$

For instance, $\# \Rightarrow_{gen} n\#n \Rightarrow_{gen} no\#on \Rightarrow_{gen} noon$ in M, so $\pi_\Delta(noon) = noon \in L(M)_{gen}$.

Second, we accept L by M. We introduce $R = \{a\#a \rightarrow \# \mid a \in \Delta\} \cup \{\varepsilon \rightarrow \#\}$ and the rewriting relation $\Rightarrow_{acc}$ over Σ^* so that for every $u, v \in \Sigma^*$, $u \Rightarrow_{acc} v$ if and only if $u = wxz$, $v = wyz$, and $x \rightarrow y \in R$. In case of language-accepting rewriting system, consider $L_{\mathcal{S}} = \Delta^*\{\#\}\Delta^*$ and $L_{\mathcal{F}} = \{\#\}$. Then, we denote the language accepted by M as $L(M)_{acc}$ and define it as

$$L(M)_{acc} = \{st \mid s\#t \Rightarrow_{acc}^* \#, s, t \in \Delta^*\}$$

To verify $L(M)_{acc} = L$, take any $\alpha \in (\{\#\} \cup \Delta)^*$. Assume that α contains two or more #s; observe that under this assumption, $\alpha \Rightarrow_{acc}^* \#$ is ruled out. Suppose that # occurs once in α, but its position is not in the middle of α; again, at this point, $\alpha \Rightarrow_{acc}^* \#$ is impossible. Consequently, considering these simple observations as well as the form of rules in R, the $\alpha \Rightarrow_{acc}^* \#$ is necessarily of the form $\alpha \Rightarrow_{acc} v\#\mathrm{reversal}(v) \Rightarrow_{acc}^* \#$ with $\alpha = v\,\mathrm{reversal}(v)$. To illustrate, $no\#on \Rightarrow n\#n \Rightarrow \#$, so

$no\#on \Rightarrow_{acc}^{*} \#$ in M. Hence, $\pi_{\Delta}(no\#on) = noon \in L(M)_{acc}$. On the other hand, $moon \notin L(M)$ because $(mo\#on, \#) \notin \Rightarrow_{acc}^{*}$. Thus, indeed, $L(M)_{acc} = L$ as desired.

Strictly speaking, based upon rewriting systems, language models represent pairs. Rarely, however, they are described in this way in language theory. Instead, we specify them as n-tuples, for some $n \geq 2$, because this alternative specification makes them easier to discuss. As a matter of fact, in the next two sections, all the types of language models are introduced in this easier-to-follow way.

In general, concerning various types of language models, we say that two of them are *equivalent* if both define the same language family. For instance, we introduce pushdown automata and context-free grammars in Sections 2.2 and 2.3, respectively. Both are equivalent because they define the same language family—the family of context-free languages. Similarly and more specifically, two instances of language models are considered as *equivalent* if both define the same language.

2.2 Automata

Conceptually speaking, a rewriting system M used as an automaton usually consists of three parts—an input tape, an auxiliary memory, and a finite state control. The input tape is divided into squares, each of which is initially occupied with an input symbol. There is an input read head, and the symbol under it is the current input symbol. The auxiliary memory can be any type of data store, such as a pushdown list. As its name suggests, the finite state control is based upon a finite set of states. It represents the heart of M because it can be thought of as a program that dictates the behavior of M as a whole. Standardly, M works by making moves generalized as rewriting in a rewriting-system view. Each move is made according to a rule that describes how the current state as well as the auxiliary memory are changed. In addition, it determines whether the current input symbol is read, and if so, the read head is shifted precisely one square to the right on the tape. M has one state defined as the start state and some states designated as final states. Let a string w be initially written on the input tape. If M can perform a sequence of moves so that starting from the start state, it reads the entire w on the tape and ends up in a final state, then M accepts w. The set of strings accepted in this way is the language accepted by M, $L(M)$.

2.2.1 Finite Automata

We start with the notion of a finite automaton, which represents a strictly finitary model because its auxiliary memory is nil.

Definition 2.2 A *general finite automaton* (GFA, see [Meduna and Zemek, 2014, Section 3.4], alternatively called *lazy finite automaton* as in [Wood, 1987, Section

2.6.2]) is a quintuple $M = (Q, \Delta, R, s, F)$, where Q is a finite set of states, Δ is an input alphabet, $Q \cap \Delta = \emptyset$, $R \subseteq Q \times \Delta^* \times Q$ is finite, $s \in Q$ is the *start state*, and $F \subsetneq Q$ is a set of *final states*. A member of R is called a *rule* of M usually written in the form $py \to q$ for $(p, y, q) \in R$. If $py \to q \in R$ implies that $|y| \leq 1$, then M is a *finite automaton* (FA). If $R \subseteq Q \times \Delta \times Q$ and for every pair (p, a) from $Q \times \Delta$ there is at most one rule in R, then M is a *deterministic FA* (DFA).

A *configuration* of M is any string in $Q\Delta^*$. If $(p, y, q) \in R$ and $x, y \in \Delta^*$, then $pyx \vdash qx$ and we say M makes a *move* or a *computational step* from pyx to qx. In the standard manner, let us extend $\vdash$ to $\vdash^n$, where $n \geq 0$; then, based on $\vdash^n$, let us define $\vdash^+$ and $\vdash^*$ (called a *sequence of moves* or a *computation*). The *language accepted by M*, denoted by $L(M)$, is defined as $L(M) = \{w \in \Delta^* \mid sw \vdash^* f,\ f \in F\}$ and a computation $sw \vdash^* f$, where $w \in \Delta^*$ and $f \in F$, is called an *accepting computation*. We say that M accepts w if and only if $w \in L(M)$. M rejects w if and only if $w \in \Delta^* - L(M)$. Two GFAs M and M' are said to be equivalent if and only if $L(M) = L(M')$.

In rewriting system point of view, $L_{\mathcal{S}} = \{s\}\Delta^*$ and $L_{\mathcal{F}} = F\{\varepsilon\} = F$ are called the set of *initial* and *final configurations*, respectivély.

Note that if we restrict the label of each transition in GFA (see Definition 2.2) to at most one symbol, we get an FA that is capable to accept a string w if and only if there is some GFA that accepts w as well.

Before going any further, we introduce a convention concerning the notion of a finite automaton.

Convention 2.3 To express that Q, Δ, R, s, and F belong to M, we specify these components as ${}_MQ$, ${}_M\Delta$, ${}_MR$, ${}_Ms$, and ${}_MF$, respectively (this M-subscript specification is primarily used when several automata are simultaneously discussed, so a confusion may arise). The analogous convention can be applied to any other rewriting system.

Sometimes (see Rozenberg and Salomaa [1997a] or Sipser [2006]), considering FA, R is replaced with the function δ from $Q(\Delta \cup \{\varepsilon\})$ to 2^Q (for DFA, $\delta\colon Q\Delta \to Q$) called *transition function* and defined by this equivalence

$$q \in \delta(p, a) \text{ if and only if } pa \to q \in R$$

where $p, q \in Q$ and $a \in \Delta \cup \{\varepsilon\}$; using this δ-specification, we define M as

$$M = (Q, \Delta, \delta, s, F)$$

As is obvious, all these kinds of specification are equivalent, and we interchangeably use them depending on what is the most appropriate and convenient notation under the given circumstances in what follows. For instance, we work with jumping finite automata (see Chapter 3), which are based on GFA that use the set of rules, and we also work with jumping $5' \to 3'$ Watson–Crick finite automata (see Section 4.4), which are based on FA that use the transition function.

When we want to visualize an FA M, we use its *state diagram* (for instance, see Figure 2.1). The state diagram is a labeled directed graph such that nodes represent

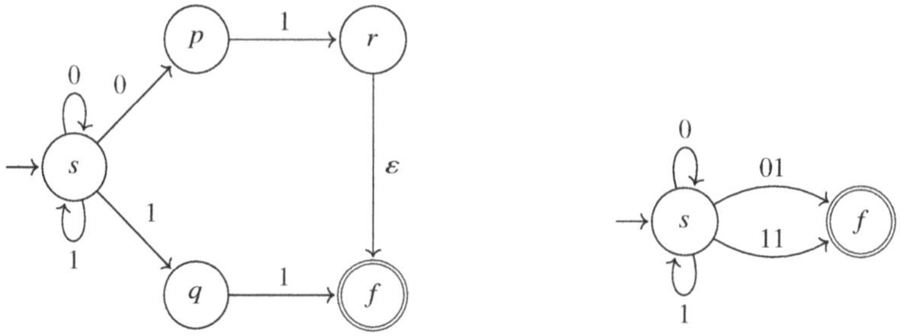

Fig. 2.1 FA M_1 (on the left), GFA M_2 (on the right).

states and each rule of the form $pa \rightarrow q$ is represented by an edge from p to q labeled by a. We mark the start state with a short arrow and final states are doubly circled.

Example 2.4 Now, according to the previous convention, we give several equivalent formal definitions of an FA, GFA, and DFA all accepting a language L over alphabet $\Delta = \{0, 1\}$ such that L consists of all terminal strings from Δ^* that end with substring 01 or 11.

First, let $M_1 = (Q_{M_1}, \Delta, R_{M_1}, s, F)$ be an FA written as a quintuple with a set of rules R_{M_1} such that $Q_{M_1} = \{s, p, q, r, f\}, \Delta = \{0, 1\}, F = \{f\}$, and $R_{M_1} = \{s0 \rightarrow s, s1 \rightarrow s, s0 \rightarrow p, s1 \rightarrow q, p1 \rightarrow r, q1 \rightarrow f, r\varepsilon \rightarrow f\}$. That is, s is the initial state of M_1 and f is the only final state of M_1. In Figure 2.1, there is a diagram for M_1 on the left, and it is obvious that $L(M_1) = L$.

Second, using GFA, we simplify M_1 to M_2 significantly such that $M_2 = (Q_{M_2}, \Delta, R_{M_2}, s, F)$, $Q_{M_2} = \{s, f\}$, and $R_{M_1} = \{s0 \rightarrow s, s1 \rightarrow s, s01 \rightarrow f, s11 \rightarrow f\}$ (as shown on the right in Figure 2.1).

To illustrate a formal definition using a transition function δ instead of the finite set of rules, $M_1 = (Q_{M_1}, \Delta, \delta, s, F)$ can be written with

$$\begin{aligned} \delta(s, 0) &= \{s, p\}, \\ \delta(s, 1) &= \{s, q\}, \\ \delta(p, 1) &= \{r\}, \\ \delta(q, 1) &= \{f\}, \\ \delta(r, \varepsilon) &= \{f\}. \end{aligned}$$

Note that if there is no rule starting in state p and reading symbol a, we skip to write $\delta(p, a) = \emptyset$.

Let 0101 be an input string. Using M_1, the accepting computation is

$$s0101 \vdash s101 \vdash s01 \vdash p1 \vdash r \vdash f$$

Alternatively, M_2 needs only three moves to accept 0101 as $s0101 \vdash s101 \vdash s01 \vdash f$.

Finally, we can illustrate DFA M_3 with $L(M_3) = L$ by the diagram in Figure 2.2.

As stated next, both FAs and GFAs have the same power.

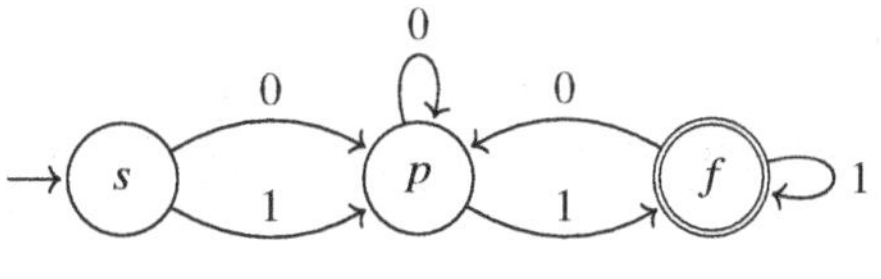

Fig. 2.2 DFA M_3.

Theorem 2.1 (see Wood [1987]) *A language is accepted by an FA if and only if it is accepted by a GFA.*

2.2.2 Pushdown Automata

A pushdown automaton is a finite automaton together with a potentially infinite pushdown list as an auxiliary memory. During its move, according to one of its rules, it reads a symbol, changes the current state, and rewrites a string of symbols occurring on the pushdown top. If it reads the entire input string, empties the pushdown list and enters a final state, the automaton accepts the input string; the set of all accepted strings in this way is the language that the automaton accepts.

As with finite automata, we define their general version—extended pushdown automata. Then, we define their special case—classical pushdown automata.

Definition 2.3 An *extended pushdown automaton* is a septuple $M = (Q, \Delta, \Gamma, R, s, S, F)$, where Q is the finite set of *states*, $\Delta \subseteq \Gamma$ is the *input alphabet*, Γ is the *pushdown alphabet*, $R \subseteq Q \times (\Delta \cup \{\varepsilon\}) \times \Gamma^* \times Q \times \Gamma^*$ is the finite set of *rules*, $s \in Q$ is the *starting state*, $S \in \Gamma$ is the *starting pushdown symbol*, and $F \subseteq Q$ is the set of *final states*. Q and Γ are pairwise disjoint. The rules are written in the form $(p, a, z) \rightarrow (q, y)$ that corresponds to $(p, a, z, q, y) \in R$, where $p, q \in Q$, $a \in \Delta \cup \{\varepsilon\}$, and $z, y \in \Gamma^*$. If every rule $(p, a, z) \rightarrow (q, y) \in R$ satisfies that $|z| = 1$, we call M a *pushdown automaton* (PDA).

In the classical definition of PDA, we do not include a total alphabet, Σ, into the list of its components, because Σ is divided into more than two subsets, such as Q, Δ, and Γ like in state grammars (see Definition 8.2).

Now, we introduce how PDA works according to its rules and what are the variants of its final configurations to accept the input string.

Definition 2.4 A *configuration* of the PDA is a triple $(p, x, \alpha) \in Q \times \Delta^* \times \Gamma^*$, where p denotes the current state, and x is a non-processed part of the input string, and α is the content of the pushdown. The *transition*, *move* or *computational step* is a binary relation $\vdash$ on $Q \times \Delta^* \times \Gamma^*$ such that $(p, aw, z\gamma) \vdash (q, w, y\gamma)$ if and only if exists $(p, a, z) \rightarrow (q, y)$ in R, where $p, q \in Q$, $a \in \Delta \cup \{\varepsilon\}$, $w \in \Delta^*$, and $z, y, \gamma \in \Gamma^*$.

A rule of M is applied to the current configuration, $(p, aw, z\gamma)$, in the following way. If p is the current state, a is the input symbol, z is a substring from the *pushdown top*, and $(p, a, z) \rightarrow (q, y) \in R$; then, M reads a from the input, changes the pushdown top from z to y, and changes the current state from p to q. Notice that if $a = \varepsilon$ in the rule $(p, a, z) \rightarrow (q, y)$, then M reads no input symbol.

In the standard way, $\vdash$ is extended to $\vdash^n$, for $n \geq 0$. As usual, $\vdash^+$ and $\vdash^*$ denote the transitive closure of $\vdash$ and the reflexive-transitive closure of $\vdash$, respectively.

The language accepted by the pushdown automaton M, $L(M)$, is defined as $L(M) = \{w \mid w \in \Delta^*, (s, w, S) \vdash^* (f, \varepsilon, \varepsilon), f \in F\}$. That is, M as a rewriting system has $L_{\mathcal{S}} = \{s\} \times \Delta^* \times \{S\}$ and $L_{\mathcal{F}} = F \times \{\varepsilon\} \times \{\varepsilon\}$ as the sets of *initial* and *final configurations*, respectively.

In addition, we have two alternative accepting computations for a (extended) PDA. Specifically, $L_e(M) = \{w \mid w \in \Delta^*, (s, w, S) \vdash^* (q, \varepsilon, \varepsilon), q \in Q\}$ and $L_f(M) = \{w \mid w \in \Delta^*, (s, w, S) \vdash^* (f, \varepsilon, z), f \in F\}$.

Alternatively, we can define PDA by a diagram similar to a diagram for FA where each edge is labeled by the relevant components from the corresponding rule. For instance, a rule $(p, a, z) \rightarrow (q, y)$ is diagrammed by an edge from state p into state q labeled as $a, z/y$.

Example 2.5 Let $M_{PDA} = (Q, \Delta, \Gamma, R, s, \$, \{f\})$ be a PDA, where $Q = \{s, p, q, f\}$, $\Delta = \{0, 1\}$, $\Gamma = \{0, 1, \$, \#\}$, such that $L(M_{PDA})$ contains all strings from Δ^* such that the number of occurences of 0s in the string is the same as of 1s. R consists of

$$\begin{aligned}
(s, 1, \$) &\rightarrow (p, \#\$),\\
(s, 0, \$) &\rightarrow (q, \#\$),\\
(p, 0, \#) &\rightarrow (p, \varepsilon),\\
(p, 1, \#) &\rightarrow (p, \#\#),\\
(p, 1, \$) &\rightarrow (p, \#\$),\\
(p, 0, \$) &\rightarrow (q, \#\$),\\
(p, \varepsilon, \$) &\rightarrow (f, \varepsilon),\\
(q, 0, \#) &\rightarrow (q, \#\#),\\
(q, 1, \#) &\rightarrow (q, \varepsilon),\\
(q, 1, \$) &\rightarrow (p, \#\$),\\
(q, 0, \$) &\rightarrow (q, \#\$),\\
(q, \varepsilon, \$) &\rightarrow (f, \varepsilon).
\end{aligned}$$

Let 0110 be an input string. Using M_{PDA}, the accepting computation is

$$(s, 0110, \$) \vdash (q, 110, \#\$) \vdash (q, 10, \$) \vdash (p, 0, \#\$) \vdash (p, \varepsilon, \$) \vdash (f, \varepsilon, \varepsilon)$$

Next, let $L = \{a^n b^m \mid n, m \geq 1, n < m\}$. We illustrate M_f with $L_f(M_f) = L$ and M_e with $L_e(M_e) = L$ in Figure 2.4. To maintain greater number of bs than as, we push all as on the pushdown and pop them while reading bs and in addition, we introduce rules $(p, b, S) \rightarrow (f, S)$ into R_{M_f} and $(p, b, S) \rightarrow (p, \varepsilon)$ into R_{M_e}, respectively. Recall that both M_e and M_f have to read the entire input string to accept it.

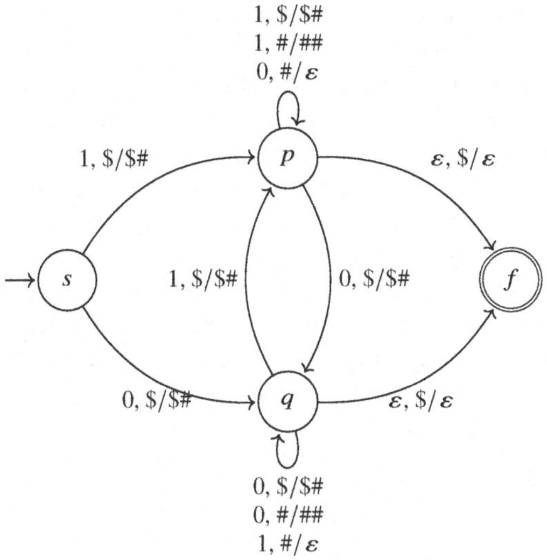

Fig. 2.3 PDA M_{PDA}.

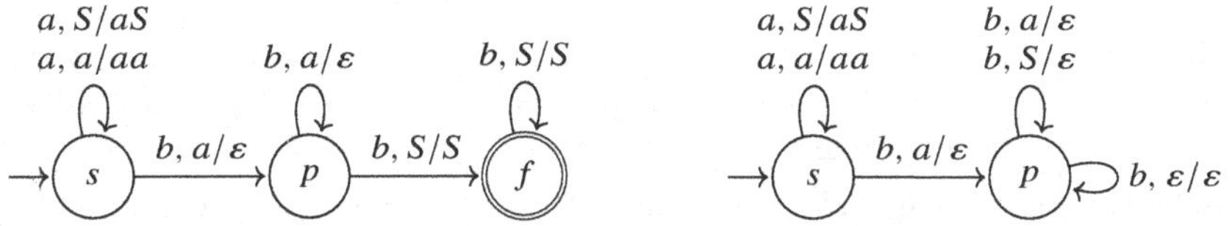

Fig. 2.4 PDA M_f and M_e.

2.2.3 Watson–Crick Finite Automaton

Reacting to the recent vivid development in molecular biology and biotechnology, theoretical computer science has introduced and studied a variety of computational models inspired by this development in order to formalize and study the new biological concepts and results in a rigorous way. The notion of a Watson–Crick (WK) automaton, introduced in Freund et al. [1997] and further discussed in Păun et al. [1998], belongs to the most important model of this kind. In essence, WK automaton represents a modified version of the notion of an FA with two reading heads working on two input tapes containing a string representing a DNA molecule.

DNA

Deoxyribonucleic acid (DNA) is a huge macromolecule consisting of millions of nucleotides—Adenine (A), Thymine (T), Cytosine (C), and Guanine (G)—arranged into a double helix with the upper and lower strand. The nucleotides are bounded in pairs between the upper and lower strand. The sequence built up by complementary pairs of nucleotides are said to be *double strands*.

In formal languages, nucleotides are straightforwardly represented by symbols A, T, C, and G, and strands are represented by strings of nucleotides. Finally, double helix is represented by two strings of nucleotides written one above the other, called *double-stranded string*. Bounded nucleotides, which are related in a complementarity way, are referred to as *pairs of symbols* and written one above the other to represent the correspondence and validity of such pairs. A substring of a double-stranded string can represent a protein or gene. Chemically, every nucleotide has two ends, (1) the 5' position corresponding to the free PO_4 group and (2) the 3' position corresponding to the free OH group. As nucleotides are stringed together, the resulting strand has one 3' end and one 5' end. In a biology environment, a strand is usually written and read from 5'-end toward its 3'-end.

Definitions

As inspired by the most prominent WK complementarity relation, the definition of complementarity relation is mathematical and more general.

Definition 2.5 Let Δ be an alphabet, $\rho \subseteq \Delta \times \Delta$ a symmetric *complementarity relation*, and $w_1, w_2 \in \Delta^*$. Then, a pair (w_1, w_2) from $\binom{\Delta^*}{\Delta^*}$ is a *double-stranded string* (DS string) and denoted as $\binom{w_1}{w_2}$. DS string $\binom{w_1}{w_2}$ is *valid* if $|w_1| = |w_2|$ and $(\text{symbol}(w_1, i), \text{symbol}(w_2, i)) \in \rho$ for all $1 \leq i \leq |w_1|$, and we denote it as $\left[\begin{smallmatrix} w_1 \\ w_2 \end{smallmatrix}\right]$.

A *Watson–Crick domain* is a set $WK_\rho(\Delta)$ which denotes all valid DS strings associated with a given alphabet Δ and ρ. Formally:

$$WK_\rho(\Delta) = \left[\begin{smallmatrix} \Delta \\ \Delta \end{smallmatrix}\right]_\rho^* \text{ where } \left[\begin{smallmatrix} \Delta \\ \Delta \end{smallmatrix}\right]_\rho = \left\{\left[\begin{smallmatrix} a \\ b \end{smallmatrix}\right] \mid a, b \in \Delta, (a, b) \in \rho\right\}$$

For instance, based on the alphabet of nucleotides $\{A, T, C, G\}$, the WK complementarity relation $\rho = \{(T, A), (A, T), (C, G), (G, C)\}$. Based on ρ, $\binom{ATC}{TCG}$ and $\left[\begin{smallmatrix} ATC \\ TAG \end{smallmatrix}\right]$ are examples of non-valid and valid DS string, respectively.

Now, we formalize an FA-based rewriting system processing valid DS strings.

Definition 2.6 A *Watson–Crick finite automaton* (WKFA) is a sextuple

$$M = (Q, \Delta, \rho, R, s, F)$$

where Q, Δ, s, and F are defined as in an FA; $Q \cap \Delta = \emptyset$, ρ is a symmetric relation on Δ, and $R \subseteq Q \times \binom{\Delta^*}{\Delta^*} \times Q$ is a finite set of rules.

A *configuration* of WKFA M is a string from $\binom{\Delta^*}{\Delta^*} Q \binom{\Delta^*}{\Delta^*}$ such that $\binom{u_1 v_1 w_1}{u_2 v_2 w_2} \in \text{WK}_\rho(\Delta)$ and $p, q \in Q$, we write

$$\binom{u_1}{u_2} p \binom{v_1}{v_2} \binom{w_1}{w_2} \vDash \binom{u_1}{u_2} \binom{v_1}{v_2} q \binom{w_1}{w_2}$$

if and only if $(p, \binom{v_1}{v_2}, q) \in R$. For lucidity, substring $\binom{\varepsilon}{\varepsilon}$ can be omitted from a configuration. Let $\models^+$ and $\models^*$ denote the transitive and the reflexive-transitive closure of $\models$, respectively.

Since M is processing the whole DS string, let $LM(M)$ denote the set of all DS strings from $\mathrm{WK}_\rho(V)$ accepted by M. In the classical theory of languages, we are interested in languages that are sets of strings, so in practice, we study the projection of $LM(M)$. Let $\uparrow_V (LM(M)) = \{w_1 \in V^* \mid \left[\begin{smallmatrix} w_1 \\ w_2 \end{smallmatrix}\right] \in LM(M),\ w_2 \in V^*\}$. Then, the language accepted by WKFA M, denoted $L(M)$, is defined as $L(M) = \uparrow_V (LM(M))$.

Formally, the language accepted by WKFA is

$$L(M) = \left\{w_1 \in \Delta^* \mid s\left[\begin{smallmatrix} w_1 \\ w_2 \end{smallmatrix}\right] \models^* \left[\begin{smallmatrix} w_1 \\ w_2 \end{smallmatrix}\right] f,\ f \in F,\ \left[\begin{smallmatrix} w_1 \\ w_2 \end{smallmatrix}\right] \in \mathrm{WK}_\rho(\Delta)\right\}$$

The family of languages accepted by WKFAs is denoted by **WK**.

It has been shown in Kuske and Weigel [2004] that the type of complementary relation does not increase the expressive power of WK automata and grammars. Moreover, Czeizler and Czeizler [2006] provide an algorithm to transform any WK automaton into an equivalent WK automaton with the relation being identity. Therefore, many models and algorithms limit themselves to work only with identity complementarity relation.

As illustrated in the following example, we can view the tape of WKFA as two tapes that are not totally independent since both such tapes are bounded by the WK relation.

Example 2.6 Let a WKFA

$$M = (\{s, q, f\}, \{a, b, c\}, \rho, R, s, \{f\})$$

where ρ is the identity relation and R is a set of rules

$$\{s\binom{a}{\varepsilon} \to s,\ s\binom{a}{\varepsilon} \to q, q\binom{b}{\varepsilon} \to q, q\binom{b}{\varepsilon} \to f,$$
$$f\binom{c}{a} \to f, f\binom{c}{b} \to f, f\binom{\varepsilon}{c} \to f\}$$

Using rules of M, we illustrate how to process $\left[\begin{smallmatrix} aabccc \\ aabccc \end{smallmatrix}\right]$.

$$s\binom{aabccc}{aabccc} \models \binom{a}{\varepsilon} s\binom{abccc}{aabccc} \models \binom{aa}{\varepsilon} q\binom{bccc}{aabccc} \models \binom{aab}{\varepsilon} f\binom{ccc}{aabccc} \models$$
$$\binom{aabc}{a} f\binom{cc}{abccc} \models \binom{aabcc}{aa} f\binom{c}{abccc} \models \binom{aabccc}{aab} f\binom{\varepsilon}{ccc} \models$$
$$\binom{aabccc}{aabc} f\binom{\varepsilon}{cc} \models \binom{aabccc}{aabcc} f\binom{\varepsilon}{c} \models \binom{aabccc}{aabccc} f$$

The language accepted by M is $L(M) = \{a^m b^n c^{m+n} \mid m, n \geq 1\}$ which is context-free language.

The following short example illustrates that WKFA can accept even some non-context-free languages.

Example 2.7 Let a WKFA $M = (\{s, p, q, f\}, \{a, b, c\}, \rho, R, s, \{f\})$, where ρ is the identity relation and R is a set of rules

$$\{s\binom{a}{\varepsilon} \to s,\ s\binom{b}{a} \to p,\ p\binom{b}{a} \to p,\ p\binom{c}{b} \to q,$$
$$q\binom{c}{b} \to q,\ q\binom{\varepsilon}{c} \to f,\ f\binom{\varepsilon}{c} \to f\}$$

Observe that $L(M) = \{a^n b^n c^n \mid n \geq 1\}$ which is non-context-free.

Variants of WK Models

By various restrictions placed on a set of states and the form of rules, there are four subclasses of WKFA (see Chapter 5 in Păun et al. [1998]).

Definition 2.7 A WKFA $M = (Q, \Delta, \rho, R, s, F)$ is

(i) *stateless* if it has only one state, so $Q = F = \{s\}$;
(ii) *all-final* if all states are final, so $Q = F$;
(iii) *simple* if at each accepting step M reads either the upper or the lower strand, so $(p, \binom{v_1}{v_2}, q) \in R$ implies $v_1 = \varepsilon$ or $v_2 = \varepsilon$;
(iv) 1-*limited* if it is simple and at every step M reads only one symbol, so $(p, \binom{v_1}{v_2}, q) \in R$ implies $|v_1 v_2| = 1$.

The families of languages accepted by stateless, all-final, simple, and 1-limited WKFAs are denoted by **NWK**, **FWK**, **SWK**, and **1WK**, respectively. Further variants such as **NS**, **FS**, **N1**, and **F1** WK automata can be defined in a straightforward way by combining multiple constraints.

The relationships between the language families accepted by variants of WKFAs are carefully investigated in Păun et al. [1998] and visualized together with the Chomsky hierarchy in Figure 2.5.

Theorem 2.2 (Păun et al. [1998])

$$\mathbf{N1WK} \subset \mathbf{NSWK} \subseteq \mathbf{NWK} \subset \mathbf{FWK} \subset \mathbf{WK} = \mathbf{SWK} = \mathbf{1WK}$$

$$\mathbf{REG} \subset \mathbf{WK}$$

$$\mathbf{REG} - \mathbf{NWK} \neq \emptyset$$

$$\mathbf{F1WK} - \mathbf{NWK} \neq \emptyset$$

$$\mathbf{NSWK} \subset \mathbf{F1WK}$$

Several additional variants and restrictions of Watson–Crick automata were introduced such as initial stateless WK finite automata, reverse WK automata, WK two-way automata, WK automata with a WK memory, and WK transducers (see Păun et al. [1998]). In addition, simple and 1-limited WK automata with bounded number of leaps between the two strands were investigated in Martín-Vide and Păun [2000].

Recently, the field of WK models was extended to grammar models as well (see Mohamad Zulkufli et al. [2016, 2017, 2018]; Hammer and Křivka [2022]). By

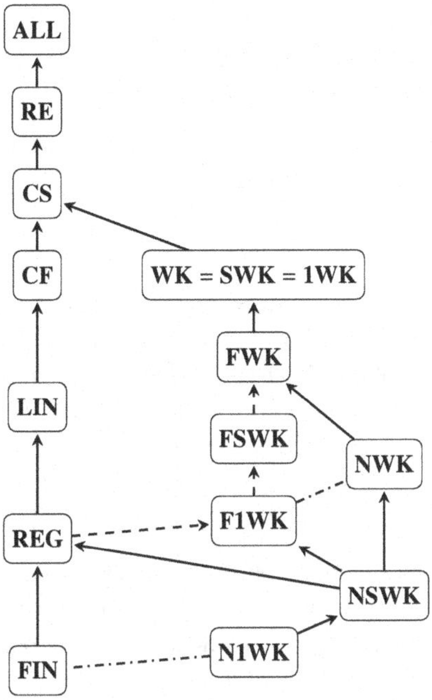

Fig. 2.5 Chomsky hierarchy and the language families defined by WKFAs.

Subramanian et al. [2012], WKFAs are equivalent in the expressive power with WK regular grammars, but it is still an open problem whether WK pushdown automata Chatterjee and Ray [2017] define the language family generated by WK context-free grammars.

2.3 Grammars

As already stated in Section 2.1, grammars represent the fundamental language-generating rewriting systems. The present section defines three basic types of grammars: context-free, context-sensitive, and unrestricted grammars, which are constantly used throughout the rest of this book. In addition, it describes the relationships, customarily called the *Chomsky hierarchy*, between the language families they generate.

Definition 2.8 An *unrestricted grammar* or *phrase-structure grammar* (PSG) is a quadruple

$$G = (\Sigma, \Delta, P, S)$$

where

Σ is the *total alphabet*,

Δ is the set of *terminals* ($\Delta \subset \Sigma$),
$P \subseteq \Sigma^*(\Sigma - \Delta)\Sigma^* \times \Sigma^*$ is a finite relation,
$S \in \Sigma - \Delta$ is the *axiom* or *starting nonterminal* or *starting symbol* of G.

The symbols in $\Sigma - \Delta$ are referred to as *nonterminals*. Furthermore, every $(x, y) \in P$ is called a *rule* or a *production rule* and written as

$$x \rightarrow y \in P$$

Accordingly, the set P is according to its content called the *set of rules* in G. Let $p: x \rightarrow y \in P$ be a rule with *label* p, then we set $\text{lhs}(p) = x$ and $\text{rhs}(p) = y$. The rewriting relation in G is called *direct derivation* or *derivation step*. It is a binary relation on Σ^* denoted by $\Rightarrow_G$ and defined in the following way. Let $p: x \rightarrow y \in P$, $u, v, z_1, z_2 \in \Sigma^*$, and $u = z_1xz_2$, $v = z_1yz_2$; then,

$$u \,_G\!\Rightarrow v \ [p]$$

When there is no danger of confusion, we simplify $u \Rightarrow_G v \ [p]$ to $u \Rightarrow_G v$. We denote the k-fold product of $\Rightarrow_G$ by $\Rightarrow_G^k$. By $\Rightarrow_G^+$ and $\Rightarrow_G^*$, we denote the transitive closure of $\Rightarrow_G$ and the reflexive-transitive closure of $\Rightarrow_G$, respectively. If $S \Rightarrow_G^* x$ for some $x \in \Sigma^*$, x is called a *sentential form*.

If there exists a derivation $S \Rightarrow_G^* w$, where $w \in \Delta^*$, $S \Rightarrow_G^* w$ is said to be a *successful derivation* in G. The *language of* G or *language generated by* G, denoted by $L(G)$, is defined as

$$L(G) = \{w \in \Delta^* \mid S \Rightarrow_G^* w\}$$

The members of $L(G)$ are called *sentences*. In general, to explicitly express that the sentences are generated by various rewritting steps, we alternatively denote the generated language by $L(G, \Rightarrow_G^*)$. In the literature, the unrestricted grammars are also often defined by listing its rules of the form

$$xAy \rightarrow xuy$$

where $u, x, y \in \Sigma^*$, $A \in \Sigma - \Delta$ (see Hopcroft and Ullman [1979]). Both definitions are interchangeable, which means that the grammars defined in these two ways generate the same language family—the family of *recursively enumerable languages*, denoted by **RE**.

In rewriting system viewpoint, the grammars work with $L_S = \{S\}$, $L_{\mathcal{F}} = \Delta^*$, and identity as the projection from $L_{\mathcal{F}}$ into the generated language. Notice that in grammars, we prefer the notion of *sentential form* instead of the notion of configuration.

Definition 2.9 An unrestricted grammar $G = (\Sigma, \Delta, P, S)$ is *context-sensitive* (CSG) if each rule in P is of the form

$$xAy \rightarrow xuy$$

where $A \in \Sigma - \Delta$, $u \in \Sigma^+$, $x, y \in \Sigma^*$. A *context-sensitive language* is the language generated by a context-sensitive grammar. The family of context-sensitive languages is denoted by **CS**.

Definition 2.10 An unrestricted grammar $G = (\Sigma, \Delta, P, S)$ is *context-free* (CFG) if each rule $x \longrightarrow y \in P$ satisfies $x \in \Sigma - \Delta$. A rule $x \longrightarrow y$ is *erasing* if $y = \varepsilon$. A CFG without erasing rules is called *ε-free*. Analogically, a *context-free language* is the language generated by a context-free grammar. The family of context-free languages is denoted by **CF**.

Importantly, **CF** is characterized by PDAs (see Section 2.2.2) and ε-free CFGs as well.

Theorem 2.3 ([Meduna, 2014, Theorem 6.55])

$$\mathbf{CF} = \{L(M) \mid M \text{ is a PDA}\}$$

Theorem 2.4 ([Meduna, 2000, Theorem 5.1.3.2.4])

$$\mathbf{CF} = \{L(G) \mid G \text{ is an } \varepsilon\text{-free CFG}\}$$

Two examples of a context-free language that cannot be generated by simpler type of grammar follow.

Example 2.8 Assume a language L over alphabet $\{0, 1\}$ such that

$$L = \{w \mid w \in \{0, 1\} \text{ and } \operatorname{occur}(w, 0) = \operatorname{occur}(w, 1)\}$$

which is the same language as in Example 2.5.

Let $G = (\Sigma, \Delta, P, S)$ where $\Delta = \{0, 1\}$, $N = \{S, A, B\}$, $\Sigma = N \cup \Delta$ and P consists of

$$\begin{array}{ll} S \longrightarrow aB, & A \longrightarrow bAA, \\ S \longrightarrow bA, & B \longrightarrow b, \\ A \longrightarrow a, & B \longrightarrow bS, \\ A \longrightarrow aS, & B \longrightarrow aBB. \end{array}$$

The proof that really $L = L(G)$ can be found, for instance, in [Meduna, 2014, page 88].

Example 2.9 Consider a CFG $G = (\Sigma = \{E, i, +, *, (,), [,]\}, \Sigma - \{E\}, P, E)$ with P consisting of

$$\begin{array}{ll} E \longrightarrow E + E, & E \longrightarrow E * E, \\ E \longrightarrow (E), & E \longrightarrow [E], \\ E \longrightarrow i & \end{array}$$

Observe that G generates the language of all well-written arithmetic expressions with parentheses (,) and [,].

When we eliminate everything but the parentheses in this language and we allow k kinds of parentheses, $k \geq 1$, we obtain a set of languages, called *semi-Dyck languages* where strings represent tree structures with different kinds of subtrees. For some $k \geq 1$, semi-Dyck language D_k is generated by a CFG with $\Delta = \{a_1, a'_1, a_2, a'_2, \ldots, a_k, a'_k\}$ (a_i and a'_i is a pair of the corresponding parentheses), start nonterminal E, and the set of rules consists of

$$
\begin{aligned}
E &\to EE, \\
E &\to a_1 E a'_1, \\
E &\to a_2 E a'_2, \\
&\vdots \\
E &\to a_k E a'_k, \\
E &\to \varepsilon
\end{aligned}
$$

Definition 2.11 A CFG $G = (\Sigma, \Delta, P, S)$ is *linear* (LG) if each rule $x \to y \in P$ satisfies $y \in \Delta^*(\Sigma - \Delta)\Delta^*$. An LG defined in this way generates a *linear language*. The family of linear languages is denoted by **LIN**.

Definition 2.12 A CFG $G = (\Sigma, \Delta, P, S)$ is *right-linear* (RLG) if each rule $x \to y \in P$ satisfies $y \in \Delta^* \cup \Delta^*(\Sigma - \Delta)$.

Definition 2.13 A CFG $G = (\Sigma, \Delta, P, S)$ is *regular* (RG) if each rule $x \to y \in P$ satisfies $y \in \Delta \cup \Delta(\Sigma, \Delta)$. A RG and a RLG define *regular* and *right-linear language*, respectively. The family of both of these types of languages is denoted as the family of regular languages by **REG**.

In addition, **REG** is characterized by FAs (see Section 2.2.1) as well.

Theorem 2.5 (see Theorem 3.38 in Meduna [2014]) *$L \in$ **REG** if and only if there is an FA M such that $L(M) = L$.*

The classes of grammars defined in this section define the language families of the well-known *Chomsky hierarchy*, diagrammed in Figure 2.5.

Theorem 2.6 FIN $\subset$ REG $\subset$ LIN $\subset$ CF $\subset$ CS $\subset$ RE $\subset$ ALL

Next, we give several important results together with references in which their proofs are to be found.

Theorem 2.7 (Sipser [2006]; Rozenberg and Salomaa [1997a]; Meduna [2007]) **REG** *is closed under union, concatenation, closure, positive closure, intersection, complementation, finite substitution, homomorphism, and regular substitution.*

Theorem 2.8 (Meduna [2007]) CF *is closed under union, concatenation, closure, complementation, reversal and homomorphism.*

The following theorem gives a characterization of the family of recursively enumerable languages by context-free languages.

Theorem 2.9 (Ginsburg et al. [1967]) *For every recursively enumerable language L, there exist two context-free languages, L_1 and L_2, and a homomorphism h such that*

$$L = h(L_1 \cap L_2)$$

Part II
Jumping Automata

This part, consisting of Chapters 3 and 4, presents the fundamentals of jumping finite automata. First, it gives an extensive and thorough coverage of jumping one-head finite automata (Chapter 3), after which it covers their multi-head versions (Chapter 4).

Chapter 3 gives a systematic body of up-to-date knowledge concerning jumping one-head finite automata, which actually originated the theory of jumping models as a whole. It demonstrates several fundamental results about these automata in most common areas of formal language theory, such as their expressive power, closure properties, infinite language family hierarchy resulting from them, and the effect resulting from various restrictions placed on the jumping direction. Although the knowledge about these automata is solidly established today, Chapter 3 points out several open questions. To complete the study of one-head jumping automata models, Chapter 3 covers one-way jumping finite automata as well.

One-head jumping finite automata obviously formalize discontinuous computation more properly than classical finite automata. Nevertheless, they always apply a single rule during every jump, thus principally failing to formalize another important feature of today's computation—parallelism. Therefore, Chapter 4 generalizes them to their multi-head versions that perform a simultaneous application of several rules during any jump, thus reflecting and formalizing discontinuous parallelism more properly than their original one-head versions. Chapter 4 defines and explores a large variety of these multi-head versions, ranging from strictly two-head jumping automata through jumping automata having any number of heads up to jumping Watson–Crick finite automata, which are frequently used in practice of today's computer science. Perhaps most importantly, concerning the Watson–Crick automata, Chapter 4 thoroughly covers their crucially important special cases—jumping Watson–Crick finite automata and jumping $5' \to 3'$ Watson–Crick finite automata, whose bioinformatically oriented applications are overwhelming at present.

Chapter 3
Jumping One-Head Automata

As computational models, finite automata are conceptualized so simply and naturally that they definitely belong to the most intensively investigated and, perhaps even more importantly, applied automata in computer science as a whole. Recently, the theory of computation has introduced their jumping versions (see Meduna and Zemek [2012] introducing jumping finite automata) as the very first jumping mechanism in this theory. As their name suggests, these automata jump across their input strings in a discontinuous way while keeping the simple concept of their classical counterparts unchanged. The fundamental reason for this introduction was that the jumping versions properly reflect and formalize discontinuous information processing, which is quite central to today's computation and which was virtually unknown in the past.

To put this reason into a historical perspective, in the previous century, most classical computer science methods were developed for continuous information processing, and the concept of classical finite automata obviously formalizes this kind of processing very well. That is, the classical finite automata work on strings, representing information, in a strictly continuous left-to-right symbol-by-symbol way. Working in this continuous way, however, makes them unable to act as adequate models of current computational methods, which often process information in an extremely discontinuous way. Indeed, within a particular running process, a typical computational step is usually performed somewhere in the middle of information, while the very next computational step is executed far away from it; therefore, before the next step is carried out, the process has to jump over a large portion of the information to the desired position of execution. As is obvious, classical finite automata cannot model discontinuous computation of this kind adequately while their jumping versions can.

To sketch the difference between both versions in greater detail, reconsider the general notion of a classical finite automaton C (see Definition 2.2). C consists of an input tape, a read head, and a finite state control. The input tape is divided into squares, each of which contains one symbol of an input string with the current input symbol right under the read head of C. The finite control is represented by a finite set of states together with a set of computational rules. C works by making moves.

Each move is made according to a computational rule that describes how the current state is changed and whether the current input symbol is read. If the symbol is read, the read head is shifted a square to the right. C has one state defined as the start state and some states designated as final states. If C can read w by making a sequence of moves from the start state to a final state, C accepts w; otherwise, C rejects w. A jumping finite automaton J is conceptualized just like C. Apart from the concept, J also works similarly to the way C does except that J does not read the input string in a symbol-by-symbol and left-to-right way. Indeed, after reading a symbol, J can jump over a portion of the tape in either direction and goes on reading from there. It is worth noting that once J reads an input symbol a, J cannot re-read it afterward; indeed, reading a actually means its replacement with ε, so all the prefixes preceding a and all the suffixes following a join each other after this erasure.

This chapter concentrates on jumping finite automata with a single read head while leaving a discussion of their multi-head versions to the next chapter. The present chapter demonstrates several key results about jumping one-head finite automata in terms of many commonly studied areas of formal language theory. Perhaps most importantly, it studies differences between them and their classical counterparts. As a whole, it gives a systematic body of knowledge concerning jumping one-head finite automata. At the same time, however, it points out several open questions regarding them, which may represent a new, attractive, and significant investigation area of automata theory in the future.

Synopsis

The chapter is divided into two sections. Section 3.1 formalizes and illustrates jumping finite automata and demonstrates their fundamental properties. Most importantly, it compares their power with the power of other well-known language-defining formal devices. In addition, this section establishes basic closure properties of the language families defined by them. In addition, it establishes an infinite hierarchy of language families resulting from these automata, one-directional jumps and various start configurations. Section 3.2 describes right one-way jumping finite automata as both natural and deterministic modification of jumping finite automata with right jumps as studied in Section 3.1.

3.1 Basic and Generalized Jumping Finite Automata

In this subsection, we define a variety of jumping finite automata discussed in this section and illustrate them by examples.

Definition 3.1 A *general jumping finite automaton* (GJFA) is a quintuple $M = (Q, \Delta, R, s, F)$, where Δ is the input alphabet of M, and Q, s, R have the same meaning as in Definition 2.2, except that $a \in \Delta^*$ for every $qa \rightarrow p \in R$. Furthermore, we define the binary *jumping relation* over $\Delta^* Q \Delta^*$, symbolically denoted by $\curvearrowright$, as follows. Let $x, z, x', z' \in \Delta^*$ such that $xz = x'z'$ and $py \rightarrow q \in R$; then, M makes a *jump* from $xpyz$ to $x'qz'$, symbolically written as $xpyz \curvearrowright x'qz'$. In the standard manner, we extend $\curvearrowright$ to $\curvearrowright^m$, where $m \geq 0$, $\curvearrowright^+$, and $\curvearrowright^*$.

The *language* accepted by M with $\curvearrowright$, denoted by $L(M, \curvearrowright)$, is defined as $L(M, \curvearrowright) = \{uv \mid u, v \in \Delta^*, usv \curvearrowright^* f, f \in F\}$. Let $w \in \Delta^*$. We say that M *accepts* w if and only if $w \in L(M, \curvearrowright)$; M *rejects* w, otherwise. Two GJFAs M and M' are said to be *equivalent* if and only if $L(M, \curvearrowright) = L(M', \curvearrowright)$.

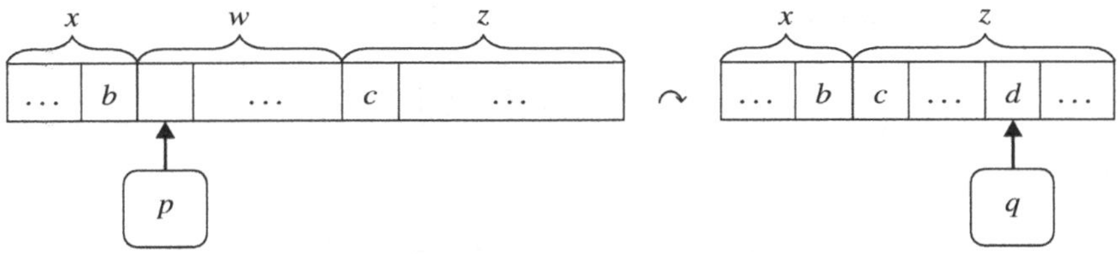

Fig. 3.1 GJFA jump.

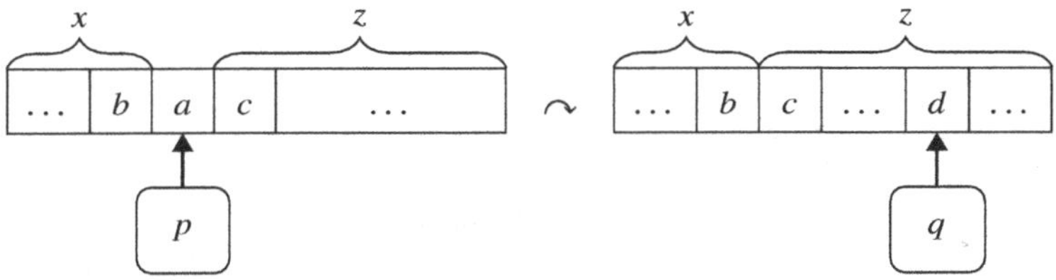

Fig. 3.2 JFA jump.

Definition 3.2 Let $M = (Q, \Delta, R, s, F)$ be a GJFA. M is an *ε-free GJFA* if $py \rightarrow q \in R$ implies that $|y| \geq 1$. M is of *degree n*, where $n \geq 0$, if $py \rightarrow q \in R$ implies that $|y| \leq n$. M is a *jumping finite automaton* (JFA) if its degree is 1.

Figures 3.1 and 3.2 schematize jumps in a GJFA and a JFA, respectively. More specifically, these figures illustrate right jumps, where x, w, z are strings, and a, b, c, d are symbols.

Definition 3.3 Let $M = (Q, \Delta, R, s, F)$ be a JFA. Analogously to a GJFA, M is an *ε-free JFA* if $py \rightarrow q \in R$ implies that $|y| = 1$. M is a *deterministic JFA* (DJFA) if (1) it is an ε-free JFA and (2) for each $p \in Q$ and each $a \in \Delta$, there is no more than one $q \in Q$ such that $pa \rightarrow q \in R$. M is a *complete JFA* (CJFA) if (1) it is a DJFA and (2) for each $p \in Q$ and each $a \in \Delta$, there is precisely one $q \in Q$ such that $pa \rightarrow q \in R$.

Definition 3.4 Let $M = (Q, \Delta, R, s, F)$ be a GJFA. The *transition graph* of M, denoted by $\Gamma(M)$, is a multi-graph, where nodes are states from Q, and there is an edge from p to q labeled with y if and only if $py \rightarrow q \in R$. A state $q \in Q$ is *reachable* if there is a walk from s to q in $\Gamma(M)$; q is *terminating* if there is a walk from q to some $f \in F$. If there is a walk from p to q, $p = q_1, q_2, \ldots, q_n = q$, for some $n \geq 2$, where $q_i y_i \rightarrow q_{i+1} \in R$ for all $i = 1, \ldots, n-1$, then we write

$$py_1y_2\cdots y_n \rightsquigarrow q$$

Next, we illustrate the previous definitions by two examples.

Example 3.1 Consider the DJFA

$$M = \left(\{s, r, t\}, \Delta, R, s, \{s\}\right)$$

where $\Delta = \{a, b, c\}$ and

$$R = \left\{sa \rightarrow r, rb \rightarrow t, tc \rightarrow s\right\}$$

Starting from s, M has to read some a, some b, and some c, entering again the start (and also the final) state s (see also Figure 3.3). All these occurrences of a, b, and c can appear anywhere in the input string. Therefore, the accepted language is clearly

$$L(M, \curvearrowright) = \left\{w \in \Delta^* \mid \text{occur}(w, a) = \text{occur}(w, b) = \text{occur}(w, c)\right\}$$

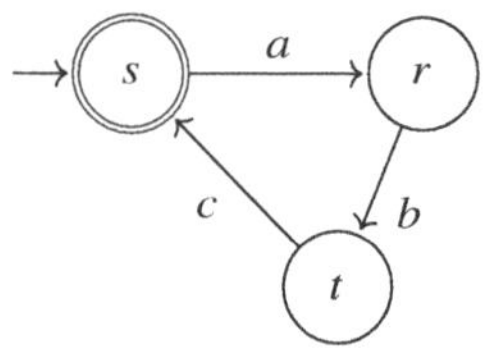

Fig. 3.3 Diagram of a finite automaton accepting $\{abc\}^*$.

Recall that $L(M, \curvearrowright)$ in Example 3.1 is a well-known non-context-free context-sensitive language.

Example 3.2 Consider the GJFA

$$M = \left(\{s, t, f\}, \{a, b\}, R, s, \{f\}\right)$$

where

$$R = \left\{sba \rightarrow f, fa \rightarrow f, fb \rightarrow f\right\}$$

Starting from s, M has to read string ba, which can appear anywhere in the input string. Then, it can read an arbitrary number of symbols a and b, including no symbols. Therefore, the accepted language is $L(M, \curvearrowright) = \{a, b\}^*\{ba\}\{a, b\}^*$.

In fact, it is easy to see that several other languages over Δ belong to **GJFA** such as

(i) $\Delta^* u \Delta^*$ where $u \in \Delta^*$ (a generalization of Example 3.2);
(ii) any semi-Dyck language D_k, for $k \geq 1$ (for the definition, see Example 2.9, and for the proof see Example 5.3 or Vorel [2018]).

Denotation of Language Families

Throughout the rest of this chapter, **GJFA**, $\mathbf{GJFA}^{-\varepsilon}$, **JFA**, $\mathbf{JFA}^{-\varepsilon}$, and **DJFA** denote the families of languages accepted by GJFAs, ε-free GJFAs, JFAs, ε-free JFAs, and DJFAs, respectively.

Properties

In this section, we discuss the generative power of GJFAs and JFAs and some other basic properties of these automata.

Theorem 3.1 *For every DJFA M, there is a CJFA M′ such that* $L(M, \curvearrowright) = L(M', \curvearrowright)$.

Proof Let $M = (Q, \Delta, R, s, F)$ be a DJFA. We next construct a CJFA M' such that $L(M, \curvearrowright) = L(M', \curvearrowright)$. Without any loss of generality, we assume that $\perp \notin Q$. Initially, set

$$M' = \left(Q \cup \{\perp\}, \Delta, R', s, F\right)$$

where $R' = R$. Next, for each $a \in \Delta$ and each $p \in Q$ such that $pa \to q \notin R$ for all $q \in Q$, add $pa \to \perp$ to R'. For each $a \in \Delta$, add $\perp a \to \perp$ to R'. Clearly, M' is a CJFA and $L(M, \curvearrowright) = L(M', \curvearrowright)$. □

Lemma 3.1 *For every GJFA M of degree* $n \geq 0$, *there is an* ε*-free GJFA M′ of degree n such that* $L(M', \curvearrowright) = L(M, \curvearrowright)$.

Proof This lemma can be demonstrated by using the standard conversion of finite automata to ε-free finite automata (see [Meduna, 2000, Algorithm 3.2.2.3]). □

Theorem 3.2 $\mathbf{GJFA} = \mathbf{GJFA}^{-\varepsilon}$

Proof $\mathbf{GJFA}^{-\varepsilon} \subseteq \mathbf{GJFA}$ follows from the definition of a GJFA (see Def. 3.1). $\mathbf{GJFA} \subseteq \mathbf{GJFA}^{-\varepsilon}$ follows from Lemma 3.1. □

Theorem 3.3 $\mathbf{JFA} = \mathbf{JFA}^{-\varepsilon} = \mathbf{DJFA}$

Proof $\mathbf{JFA} = \mathbf{JFA}^{-\varepsilon}$ can be proved by analogy with the proof of Theorem 3.2, so we only prove that $\mathbf{JFA}^{-\varepsilon} = \mathbf{DJFA}$. $\mathbf{DJFA} \subseteq \mathbf{JFA}^{-\varepsilon}$ follows from the definition of a DJFA (see Def. 3.3). The converse inclusion can be proved by using the standard technique of converting ε-free finite automata to deterministic finite automata (see [Meduna, 2000, Algorithm 3.2.3.1]). □

The next theorem shows a property of languages accepted by GJFAs with unary input alphabets.

Theorem 3.4 *Let* $M = (Q, \Delta, R, s, F)$ *be a GJFA such that* $\mathrm{card}(\Delta) = 1$. *Then,* $L(M, \curvearrowright)$ *is regular.*

Proof Let $M = (Q, \Delta, R, s, F)$ be a GJFA such that $\mathrm{card}(\Delta) = 1$. Since $\mathrm{card}(\Delta) = 1$, without any loss of generality, we can assume that the acceptance process for $w \in \Delta^*$ starts from the configuration sw and M does not jump over any symbols. Therefore, we can treat M as an equivalent *general finite automaton* defined just like an ordinary finite automaton except that it can read a string, not just a symbol, during a single move (see [Meduna and Zemek, 2014, Definition 3.4.1]). As general finite automata accept only regular languages (see [Meduna and Zemek, 2014, Theorem 3.4.4]), $L(M, \curvearrowright)$ is regular. □

As a consequence of Theorem 3.4, we obtain the following corollary (recall that K below is not regular).

Corollary 3.1 *The language* $K = \{a^p \mid p \text{ is a prime number}\}$ *cannot be accepted by any GJFA.*

The following theorem gives a necessary condition for a language to be in **JFA**.

Theorem 3.5 *Let* K *be an arbitrary language. Then,* $K \in \mathbf{JFA}$ *only if* $K = \mathrm{perm}(K)$.

Proof Let $M = (Q, \Delta, R, s, F)$ be a JFA. Without any loss of generality, we assume that M is a DJFA (recall that **JFA** = **DJFA** by Theorem 3.3). Let $w \in L(M, \curvearrowright)$. We next prove that $\mathrm{perm}(w) \subseteq L(M, \curvearrowright)$. If $w = \varepsilon$, then $\mathrm{perm}(\varepsilon) = \varepsilon \in L(M, \curvearrowright)$, so we assume that $w \neq \varepsilon$. Then, $w = a_1 a_2 \cdots a_n$, where $a_i \in \Delta$ for all $i = 1, \ldots, n$, for some $n \geq 1$. Since $w \in L(M, \curvearrowright)$, R contains

$$\begin{array}{ll} s a_{i_1} & \rightarrow s_{i_1} \\ s_{i_1} a_{i_2} & \rightarrow s_{i_2} \\ & \vdots \\ s_{i_{n-1}} a_{i_n} & \rightarrow s_{i_n} \end{array}$$

where $s_j \in Q$ for all $j \in \{i_1, i_2, \ldots, i_n\}$, $(i_1, i_2, \ldots, i_n)$ is a permutation of $(1, 2, \ldots, n)$, and $s_{i_n} \in F$. However, this implies that $a_{k_1} a_{k_2} \cdots a_{k_n} \in L(M, \curvearrowright)$, where $(k_1, k_2, \ldots, k_n)$ is a permutation of $(1, 2, \ldots, n)$, so $\mathrm{perm}(w) \subseteq L(M, \curvearrowright)$. □

From Theorem 3.5, we obtain the following two corollaries, which are used in subsequent proofs.

Corollary 3.2 *There is no JFA that accepts* $\{ab\}^*$.

Corollary 3.3 *There is no JFA that accepts* $\{a, b\}^* \{ba\} \{a, b\}^*$.

Consider the language of primes K from Corollary 3.1. Since $K = \mathrm{perm}(K)$, the condition from Theorem 3.5 is not sufficient for a language to be in **JFA**. This is stated in the following corollary.

Corollary 3.4 *There is a language K satisfying $K = \mathrm{perm}(K)$ that cannot be accepted by any JFA.*

The next theorem gives both a necessary and sufficient condition for a language to be accepted by a JFA.

Theorem 3.6 *Let L be an arbitrary language. $L \in$ **JFA** if and only if $L = \mathrm{perm}(K)$, where K is a regular language.*

Proof The proof is divided into the only-if part and the if part.

Only If. Let M be a JFA. Consider M as a finite automaton M'. Set $K = L(M')$. K is regular, and $L(M, \curvearrowright) = \mathrm{perm}(K)$. Hence, the only-if part holds.

If. Take $\mathrm{perm}(K)$, where K is any regular language. Let $K = L(M)$, where M is a finite automaton. Consider M as a JFA M'. Observe that $L(M', \curvearrowright) = \mathrm{perm}(K)$, which proves the if part of the proof. □

Inspired by the pumping lemma for regular languages, we can formulate corresponding lemma for JFAs.

Lemma 3.2 (Chigahara et al. [2016]) *For any language L over an alphabet Δ ($\mathrm{card}(\Delta) = n$) accepted by a JFA, there exists a constant k such that for all strings $w \in L$ with $|w| \geq k$ and Parikh image $\psi_\Delta(w) = (m_1, m_2, \ldots, m_n)$ there exists a vector $(t_1, t_2, \ldots, t_n)$ which satisfies the following criteria:*

(1) $t_i \leq m_i$, for all i with $1 \leq i \leq n$;
(2) $\sum_{i=1}^{n} t_n \leq k$;
(3) all strings with Parikh vector $(m_1 + i \cdot t_1, m_2 + i \cdot t_2, \ldots, m_n + i \cdot t_n)$ are in L, for all integers $i \geq -1$.

As opposed to the standard versions of FAs and GFAs, which are equally powerful (see Theorem 2.1), we next show that GJFAs are stronger than JFAs.

Theorem 3.7 JFA $\subset$ GJFA

Proof **JFA** $\subseteq$ **GJFA** follows from the definition of a JFA (see Definition 3.2). From Corollary 3.3, **GJFA** $-$ **JFA** $\neq \emptyset$, because $\{a, b\}^*\{ba\}\{a, b\}^*$ is accepted by the GJFA from Example 3.2. □

Theorem 3.6 gives a necessary and sufficient condition concerning the membership of any language in **JFA**. Concerning **GJFA**, however, so far, only a necessary condition has been achieved (see Vorel [2018]).

Open Problem Is there a necessary and sufficient condition for a language to be in **GJFA**? □

Relationships with Well-Known Language Families

In this section, we establish relationships between **GJFA**, **JFA**, and some well-known language families, including **FIN**, **REG**, **CF**, and **CS**.

Theorem 3.8 FIN ⊂ GJFA

Proof Let $K \in$ **FIN**. Since K is a finite, there exists $n \geq 0$ such that $\text{card}(K) = n$. Therefore, we can express K as $K = \{w_1, w_2, \ldots, w_n\}$. Define the GJFA

$$M = \big(\{s, f\}, \Delta, R, s, \{f\}\big)$$

where $\Delta = \text{symbols}(K)$ and $R = \{sw_1 \rightarrow f, sw_2 \rightarrow f, \ldots, sw_n \rightarrow f\}$. Clearly, $L(M, \curvearrowright) = K$. Therefore, **FIN** ⊆ **GJFA**. From Example 3.1, **GJFA** − **FIN** $\neq \emptyset$, which proves the theorem. □

Lemma 3.3 *There is no GJFA that accepts* $\{a\}^*\{b\}^*$.

Proof (*by contradition*) Let $K = \{a\}^*\{b\}^*$. For the sake of contradiction, assume that there is a GJFA, $M = (Q, \Delta, R, s, F)$, such that $L(M, \curvearrowright) = K$. Let $w = a^n b$, where n is the degree of M. Since $w \in K$, during an acceptance of w, a rule, $pa^i b \rightarrow q \in R$, where $p, q \in Q$ and $0 \leq i < n$, has to be used. However, then M also accepts from the configuration $a^i bsa^{n-i}$. Indeed, as $a^i b$ is read in a single step, and all the other symbols in w are just as, $a^i ba^{n-i}$ may be accepted by using the same rules as during an acceptance of w. This implies that $a^i ba^{n-i} \in K$—a contradiction with the assumption that $L(M, \curvearrowright) = K$. Therefore, there is no GJFA that accepts $\{a\}^*\{b\}^*$. □

Theorem 3.9 REG *and* **GJFA** *are incomparable.*

Proof **GJFA** ⊈ **REG** follows from Example 3.1. **REG** ⊈ **GJFA** follows from Lemma 3.3. □

Theorem 3.10 CF *and* **GJFA** *are incomparable.*

Proof **GJFA** ⊈ **CF** follows from Example 3.1, and **CF** ⊈ **GJFA** follows from Lemma 3.3. □

Theorem 3.11 GJFA ⊂ CS

Proof Clearly, jumps of GJFAs can be simulated by context-sensitive grammars, so **GJFA** ⊆ **CS**. From Lemma 3.3, it follows that **CS** − **GJFA** $\neq \emptyset$. □

Theorem 3.12 FIN *and* **JFA** *are incomparable.*

Proof **JFA** ⊈ **FIN** follows from Example 3.1. Consider the finite language $K = \{ab\}$. By Theorem 3.5, $K \notin$ **JFA**, so **FIN** ⊈ **JFA**. □

Closure Properties

In this section, we show the closure properties of the families **GJFA** and **JFA** under various operations. The basic study is to be found in Meduna and Zemek [2012] and Vorel [2016, 2017, 2018] that continue the investigation of decidability and closure properties.

Theorem 3.13 *Both* **GJFA** *and* **JFA** *are not closed under endmarking.*

Proof Consider the language $K = \{a\}^*$. Clearly, $K \in$ **JFA**. A proof that no GJFA accepts $K\{\#\}$, where # is a symbol such that $\# \neq a$, can be made by analogy with the proof of Lemma 3.3. □

Theorem 3.13 implies that both families are not closed under concatenation. Indeed, observe that the JFA

$$M = (\{s, f\}, \{\#\}, \{s\# \rightarrow f\}, s, \{f\})$$

accepts $\{\#\}$.

Corollary 3.5 *Both* **GJFA** *and* **JFA** *are not closed under concatenation.*

Theorem 3.14 **JFA** *is closed under shuffle and iterated shuffle.*

Proof Let $M_1 = (Q_1, \Delta_1, R_1, s_1, F_1)$ and $M_2 = (Q_2, \Delta_2, R_2, s_2, F_2)$ be two JFAs. Without any loss of generality, we assume that $Q_1 \cap Q_2 = \emptyset$. Define the JFA

$$H = (Q_1 \cup Q_2, \Delta_1 \cup \Delta_2, R_1 \cup R_2 \cup \{f \rightarrow s_2 \mid f \in F_1\}, s_1, F_2)$$

To see that $L(H) = ⧢(L(M_1, \curvearrowright), L(M_2, \curvearrowright))$, observe how H works. On an input string, $w \in (\Delta_1 \cup \Delta_2)^*$, H first runs M_1 on w, and if it ends in a final state, then it runs M_2 on the rest of the input. If M_2 ends in a final state, H accepts w. Otherwise, it rejects w. By Theorem 3.5, $L(M_i, \curvearrowright) = \text{perm}(L(M_i, \curvearrowright))$ for all $i \in \{1, 2\}$. Based on these observations, since H can jump anywhere after a symbol is read, we see that $L(H) = ⧢(L(M_1, \curvearrowright), L(M_2, \curvearrowright))$. In addition, as proved in Fernau et al. [2017], the power of JFAs coincide to α-SHUF expressions so **JFA** is closed under iterated shuffle as well. □

Notice that the construction used in the previous proof coincides with the standard construction of a concatenation of two finite automata (see Meduna [2000]).

Theorem 3.15 (Fernau et al. [2017]) *If $L \in$* **JFA**, *then L is closed under permutation, i.e., $L = \text{perm}(L)$.*

Theorem 3.16 *Both* **GJFA** *and* **JFA** *are closed under union.*

Proof Let $M_1 = (Q_1, \Delta_1, R_1, s_1, F_1)$ and $M_2 = (Q_2, \Delta_2, R_2, s_2, F_2)$ be two GJFAs. Without any loss of generality, we assume that $Q_1 \cap Q_2 = \emptyset$ and $s \notin (Q_1 \cup Q_2)$. Define the GJFA

$$H = \left(Q_1 \cup Q_2 \cup \{s\}, \Delta_1 \cup \Delta_2, R_1 \cup R_2 \cup \{s \to s_1, s \to s_2\}, s, F_1 \cup F_2\right)$$

Clearly, $L(H) = L(M_1, \curvearrowright) \cup L(M_2, \curvearrowright)$, and if both M_1 and M_2 are JFAs, then H is also a JFA. □

Theorem 3.17 **GJFA** *is not closed under complement.*

Proof Consider the GJFA M from Example 3.2. Observe that the complement of $L(M, \curvearrowright)$ (with respect to $\{a, b\}^*$) is $\{a\}^*\{b\}^*$, which cannot be accepted by any GJFA (see Lemma 3.3). □

Theorem 3.18 **JFA** *is closed under complement.*

Proof Let $M = (Q, \Delta, R, s, F)$ be a JFA. Without any loss of generality, we assume that M is a CJFA (**JFA** = **DJFA** by Theorem 3.3 and every DJFA can be converted to an equivalent CJFA by Theorem 3.1). Then, the JFA

$$M' = \left(Q, \Delta, R, s, Q - F\right)$$

accepts $\sim L(M, \curvearrowright)$. □

Lemma 3.4 (Vorel [2018]) *For* $\Delta = \{a, b\}$, $\{ab\}^* \notin$ **GJFA**.

By using De Morgan's laws, we obtain the following two corollaries of Theorems 3.16, 3.17, and 3.18.

Corollary 3.6 **GJFA** *is not closed under intersection.*

Proof Consider any $M = (\{s, f\}, \{a, b\}, \{sba \to s, sab \to f\}, s, \{f\})$ and any semi-Dyck language $D_1 \in$ **GJFA** (see Example 3.2). Observe that $D_1 \cap L(M, \curvearrowright) = \{ab\}^*$, which is out of **GJFA** by Lemma 3.4. □

Corollary 3.7 **JFA** *is closed under intersection.*

Theorem 3.19 *Both* **GJFA** *and* **JFA** *are not closed under intersection with regular languages.*

Proof Consider the language $J = \{a, b\}^*$, which can be accepted by both GJFAs and JFAs. Consider the regular language $K = \{a\}^*\{b\}^*$. Since $J \cap K = K$, this theorem follows from Lemma 3.3. □

Theorem 3.20 **JFA** *is closed under reversal.*

Proof Let $K \in$ **JFA**. Since $\text{perm}(w) \subseteq K$ by Theorem 3.5 for all $w \in K$, also $\text{reversal}(w) \in K$ for all $w \in K$, so the theorem holds. □

Theorem 3.21 **JFA** *is not closed under Kleene star or under Kleene plus.*

Proof Consider the language $K = \{ab, ba\}$, which is accepted by the JFA

$$M = (\{s, r, f\}, \{a, b\}, \{sa \to r, rb \to f\}, s, \{f\})$$

However, by Theorem 3.5, there is no JFA that accepts K^* or K^+ (notice that, for example, $abab \in K^+$, but $aabb \notin K^+$). □

Lemma 3.5 *There is no GJFA that accepts* $\{a\}^*\{b\}^* \cup \{b\}^*\{a\}^*$.

Proof This lemma can be proved by analogy with the proof of Lemma 3.3. □

Theorem 3.22 *Both* **GJFA** *and* **JFA** *are not closed under substitution.*

Proof Consider the language $K = \{ab, ba\}$, which is accepted by the JFA M from the proof of Theorem 3.21. Define the substitution σ from $\{a, b\}^*$ to power($\{a, b\}^*$) as $\sigma(a) = \{a\}^*$ and $\sigma(b) = \{b\}^*$. Clearly, both $\sigma(a)$ and $\sigma(b)$ can be accepted by JFAs. However, $\sigma(K)$ cannot be accepted by any GJFA (see Lemma 3.5). □

Since the substitution σ in the proof of Theorem 3.22 is regular, we obtain the following corollary.

Corollary 3.8 *Both* **GJFA** *and* **JFA** *are not closed under regular substitution.*

Theorem 3.23 **JFA** *is not closed under* ε*-free homomorphism.*

Proof Define the ε-free homomorphism ϕ from $\{a\}$ to $\{a, b\}^+$ as $\phi(a) = ab$, and consider the language $\{a\}^*$, which is accepted by the JFA

$$M = (\{s\}, \{a\}, \{sa \to s\}, \{s\})$$

Notice that $\phi(L(M, \curvearrowright)) = \{ab\}^*$, which cannot be accepted by any JFA (see Corollary 3.2).

The analogous result was proved for GJFAs in Vorel [2018].

Theorem 3.24 ([Vorel, 2018, Theorem 14]) **GJFA** *is not closed under* ε*-free homomorphism.*

Since ε-free homomorphism is a special case of homomorphism, and since homomorphism is a special case of finite substitution, we obtain the following corollary of Theorems 3.23 and 3.24.

Corollary 3.9 **GJFA** *and* **JFA** *are not closed under homomorphism.*

Corollary 3.10 **GJFA** *and* **JFA** *are not closed under finite substitution.*

Theorem 3.25 **JFA** *is closed under inverse homomorphism.*

Proof Let $M = (Q, \Delta, R, s, F)$ be a JFA, Δ' be an alphabet, and ϕ be a homomorphism from Δ'^* to Δ^*. We next construct a JFA M' such that $L(M', \curvearrowright) = \phi^{-1}(L(M, \curvearrowright))$. Define

$$M' = \left(Q, \Delta', R', s, F\right)$$

where

$$R' = \left\{pa \to q \mid a \in \Delta', p\phi(a) \rightsquigarrow q \text{ in } \Gamma(M)\right\}$$

Observe that $w_1 s w_2 \curvearrowright^* q$ in M if and only if $w'_1 s w'_2 \curvearrowright^* q$ in M', where $w_1 w_2 = \phi(w'_1 w'_2)$ and $q \in Q$, so $L(M', \curvearrowright) = \phi^{-1}(L(M, \curvearrowright))$. A fully rigorous proof is left to the reader. □

However, the same does not hold for GJFAs.

Theorem 3.26 ([Vorel, 2018, Theorem 15]) GJFA *is not closed under inverse homomorphism.*

Moreover, in Vorel [2018] it was shown that **GJFA** is not close under shuffle, Kleene star, and Kleene plus, while it is closed under reversal.

Theorem 3.27 ([Vorel, 2018, Theorem 14 and Theorem 16]) GJFA *is not closed under shuffle, Kleene star, and Kleene plus.*

Theorem 3.28 ([Vorel, 2018, Theorem 18]) GJFA *is closed under reversal.*

The summary of closure properties of the families **GJFA** and **JFA** is given in Table 3.1, where + marks closure and − marks non-closure. It is worth noting that **REG**, characterized by finite automata, is closed under all of these operations.

	GJFA	**JFA**
endmarking	−	−
concatenation	−	−
shuffle	−	+
union	+	+
complement	−	+
intersection	−	+
int. with regular languages	−	−
Kleene star	−	−
Kleene plus	−	−
mirror image	+	+
substitution	−	−
regular substitution	−	−
finite substitution	−	−
homomorphism	−	−
ε-free homomorphism	−	−
inverse homomorphism	−	+

Table 3.1 Closure properties of **GJFA** and **JFA**.

Decidability

In this section, we prove the decidability of some decision problems with regard to **GJFA** and **JFA**.

Lemma 3.6 *Let $M = (Q, \Delta, R, s, F)$ be a GJFA. Then, $L(M, \curvearrowright)$ is infinite if and only if $py \rightsquigarrow p$ in $\Gamma(M)$, for some $y \in \Delta^+$ and $p \in Q$ such that p is both reachable and terminating in $\Gamma(M)$.*

Proof *If.* Let $M = (Q, \Delta, R, s, F)$ be a GJFA such that $py \rightsquigarrow p$ in $\Gamma(M)$, for some $y \in \Delta^+$ and $p \in Q$ such that p is both reachable and terminating in $\Gamma(M)$. Then,

$$w_1 s w_2 \curvearrowright^* upv \curvearrowright^+ xpz \curvearrowright^* f$$

where $w_1 w_2 \in L(M, \curvearrowright)$, $u, v, x, z \in \Delta^*$, $p \in Q$, and $f \in F$. Consequently,

$$w_1 s w_2 \curvearrowright^* upvy' \curvearrowright^+ xpz \curvearrowright^* f$$

where $y' = y^n$ for all $n \geq 0$. Therefore, $L(M, \curvearrowright)$ is infinite, so the if part holds.

Only If. Let $M = (Q, \Delta, R, s, F)$ be a GJFA such that $L(M, \curvearrowright)$ is infinite. Without any loss of generality, we assume that M is ε-free (see Lemma 3.1). Then,

$$w_1 s w_2 \curvearrowright^* upv \curvearrowright^+ xpz \curvearrowright^* f$$

for some $w_1 w_2 \in L(M, \curvearrowright)$, $u, v, x, z \in \Delta^*$, $p \in Q$, and $f \in F$. This implies that p is both terminating and reachable in $\Gamma(M)$. Let $y \in \Delta^+$ be a string read by M during $upv \curvearrowright^+ xpz$. Then, $py \rightsquigarrow p$ in $\Gamma(M)$, so the only-if part holds. □

Theorem 3.29 *Both finiteness and infiniteness are decidable for* **GJFA**.

Proof Let $M = (Q, \Delta, R, s, F)$ be a GJFA. By Lemma 3.6, $L(M, \curvearrowright)$ is infinite if and only if $py \rightsquigarrow p$ in $\Gamma(M)$, for some $y \in \Delta^+$ and $p \in Q$ such that p is both reachable and terminating in $\Gamma(M)$. This condition can be checked by any graph searching algorithm, such as breadth-first search (see [Russell and Norvig, 2002, page 73]). Therefore, the theorem holds. □

Corollary 3.11 *Both finiteness and infiniteness are decidable for* **JFA**.

Observe that since there is no deterministic version of a GJFA, the following proof of Theorem 3.30 is not as straightforward as in terms of regular languages and classical deterministic finite automata.

Theorem 3.30 *The membership problem is decidable for* **GJFA**.

Proof Let $M = (Q, \Delta, R, s, F)$ be a GJFA, and let $x \in \Delta^*$. Without any loss of generality, we assume that M is ε-free (see Theorem 3.2). If $x = \varepsilon$, then $x \in L(M, \curvearrowright)$ if and only if $s \in F$, so assume that $x \neq \varepsilon$. Set

$$\Psi = \{(x_1, x_2, \ldots, x_n) \mid x_i \in \Delta^+, 1 \leq i \leq n, x_1 x_2 \cdots x_n = x, n \geq 1\}$$

and

$$\Psi_p = \{(y_1, y_2, \ldots, y_n) \mid (x_1, x_2, \ldots, x_n) \in \Psi, n \geq 1, (y_1, y_2, \ldots, y_n) \text{ is a permutation of } (x_1, x_2, \ldots, x_n)\}$$

If there exist $(y_1, y_2, \ldots, y_n) \in \Psi_p$ and $q_1, q_2, \ldots, q_{n+1} \in Q$, for some n, $1 \leq n \leq |x|$, such that $s = q_1$, $q_{n+1} \in F$, and $q_i y_i \rightarrow q_{i+1} \in R$ for all $i = 1, 2, \ldots, n$, then $x \in L(M, \curvearrowright)$; otherwise, $x \notin L(M, \curvearrowright)$. Since both Q and Ψ_p are finite, this check can be performed in finite time. □

Corollary 3.12 *The membership problem is decidable for* **JFA**.

Theorem 3.31 *The emptiness problem is decidable for* **GJFA**.

Proof Let $M = (Q, \Delta, R, s, F)$ be a GJFA. Then, $L(M, \curvearrowright)$ is empty if and only if no $f \in F$ is reachable in $\Gamma(M)$. This check can be done by any graph searching algorithm, such as breadth-first search (see [Russell and Norvig, 2002, page 73]). □

Corollary 3.13 *The emptiness problem is decidable for* **JFA**.

	GJFA	JFA
membership	+	+
emptiness	+	+
finiteness	+	+
infiniteness	+	+

Table 3.2 Decidability properties.

The summary of decidability properties of the families **GJFA** and **JFA** is given in Table 3.2, where + marks decidability. Further, Fernau et al. [2017] presents several results concerning computational hardness and algorithms for parsing and other basic tasks concerning JFAs and GJFAs.

In addition, Beier et al. [2017, 2019] study their operational state complexity and decidability of JFAs; in addition, these studies relate JFAs to semilinear sets and Parikh images of regular sets.

An Infinite Hierarchy of Language Families

In this section, we establish an infinite hierarchy of language families resulting from GJFAs of degree n, where $n \geq 0$. Let $\mathbf{GJFA}_n$ and $\mathbf{GJFA}_n^{-\varepsilon}$ denote the families of languages accepted by GJFAs of degree n and by ε-free GJFAs of degree n, respectively. Observe that $\mathbf{GJFA}_n = \mathbf{GJFA}_n^{-\varepsilon}$ by the definition of a GJFA (see Def. 3.1) and by Lemma 3.1, for all $n \geq 0$.

Lemma 3.7 *Let* Δ *be an alphabet such that* $\text{card}(\Delta) \geq 2$. *Then, for any* $n \geq 1$, *there is a GJFA of degree* n, $M_n = (Q, \Delta, R, s, F)$, *such that* $L(M_n, \curvearrowright)$ *cannot be accepted by any GJFA of degree* $n - 1$.

Proof Let Δ be an alphabet such that $\text{card}(\Delta) \geq 2$, and let $a, b \in \Delta$ such that $a \neq b$. The case when $n = 1$ follows immediately from the definition of a JFA (see Definition 3.2), so we assume that $n \geq 2$. Define the GJFA of degree n

$$M_n = \big(\{s, f\}, \Delta, \{sw \to f\}, s, \{f\}\big)$$

where $w = ab(a)^{n-2}$. Clearly, $L(M_n, \curvearrowright) = \{w\}$. We next prove that $L(M_n, \curvearrowright)$ cannot be accepted by any GJFA of degree $n - 1$.

Suppose, for the sake of contradiction, that there is a GJFA of degree $n - 1$, $H = (Q, \Delta, R, s', F)$, such that $L(H) = L(M_n, \curvearrowright)$. Without any loss of generality, we assume that H is ε-free (see Lemma 3.1). Since $L(H) = L(M_n, \curvearrowright) = \{w\}$ and $|w| > n - 1$, there has to be

$$us'xv \curvearrowright^m f$$

in H, where $w = uxv$, $u, v \in \Delta^*$, $x \in \Delta^+$, $f \in F$, and $m \geq 2$. Thus,

$$s'xuv \curvearrowright^m f$$

and

$$uvs'x \curvearrowright^m f$$

in H, which contradicts the assumption that $L(H) = \{w\}$. Therefore, $L(M_n, \curvearrowright)$ cannot be accepted by any GJFA of degree $n - 1$. □

Theorem 3.32 $\mathbf{GJFA}_n \subset \mathbf{GJFA}_{n+1}$ *for all* $n \geq 0$.

Proof $\mathbf{GJFA}_n \subseteq \mathbf{GJFA}_{n+1}$ follows from the definition of a GJFA of degree n (see Def. 3.2), for all $n \geq 0$. From Lemma 3.7, $\mathbf{GJFA}_{n+1} - \mathbf{GJFA}_n \neq \emptyset$, which proves the theorem. □

Taking Lemma 3.1 into account, we obtain the following corollary of Theorem 3.32.

Corollary 3.14 $\mathbf{GJFA}_n^{-\varepsilon} \subset \mathbf{GJFA}_{n+1}^{-\varepsilon}$ *for all* $n \geq 0$.

Left and Right Jumps

We define two special cases of the jumping relation.

Definition 3.5 Let $M = (Q, \Delta, R, s, F)$ be a GJFA. Let $w, x, y, z \in \Delta^*$, and $py \to q \in R$; then, (1) M makes a *left jump* from $wxpyz$ to $wqxz$, symbolically written as

$$wxpyz \;{}_l\!\curvearrowright\; wqxz$$

and (2) M makes a *right jump* from $wpyxz$ to $wxqz$, written as

$$wpyxz \; {}_r\curvearrowright \; wxqz$$

Let $u, v \in \Delta^*Q\Delta^*$; then, $u \curvearrowright v$ if and only if $u \; {}_l\curvearrowright \; v$ or $u \; {}_r\curvearrowright \; v$. Extend ${}_l\curvearrowright$ and ${}_r\curvearrowright$ to ${}_l\curvearrowright^m$, ${}_l\curvearrowright^*$, ${}_l\curvearrowright^+$, ${}_r\curvearrowright^m$, ${}_r\curvearrowright^*$, and ${}_r\curvearrowright^+$, where $m \geq 0$, by analogy with extending $\curvearrowright$. Set

$${}_lL(M, \curvearrowright) = \left\{uv \mid u, v \in \Delta^*, usv \; {}_l\curvearrowright^* \; f \text{ with } f \in F\right\}$$

and

$${}_rL(M, \curvearrowright) = \left\{uv \mid u, v \in \Delta^*, usv \; {}_r\curvearrowright^* \; f \text{ with } f \in F\right\}$$

Let ${}_l$**GJFA**, ${}_l$**JFA**, ${}_r$**GJFA**, and ${}_r$**JFA** denote the families of languages accepted by GJFAs using only left jumps, JFAs using only left jumps, GJFAs using only right jumps, and JFAs using only right jumps, respectively.

Theorem 3.33 ${}_r$**GJFA** = ${}_r$**JFA** = **REG**

Proof We first prove that ${}_r$**JFA** = **REG**. Consider any JFA, $M = (Q, \Delta, R, s, F)$. Observe that if M occurs in a configuration of the form xpy, where $x \in \Delta^*$, $p \in Q$, and $y \in \Delta^*$, then it cannot read the symbols in x anymore because M can make only right jumps. Also, observe that this covers the situation when M starts to accept $w \in \Delta^*$ from a different configuration than sw. Therefore, to read the whole input, M has to start in configuration sw, and it cannot jump to skip some symbols. Consequently, M behaves like an ordinary finite automaton, reading the input from the left to the right, so $L(M, \curvearrowright)$ is regular and, therefore, ${}_r$**JFA** $\subseteq$ **REG**. Conversely, any finite automaton can be viewed as a JFA that starts from configuration sw and does not jump to skip some symbols. Therefore, **REG** $\subseteq$ ${}_r$**JFA**, which proves that ${}_r$**JFA** = **REG**. ${}_r$**GJFA** = **REG** can be proved by the same reasoning using general finite automata instead of finite automata. □

Next, we show that JFAs using only left jumps accept some non-regular languages.

Theorem 3.34 ${}_l$**JFA** − **REG** $\neq \emptyset$

Proof Consider the JFA

$$M = \left(\{s, p, q\}, \{a, b\}, R, s, \{s\}\right)$$

where

$$R = \left\{sa \to p, pb \to s, sb \to q, qa \to s\right\}$$

We argue that

$${}_lL(M, \curvearrowright) = \left\{w \mid \text{occur}(w, a) = \text{occur}(w, b)\right\}$$

With $w \in \{a, b\}^*$ on its input, M starts over the last symbol. M reads this symbol by using $sa \to p$ or $sb \to q$, and jumps to the left in front of the rightmost occurrence of b or a, respectively. Then, it consumes it by using $pb \rightarrow s$ or $qa \rightarrow s$, respectively. If this read symbol was the rightmost one, it jumps one symbol to the left and repeats the process. Otherwise, it makes no jumps at all. Observe that in this way, every configuration is of the form urv, where $r \in \{s, p, q\}$, $u \in \{a, b\}^*$, and either $v \in \{a, \varepsilon\}\{b\}^*$ or $v \in \{b, \varepsilon\}\{a\}^*$.

Based on the previous observations, we see that

$$_{l}L(M, \curvearrowright) = \{w \mid \text{occur}(w, a) = \text{occur}(w, b)\}$$

Since $L(M, \curvearrowright)$ is not regular, $_{l}$**JFA** − **REG** $\neq \emptyset$, so the theorem holds. □

Open Problem Study the effect of left jumps to the acceptance power of JFAs and GJFAs. □

Figure 3.4 summarizes the achieved results on jumping automata in this chapter.

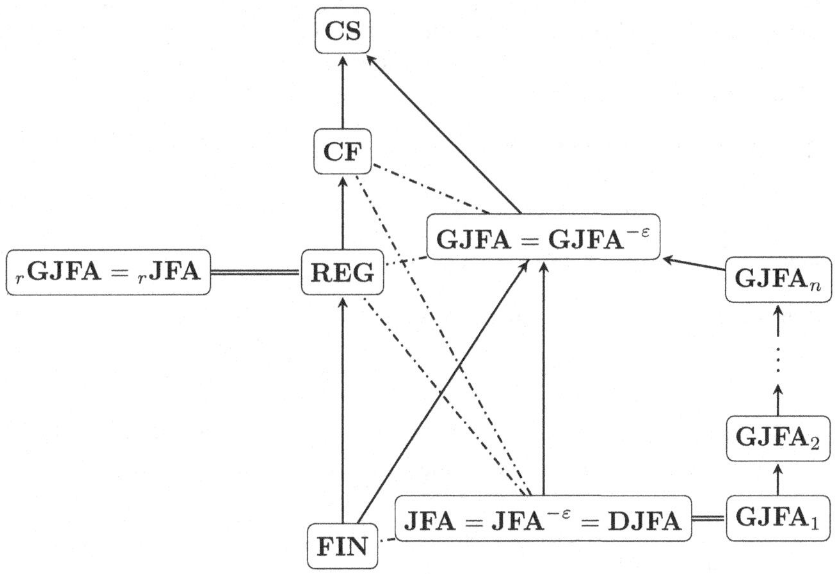

Fig. 3.4 Relationships between **JFA**, **GJFA**, and the Chomsky hierarchy.

A Variety of Start Configurations

In general, a GJFA can start its computation anywhere in the input string (see Definition 3.1). In this section, we consider the impact of various start configurations on the acceptance power of GJFAs and JFAs.

Definition 3.6 Let $M = (Q, \Delta, R, s, F)$ be a GJFA. Set

$$^{b}L(M, \curvearrowright) = \{w \in \Delta^* \mid sw \curvearrowright^* f \text{ with } f \in F\}$$
$$^{a}L(M, \curvearrowright) = \{uv \mid u, v \in \Delta^*, usv \curvearrowright^* f \text{ with } f \in F\}$$
$$^{e}L(M, \curvearrowright) = \{w \in \Delta^* \mid ws \curvearrowright^* f \text{ with } f \in F\}$$

Intuitively, b, a, and e stand for *beginning*, *anywhere*, and *end*, respectively; in this way, we express where the acceptance process starts. Observe that we simplify $^{a}L(M, \curvearrowright)$ to $L(M, \curvearrowright)$ because we pay a principal attention to the languages accepted in this way in this chapter. Let ^{b}**GJFA**, ^{a}**GJFA**, ^{e}**GJFA**, ^{b}**JFA**, ^{a}**JFA**, and ^{e}**JFA** denote the families of languages accepted by GJFAs starting at the beginning, GJFAs starting anywhere, GJFAs starting at the end, JFAs starting at the beginning, JFAs starting anywhere, and JFAs starting at the end, respectively.

We show that

(1) starting at the beginning increases the acceptance power of GJFAs and JFAs, and
(2) starting at the end does not increase the acceptance power of GJFAs and JFAs.

Theorem 3.35 ^{a}**JFA** $\subset$ ^{b}**JFA**

Proof Let $M = (Q, \Delta, R, s, F)$ be a JFA. The JFA

$$M' = \big(Q, \Delta, R \cup \{s \rightarrow s\}, s, F\big)$$

clearly satisfies $^{a}L(M, \curvearrowright) = {}^{b}L(M', \curvearrowright)$, so ^{a}**JFA** $\subseteq$ ^{b}**JFA**. We prove that this inclusion is, in fact, proper. Consider the language $K = \{a\}\{b\}^*$. The JFA

$$H = \big(\{s, f\}, \{a, b\}, \{sa \rightarrow f, fb \rightarrow f\}, s, \{f\}\big)$$

satisfies $^{b}L(H) = K$. However, observe that $^{a}L(H) = \{b\}^*\{a\}\{b\}^*$, which differs from K. By Theorem 3.5, for every JFA N, it holds that $^{a}L(N) \neq K$. Hence, ^{a}**JFA** $\subset$ ^{b}**JFA**. □

Theorem 3.36 ^{a}**GJFA** $\subset$ ^{b}**GJFA**

Proof This theorem can be proved by analogy with the proof of Theorem 3.35. □

Lemma 3.8 *Let M be a GJFA of degree $n \geq 0$. Then, there is a GJFA M' of degree n such that* $^{a}L(M, \curvearrowright) = {}^{e}L(M', \curvearrowright)$.

Proof Let $M = (Q, \Delta, R, s, F)$ be a GJFA of degree n. Then, the GJFA

$$M' = \left(Q, \Delta, R \cup \{s \rightarrow s\}, s, F\right)$$

is of degree n and satisfies ${}^{a}L(M, \curvearrowright) = {}^{e}L(M', \curvearrowright)$. □

Lemma 3.9 *Let M be a GJFA of degree $n \geq 0$. Then, there is a GJFA $\hat{M}$ of degree n such that ${}^{e}L(M, \curvearrowright) = {}^{a}L(\hat{M})$.*

Proof Let $M = (Q, \Delta, R, s, F)$ be a GJFA of degree n. If ${}^{e}L(M, \curvearrowright) = \emptyset$, then the GJFA

$$M' = \left(\{s\}, \Delta, \emptyset, s, \emptyset\right)$$

is of degree n and satisfies ${}^{a}L(M', \curvearrowright) = \emptyset$. If ${}^{e}L(M, \curvearrowright) = \{\varepsilon\}$, then the GJFA

$$M'' = \left(\{s\}, \Delta, \emptyset, s, \{s\}\right)$$

is of degree n and satisfies ${}^{a}L(M'', \curvearrowright) = \{\varepsilon\}$. Therefore, assume that $w \in {}^{e}L(M, \curvearrowright)$, where $w \in \Delta^{+}$. Then, $s \rightarrow p \in R$, for some $p \in Q$. Indeed, observe that either ${}^{e}L(M, \curvearrowright) = \emptyset$ or ${}^{e}L(M, \curvearrowright) = \{\varepsilon\}$, which follows from the observation that if M starts at the end of an input string, then it first has to jump to the left to be able to read some symbols.

Define the GJFA $\hat{M} = (Q, \Delta, \hat{R}, s, F)$, where

$$\hat{R} = R - \left\{su \rightarrow q \mid u \in \Delta^{+}, q \in Q, \text{ and there is no } x \in \Delta^{+} \text{ such that } sx \rightsquigarrow s \text{ in } \Gamma(M)\right\}$$

The reason for excluding such $su \rightarrow q$ from $\hat{R}$ is that M first has to use a rule of the form $s \rightarrow p$, where $p \in Q$ (see the argumentation above). However, since $\hat{M}$ starts anywhere in the input string, we need to force it to use $s \rightarrow p$ as the first rule, thus changing the state from s to p, just like M does.

Clearly, $\hat{M}$ is of degree n and satisfies ${}^{e}L(M, \curvearrowright) = {}^{a}L(\hat{M})$, so the lemma holds. □

Theorem 3.37 ^{e}**GJFA** = ^{a}**GJFA** *and* ^{e}**JFA** = ^{a}**JFA**

Proof This theorem follows from Lemmas 3.8 and 3.9. □

We also consider combinations of left jumps, right jumps, and various start configurations. For this purpose, by analogy with the previous denotations, we define ${}^{b}_{l}$**GJFA**, ${}^{a}_{l}$**GJFA**, ${}^{e}_{l}$**GJFA**, ${}^{b}_{r}$**GJFA**, ${}^{a}_{r}$**GJFA**, ${}^{e}_{r}$**GJFA**, ${}^{b}_{l}$**JFA**, ${}^{a}_{l}$**JFA**, ${}^{e}_{l}$**JFA**, ${}^{b}_{r}$**JFA**, ${}^{a}_{r}$**JFA**, and ${}^{e}_{r}$**JFA**. For example, ${}^{b}_{r}$**GJFA** denotes the family of languages accepted by GJFAs that perform only right jumps and starts at the beginning.

Theorem 3.38 ${}^{a}_{r}$**GJFA** = ${}^{a}_{r}$**JFA** = ${}^{b}_{r}$**GJFA** = ${}^{b}_{r}$**JFA** = ${}^{b}_{l}$**GJFA** = ${}^{b}_{l}$**JFA** = **REG**

Proof Theorem 3.33, in fact, states that ${}^{a}_{r}$**GJFA** = ${}^{a}_{r}$**JFA** = **REG**. Furthermore, ${}^{b}_{r}$**GJFA** = ${}^{b}_{r}$**JFA** = **REG** follows from the proof of Theorem 3.33 because M has to start the acceptance process of a string w from the configuration sw—that is, it starts at the beginning of w. ${}^{b}_{l}$**GJFA** = ${}^{b}_{l}$**JFA** = **REG** can be proved analogously. □

Theorem 3.39 ${}_{r}^{e}$**GJFA** = ${}_{r}^{e}$**JFA** = $\{\emptyset, \{\varepsilon\}\}$

Proof Consider JFAs $M = (\{s\}, \{a\}, \emptyset, s, \emptyset)$ and $M' = (\{s\}, \{a\}, \emptyset, s, \{s\})$ to see that $\{\emptyset, \{\varepsilon\}\} \subseteq {}_{r}^{e}$**GJFA** and $\{\emptyset, \{\varepsilon\}\} \subseteq {}_{r}^{e}$**JFA**. The converse inclusion also holds. Indeed, any GJFA that starts the acceptance process of a string w from ws and that can make only right jumps accepts either $\emptyset$ or $\{\varepsilon\}$. □

Open Problem What are the properties of ${}_{l}^{e}$**GJFA** and ${}_{l}^{e}$**JFA**? □

Notice that Open Problem, in fact, suggests an investigation of the properties of ${}_{l}^{a}$**GJFA** and ${}_{l}^{a}$**JFA**.

Open Problems

Within the previous sections, we have already pointed out several specific open problems concerning them. We close the present chapter by pointing out some crucially important open problem areas as suggested topics of future investigations.

(I) Concerning closure properties, study the closure of **GJFA** under shuffle, Kleene star, Kleene plus, and under reversal.

(II) Regarding decision problems, investigate other decision properties of **GJFA** and **JFA**, like equivalence, universality, inclusion, or regularity. Furthermore, study their computational complexity. Do there exist undecidable problems for **GJFA** or **JFA**?

(III) Section 3.1 has demonstrated that GJFAs and JFAs using only right jumps define the family of regular languages. How precisely do left jumps affect the acceptance power of JFAs and GJFAs?

(IV) Broaden the results of Section 3.1 concerning various start configurations by investigating the properties of ${}_{l}^{e}$**GJFA** and ${}_{l}^{e}$**JFA**.

(V) Determinism represents a crucially important investigation area in terms of all types of automata. In essence, the nondeterministic versions of automata can make several different moves from the same configuration while their deterministic counterparts cannot—that is, they make no more than one move from any configuration. More specifically, the deterministic version of classical finite automata require that for any state q and any input symbol a, there exists no more than one rule with qa on its left-hand side; in this way, they make no more than one move from any configuration. As a result, with any input string w, they make a unique sequence of moves. As should be obvious, in terms of jumping finite automata, this requirement does not guarantee their determinism in the above sense. Modify the requirement so it guarantees the determinism.

Other models that characterize GJFA and JFA

As pointed out in Fernau et al. [2015, 2017], there exist several formalisms that characterize **GJFA** and **JFA** including shuffle expressions, α-shuffle expressions, commutative context-free grammars, letter bounded languages, and regular expressions over comutative monoids. None of them, however, works as acceptors while JFAs and GJFAs do, thus resembling the way ordinary FAs work. This resemblance is probably the key reason why the automata theory has recently paid greater attention to them than the other formalisms that define **GJFA** and **JFA**. Moreover, in Vorel [2018], the connection of GJFAs with graph-controlled insertion systems and Galiukschov semicontextual grammars is established.

3.2 One-Way Jumping Finite Automata

At a first and somewhat hasty glance, the definitions of the previous two models might produce a wrong impression that jumping models always work in an inherently nondeterministic way. However, this is not the case at all as demonstrated, for instance, by one-way jumping finite automata introduced in Chigahara et al. [2015, 2016].

Although in many respects, one-way jumping finite automata make their jumps similarly to the way JFAs do, these jumps are performed in a slightly different manner, which subsequently implies their determinism. To explain this determinism, consider any one-way jumping finite automaton, M. Concerning an individual jump performance in M on a tape containing some symbols, there are three situations to be distinguished—(1) if a rule is defined for the current state and input symbol, it is applied there; otherwise, (2) the reading head jumps to the right to the nearest possible symbol where a rule is applicable; and (3) if no symbol like this occurs on the tape, M gets stuck. Starting from the input tape beginning, M performs jumps in the way sketched above only in one direction from left to right on its cyclic tape (see Figure 3.5), possibly skipping over some of its parts. This reading process is cyclically repeated over the tape until M either reads all the symbols, thus accepting the input string, or gets stuck, thus rejecting the input. As a result, M works in an utterly deterministic way.

Definitions and Examples

Let us now formally define two types of one-way jumping finite automata.

Definition 3.7 A *right one-way jumping finite automaton* (ROWJFA) is a quintuple $M = (Q, \Delta, R, s, F)$, where Q is a finite set of states, Δ is an input alphabet of M, $Q \cap \Delta = \emptyset$, $s \in Q$ is the start state, $F \subseteq Q$ is a set of final states, and $R \subseteq Q \times \Delta \times Q$ is finite set of rules. R differs from FA (see Definition 2.2) such that $a \in \Delta$ for every $qa \rightarrow p \in R$, and no two rules in R have the same left-hand side. A configuration of M is simply any string in $Q\Delta^*$. Furthermore, we define the *right one-way jumping relation* over $Q\Delta^*$, symbolically denoted by $\circlearrowright$, as follows. Let $x, y \in \Delta^*$, $a \in \Delta$,

$p, q \in Q$ and $pa \to q \in R$. Then M makes a jump from $pxay$ to qyx, symbolically written as

$$pxay \circlearrowright qyx$$

if $x \in (\Delta - \Delta_p)^*$ where $\Delta_p = \{b \in \Delta \mid pb \to b \in R\}$. A right one-way jump is illustrated in Figure 3.5. In the standard manner, we extend $\circlearrowright$ to $\circlearrowright^m$ where $m \geq 0$, $\circlearrowright^+$ and $\circlearrowright^*$. The language accepted by M, denoted by $L(M, \circlearrowright)$, is defined as

$$L(M, \circlearrowright) = \{w \in \Delta^* \mid sw \circlearrowright^* f \text{ for some } f \in F\}.$$

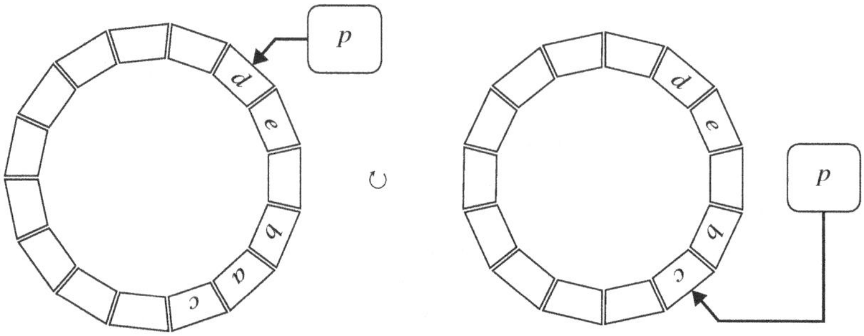

Fig. 3.5 A ROWJFA jump.

Definition 3.8 A *left one-way jumping finite automaton* (LOWJFA) is a quintuple $M = (Q, \Delta, R, s, F)$ where Q, Δ, R, s, and F are defined as in a ROWJFA. A configuration of M is any string in $\Sigma^* Q$. The binary *left one-way jumping relation*, symbolically denoted by $\circlearrowleft$, over $\Sigma^* Q$, is defined as follows. Let $x, y \in \Sigma^*$, $a \in \Sigma$, $p, q \in Q$, and $pa \to q \in R$. Then, M makes a jump from $yaxp$ to xyq, symbolically written as

$$yaxp \circlearrowleft xyq$$

if $x \in (\Delta - \Delta_p)^*$ where $\Delta_p = \{b \in \Delta \mid pb \to b \in R\}$.

In a straightforward analogy with a ROWJFA, we can define $\circlearrowleft^m$ where $m \geq 0$, $\circlearrowleft^+$, $\circlearrowleft^*$, and $L(M)$.

We denote the families of languages accepted by ROWJFAs and LOWJFA by **ROWJFA** and **LOWJFA**, respectively.

Observe that when M applies a rule $pa \to q$, it first jumps to the appropriate position while skipping the symbols no rule in p can read and, then, M reads a which is different from JFAs.

Notice that the majority of results study a ROWJFA instead of a LOWJFA.

Example 3.3 Let a ROWJFA $M = (\{s, f\}, \{a, b\}, R, s, \{s, f\})$, where R consists of

$$\{sa \to s,\ sb \to f,\ fb \to f\}$$

M works on aab as follows

$$saab \curvearrowright sab \curvearrowright sb \curvearrowright f$$

But M rejects $aaba$. See, for instance, the following sequence of steps

$$saaba \curvearrowright saba \curvearrowright sba \curvearrowright fa$$

Since both a and b can be read in the start state, M cannot skip any a or b, and after reading first b, M cannot read a anymore. Hence, M accepts $L(M) = \{a\}^*\{b\}^*$ which is accepted neither by an JFA nor a GJFA (see Lemma 3.3).

Example 3.4 Consider a ROWJFA $M = (\{s, p, q\}, \Delta = \{a, b, c\}, R, s, \{s\})$, where R consists of

$$\{sa \to p,\ pb \to q,\ qc \to s\}$$

Although M can deterministically jump only to the right, thanks to implicit continuation of the input string from the end back to the beginning, M accepts, for instance, $bcaacb$ as follows

$$sbcaacb \curvearrowright pacbbc \curvearrowright qbcac \curvearrowright sacb \curvearrowright pcb \curvearrowright qc \curvearrowright s$$

Obviously, M accepts $L(M) = \{w \in \{a, b, c\}^* \mid \text{occur}(w, a) = \text{occur}(w, b) = \text{occur}(w, c)\}$ which is another non-context-free language.

Note that it is straighforward to add more states and more rules to handle a balanced number of occurrences of symbols in Δ such that $\text{card}(\Delta) \geq 2$. On the other hand, Beier and Holzer [2019] prove that $\{w \in \{a, b\}^* \mid \text{occur}(w, a) \neq \text{occur}(w, b)\} \notin$ **ROWJFA**.

Results and Properties

Now, we investigate results concerning the accepting power of ROWJFAs and LOWJFAs and their closure properties as they are significantly different from DJFAs.

Theorem 3.40 **ROWJFA** *and* **LOWJFA** *are incomparable.*

Proof (sketch) We use slightly modified language from Example 3.4. Consider $L = \{aw \in \{a, b\}^* \mid \text{occur}(w, a) = \text{occur}(w, b)\}$. There is an accepting ROWJFA $M = (\{s, t, q, f\}, \{a, b\}, R, s, \{f\})$, where R consists of

$$\{sb \to t,\ sa \to q,\ qb \to f,\ fa \to q\}$$

Obviously, t has a role of a trap state, so M cannot accept the input string after entering t. The detailed proof that L is accepted by no LOWJFA so $L \in$ **ROWJFA** $-$ **LOWJFA** is in Chigahara et al. [2016]. On the other hand, $L' = \{wa \in \{a, b\}^* \mid \text{occur}(w, a) = \text{occur}(w, b)\} \in$ **LOWJFA** $-$ **ROWJFA**. □

Similarly to Theorem 3.4, every language accepted by a ROWJFA working with a unary alphabet is regular.

Theorem 3.41 (Chigahara et al. [2016]) *Let* $M = (Q, \Delta, R, s, F)$ *be a ROWJFA such that* $\mathrm{card}(\Delta) = 1$. *Then,* $L(M)$ *is regular.*

Corollary 3.15 (Chigahara et al. [2016]) $\{a^p \mid p \text{ is a prime number}\} \notin$ **ROWJFA.**

Based on the properties of right one-way jumping relation, there is a corollary in Chigahara et al. [2016] that resembles the pumping lemma for regular languages (see [Meduna, 2000, Lemma 4.1.1]).

Corollary 3.16 (Chigahara et al. [2016]) *For any* $L \in$ **ROWJFA** *there is a constant* $k \in \mathbb{N}$ *such that for every string* $w \in L$ *with* $|w| \geq k$, *there exists* $xyz \in \mathrm{perm}(w)$ *satisfying the following three conditions:*

(1) $y \neq \varepsilon$;
(2) $|xy| \leq k$;
(3) $xy^m z \in L$, *for all* $m \geq 0$.

Corollary 3.17 (Beier and Holzer [2019])

(i) **REG** $\subset$ **ROWJFA** $\subset$ **CS.**
(ii) **ROWJFA** *and* **JFA** *are incomparable.*
(iii) Every language $L \in$ **ROWJFA** *is semilinear.*

Corollary 3.18 (Chigahara et al. [2016]) $\{a^n b^n \mid n \geq 0\} \notin$ **ROWJFA**

Theorem 3.42 **ROWJFA** *is not closed under Kleene star and Kleene plus.*

Proof (sketch) Consider $L = \{cw \in \{a, b, c\}^* \mid \mathrm{occur}(w, a) = \mathrm{occur}(w, b), w \in \{a, b\}^*\}$. There is a ROWJFA M that accepts L such that $M = (\{s, t, q, f\}, \{a, b, c\}, R, s, \{f\})$, where R consists of

$$\{sa \to t, sb \to t, sc \to f, fa \to q, qb \to f\}$$

Similarly to the proof of Theorem 3.40, t represents a trap state, so again M cannot accept the input string after entering t. Clearly, $L^* \notin$ **ROWJFA** and $L^+ \notin$ **ROWJFA** that is proved in details in Chigahara et al. [2016]. □

The summary of closure properties of **ROWJFA** family compared with the properties of **DJFA** (see Theorem 3.3 and Table 3.1) are given in Table 3.3, where + and − mark closure and non-closure, respectively. These results are proved in Chigahara et al. [2016] and Beier and Holzer [2019].

	ROWJFA	DJFA
concatenation	−	−
union	−	+
complement	−	+
intersection	−	+
int. with regular languages	−	−
Kleene star	−	−
mirror image	−	+
substitution	−	−
homomorphism	−	−
inverse homomorphism	−	+

Table 3.3 Closure properties of **ROWJFA** compared with **JFA**.

Conclusion

Naturally, the research on ROWJFAs and LOWJFAs continues. As seen from the previous results, Chigahara et al. [2016] study the accepting power and closure properties, and they also define pumping lemmas for the resulting language families. In Fazekas and Yamamura [2016], the sufficient conditions for the resulting language to be regular are studied.

Beier and Holzer [2018b] study inclusion relations and closure properties. Beier and Holzer [2018a] is a continuation of Beier and Holzer [2018b] that focuses on decision problems. It shows that most of the classical problems are decidable for ROWJFAs, and it discusses some complexity results for the considered decision problems. Beier and Holzer [2019] characterize the family of permutation closed languages accepted by ROWJFAs in terms of Myhill-Nerode equivalence classes. Using this, it investigates closure and non-closure properties as well as inclusion relationships between all related language families. Furthermore, it gives more characterizations of languages accepted by ROWJFAs in the case that the language is given as the concatenation of two languages. Recently in Beier and Holzer [2022], nondeterministic versions of right one-way jumping finite automata were introduced and their computational power was investigated including the relationship to **JFA**.

Lastly, Fazekas et al. [2019] compare the deterministic and nondeterministic finite automata and pushdown automata when they use standard, jumping, and one-way jumping steps. Then, the same authors investigated two-way jumping automata as strictly more powerful model in Fazekas et al. [2021]. Further, Fazekas et al. [2022] discuss asymptotically bounded computation in terms of one-way jumping finite automata with a principal focus on the study of its complexity.

Other Jumping Models

Apart from the most influential models mentioned in this part, there are also other papers that study the jumping mechanism further in more advanced automata-based models:

- Two-dimensional jumping finite automata (see Immanuel and Thomas [2016b]; Madejski and Szepietowski [2017]; Immanuel and Thomas [2017]);
- Jumping restarting automata (see Wang and Li [2018]);
- Jumping multi-head automata (see Kuperberg et al. [2019]);
- Jumping automata over infinite words (see Shaull and Omer [2023]).

Note that it may seem, from the name of jumping multi-head automata, that this model is similar to the models studied later in this book. However, it falls into the category (PA.1) of parallelism in finite automata. On the other hand, most finite automata studied in this book fall into the category (PA.2), which is a fundamentally different behavior.

Chapter 4
Jumping Multi-Head Automata

To place the subject of this chapter into a general and historical context, recall that early computer programs were always executed strictly sequentially. Indeed, to perform a computational task, an algorithm was written and implemented as an instruction sequence executed on a central processing unit of a single computer. Only one instruction was executed at a time, so after this instruction was completed, the next instruction was executed until all the sequence of instructions was performed in this unbearably slow way. In the mid-1980s or so, however, computer programmers started to write their first pioneer programs that performed several parts of a single computational task simultaneously. As a result, around that time, parallel computation emerged in computer science.

Generally speaking, seen from today's perspective, parallel computation can be categorized as any type of computation in which many computational processes are carried out simultaneously while taking advantage of mutually cooperating multiprocessor computers. From a hardware standpoint, parallel computation is often executed on various computers, such as a single computer with multiple processors or several networked computers with specialized hardware, and it may simultaneously process quite diverse data. It can be performed at various levels, ranging from bit-level through instruction-level up to task-level parallelism. Over the past few years, parallel computing has become the dominant paradigm in computer architecture, mainly in the form of multi-core processors. From a software standpoint, parallel computation is conceptually accomplished by breaking a single computational task into many independent subtasks so that each subtask can be simultaneously executed with the others. It thus comes as no surprise that today the investigation of parallel computation fulfills a central role within computer science as a whole.

Of course, discontinuous computation, whose models represent the principal subject of this book, is often executed in parallel, too. Building up a systematized body of knowledge about this kind of computation obviously necessitates an introduction of its proper formalization in the first place. In terms of jumping automata, this investigation trend leads to a generalization of one-head jumping automata, covered in Chapter 3, to their multi-head versions, which can act as an automaton-based formalization of discontinuous parallelism much more properly. To see the principal reason why the multi-head jumping automata represent appropriate models of discontinuous computation in parallel, recall that their original one-head counterparts always apply a single rule during every jump, so they obviously fail to formalize any kind of computational parallelism. On the other hand, their multi-head versions can perform a simultaneous application of several rules during any jump, thus reflecting and formalizing discontinuous parallelism more adequately. That is also why the present chapter carefully explores a large variety of these versions.

The introduction of parallel mechanisms such as multiple reading heads influence the properties of jumping automata significantly in various ways such as increase of their accepting power (see Section 4.2) or even fundamental change of the behavior such that the jumping concept utilizes multiple heads, the heads can naturally jump at specific positions on the tape, and thus they can easily work on different places at once in parallel, although their heads cooperate on a single tape and, therefore, process a single input string. From a practical point of view, the deterministic variants and scalable splitting the work into more or less independent tasks are of interest as well.

More specifically, this four-section chapter opens its discussion by investigating two-head jumping automata in Section 4.1, which are generalized to multi-head jumping automata in Section 4.2. Section 4.3 explores jumping Watson–Crick finite automata, which represent biology-related model processing double-stranded inputs. Finally, Section 4.4 deals with their special cases—jumping $5' \rightarrow 3'$ Watson–Crick finite automata that read the double-stranded string from opposite ends so it is closer to the real processing of DNA.

Categories of Parallelism

When we talk about parallelism in modern computer science, we almost automatically mean some form of parallel processing or parallel computing. By these terms we refer to situations where we want to split some large task into smaller chunks of work in such a way that the chunks can be executed in parallel on separate processing units, and the whole task can thus be computed faster than if it was executed completely sequentially on a single processing unit.

Nonetheless, this perception of the notion of parallelism can change quite rapidly when we wander into more theoretical branches of computer science; especially if we consider the basic research in the theory of formal languages. There are many formal models in this area that incorporate some form of parallelism, but they utilize very diverse mechanics in the background to achieve their goal. If we take a broader look at these formal models and the basic research in general, we can roughly divide parallelism in formal language theory into the following three categories:

(P.1) *Power-increasing Parallelism* that increases the expressive power of the model;

(P.2) *Behavior-changing Parallelism* that is a fundamental part of the behavior of the model;

(P.3) *Work-distributing Parallelism* that splits the work of the task.

Power-increasing Parallelism. The most commonly studied category in the basic research is probably category (P.1). This is especially noticeable in formal grammars. Considering classical formal grammars in general, there is a big difference if a model can use only context-free rules or also non-context-free rules. It is much harder to deal with the non-context-free rules from both the theoretical and practical points of view. Therefore, there is a large incentive to study models that can use only the context-free (or even more restricted) rules but that also incorporate some additional mechanisms which further increase their generative power.

In formal grammars, the models can incorporate parallelism in such a way that, in each step of the rewriting process, the grammar rewrites several symbols in the sentential form at once in parallel. Let us mention some well-known models that match this description:

- scattered context grammars (see Definition 6.1);
- n-parallel (right-)linear grammars (see Definition 4.3);
- simple matrix grammars (see Ibarra [1970] and Rosebrugh and Wood [1974]);
- unordered scattered context grammars (see Mayer [1972]);
- substitution selective grammars (see Kleijn [1983]).

In the case of finite automata, we can imagine the parallelism of category (P.1) as a parallel cooperation of multiple heads. There are several well-known models of finite automata that utilize more than one head; nonetheless, their behavior does not fall precisely into one specific category of parallelism. So we will leave their description for later.

A very common property of models from this category is that we can freely select their degree of parallelism. More specifically, we can choose n which represents the number of symbols or heads that are considered together in a single step of the model. Then, if $n = 1$, we get the power of a classical non-augmented model (e.g., the power of context-free grammars); and, for $n > 1$, we either get an infinite hierarchy of more powerful models or the power of the model increases at first but then stabilizes.

Behavior-changing Parallelism. Considering category (P.2), we are looking at the models that have parallelism rooted inseparably into their core structure. From our exploration of this topic, it seems that the models which fall into this category are usually related to biology.

On the one hand, there are massively parallel models such as Lindenmayer systems (see Rozenberg and Salomaa [1980, 1997a]; Meduna and Švec [2005]; Meduna and Zemek [2014]; Meduna and Soukup [2017b]) that are based on the evolution process. In these models, all eligible symbols in the sentential form are always rewritten together at once in parallel. Consequently, it is not possible to select a constant degree of parallelism for these models since the conditions continuously change depending on the current task. Indian grammars (see Siromoney and Krithivasan [1974]) represent another grammatical parallelism of this kind: during every derivation step, they select any rule and simultaneously apply it to all occurrences of its left-hand side in the current sentential form.

On the other hand, there are also models with a fixed degree of parallelism such as Watson–Crick finite automata (see Păun et al. [1998]). These automaton models use two heads in parallel in such a way that each head processes one strand of a double-stranded DNA input sequence. Consequently, the degree of parallelism of Watson–Crick finite automata is always two.

Work-distributing Parallelism. Lastly, if we consider category (P.3) in the basic research, it seems that there is not much interest to study possibilities how to split the work for the given tasks. This may not be that surprising because in the basic research we usually study characteristics like the expressive power, closure properties, and the decidability and complexity of various operations; and, of course, these results are not affected by parallelism that is primarily applied to speed up the computation without changing the result. In basic research, we often even prefer approaches that are completely sequential because it makes the subsequent proof techniques much easier in many cases. When we do consider parallelism that splits the work of the tasks (see Rozenberg and Salomaa [1997a,b]), we usually just simply conclude that if the model behaves nondeterministically, then we can explore different cases in parallel, and if the model uses only context-free rules, then we can trivially split the generation process into multiple independent parts.

It is possible to find some theoretical papers that explore this role of parallelism further in certain areas, e.g., in biomolecular computing (see Loos and Nagy [2011]); but a thorough study is usually left for practical applications such as parsing (see Grune and Jacobs [2008]), formal verification, and others.

Parallelism and Finite Automata

The situation around the types of parallelism gets more complex if we look at finite automata. Thus, we introduce some additional categorization.

There are some finite automaton models that have the same expressive power as grammars from category (P.1). For example, self-regulating finite automata (see Meduna and Masopust [2007]), pure multi-pushdown automata that perform complete pushdown pops (see Masopust and Meduna [2009]), and finite-turn checking automata (see Siromoney [1971]), which are connected to the various versions of simple matrix, equal matrix, and n-parallel right-linear grammars. However, we do not consider these models to be parallel. This is due to the fact that, up until quite recently, automaton models always read the input tape almost exclusively in the strictly continuous (left-to-right) symbol-by-symbol way. The mentioned models are no exceptions, and thus they use various kinds of stacks to match the expressive power of the parallel grammars but otherwise work strictly continuously on the input tape in a completely non-parallel way.

As we have already pointed out, we can imagine parallelism in finite automata as a parallel cooperation of multiple heads. There is indeed the well-known concept of Turing machines with multiple tapes and multiple heads; which was also adapted and studied in terms of finite automaton models. Nonetheless, not all such models necessarily work in a parallel way. Considering multi-head finite automata that actually do work in a parallel way, we can find two distinct categories of their behavior:

(PA.1) Multi-head automata where each head works on an independent copy of the input;
(PA.2) Multi-head automata where heads cooperate to process the single input.

The first category seems to be the most studied one so far. Let us mention some prominent models that fit into this description: classical Watson–Crick finite automata (see Section 2.2.3), multi-head finite automata (see Rosenberg [1965]; Inoue et al. [1979]; Ďuriš and Hromkovič [1983]; Holzer et al. [2009]), and parallel communicating finite automata systems (see Holzer et al. [2009]). In these models, the heads can work in parallel; however, their behavior can be hardly seen as parallel processing since it does not speed up the task in any way. In most cases, there is a single read-only input tape that must be completely traversed with all heads until the conclusion about the acceptance of the input is reached.

We only know about a few models that fall into the second category. These are finite automaton models introduced by Nagy that utilize two heads with the following behavior. The first head reads the input from left to right, the second head reads the input from right to left, and the processing of the input ends when the heads meet each other on the tape. This concept was explored several times in various models:

- Two-head finite automata (see Nagy [2012]);
- $5' \rightarrow 3'$ Watson–Crick finite automata (see Nagy [2008, 2009, 2010, 2013]; Nagy et al. [2017]; Parchami and Nagy [2018]; Nagy and Parchami [2020]);
- Multicounter $5' \rightarrow 3'$ Watson–Crick finite automata (see Eğecioğlu et al. [2010]; Nagy et al. [2011]; Hegedüs et al. [2012]);
- Two-head finite-state acceptors with translucent letters (see Nagy and Otto [2019, 2020]).

In these models, the heads truly cooperate in parallel on a single tape such that each head exclusively process only some portion of the input string; thus, this behavior can be seen as parallel processing. Naturally, their degree of parallelism is always two.

In this chapter, apart from jumping Watson–Crick finite automata that belongs into (PA.1) category, all remaining studied models in this chapter fall into (PA.2) category, since each head of these automata typically processes only a part of the input string.

Synopsis

While Chapter 3 has explored one-head jumping finite automata (JFA), the present four-section chapter is devoted to JFAs having several heads.

Section 4.1 modifies the way the basic model of a JFA works so it simultaneously performs two jumps according to the same rule. For either of the two jumps, it always considers three directions—(1) to the left, (2) to the right, and (3) in either direction. In correspondence to these three directions, this section investigates the mutual relation between the language families resulting from JFAs working in these ways and well-known language families, including the families of regular, linear, context-free, and context-sensitive languages. In essence, it demonstrates that most of these language families are pairwise incomparable—that is, they are not subfamilies of each other, but they are not disjoint either. In addition, this section establishes several closure as well as non-closure properties concerning the language families under discussion.

Section 4.2 covers n-parallel jumping finite automata, whose input is divided into several parts separately processed by distinct synchronized heads. Under this parallel mechanism, each part can be read discontinuously, but the order between parts is preserved; from this viewpoint, this model actually combines both discontinuous and continuous ways of reading.

More precisely, the n-parallel jumping finite automata utilize jumping only during the initialization when heads jump to their starting positions. After that, all heads read their parts of the input continuously in a left-to-right way. Section 4.2 compares these automata with n-parallel right linear grammars and shows that both models actually define the same language families. Consequently, making use of well-known results about n-parallel right linear grammars, Section 4.2 establishes several properties of n-parallel jumping finite automata.

Sections 4.3 and 4.4 demonstrate a close relation between two-head jumping automata discussed in Section 4.2 and Watson–Crick automata (see Section 2.2.3), which fulfill a crucially important role in many biologically oriented research areas, particularly, in DNA computation. In essence, Watson–Crick automata work with DNA information represented by two strings, referred to as strands, bounded with symmetric Watson–Crick relation and read by their heads. As is obvious, this fundamental conceptualization strongly resembles that of two-head jumping automata, and this resemblance gives rise to introducing combined versions of both types of automata—the principal subject of these two sections. Both sections concentrate their attention on the accepting power of the resulting combined versions of Watson–Crick and jumping automata, including a large variety of their restricted versions. From a more practical standpoint, it is worth making a prediction: as the biological applications frequently make use of original versions of Watson–Crick automata as their models, the future applications of this kind are highly likely to pay a significant attention to their jumping versions as well as sketched in Section 9.1.

4.1 Double-Jumping Finite Automata

The present section investigates two-head JFAs that work over a single tape. To give an insight into this, let us first recall the notion of a classical finite automaton (see

Section 2.2.1), M, which consists of an input tape, a read head, and a finite state control. The input tape is divided into squares. Each square contains one symbol of an input string. The symbol under the read head, a, is the current input symbol. The finite control is represented by a finite set of states together with a control relation, which is usually specified as a set of computational rules. M computes by making a sequence of moves. Each move is made according to a computational rule that describes how the current state is changed and whether the current input symbol is read. If the symbol is read, the read head is shifted precisely one square to the right. M has one state defined as the start state and some states designated as final states. If M can read entire w by making a sequence of moves from the start state to a final state, M accepts w; otherwise, M rejects w.

As discussed in Chapter 3, a JFA works just like a classical finite automaton except it does not read the input string in a symbol-by-symbol left-to-right way: after reading a symbol, M can jump over a portion of the tape in either direction and continue making moves from there. Once an occurrence of a symbol is read on the tape, it cannot be re-read again later during the computation of M. Otherwise, it coincides with the standard notion of a finite automaton.

Consider the notion of a JFA M sketched above. The present section based on Kocman et al. [2016, 2018] modifies the way M works so it simultaneously performs two jumps according to the same rule. For either of the two jumps, it always considers three natural directions—(1) to the left, (2) to the right, and (3) in either direction. In correspondence to this jumping-direction three-part classification, the section investigates the mutual relation between the language families resulting from JFAs working in these ways and the families of regular, linear, context-free, and context-sensitive languages. In essence, it demonstrates that most of these language families are pairwise insmparable—that is, they are not subfamilies of each other and, simultaneously, they are not disjoint either. In addition, the section establishes several closure and non-closure properties concerning the language families defined by JFAs working in the three ways sketched above.

Definitions and Examples

Recall from Section 3.1 that a *general jumping finite automaton* (GJFA) is a quintuple $M = (Q, \Delta, R, s, F)$, where Q, Δ, R, s, and F are defined as in a general finite automaton (see Section 2.2.1). According to Convention 2.1, we sometimes denote a rule $py \to q$ with a unique label h as $h : py \to q$, so we can write h instead of $py \to q$. A *configuration* of M is any string in $\Delta^* Q \Delta^*$. To make the notation of jumping relation consistent with the rest of this section, instead of $\curvearrowright$, we denote the binary *jumping relation* by ${}_{\blacklozenge}\curvearrowright$, over $\Delta^* Q \Delta^*$, and ${}_{\blacklozenge}\curvearrowright$ is defined as follows. Let $x, z, x', z' \in \Delta^*$ such that $xz = x'z'$ and $h : (p, y, q) \in R$; then, M makes a *jump* from $xpyz$ to $x'qz'$, symbolically written as $xpyz \; {}_{\blacklozenge}\curvearrowright \; x'qz' \; [h]$. When the specification of the rule h is immaterial, we can omit $[h]$.

We define a new mode for GJFAs that performs two single jumps simultaneously. In this mode, both single jumps follow the same rule; however, they are performed on two different positions on the tape and thus handle different parts of the input string. Moreover, these two jumps cannot ever cross each other—their initial mutual order is preserved during the whole process. As a result, when needed, we can specifically denote them as the *first jump* and the *second jump*. Furthermore, this section considers three possible types of single jumps that can be used in this new *double-jumping mode*. Besides the unrestricted single jump $_{\blacklozenge}\!\curvearrowright$ from the original definition, we also define and use two restricted single jumps with limited movement. The definition of restricted jumps is modified from the original paper Meduna and Zemek [2012] (see Definition 3.5) in order to get a more consistent behavior. The restricted single jumps now read strings from the configuration on the specific side of the state depending on the actual direction of their jumping.

Let $M = (Q, \Delta, R, s, F)$ be a GJFA. Let $w, x, y, z \in \Delta^*$ and $h: (p, y, q) \in R$; then, $wpyxz \,_{\blacktriangleright}\!\curvearrowright wxqz \; [h]$ and $wxypz \,_{\blacktriangleleft}\!\curvearrowright wqxz \; [h]$ in M.

Consider the jumping relation (see Definition 3.1) and right and left jumps (see Definition 3.5). Based on the jumping relation, we next introduce the notion of an unrestricted 2-jumping relation (see Figure 4.1). In addition, based on the combination of left jumps and right jumps, we define four new types of restricted 2-jumping relations, such as left-right 2-jumping relation in Figure 4.2.

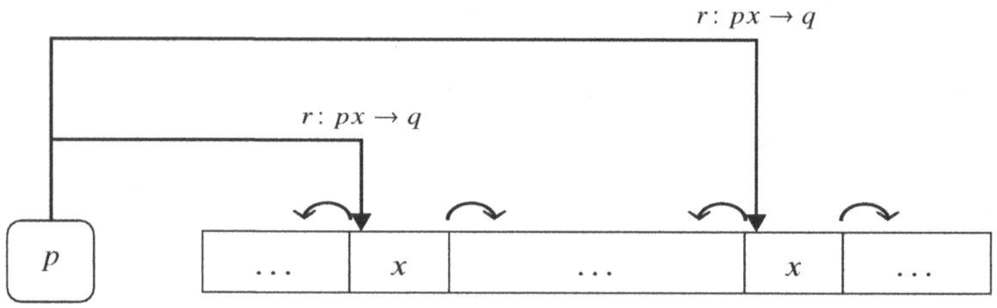

Fig. 4.1 GJFA with 2-jumping relation $_{\blacklozenge\blacklozenge}\!\curvearrowright$.

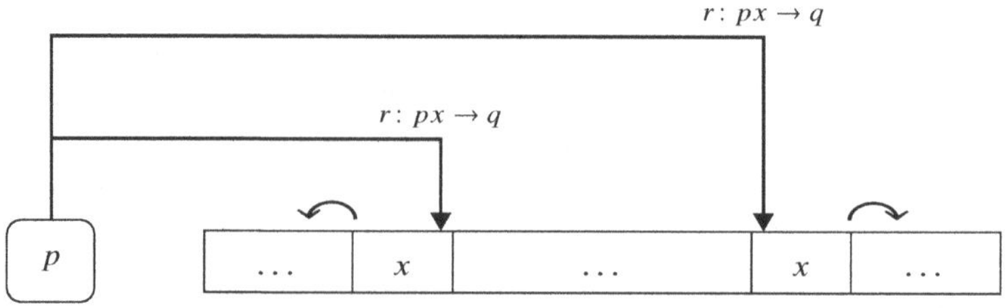

Fig. 4.2 GJFA with 2-jumping relation $_{\blacktriangleleft\blacktriangleright}\!\curvearrowright$.

An investigation of these new relations represents the central subject of this section, which demonstrates a significant impact on the behavior of the jumping automata under consideration. In the correspondence to these relations, it describes and compares the language families accepted by these automata and studies closure properties of these families.

Definition 4.1 Let X denote the set of all configurations of M. A *2-configuration* of M is any string in XX. Let X^2 denote the set of all 2-configurations of M. For brevity, let $t_1t_2 \in \{\blacklozenge\blacklozenge, \blacktriangleright\blacktriangleright, \blacktriangleright\blacktriangleleft, \blacktriangleleft\blacktriangleright, \blacktriangleleft\blacktriangleleft\}$ such that $t_1, t_2 \in \{\blacklozenge, \blacktriangleright, \blacktriangleleft\}$. The binary t_1t_2 *2-jumping relation*, symbolically denoted by ${}_{t_1t_2}\curvearrowright$, over X^2, is defined as follows. Let $\zeta_1\zeta_2, \vartheta_1\vartheta_2 \in X^2$, where $\zeta_1, \zeta_2, \vartheta_1, \vartheta_2 \in X$, and $h \in R$; then, M makes a t_1t_2 *2-jump* from $\zeta_1\zeta_2$ to $\vartheta_1\vartheta_2$ according to h, symbolically written as $\zeta_1\zeta_2 \ {}_{t_1t_2}\curvearrowright \ \vartheta_1\vartheta_2 \ [h]$ if and only if $\zeta_1 \ {}_{t_1}\curvearrowright \vartheta_1 \ [h]$ and $\zeta_2 \ {}_{t_2}\curvearrowright \vartheta_2 \ [h]$. Depending on the specific type of jumps $\blacklozenge\blacklozenge$, $\blacktriangleright\blacktriangleright$, $\blacktriangleright\blacktriangleleft$, $\blacktriangleleft\blacktriangleright$, $\blacktriangleleft\blacktriangleleft$, we use the following naming: unrestricted, right-right, right-left, left-right, left-left 2-jumping relation (or 2-jump), respectively.

Let o be any of the jumping direct relations introduced above. In the standard way, extend o to o^m, $m \geq 0$; o^+; and o^*. To express that M only performs jumps according to o, write M_o. If o is one of the relations ${}_{\blacklozenge}\curvearrowright$, ${}_{\blacktriangleright}\curvearrowright$, ${}_{\blacktriangleleft}\curvearrowright$, set $L(M_o) = \{uv \mid u, v \in \Delta^*, \ usv \ \ o^* \ f, \ f \in F\}$. In fact, by Definition 3.1, **GJFA** coincides to $\{L(M_{\blacklozenge\curvearrowright}) \mid M \text{ is a GJFA}\}$, ${}_l$**GJFA** to $\{L(M_{\blacktriangleleft\curvearrowright}) \mid M \text{ is a GJFA}\}$, and ${}_r$**GJFA** to $\{L(M_{\blacktriangleright\curvearrowright}) \mid M \text{ is a GJFA}\}$.

If o is one of the relations ${}_{\blacklozenge\blacklozenge}\curvearrowright$, ${}_{\blacktriangleright\blacktriangleright}\curvearrowright$, ${}_{\blacktriangleright\blacktriangleleft}\curvearrowright$, ${}_{\blacktriangleleft\blacktriangleright}\curvearrowright$, ${}_{\blacktriangleleft\blacktriangleleft}\curvearrowright$, we call M_o a *double-jumping finite automaton* and set $L(M_o) = \{uvw \mid u, v, w \in \Delta^*, \ usvsw \ \ o^* \ ff, \ f \in F\}$. $L(M_o)$ is referred to as the *language of* M_o.

To illustrate this terminology, take $o = {}_{\blacklozenge\blacklozenge}\curvearrowright$. Consider $M_{\blacklozenge\blacklozenge\curvearrowright}$. Notice that $L(M_{\blacklozenge\blacklozenge\curvearrowright}) = \{uvw \mid u, v, w \in \Delta^*, \ usvsw \ \ {}_{\blacklozenge\blacklozenge}\curvearrowright^* \ ff, \ f \in F\}$. $L(M_{\blacklozenge\blacklozenge\curvearrowright})$ is referred to as the *language of* $M_{\blacklozenge\blacklozenge\curvearrowright}$. Set $\mathbf{DJFA}_{\blacklozenge\blacklozenge} = \{L(M_{\blacklozenge\blacklozenge\curvearrowright}) \mid M \text{ is a GJFA}\}$; $\mathbf{DJFA}_{\blacklozenge\blacklozenge}$ is referred to as the *language family accepted by GJFAs according to* ${}_{\blacklozenge\blacklozenge}\curvearrowright$.

Furthermore, set $\mathbf{DJFA}_2 = \mathbf{DJFA}_{\blacklozenge\blacklozenge} \cup \mathbf{DJFA}_{\blacktriangleright\blacktriangleright} \cup \mathbf{DJFA}_{\blacktriangleright\blacktriangleleft} \cup \mathbf{DJFA}_{\blacktriangleleft\blacktriangleright} \cup \mathbf{DJFA}_{\blacktriangleleft\blacktriangleleft}$.

Example 4.1 Let $M = (\{s\}, \{a, b\}, R, s, \{s\})$ be very simple GJFA, where R consists of a single rule $1: sab \to s$. Let us explore M working with some 2-jumping relations for an input $aabbabab$.

First, see M accepts $aabbabab$ by ${}_{\blacklozenge\blacklozenge}\curvearrowright$:

$$asabb \ sabab \ {}_{\blacklozenge\blacklozenge}\curvearrowright \ sab \ sab \ {}_{\blacklozenge\blacklozenge}\curvearrowright \ ss$$

We get a different behavior for ${}_{\blacktriangleleft\blacktriangleright}\curvearrowright$:

$$asabb \ sabab \ {}_{\blacktriangleleft\blacktriangleright}\curvearrowright \ asb \ sab$$

Observe that $M_{\blacktriangleleft\blacktriangleright\curvearrowright}$ is stuck since we need to move the first head one position to the right as we need to reach configuration $abssab$ to be able to apply rule 1 again.

The similar situation happens if we consider M working by ${}_{\blacktriangleright\blacktriangleleft}\curvearrowright$:

$$asabb \ ababs \ {}_{\blacktriangleright\blacktriangleleft}\curvearrowright \ asb \ abs$$

Again, the first head is stuck since $M_{\blacktriangleright\blacktriangleleft\curvearrowright}$ reads from s to the right, but it cannot jump to the left to move s at the position of first a.

Therefore, it is easy to see that $L(M_{\blacklozenge\blacklozenge\curvearrowright}) \subset L(M_{\blacktriangleleft\blacktriangleright\curvearrowright}) = L(M_{\blacktriangleright\blacktriangleleft\curvearrowright}) = \{abab\}^*$.

Lastly, we define an auxiliary subfamily of the family of regular languages that will be useful to the study of the accepting power of GJFAs that perform right-left and left-right 2-jumps.

Definition 4.2 Let $L_{m,n}$ be a *simply expandable language* (SEL) over an alphabet Δ if it can be written as follows. Let m and n be positive integers; then, $L_{m,n} = \bigcup_{h=1}^{m} \left\{ u_{h,1}u_{h,2} \dots u_{h,n}v_h^i v_h^i u_{h,n} \dots u_{h,2}u_{h,1} \mid i \geq 0,\ u_{h,k}, v_h \in \Delta^*,\ 1 \leq k \leq n \right\}$.

For the sake of clarity, let us note that, in the previous definition, v_h and all $u_{h,k}$ are fixed strings that only vary for different values of h.

Throughout the rest of this section, **SEL** denotes the family of SELs. Furthermore, for any language family $\mathcal{F}$, $\mathcal{F}_{\text{even}} = \{K \mid K$ is the maximal subset of L in which every string has an even length, $L \in \mathcal{F}\}$. Specifically, we make use of $\mathbf{FIN}_{\text{even}}$, $\mathbf{REG}_{\text{even}}$, $\mathbf{LIN}_{\text{even}}$, $\mathbf{CF}_{\text{even}}$, and $\mathbf{CS}_{\text{even}}$ in what follows.

Example 4.2 Let $\Delta = \{a, b, c\}$. Consider the GJFA $M_{\blacklozenge\blacklozenge\curvearrowright} = (\{s, f\}, \Delta, R, s, \{f\})$, where R consists of the rules $1\colon sab \rightarrow f$ and $2\colon fc \rightarrow f$. Starting from s, M has to read two times some ab, entering the final state f; then, M can arbitrarily many times read two times some c. Consequently, if we work with the unrestricted 2-jumps, the input must always contain two separate strings ab, and the symbols c can be anywhere around these two strings. For instance, M works on $cabcabcc$ as follows.

$$csabcsabcc \;{}_{\blacklozenge\blacklozenge}\!\curvearrowright fcccfc\ [1] \;{}_{\blacklozenge\blacklozenge}\!\curvearrowright fcfc\ [2] \;{}_{\blacklozenge\blacklozenge}\!\curvearrowright ff\ [2]$$

Therefore, the accepted language is $L(M_{\blacklozenge\blacklozenge\curvearrowright}) = \{c^k abc^m abc^n \mid k + m + n$ is an even integer, $k, m, n \geq 0\}$.

General Results

This section studies the accepting power of GJFAs making their computational steps by unrestricted, right-left, left-right, right-right, and left-left 2-jumps.

On the unrestricted 2-jumping relation

Lemma 4.1 *For every language $L \in \mathbf{DJFA}_2$, there is no $x \in L$ such that $|x|$ is an odd number; furthermore, there is no symbol a for which* occur(x, a) *is an odd number.*

Proof By the definition of 2-jumps, any GJFA that uses 2-jumps always performs two single jumps simultaneously, and they both follow the same rule; therefore, there is no way how to read an odd number of symbols from the input string. □

Lemma 4.2 *There is no GJFA* $M_{\blacklozenge\curvearrowright}$ *that accepts* $\{c^k abc^m abc^n \mid k+m+n$ *is an even integer,* $k, m, n \geq 0\}$.

Proof Since GJFA $M_{\blacklozenge\curvearrowright}$ works as a GJFA (see Definitions 3.1 and 4.1), we follow Lemma 3.3 which effectively shows that a GJFA $M_{\blacklozenge\curvearrowright}$ can maintain a specific order of symbols only in the sole context of a rule. Let $K = \{c^k abc^m abc^n \mid k+m+n$ be an even integer, $k, m, n \geq 0\}$. For the sake of contradiction, assume that there is a GJFA $M_{\blacklozenge\curvearrowright}$ such that $L(M_{\blacklozenge\curvearrowright}) = K$. If M uses two times a rule reading ab, then it can also accept input $aabb$; and clearly $aabb \notin K$. Consequently, M has to always read the whole sequence $abc^m ab$ with a single rule; however, number m is unbounded and thus there cannot be finitely many rules that cover all possibilities—a contradiction with the assumption that $L(M_{\blacklozenge\curvearrowright}) = K$ exists. Therefore, there is no GJFA $M_{\blacklozenge\curvearrowright}$ that accepts $\{c^k abc^m abc^n \mid k+m+n$ is an even integer, $k, m, n \geq 0\}$.□

Theorem 4.1 **GJFA** *and* $\mathbf{DJFA}_{\blacklozenge\blacklozenge}$ *are incomparable.*

Proof $\mathbf{GJFA} \not\subseteq \mathbf{DJFA}_{\blacklozenge\blacklozenge}$ follows from $\mathbf{FIN} \subset \mathbf{GJFA}$ (see Theorem 3.8) and Lemma 4.1. $\mathbf{DJFA}_{\blacklozenge\blacklozenge} \not\subseteq \mathbf{GJFA}$ follows from Example 4.2 and Lemma 4.2. Moreover, both $\mathbf{DJFA}_{\blacklozenge}$ and $\mathbf{DJFA}_{\blacklozenge\blacklozenge}$ clearly contain the simple finite language $\{aa\}$. □

On the right-left 2-jumping relation

Lemma 4.3 *Let* $M = (Q, \Delta, R, s, F)$ *be a GJFA; then, every* $x \in L(M_{\blacktriangleright\blacktriangleleft\curvearrowright})$ *can be written as* $x = u_1 u_2 \ldots u_n u_n \ldots u_2 u_1$*, where* $n \in \mathbb{N}$*, and* $u_i \in \Delta^*$*,* $1 \leq i \leq n$.

Proof Consider any GJFA $M_{\blacktriangleright\blacktriangleleft\curvearrowright} = (Q, \Delta, R, s, F)$. Since we work with the right-left 2-jumps, the first jump can move only to the right, the second jump can move only to the left, and both jumps cannot cross each other. Observe that if the configuration of M is of the form $upvpw$, where $u, v, w \in \Delta^*$, and $p \in Q$, then M cannot read the symbols in u and w anymore. Also, observe that this covers the situation when M starts to accept $x \in \Delta^*$ from any other configuration than sxs. Therefore, to read the whole input string, M has to start in the configuration sxs, and it cannot jump over any symbols during the whole process. Consequently, since both jumps always follow the same rule, they have to read the same corresponding strings and, at the end, meet in the middle of the input string. Therefore, every $x \in L(M_{\blacktriangleright\blacktriangleleft\curvearrowright})$ can be surely written as $x = u_1 u_2 \ldots u_n u_n \ldots u_2 u_1$, where $n \in \mathbb{N}$, and $u_i \in \Delta^*$, $1 \leq i \leq n$.□

Lemma 4.4 *For every GJFA M, there is a linear grammar G such that* $L(M_{\blacktriangleright\blacktriangleleft\curvearrowright}) = L(G)$.

Proof Consider any GJFA $M_{\blacktriangleright\blacktriangleleft\curvearrowright} = (Q, \Delta, R, s, F)$. Define the linear grammar $G = (Q, \Delta, P, s)$, where P is constructed in the following way:

1. For each $(p, y, q) \in R$, add $p \rightarrow yqy$ to P.
2. For each $p \in F$, add $p \rightarrow \varepsilon$ to P.

We follow Lemma 4.3 and its proof. Let $p, q \in Q$, $f \in F$, and $y, u, v, w \in \Delta^*$. Observe that every time M can make a 2-jump $pywyp \; {}_{\blacktriangleright\blacktriangleleft}\!\curvearrowright \; qwq$ according to $(p, y, q) \in P$, G can also make the derivation step $upv \Rightarrow uyqyv$ according to $p \rightarrow yqy \in P$. Moreover, every time M is in a final state f, G can finish the string with $f \rightarrow \varepsilon \in P$. Finally, observe that G cannot do any other action; therefore, $L(M_{\blacktriangleright\blacktriangleleft\curvearrowright}) = L(G)$. □

Theorem 4.2 $\mathbf{DJFA}_{\blacktriangleright\blacktriangleleft} \subset \mathbf{LIN}_{even}$.

Proof $\mathbf{DJFA}_{\blacktriangleright\blacktriangleleft} \subseteq \mathbf{LIN}_{\mathrm{even}}$ follows from Lemma 4.4 and the structure of its proof. $\mathbf{LIN}_{\mathrm{even}} \not\subseteq \mathbf{DJFA}_{\blacktriangleright\blacktriangleleft}$ follows from Lemma 4.1. □

Lemma 4.5 *There is a GJFA M such that $L(M_{\blacktriangleright\blacktriangleleft\curvearrowright}) = \{w \in \Delta^* \mid w$ is an even palindrome$\}$.*

Proof Consider an arbitrary alphabet Δ. Define the GJFA $M_{\blacktriangleright\blacktriangleleft\curvearrowright} = (\{f\}, \Delta, R, f, \{f\})$ where $R = \{(f, a, f) \mid a \in \Delta\}$. We follow Lemma 4.3 and its proof, which shows that every $x \in L(M_{\blacktriangleright\blacktriangleleft\curvearrowright})$ can be written as $x = u_1u_2 \ldots u_nu_n \ldots u_2u_1$, where $n \in \mathbb{N}$, and $u_i \in \Delta^*$, $1 \leq i \leq n$. Observe that we use only rules reading single symbols, thus we can even say that $u_i \in (\Delta \cup \{\varepsilon\})$, $1 \leq i \leq n$, which, in fact, models the string pattern of the even palindrome. Moreover, we use only one sole state that can accept all symbols from Δ; therefore, $L(M_{\blacktriangleright\blacktriangleleft\curvearrowright}) = \{w \in \Delta^* \mid w$ is an even palindrome$\}$. □

Lemma 4.6 *For every SEL $K_{m,n}$, there is a GJFA M such that $K_{m,n}$=$L(M_{\blacktriangleright\blacktriangleleft\curvearrowright})$.*

Proof Let m and n be positive integers. Consider any SEL over an alphabet Δ, $K_{m,n} = \bigcup_{h=1}^{m} \left\{u_{h,1}u_{h,2} \ldots u_{h,n}v_h^iv_h^iu_{h,n} \ldots u_{h,2}u_{h,1} \mid i \geq 0,\ u_{h,k}, v_h \in \Delta^*,\ 1 \leq k \leq n\right\}$. Define the GJFA $M_{\blacktriangleright\blacktriangleleft\curvearrowright} = (Q, \Delta, R, \langle s \rangle, F)$, where Q, R, and F are constructed in the following way:

1. Add $\langle s \rangle$ to Q.
2. Add $\langle h, k \rangle$ to Q, for all $1 \leq h \leq m$, $1 \leq k \leq n + 1$.
3. Add $\langle h, n + 1 \rangle$ to F, for all $1 \leq h \leq m$.
4. Add $(\langle s \rangle, \varepsilon, \langle h, 1 \rangle)$ to R, for all $1 \leq h \leq m$.
5. Add $(\langle h, k \rangle, u_{h,k}, \langle h, k + 1 \rangle)$ to R, for all $1 \leq h \leq m$, $1 \leq k \leq n$.
6. Add $(\langle h, n + 1 \rangle, v_h, \langle h, n + 1 \rangle)$ to R, for all $1 \leq h \leq m$.

We follow Lemma 4.3 and its proof. Observe that M starts from $\langle s \rangle$ by jumping to an arbitrary state $\langle h, 1 \rangle$, where $1 \leq h \leq m$. Then, the first jump consecutively reads $u_{h,1}u_{h,2} \ldots u_{h,n}$, and the second jump consecutively reads $u_{h,n} \ldots u_{h,2}u_{h,1}$, until M ends up in the final state $\langle h, n + 1 \rangle$. Here, both jumps can arbitrarily many times read v_h. As a result, M accepts $u_{h,1}u_{h,2} \ldots u_{h,n}v_h^iv_h^iu_{h,n} \ldots u_{h,2}u_{h,1}$, for all $1 \leq h \leq m$, where $i \geq 0$, $u_{h,k}, v_h \in \Delta^*$, $1 \leq k \leq n$; therefore, $K_{m,n} = L(M_{\blacktriangleright\blacktriangleleft\curvearrowright})$. □

Lemma 4.7 *For every SEL $K_{m,n}$, there is a right-linear grammar G such that $K_{m,n} = L(G)$.*

Proof Let m and n be positive integers. Consider any SEL over an alphabet Δ, $K_{m,n} = \bigcup_{h=1}^{m} \{u_{h,1}u_{h,2} \dots u_{h,n}v_h^i v_h^i u_{h,n} \dots u_{h,2}u_{h,1} \mid i \geq 0,\ u_{h,k}, v_h \in \Delta^*,\ 1 \leq k \leq n\}$. Define the right-linear grammar $G = (N, \Delta, P, \langle s \rangle)$, where N and P are constructed in the following way:

1. Add $\langle s \rangle$ to N.
2. Add $\langle h, 1 \rangle$ and $\langle h, 2 \rangle$ to N, for all $1 \leq h \leq m$.
3. Add $\langle s \rangle \rightarrow \langle h, 1 \rangle$ to P, for all $1 \leq h \leq m$.
4. Add $\langle h, 1 \rangle \rightarrow u_{h,1}u_{h,2} \dots u_{h,n}\langle h, 2 \rangle$ to P, for all $1 \leq h \leq m$.
5. Add $\langle h, 2 \rangle \rightarrow v_n v_n \langle h, 2 \rangle$ to P, for all $1 \leq h \leq m$.
6. Add $\langle h, 2 \rangle \rightarrow u_{h,n} \dots u_{h,2}u_{h,1}$ to P, for all $1 \leq h \leq m$.

Observe that at the beginning, G has to change nonterminal $\langle s \rangle$ to an arbitrary nonterminal $\langle h, 1 \rangle$, where $1 \leq h \leq m$. Then, it generates $u_{h,1}u_{h,2} \dots u_{h,n}$ and nonterminal $\langle h, 2 \rangle$. Here, it can arbitrarily many times generate $v_n v_n$ and ultimately finish the generation with $u_{h,n} \dots u_{h,2}u_{h,1}$. As a result, G generates $u_{h,1}u_{h,2} \dots u_{h,n}(v_h v_h)^i u_{h,n} \dots u_{h,2}u_{h,1}$, for all $1 \leq h \leq m$, where $i \geq 0$, $u_{h,k}, v_h \in \Delta^*$, $1 \leq k \leq n$, which is indistinguishable from $u_{h,1}u_{h,2} \dots u_{h,n}v_h^i v_h^i u_{h,n} \dots u_{h,2}u_{h,1}$; therefore, $K_{m,n} = L(G)$. □

Theorem 4.3 $\mathbf{SEL} \subset \mathbf{REG}_{even}$.

Proof $\mathbf{SEL} \subseteq \mathbf{REG}_{\text{even}}$ follows from Lemma 4.7 and the structure of its proof. $\mathbf{REG}_{\text{even}} \not\subseteq \mathbf{SEL}$ follows from Lemma 4.6 and Lemma 4.1. □

Theorem 4.4 $\mathbf{SEL} \subset \mathbf{DJFA}_{\blacktriangleright\blacktriangleleft}$.

Proof $\mathbf{SEL} \subseteq \mathbf{DJFA}_{\blacktriangleright\blacktriangleleft}$ follows from Lemma 4.6. $\mathbf{DJFA}_{\blacktriangleright\blacktriangleleft} \not\subseteq \mathbf{SEL}$ follows from Theorem 4.3 and Lemma 4.5 because a subfamily of the family of regular languages surely cannot contain a non-trivial language of all even palindromes. □

Theorem 4.5 *The following pairs of language families are incomparable:*

(i) $\mathbf{DJFA}_{\blacktriangleright\blacktriangleleft}$ *and* $\mathbf{REG}$ *(*$\mathbf{REG}_{even}$*);*
(ii) $\mathbf{DJFA}_{\blacktriangleright\blacktriangleleft}$ *and* $\mathbf{FIN}$ *(*$\mathbf{FIN}_{even}$*).*

Proof $\mathbf{DJFA}_{\blacktriangleright\blacktriangleleft} \not\subseteq \mathbf{REG}$ $(\mathbf{REG}_{\text{even}})$ and $\mathbf{DJFA}_{\blacktriangleright\blacktriangleleft} \not\subseteq \mathbf{FIN}$ $(\mathbf{FIN}_{\text{even}})$ follow from Lemma 4.5, Theorem 4.3, and Theorem 4.4 (and Lemma 4.1). $\mathbf{REG}$ $(\mathbf{REG}_{\text{even}}) \not\subseteq \mathbf{DJFA}_{\blacktriangleright\blacktriangleleft}$ and $\mathbf{FIN}$ $(\mathbf{FIN}_{\text{even}}) \not\subseteq \mathbf{DJFA}_{\blacktriangleright\blacktriangleleft}$ follow from Lemma 4.1. Moreover, $\mathbf{DJFA}_{\blacktriangleright\blacktriangleleft}$ clearly contains the regular language $\{a^{2n} \mid n \geq 0\}$ and finite language $\{aa\}$. □

Open Problem $(\mathbf{DJFA}_{\blacktriangleright\blacktriangleleft} - \mathbf{SEL}) \cap \mathbf{REG} = \emptyset$? □

On the left-right 2-jumping relation

Lemma 4.8 *Let* $M = (Q, \Delta, R, s, F)$ *be a GJFA; then, every* $x \in L(M_{\blacktriangleleft\blacktriangleright\curvearrowright})$ *can be written as* $x = u_n \dots u_2u_1u_1u_2 \dots u_n$*, where* $n \in \mathbb{N}$*, and* $u_i \in \Delta^*$*,* $1 \leq i \leq n$*.*

Proof Consider any GJFA $M_{\blacktriangleleft\blacktriangleright\curvearrowright} = (Q, \Delta, R, s, F)$. Since we work with the left-right 2-jumps, the first jump can move only to the left, and the second jump can move only to the right. Observe that if the configuration of M is of the form $upvpw$, where $u, v, w \in \Delta^*$, and $p \in Q$, then M cannot read the symbols in v anymore. Also, observe that this covers the situation when M starts to accept $x \in \Delta^*$ from any other configuration than $yssz$, where $y, z \in \Delta^*$ such that $x = yz$. Therefore, to read the whole input string, M has to start in the configuration $yssz$, and it cannot jump over any symbols during the whole process. Consequently, since both jumps follow the same rule, they have to read the same corresponding strings and ultimately finish at the ends of the input string. Therefore, every $x \in L(M_{\blacktriangleleft\blacktriangleright\curvearrowright})$ can be written as $x = u_n \dots u_2 u_1 u_1 u_2 \dots u_n$, where $n \in \mathbb{N}$, and $u_i \in \Delta^*$, $1 \le i \le n$. □

Lemma 4.9 *For every GJFA M, there is a GJFA N such that $L(M_{\blacktriangleleft\blacktriangleright\curvearrowright}) = L(N_{\blacktriangleright\blacktriangleleft\curvearrowright})$.*

Proof Consider any $GJFA$ $M_{\blacktriangleleft\blacktriangleright\curvearrowright} = (Q, \Delta, R_1, s_1, F)$. Without a loss of generality, assume that $s_2 \notin Q$. Define the GJFA $N_{\blacktriangleright\blacktriangleleft\curvearrowright} = (Q \cup \{s_2\}, \Delta, R_2, s_2, \{s_1\})$, where R_2 is constructed in the following way:

1. For each $(p, y, q) \in R_1$, add (q, y, p) to R_2.
2. For each $f \in F$, add (s_2, ε, f) to R_2.

Note that this construction resembles the well-known conversion technique for finite automata which creates a finite automaton that accepts the reversal of the original language. However, in this case, the effect is quite different. We follow Lemmas 4.3 and 4.8. Consider any $x \in L(M_{\blacktriangleleft\blacktriangleright\curvearrowright})$. We can surely find $x = u_n \dots u_2 u_1 u_1 u_2 \dots u_n$, where $n \in \mathbb{N}$, and $u_i \in \Delta^*$, $1 \le i \le n$, such that N reads $u_n \dots u_2 u_1$ and $u_1 u_2 \dots u_n$ in the reverse order. Moreover, in N, both jumps have their direction reversed, compared to jumps in M, and thus they start on the opposite ends of their parts, which is demonstrated in the mentioned claims. Consequently, if each jump in N reads its part reversely and from the opposite end, then N reads the same $u_n \dots u_2 u_1 u_1 u_2 \dots u_n$ as M. Finally, N surely cannot accept anything new that is not accepted by M. Thus, $L(M_{\blacktriangleleft\blacktriangleright\curvearrowright}) = L(N_{\blacktriangleright\blacktriangleleft\curvearrowright})$. □

Lemma 4.10 *For every GJFA M, there is a GJFA N such that $L(M_{\blacktriangleright\blacktriangleleft\curvearrowright}) = L(N_{\blacktriangleleft\blacktriangleright\curvearrowright})$.*

Proof The construction and reasoning is exactly the same as in Lemma 4.9. □

Theorem 4.6 $\mathbf{DJFA}_{\blacktriangleleft\blacktriangleright} = \mathbf{DJFA}_{\blacktriangleright\blacktriangleleft}$.

Proof $\mathbf{DJFA}_{\blacktriangleleft\blacktriangleright} \subseteq \mathbf{DJFA}_{\blacktriangleright\blacktriangleleft}$ follows from Lemma 4.9. $\mathbf{DJFA}_{\blacktriangleright\blacktriangleleft} \subseteq \mathbf{DJFA}_{\blacktriangleleft\blacktriangleright}$ follows from Lemma 4.10. □

Other properties of this language family thus coincide with Section 4.1.

On the right-right 2-jumping relation

Example 4.3 Consider the GJFA $M_{\blacktriangleright\blacktriangleright\curvearrowright} = (\{s, p, f\}, \Delta, R, s, \{f\})$, where $\Delta = \{a, b, c\}$ and R consists of the rules (s, ab, p) and (p, c, f). Starting from s, M

has to read two times ab and two times c. Observe that if the first jump skips (jumps over) some symbols, then they cannot be ever read afterward. However, the second jump is not so harshly restricted and can potentially skip some symbols which will be read later by the first jump. Therefore, the accepted language is $L(M_{\blacktriangleright\blacktriangleright\curvearrowright}) = \{ababcc, abcabc\}$.

Example 4.4 Consider the GJFA $M_{\blacktriangleright\blacktriangleright\curvearrowright} = (\{s, f\}, \Delta, R, s, \{f\})$, where $\Delta = \{a, b\}$ and R consists of the rules (s, b, f) and (f, a, f). Starting from s, M has to read two times b and then it can arbitrarily many times read two times a. Both jumps behave in the same way as in Example 4.3. Observe that when we consider no skipping of symbols, then M reads ba^nba^n, $n \geq 0$. Nevertheless, when we consider the skipping with the second jump, then the second b can also occur arbitrarily closer to the first b; until they are neighbors, and M reads bba^{2n}, $n \geq 0$. When combined together, the accepted language is $L(M_{\blacktriangleright\blacktriangleright\curvearrowright}) = \{ba^nba^na^{2m} \mid n, m \geq 0\}$. Observe that this is clearly a non-regular context-free language.

Example 4.5 Consider the GJFA $M_{\blacktriangleright\blacktriangleright\curvearrowright} = (\{s, f\}, \Delta, R, s, \{f\})$, where $\Delta = \{a, b, c, d\}$ and $R = \{(s, y, f) \mid y \in \Delta\} \cup \{(f, y, f) \mid y \in \Delta\}$. Starting from s, M has to read two times some symbol from Δ, and then it can arbitrarily many times read two times any symbols from Δ. Again, both jumps behave in the same way as in Example 4.3. Consider the special case when the second jump consistently jumps over one symbol each time (except the last step) during the whole process. In such a case, the accepted strings can be written as $u_1u'_1u_2u'_2 \ldots u_nu'_n$, where $n \in \mathbb{N}$, $u_i, u'_i \in \Delta$, $u_i = u'_i$, $1 \leq i \leq n$. Observe that the symbols without primes are read by the first jump, and the symbols with primes are read by the second jump. Moreover, such strings can be surely generated by a right-linear grammar. Nevertheless, now consider no special case. Observe that, in the accepted strings, the symbols with primes can be arbitrarily shifted to the right over symbols without primes; this creates a more complex structure, due to $u_i = u'_i$, with multiple crossed agreements. Lastly, consider the other border case with no skipping of any symbols at all. Then, the accepted strings can be written as ww, where $w \in \Delta^+$. Such strings represent the reduplication phenomenon—the well-known example of non-context-free languages (see Chapter 3.1 in Rozenberg and Salomaa [1997b]). As a result, due to the unbound number of crossed agreements, we can safely state that $L(M_{\blacktriangleright\blacktriangleright\curvearrowright})$ is a non-context-free language.

This statement can be formally proven by contradiction. Assume that $L(M_{\blacktriangleright\blacktriangleright\curvearrowright})$ is a context-free language. The family of context-free languages is closed under intersection with regular sets. Let $K = L(M_{\blacktriangleright\blacktriangleright\curvearrowright}) \cap ab^+c^+dab^+c^+d$. Consider the previous description. Observe that this selects strings where $u_1 = a$ and $u'_n = d$. Since there are only exactly two symbols a and two symbols d in each selected string, we know where precisely both jumps start and end. And since the second jump starts after the position where the first jump ends, we also know that this, in fact, follows the special border case of behavior with no skipping of any symbols at all. Consequently, $K = \{ab^nc^mdab^nc^md \mid n, m \geq 1\}$. However, K is clearly a non-context-free language (see Chapter 3.1 in Rozenberg and Salomaa [1997b])—a contradiction with the assumption that $L(M_{\blacktriangleright\blacktriangleright\curvearrowright})$ is a context-free language. Therefore, $L(M_{\blacktriangleright\blacktriangleright\curvearrowright})$ is a non-context-free language.

Theorem 4.7 $\mathbf{DJFA}_{\blacktriangleright\blacktriangleright} \subset \mathbf{CS}_{even}$.

Proof Clearly, any GJFA $M_{\blacktriangleright\blacktriangleright\curvearrowright}$ can be simulated by linear bounded automata, so $\mathbf{DJFA}_{\blacktriangleright\blacktriangleright} \subseteq \mathbf{CS}$. Due to Lemma 4.1, we can safely exclude all languages containing odd-length strings. $\mathbf{CS}_{\text{even}} \not\subseteq \mathbf{DJFA}_{\blacktriangleleft\blacktriangleleft}$ also follows from Lemma 4.1. □

Lemma 4.11 *Let $n \in \mathbb{N}$, and let M be any GJFA. Furthermore, let every $x \in L(M_{\blacktriangleright\blacktriangleright\curvearrowright})$ satisfy either $|x| \leq n$ or* $\text{symbols}(x) = 1$. *Then, there exists a right-linear grammar G such that $L(M_{\blacktriangleright\blacktriangleright\curvearrowright}) = L(G)$.*

Proof Let $n \in \mathbb{N}$. Consider any GJFA $M_{\blacktriangleright\blacktriangleright\curvearrowright}$ where every $x \in L(M_{\blacktriangleright\blacktriangleright\curvearrowright})$ satisfy either $|x| \leq n$ or $\text{symbols}(x) = 1$. Define the right-linear grammar G in the following way: Observe that the number of x for which holds $|x| \leq n$ must be finite; therefore, for each such x, we can create a separate rule that generates x in G. On the other hand, the number of x for which holds $\text{symbols}(x) = 1$ can be infinite; however, every such x is defined by the finite number of rules in M. And we can surely convert these rules (p, y, q) from M into rules in G in such a way that they generate y^2 and simulate the state transitions of M. Consequently, since the position of symbols here is ultimately irrelevant, these rules properly simulate results of 2-jumps in M. Therefore, $L(M_{\blacktriangleright\blacktriangleright\curvearrowright}) = L(G)$. □

Theorem 4.8 *The following pairs of language families are incomparable:*

(i) $\mathbf{DJFA}_{\blacktriangleright\blacktriangleright}$ *and* $\mathbf{CF}$ *(*$\mathbf{CF}_{even}$*);*
(ii) $\mathbf{DJFA}_{\blacktriangleright\blacktriangleright}$ *and* $\mathbf{REG}$ *(*$\mathbf{REG}_{even}$*);*
(iii) $\mathbf{DJFA}_{\blacktriangleright\blacktriangleright}$ *and* $\mathbf{FIN}$ *(*$\mathbf{FIN}_{even}$*).*

Proof $\mathbf{DJFA}_{\blacktriangleright\blacktriangleright} \not\subseteq \mathbf{CF}$ ($\mathbf{CF}_{\text{even}}$), $\mathbf{DJFA}_{\blacktriangleright\blacktriangleright} \not\subseteq \mathbf{REG}$ ($\mathbf{REG}_{\text{even}}$), and $\mathbf{DJFA}_{\blacktriangleright\blacktriangleright} \not\subseteq \mathbf{FIN}$ ($\mathbf{FIN}_{\text{even}}$) follow from Example 4.5. $\mathbf{CF}$ ($\mathbf{CF}_{\text{even}}$) $\not\subseteq \mathbf{DJFA}_{\blacktriangleright\blacktriangleright}$, $\mathbf{REG}$ ($\mathbf{REG}_{\text{even}}$) $\not\subseteq \mathbf{DJFA}_{\blacktriangleright\blacktriangleright}$, and $\mathbf{FIN}$ ($\mathbf{FIN}_{\text{even}}$) $\not\subseteq \mathbf{DJFA}_{\blacktriangleright\blacktriangleright}$ follow from Lemma 4.1. Moreover, observe that $\mathbf{DJFA}_{\blacktriangleright\blacktriangleright}$ clearly contains the context-free language from Example 4.4, regular language $\{a^{2n} \mid n \geq 0\}$, and finite language from Example 4.3. □

On the left-left 2-jumping relation

Example 4.6 Consider the GJFA $M_{\blacktriangleleft\blacktriangleleft\curvearrowright} = (\{s, p, f\}, \Delta, R, s, \{f\})$, where $\Delta = \{a, b, c\}$ and R consists of the rules (s, c, p) and (p, ab, f). Starting from s, M has to read two times c and two times ab. Observe that if the second jump skips some symbols, then they cannot be ever read afterward. However, the first jump is not so harshly restricted and can potentially skip some symbols which will be read later by the second jump. Note that this precisely resembles the inverted behavior of the right-right 2-jumping relation. As a result, the language is $L(M_{\blacktriangleleft\blacktriangleleft\curvearrowright}) = \{ababcc, abacbc, abcabc\}$.

Example 4.7 Consider the GJFA $M_{\blacktriangleleft\blacktriangleleft\curvearrowright} = (\{s, f\}, \Delta, R, s, \{f\})$, where $\Delta = \{a, b\}$ and R consists of the rules (s, a, s) and (s, b, f). Starting from s, M can arbitrarily many times read two times a and, at the end, it has to read two times b. Both jumps behave in the same way as in Example 4.6. Observe that when we consider no skipping of symbols, then M reads $ba^n ba^n$, $n \geq 0$. Nevertheless, when we consider the skipping with the first jump, then the second b can also occur arbitrarily closer to the first b, since the first jump can now read symbols a also behind this second b. Consequently, the accepted language is $L(M_{\blacktriangleleft\blacktriangleleft\curvearrowright}) = \{ba^n ba^n a^{2m} \mid n, m \geq 0\}$. Note that this is the same language as in Example 4.4.

Example 4.8 Consider the GJFA $M_{\blacktriangleleft\blacktriangleleft\curvearrowright} = (\{s, f\}, \Delta, R, s, \{f\})$, where $\Delta = \{a, b, c, d\}$ and $R = \{(s, y, f) \mid y \in \Delta\} \cup \{(f, y, f) \mid y \in \Delta\}$. Starting from s, M has to read two times some symbol from Δ, and then it can arbitrarily many times read two times any symbols from Δ. Both jumps behave in the same way as in Example 4.6, and the overall behavior tightly follows Example 4.5. In the special case where the first jump consistently jumps over one symbol each time (except the last step) during the whole process, the accepted strings can be written as $u'_n u_n \ldots u'_2 u_2 u'_1 u_1$, where $n \in \mathbb{N}$, $u'_i, u_i \in \Delta$, $u'_i = u_i$, $1 \leq i \leq n$. The symbols with primes are read by the first jump, and the symbols without primes are read by the second jump. With no special case, the symbols with primes can be arbitrarily shifted to the left over the symbols without primes, which creates a more complex structure with multiple crossed agreements and ultimately also the structure of the reduplication phenomenon. As a result, we can safely state that $L(M_{\blacktriangleleft\blacktriangleleft\curvearrowright})$ is a non-context-free language, and this statement can be formally proven in the same way as in Example 4.5.

Theorem 4.9 $\mathbf{DJFA}_{\blacktriangleleft\blacktriangleleft} \subset \mathbf{CS}_{even}$.

Proof The reasoning is identical to Theorem 4.7. □

Lemma 4.12 *Let $n \in \mathbb{N}$, and let M be any GJFA. Furthermore, let every $x \in L(M_{\blacktriangleleft\blacktriangleleft\curvearrowright})$ satisfy either $|x| \leq n$ or* symbols$(x) = 1$. *Then, there exists a right-linear grammar G such that $L(M_{\blacktriangleleft\blacktriangleleft\curvearrowright}) = L(G)$.*

Proof The reasoning is exactly the same as in Lemma 4.11. □

Theorem 4.10 *The following pairs of language families are incomparable:*

(i) $\mathbf{DJFA}_{\blacktriangleleft\blacktriangleleft}$ *and* **CF** *(*$\mathbf{CF}_{even}$*);*
(ii) $\mathbf{DJFA}_{\blacktriangleleft\blacktriangleleft}$ *and* **REG** *(*$\mathbf{REG}_{even}$*);*
(iii) $\mathbf{DJFA}_{\blacktriangleleft\blacktriangleleft}$ *and* **FIN** *(*$\mathbf{FIN}_{even}$*).*

Proof $\mathbf{DJFA}_{\blacktriangleleft\blacktriangleleft} \not\subseteq \mathbf{CF}$ ($\mathbf{CF}_{\text{even}}$), $\mathbf{DJFA}_{\blacktriangleleft\blacktriangleleft} \not\subseteq \mathbf{REG}$ ($\mathbf{REG}_{\text{even}}$), and $\mathbf{DJFA}_{\blacktriangleleft\blacktriangleleft} \not\subseteq \mathbf{FIN}$ ($\mathbf{FIN}_{\text{even}}$) follow from Example 4.8. **CF** ($\mathbf{CF}_{\text{even}}$) $\not\subseteq \mathbf{DJFA}_{\blacktriangleleft\blacktriangleleft}$, **REG** ($\mathbf{REG}_{\text{even}}$) $\not\subseteq \mathbf{DJFA}_{\blacktriangleleft\blacktriangleleft}$, and **FIN** ($\mathbf{FIN}_{\text{even}}$) $\not\subseteq \mathbf{DJFA}_{\blacktriangleleft\blacktriangleleft}$ follow from Lemma 4.1. Moreover, $\mathbf{DJFA}_{\blacktriangleleft\blacktriangleleft}$ contains the context-free language from Example 4.7, regular language $\{a^{2n} \mid n \geq 0\}$, and finite language from Example 4.6. □

Lemma 4.13 *There is no GJFA $M_{\blacktriangleright\blacktriangleright\curvearrowright}$ that accepts $\{ababcc, abacbc, abcabc\}$.*

Proof (*by contradition*) Let $K = \{ababcc, abacbc, abcabc\}$. For the sake of contradiction, assume that there is a GJFA M such that $L(M_{\blacktriangleright\blacktriangleright\curvearrowright}) = K$. Observe that each string in K contains three pairs of symbols; therefore, to effectively read such a string, we need a maximum of three chained rules in M or less. (Note that additional rules reading ε do not affect results.) Moreover, due to the nature of strings in K, we need to consider only such chains of rules where, in the result, a precedes b, and b precedes c. Therefore, we can easily try all possibilities and calculate their resulting sets. Surely, $L(M_{\blacktriangleright\blacktriangleright\curvearrowright})$ must be a union of some of these sets:

(i) if M reads abc, the set is $\{abcabc\}$;
(ii) if M reads ab, and c, the set is $\{ababcc, abcabc\}$;
(iii) if M reads a, and bc, the set is $\{aabcbc, abacbc, abcabc\}$;
(iv) if M reads a, b, and c, the set is $\{aabbcc, ababcc, aabcbc, abacbc, abcabc\}$.

Clearly, no union of these sets can result in K—a contradiction with the assumption that $L(M_{\blacktriangleright\blacktriangleright\curvearrowright}) = K$ exists. Therefore, there is no GJFA $M_{\blacktriangleright\blacktriangleright\curvearrowright}$ that accepts $\{ababcc, abacbc, abcabc\}$. □

Lemma 4.14 *There is no GJFA $M_{\blacktriangleleft\blacktriangleleft\curvearrowright}$ that accepts $\{ababcc, abcabc\}$.*

Proof (*by contradition*) Let $K = \{ababcc, abcabc\}$. For the sake of contradiction, assume that there is a GJFA M such that $L(M_{\blacktriangleleft\blacktriangleleft\curvearrowright}) = K$. By the same reasoning as in the proof of Lemma 4.13, $L(M_{\blacktriangleleft\blacktriangleleft\curvearrowright})$ must be a union of some of these sets:

(i) if M reads abc, the set is $\{abcabc\}$;
(ii) if M reads c, and ab, the set is $\{ababcc, abacbc, abcabc\}$;
(iii) if M reads bc, and a, the set is $\{aabcbc, abcabc\}$;
(iv) if M reads c, b, and a, the set is $\{aabbcc, aabcbc, ababcc, abacbc, abcabc\}$.

Clearly, no union of these sets can result in K. Therefore, there is no GJFA $M_{\blacktriangleleft\blacktriangleleft\curvearrowright}$ that accepts $\{ababcc, abcabc\}$. □

Theorem 4.11 $\mathbf{DJFA}_{\blacktriangleright\blacktriangleright}$ *and* $\mathbf{DJFA}_{\blacktriangleleft\blacktriangleleft}$ *are incomparable.*

Proof $\mathbf{DJFA}_{\blacktriangleright\blacktriangleright} \not\subseteq \mathbf{DJFA}_{\blacktriangleleft\blacktriangleleft}$ follows from Example 4.3 and Lemma 4.14. $\mathbf{DJFA}_{\blacktriangleleft\blacktriangleleft} \not\subseteq \mathbf{DJFA}_{\blacktriangleright\blacktriangleright}$ follows from Example 4.6 and Lemma 4.13. Moreover, both $\mathbf{DJFA}_{\blacktriangleright\blacktriangleright}$ and $\mathbf{DJFA}_{\blacktriangleleft\blacktriangleleft}$ clearly contain the same language from Examples 4.4 and 4.7. □

The results concerning the accepting power of GJFAs that perform right-left, left-right, right-right, and left-left 2-jumps are summarized in Figure 4.3.

Closure Properties

In this section, we show the closure properties of $\mathbf{DJFA}_{\blacktriangleright\blacktriangleleft}$, $\mathbf{DJFA}_{\blacktriangleleft\blacktriangleright}$, $\mathbf{DJFA}_{\blacktriangleright\blacktriangleright}$, and $\mathbf{DJFA}_{\blacktriangleleft\blacktriangleleft}$ under various operations. Recall that, by Theorem 4.6, $\mathbf{DJFA}_{\blacktriangleright\blacktriangleleft}$ and $\mathbf{DJFA}_{\blacktriangleleft\blacktriangleright}$ are equivalent, and so their closure properties coincide.

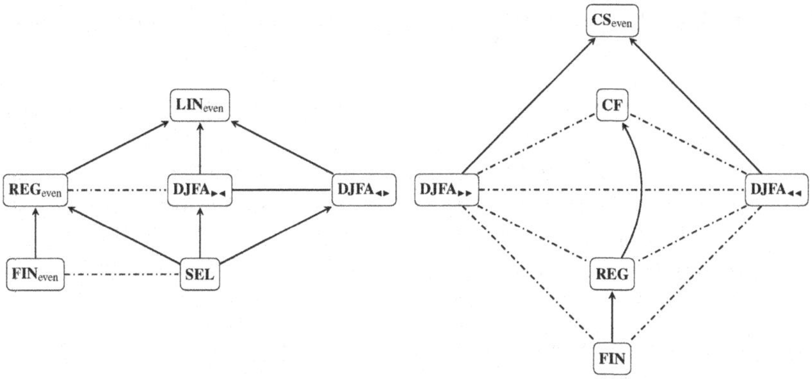

Fig. 4.3 Relationships between $\mathbf{DJFA}_{\blacktriangleright\blacktriangleright}$, $\mathbf{DJFA}_{\blacktriangleleft\blacktriangleleft}$, and other language families.

Theorem 4.12 *All* $\mathbf{DJFA}_{\blacktriangleright\blacktriangleleft}$ *(*$\mathbf{DJFA}_{\blacktriangleleft\blacktriangleright}$*),* $\mathbf{DJFA}_{\blacktriangleright\blacktriangleright}$*, and* $\mathbf{DJFA}_{\blacktriangleleft\blacktriangleleft}$ *are not closed under endmarking.*

Proof This result directly follows from Lemma 4.1—the inability to read an odd number of symbols from the input string. □

Theorem 4.13 $\mathbf{DJFA}_{\blacktriangleright\blacktriangleleft}$ *(*$\mathbf{DJFA}_{\blacktriangleleft\blacktriangleright}$*) is closed under endmarking on both sides.*

Proof Consider any GJFA $M_{\blacktriangleright\blacktriangleleft\curvearrowright} = (Q, \Delta, R, s, F)$. Without a loss of generality, assume that $s' \notin Q$ and $\# \notin \Delta$. Define GJFA $N_{\blacktriangleright\blacktriangleleft\curvearrowright} = (Q \cup \{s'\}, \Delta \cup \{\#\}, R \cup \{(s', \#, s)\}, s', F)$. Then, by Lemma 4.3, every $x \in L(N_{\blacktriangleright\blacktriangleleft\curvearrowright})$ can be surely written as $x = \#u_2u_3 \dots u_nu_n \dots u_3u_2\#$, where $n \in \mathbb{N}$, and $u_i \in \Delta^*$, $2 \leq i \leq n$ □

Theorem 4.14 *Both* $\mathbf{DJFA}_{\blacktriangleright\blacktriangleright}$ *and* $\mathbf{DJFA}_{\blacktriangleleft\blacktriangleleft}$ *are not closed under endmarking on both sides.*

Proof Since both jumps always read the same strings in the same direction, they clearly cannot reliably define the endmarking on the opposite sides of the input string in the general case. □

Theorem 4.15 *All* $\mathbf{DJFA}_{\blacktriangleright\blacktriangleleft}$ *(*$\mathbf{DJFA}_{\blacktriangleleft\blacktriangleright}$*),* $\mathbf{DJFA}_{\blacktriangleright\blacktriangleright}$*, and* $\mathbf{DJFA}_{\blacktriangleleft\blacktriangleleft}$ *are not closed under concatenation.*

Proof This can be easily proven by contradiction. Consider two simple languages $\{aa\}$ and $\{bb\}$, which clearly belong into $\mathbf{DJFA}_{\blacktriangleright\blacktriangleleft}$, $\mathbf{DJFA}_{\blacktriangleright\blacktriangleright}$, and $\mathbf{DJFA}_{\blacktriangleleft\blacktriangleleft}$. Assume that $\mathbf{DJFA}_{\blacktriangleright\blacktriangleleft}$, $\mathbf{DJFA}_{\blacktriangleright\blacktriangleright}$, and $\mathbf{DJFA}_{\blacktriangleleft\blacktriangleleft}$ are closed under concatenation. Therefore, the resulting language $\{aabb\}$ also has to belong into $\mathbf{DJFA}_{\blacktriangleright\blacktriangleleft}$, $\mathbf{DJFA}_{\blacktriangleright\blacktriangleright}$, and $\mathbf{DJFA}_{\blacktriangleleft\blacktriangleleft}$. However, such a language does not satisfy the string form for $\mathbf{DJFA}_{\blacktriangleright\blacktriangleleft}$ from Lemma 4.3, and there is no GJFA $M_{\blacktriangleright\blacktriangleright\curvearrowright}$ or GJFA $N_{\blacktriangleleft\blacktriangleleft\curvearrowright}$ that can define such a language. Observe that M and N cannot accept $aabb$ with a single 2-jump, and that the rules for multiple 2-jumps define broader languages, e.g., $\{abab, aabb\}$. □

Theorem 4.16 *All* $\mathbf{DJFA}_{\blacktriangleright\blacktriangleleft}$ *(*$\mathbf{DJFA}_{\blacktriangleleft\blacktriangleright}$*),* $\mathbf{DJFA}_{\blacktriangleright\blacktriangleright}$*, and* $\mathbf{DJFA}_{\blacktriangleleft\blacktriangleleft}$ *are not closed under square.*

Proof Consider language $L = \{aa, bb\}$, which clearly belongs into $\mathbf{DJFA}_{\blacktriangleright\blacktriangleleft}$, $\mathbf{DJFA}_{\blacktriangleright\blacktriangleright}$, and $\mathbf{DJFA}_{\blacktriangleleft\blacktriangleleft}$. Therefore, $L^2 = \{aaaa, aabb, bbaa, bbbb\}$ should also belong into these language families. However, observe string $aabb$; it causes the same problems as in the proof of Theorem 4.15. This string does not satisfy the string form for $\mathbf{DJFA}_{\blacktriangleright\blacktriangleleft}$ from Lemma 4.3. Moreover, there is no GJFA $M_{\blacktriangleright\blacktriangleright\curvearrowright}$ or GJFA $N_{\blacktriangleleft\blacktriangleleft\curvearrowright}$ that can simultaneously accept required string $aabb$ and reject unwanted string $abab$. □

Theorem 4.17 *All* $\mathbf{DJFA}_{\blacktriangleright\blacktriangleleft}$ *(*$\mathbf{DJFA}_{\blacktriangleleft\blacktriangleright}$*),* $\mathbf{DJFA}_{\blacktriangleright\blacktriangleright}$*, and* $\mathbf{DJFA}_{\blacktriangleleft\blacktriangleleft}$ *are not closed under shuffle.*

Proof Consider two simple languages $\{aa\}$ and $\{bb\}$, which clearly belong into $\mathbf{DJFA}_{\blacktriangleright\blacktriangleleft}$, $\mathbf{DJFA}_{\blacktriangleright\blacktriangleright}$, and $\mathbf{DJFA}_{\blacktriangleleft\blacktriangleleft}$. Therefore, the resulting language of their shuffle $\{aabb, abab, baab, abba, baba, bbaa\}$ should also belong into these language families. However, several strings from this language do not satisfy the string form for $\mathbf{DJFA}_{\blacktriangleright\blacktriangleleft}$ from Lemma 4.3. Moreover, there is surely no GJFA $M_{\blacktriangleright\blacktriangleright\curvearrowright}$ or GJFA $N_{\blacktriangleleft\blacktriangleleft\curvearrowright}$ that can accept string $baab$ or $abba$, since these strings do not contain two identical sequences of symbols that could be properly synchronously read. □

Theorem 4.18 *All* $\mathbf{DJFA}_{\blacktriangleright\blacktriangleleft}$ *(*$\mathbf{DJFA}_{\blacktriangleleft\blacktriangleright}$*),* $\mathbf{DJFA}_{\blacktriangleright\blacktriangleright}$*, and* $\mathbf{DJFA}_{\blacktriangleleft\blacktriangleleft}$ *are closed under union.*

Proof Let o be one of the relations ${}_{\blacktriangleright\blacktriangleleft}\curvearrowright$, ${}_{\blacktriangleright\blacktriangleright}\curvearrowright$, and ${}_{\blacktriangleleft\blacktriangleleft}\curvearrowright$; and $M_o = (Q_1, \Delta_1, R_1, s_1, F_1)$, and $N_o = (Q_2, \Delta_2, R_2, s_2, F_2)$ be two GJFAs. Without a loss of generality, assume that $Q_1 \cap Q_2 = \emptyset$ and $s \notin (Q_1 \cup Q_2)$. Define the GJFA $H_o = (Q_1 \cup Q_2 \cup \{s\}, \Delta_1 \cup \Delta_2, R_1 \cup R_2 \cup \{(s, \varepsilon, s_1), (s, \varepsilon, s_2)\}, s, F_1 \cup F_2)$. Observe that $L(H_o) = L(M_o) \cup L(N_o)$ holds in all modes. Indeed, the leading 2-jump only selects whether H_o enters M_o or N_o, and this leading 2-jump introduces no other new configuration to the configurations of M_o and N_o. □

Theorem 4.19 *All* $\mathbf{DJFA}_{\blacktriangleright\blacktriangleleft}$ *(*$\mathbf{DJFA}_{\blacktriangleleft\blacktriangleright}$*),* $\mathbf{DJFA}_{\blacktriangleright\blacktriangleright}$*, and* $\mathbf{DJFA}_{\blacktriangleleft\blacktriangleleft}$ *are not closed under complement.*

Proof Consider Lemma 4.1—that all 2-jumping modes can only accept even-length input strings. As a result, every complement has to contain at least all odd-length strings, and thus it cannot be defined by any 2-jumping mode. □

Theorem 4.20 $\mathbf{DJFA}_{\blacktriangleright\blacktriangleleft}$ *(*$\mathbf{DJFA}_{\blacktriangleleft\blacktriangleright}$*) is closed under intersection with regular languages.*

Proof Consider any GJFA $M_{\blacktriangleright\blacktriangleleft\curvearrowright} = (Q_1, \Delta, R_1, s_1, F_1)$ and FA $N = (Q_2, \Delta, R_2, s_2, F_2)$. We can define a new GJFA $H_{\blacktriangleright\blacktriangleleft\curvearrowright} = (Q_3, \Delta, R_3, s_3, F_3)$ that simulates both M and N in the same time and that accepts the input string x if and only if both M and N also accept x. Note that the requirement of identical Δ does not affect the generality of the result. We are going to use two auxiliary functions that will help us with the construction of H. First, $\mathrm{Fw}(N, p, str)$ accepts three parameters: N which is some FA, p which is some state of N, and str which is some string. This function returns the set of states in which N can end up if N is in state p and reads str. Second, $\mathrm{Bw}(N, p, str)$ that also accepts the same parameters: N which is some FA, p which is some state of N, and str which is some string. This function returns the set of states from which N reads str and ends in state p. We are not giving full details of these functions here since they only incorporate the well-known standard techniques for finite automata. With this, we construct Q_3, R_3, and F_3 in the following way:

1. Add s_3 to Q_3.
2. Add $\langle p, q, r\rangle$ to Q_3, for all $(p, q, r) \in Q_1 \times Q_2 \times Q_2$.
3. Add $\langle p, q, q\rangle$ to F_3, for all $(p, q) \in F_1 \times Q_2$.
4. Add $(s_3, \varepsilon, \langle s_1, s_2, f\rangle)$ to R_3, for all $f \in F_2$.
5. For each $(p, a, q) \in R_1$ and $r_1, t_1 \in Q_2$, add $(\langle p, r_1, t_1\rangle, a, \langle q, r_2, t_2\rangle)$ to R_3, for all $(r_2, t_2) \in \mathrm{Fw}(N, r_1, a) \times \mathrm{Bw}(N, t_1, a)$.

Observe that H handles three distinct things in its states $\langle p, q, r\rangle$: p represents the original state of M, q simulates the first part of N in the classical forward way, and r simulates the second part of N in the backward way. At the beginning, H makes a 2-jump from the initial state s_3 into one of the states $\langle s_1, s_2, f\rangle$, where $f \in F_2$, and the main part of the simulation starts. In each following step, H can only make a 2-jump if the similar 2-jump is also in M and if N can read the same string as M from both opposite sides with the current states. This part ends when there are no valid 2-jumps or when H reads the whole input string. If H processes the whole input string, we can recognize valid final state $\langle p, q, r\rangle$ in the following way: p has to be the original final state of M, and q must be the same as r so that the simulation of N from the two opposite sides can be connected in the middle. As a result, $L(H_{\blacktriangleright\blacktriangleleft\curvearrowright}) = L(M_{\blacktriangleright\blacktriangleleft\curvearrowright}) \cap L(N)$. □

Theorem 4.21 DJFA$_{\blacktriangleright\blacktriangleleft}$ *(***DJFA$_{\blacktriangleleft\blacktriangleright}$***) is closed under intersection.*

Proof Consider any GJFA $M_{\blacktriangleright\blacktriangleleft\curvearrowright} = (Q_1, \Delta, R_1, s_1, F_1)$ and GJFA $N_{\blacktriangleright\blacktriangleleft\curvearrowright} = (Q_2, \Delta, R_2, s_2, F_2)$. We can define a new GJFA $H_{\blacktriangleright\blacktriangleleft\curvearrowright} = (Q, \Delta, R, s, F)$ that simulates both M and N in the same time such that $L(H_{\blacktriangleright\blacktriangleleft\curvearrowright}) = L(M_{\blacktriangleright\blacktriangleleft\curvearrowright}) \cap L(N_{\blacktriangleright\blacktriangleleft\curvearrowright})$. To support the construction of Q and R, define $\Delta^{\leq h} = \bigcup_{i=0}^{h} \Delta^i$, and let k be the maximum length of the right-hand sides of the rules from $R_1 \cup R_2$. First, set Q to $\{\langle q_1, x, x', q_2, y, y'\rangle \mid q_1 \in Q_1,\ q_2 \in Q_2,\ x, x', y, y' \in \Delta^{\leq 2k-1}\}$, F to $\{\langle f_1, \varepsilon, \varepsilon, f_2, \varepsilon, \varepsilon\rangle \mid f_1 \in F_1, f_2 \in F_2\}$, and $s = \langle s_1, \varepsilon, \varepsilon, s_2, \varepsilon, \varepsilon\rangle$. Then, we construct R in the following way:

(I) Add $(\langle p, x, x', q, y, y'\rangle, a, \langle p, xa, ax', q, ya, ay'\rangle)$ to R, for all $a \in \Delta^{\leq k}$, $p \in Q_1$, $q \in Q_2$, and $x, x', y, y' \in \Delta^{\leq 2k-1-|a|}$.
(II) For each $(p, a, p') \in R_1$, add $(\langle p, ax, x'a, q, y, y'\rangle, \varepsilon, \langle p', x, x', q, y, y'\rangle)$ to R, for all $x, x' \in \Delta^{\leq 2k-1-|a|}$, $q \in Q_2$, and $y, y' \in \Delta^{\leq 2k-1}$.
(III) For each $(q, b, q') \in R_2$, add $(\langle p, x, x', q, by, y'b\rangle, \varepsilon, \langle p, x, x', q', y, y'\rangle)$ to R, for all $p \in Q_1$, $x, x' \in \Delta^{\leq 2k-1}$, and $y, y' \in \Delta^{\leq 2k-1-|b|}$.

Observe that H stores six pieces of information in its compound states: (1) the state of M, (2) the buffered string (so-called buffer) with up to $2k - 1$ symbols read from the beginning of the input string to simulate the work of M on it, (3) the buffered string with up to $2k - 1$ symbols read from the end of the input string to simulate the work of M on it, and pieces (4), (5), and (6) are analogous to (1), (2), and (3) but for N, respectively.

Next, by the same reasoning as in the proof of Lemma 4.3, we can assume that M and N start from configurations s_1ws_1 and s_2ws_2, respectively, and neither of them can jump over any symbol during the reading. Using these assumptions, H simulates the work of M and N as follows. First, it reads by the rules from (I) a part of the input string and stores it in the buffers. Then, by the rules from (II) and (III), H processes the symbols from the buffers by the simulation of the rules from M and N. Whenever needed, H reads from the input string some additional symbols using the rules from (I). The input string is accepted by H if and only if the whole input string is read, all buffers are processed and emptied, and both (1) and (4) are final states of M and N, respectively.

To justify the maximum size of the buffers in (2), (3), (5), and (6), consider the situation when the simulation of M needs to read the input string by the strings of length k, but the N's right-hand sides of the simulated rules alternate between 1 and k symbols. Then, we can observe a situation when a buffer contains $k - 1$ symbols and we have to read k additional symbols from the input string before we can process the first (or the last) k symbols of the buffer. The question remains, however, whether we can reliably exclude some of these situations and possibly further decrease the size of the buffers in the states of H.

The rigorous proof of $L(H_{\blacktriangleright\blacktriangleleft\curvearrowright}) = L(M_{\blacktriangleright\blacktriangleleft\curvearrowright}) \cap L(N_{\blacktriangleright\blacktriangleleft\curvearrowright})$ is left to the reader. □

Theorem 4.22 *Both* $\mathbf{DJFA}_{\blacktriangleright\blacktriangleright}$ *and* $\mathbf{DJFA}_{\blacktriangleleft\blacktriangleleft}$ *are not closed under intersection and intersection with regular languages.*

Proof Consider two GJFAs:

$$M_{\blacktriangleright\blacktriangleright\curvearrowright} = (\{s, r, p, f\}, \{a, b\}, \{(s, a, r), (r, bb, p), (p, a, f)\}, s, \{f\});$$
$$L(M_{\blacktriangleright\blacktriangleright\curvearrowright}) = \{abbaabba, abbabbaa, abababba, ababbbaa, aabbabba, aabbbbaa\},$$
and $N_{\blacktriangleright\blacktriangleright\curvearrowright} = (\{s, r, p, f\}, \{a, b\}, \{(s, a, r), (r, b, p), (p, ba, f)\}, s, \{f\});$
$$L(N_{\blacktriangleright\blacktriangleright\curvearrowright}) = \{abbaabba, abbababa, abababba, ababbaba, aabbabba, aabbbaba\}.$$

The intersection $L_\cap = L(M_{\blacktriangleright\blacktriangleright\curvearrowright}) \cap L(N_{\blacktriangleright\blacktriangleright\curvearrowright}) = \{abbaabba, abababba, aabbabba\}$ should also belong into $\mathbf{DJFA}_{\blacktriangleright\blacktriangleright}$. However, consider the simplest GJFA $P_{\blacktriangleright\blacktriangleright\curvearrowright}$ that can accept string $aabbabba$; it surely has to start with reading two times only one symbol a, then it can read two times bb together, and then it finishes by reading two times symbol a. However, this is exactly the behavior of $M_{\blacktriangleright\blacktriangleright\curvearrowright}$, and we see that $L(M_{\blacktriangleright\blacktriangleright\curvearrowright})$ is a proper superset of $L_\cap$. Therefore, there cannot be any GJFA $H_{\blacktriangleright\blacktriangleright\curvearrowright}$ that defines $L_\cap$. Trivially, both $L(M_{\blacktriangleright\blacktriangleright\curvearrowright})$ and $L(N_{\blacktriangleright\blacktriangleright\curvearrowright})$ are also regular languages. The similar proof for $\mathbf{DJFA}_{\blacktriangleleft\blacktriangleleft}$ is left to the reader. □

Theorem 4.23 $\mathbf{DJFA}_{\blacktriangleright\blacktriangleleft}$ *(*$\mathbf{DJFA}_{\blacktriangleleft\blacktriangleright}$*) is closed under reversal.*

Proof Consider any GJFA $M_{\blacktriangleright\blacktriangleleft\curvearrowright} = (Q, \Delta, R_1, s, F)$. Define the GJFA $N_{\blacktriangleright\blacktriangleleft\curvearrowright} = (Q, \Delta, R_2, s, F)$, where R_2 is constructed in the following way. For each $(p, a, q) \in R_1$, add $(p, \text{reversal}(a), q)$ to R_2. Note that by Lemma 4.3 and its proof, every $x \in L(M_{\blacktriangleright\blacktriangleleft\curvearrowright})$ can be written as $x = u_1u_2 \dots u_nu_n \dots u_2u_1$, where $n \in \mathbb{N}$, and $u_i \in \Delta^*$, $1 \leq i \leq n$; and where each u_i represents string a from a certain rule. Observe that each x almost resembles an even palindrome. We just need to resolve the individual parts $|u_i| > 1$ for which the palindrome statement does not hold. Nevertheless, observe that if we simply reverse each u_i individually, it will create the reversal of the whole x. As a result, $L(N_{\blacktriangleright\blacktriangleleft\curvearrowright})$ is a reversal of $L(M_{\blacktriangleright\blacktriangleleft\curvearrowright})$. □

Theorem 4.24 *Both* $\mathbf{DJFA}_{\blacktriangleright\blacktriangleright}$ *and* $\mathbf{DJFA}_{\blacktriangleleft\blacktriangleleft}$ *are not closed under reversal.*

Proof Consider language $K = \{ababcc, abcabc\}$, which is accepted by the GJFA $M_{\blacktriangleright\blacktriangleright\curvearrowright} = (\{s, r, f\}, \{a, b, c\}, \{(s, ab, r), (r, c, f)\}, s, \{f\})$. Therefore, the mirror language $K_{mi} = \{ccbaba, cbacba\}$ should also belong into $\mathbf{DJFA}_{\blacktriangleright\blacktriangleright}$. However, consider the simplest GJFA $N_{\blacktriangleright\blacktriangleright\curvearrowright}$ that can accept string $ccbaba$; it surely has to start with reading two times only symbol c, then it can read two times ba together. Even in such a case $L(N_{\blacktriangleright\blacktriangleright\curvearrowright}) = \{ccbaba, cbcaba, cbacba\}$; which is a proper superset of K_{mi}. Therefore, there cannot be any GJFA $H_{\blacktriangleright\blacktriangleright\curvearrowright}$ that defines K_{mi}. The similar proof for $\mathbf{DJFA}_{\blacktriangleleft\blacktriangleleft}$ is left to the reader. □

Theorem 4.25 *All* $\mathbf{DJFA}_{\blacktriangleright\blacktriangleleft}$ *(*$\mathbf{DJFA}_{\blacktriangleleft\blacktriangleright}$*),* $\mathbf{DJFA}_{\blacktriangleright\blacktriangleright}$*, and* $\mathbf{DJFA}_{\blacktriangleleft\blacktriangleleft}$ *are not closed under finite substitution.*

Proof Consider language $L = \{a^{2n} \mid n \geq 0\}$, which clearly belongs into $\mathbf{DJFA}_{\blacktriangleright\blacktriangleleft}$, $\mathbf{DJFA}_{\blacktriangleright\blacktriangleright}$, and $\mathbf{DJFA}_{\blacktriangleleft\blacktriangleleft}$. Define the finite substitution $\varphi : \{a\}^* \to 2^{\{a\}^*}$ as $\varphi(a) = \{\varepsilon, a\}$. Observe that $\varphi(L)$ contains odd-length strings. However, in consequence of Lemma 4.1, we know that no 2-jumping mode can accept such strings. □

Theorem 4.26 $\mathbf{DJFA}_{\blacktriangleright\blacktriangleleft}$ *(*$\mathbf{DJFA}_{\blacktriangleleft\blacktriangleright}$*) is closed under homomorphism and* ε*-free homomorphism.*

Proof Consider any GJFA $M_{\blacktriangleright\blacktriangleleft\curvearrowright} = (Q, \Delta, R_1, s, F)$ and arbitrary homomorphism $\varphi : \Delta^* \to \Delta'^*$. Define the GJFA $N_{\blacktriangleright\blacktriangleleft\curvearrowright} = (Q, \Delta', R_2, s, F)$, where R_2 is constructed in the following way. For each $(p, a, q) \in R_1$, add $(p, \varphi(a), q)$ to R_2. Observe that by Lemma 4.3 and its proof, every $x \in L(M_{\blacktriangleright\blacktriangleleft\curvearrowright})$ can be written as $x = u_1u_2 \dots u_nu_n \dots u_2u_1$, where $n \in \mathbb{N}$, and $u_i \in \Delta^*$, $1 \leq i \leq n$; and where each u_i represents string a from a certain rule. Then, every $y \in L(N_{\blacktriangleright\blacktriangleleft\curvearrowright})$ can be surely written as $y = \varphi(u_1)\varphi(u_2) \dots \varphi(u_n)\varphi(u_n) \dots \varphi(u_2)\varphi(u_1)$, and clearly $\varphi(L(M_{\blacktriangleright\blacktriangleleft\curvearrowright})) = L(N_{\blacktriangleright\blacktriangleleft\curvearrowright})$. □

Theorem 4.27 *Both* $\mathbf{DJFA}_{\blacktriangleright\blacktriangleright}$ *and* $\mathbf{DJFA}_{\blacktriangleleft\blacktriangleleft}$ *are not closed under homomorphism and* ε*-free homomorphism.*

Proof Consider language $K = \{abab, aabb\}$, which is accepted by the GJFA $M_{\blacktriangleright\blacktriangleright\curvearrowright} = (\{s, r, f\}, \{a, b\}, \{(s, a, r), (r, b, f)\}, s, \{f\})$. Define the ε-free homomorphism $\varphi : \{a, b\}^+ \to \{a, b, c\}^+$ as $\varphi(a) = a$ and $\varphi(b) = bc$. By applying φ to K, we get $\varphi(K) = \{abcabc, aabcbc\}$. Consider the simplest GJFA $N_{\blacktriangleright\blacktriangleright\curvearrowright}$

that can accept string $aabcbc$; it surely has to start with reading two times only symbol a, then it can read two times bc together. However, even in such a case $L(N_{\blacktriangleright\blacktriangleright\curvearrowright}) = \{abcabc, abacbc, aabcbc\}$; which is a proper superset of $\varphi(K)$. Therefore, there cannot be any GJFA $H_{\blacktriangleright\blacktriangleright\curvearrowright}$ that defines $\varphi(K)$. Trivially, φ is also a general homomorphism. The similar proof for $\mathbf{DJFA}_{\blacktriangleleft\blacktriangleleft}$ is left to the reader. □

Theorem 4.28 *All* $\mathbf{DJFA}_{\blacktriangleright\blacktriangleleft}$ *(*$\mathbf{DJFA}_{\blacktriangleleft\blacktriangleright}$*),* $\mathbf{DJFA}_{\blacktriangleright\blacktriangleright}$*, and* $\mathbf{DJFA}_{\blacktriangleleft\blacktriangleleft}$ *are not closed under inverse homomorphism.*

Proof Consider language $L = \{aa\}$, which clearly belongs into $\mathbf{DJFA}_{\blacktriangleright\blacktriangleleft}$, $\mathbf{DJFA}_{\blacktriangleright\blacktriangleright}$, and $\mathbf{DJFA}_{\blacktriangleleft\blacktriangleleft}$. Define the homomorphism $\varphi : \{a\}^* \to \{a\}^*$ as $\varphi(a) = aa$. By applying φ^{-1} to L, we get $\varphi^{-1}(L) = \{a\}$. However, in consequence of Lemma 4.1, we know that no 2-jumping mode can define such a language. □

The summary of closure properties of $\mathbf{DJFA}_{\blacktriangleright\blacktriangleleft}$, $\mathbf{DJFA}_{\blacktriangleleft\blacktriangleright}$, $\mathbf{DJFA}_{\blacktriangleright\blacktriangleright}$, and $\mathbf{DJFA}_{\blacktriangleleft\blacktriangleleft}$ is given in Figure 4.4, where + marks closure, and – marks non-closure.

	$\mathbf{DJFA}_{\blacktriangleright\blacktriangleleft}$, $\mathbf{DJFA}_{\blacktriangleleft\blacktriangleright}$	$\mathbf{DJFA}_{\blacktriangleright\blacktriangleright}$	$\mathbf{DJFA}_{\blacktriangleleft\blacktriangleleft}$
endmarking (both sides)	– (+)	– (–)	– (–)
concatenation	–	–	–
square (L^2)	–	–	–
shuffle	–	–	–
union	+	+	+
complement	–	–	–
intersection	+	–	–
int. with regular languages	+	–	–
reversal	+	–	–
finite substitution	–	–	–
homomorphism	+	–	–
ε-free homomorphism	+	–	–
inverse homomorphism	–	–	–

Fig. 4.4 Summary of closure properties.

Remarks and Conclusion

We would like to remark that the resulting behavior of right-left 2-jumps has proven to be very similar to the behaviors of 2-head finite automata accepting linear languages (see Nagy [2012]) and $5' \to 3'$ sensing Watson–Crick finite automata (see Nagy [2008, 2010, 2013]). Although these models differ in details, the general concept of their reading remains the same—all three mentioned models read simultaneously from the two different positions on the opposite sides of the input string. The main difference comes in the form of their rules. The other two models use more complex rules that allow them to read two different strings on their reading positions. Consequently, the resulting language families of these models differ from the language family defined by right-left 2-jumps. Nonetheless, the connection to Watson–Crick models shows that the concept of synchronized jumping could potentially find its use in the fields that study the correlations of several patterns such as biology or computer graphics. A further study of the combined model of jumping and $5' \rightarrow 3'$ Watson–Crick finite automata can be found in Section 4.4.

At the end, we propose some future investigation areas concerning JFAs that link several jumps together. Within the previous sections, we have already pointed out one open problem concerning right-left (and left-right) 2-jumps (Open Problem). This section continues with other more general suggestions.

(I) Study decidability properties of the newly defined jumping modes.
(II) Investigate remaining possible variants of 2-jumps where the unrestricted single jumps and the restricted single jumps are combined together.
(III) Extend the definition of 2-jumps to the general definition of n-jumps, where $n \in \mathbb{N}$. Can we find some interesting general results about these multi-jumps?
(IV) Study relaxed versions of 2-jumps where the single jumps do not have to follow the same rule and where each single jump has its own state.
(V) Use the newly defined jumping modes in JFAs in which rules read single symbols rather than whole strings (JFA—see Definition 3.2).
(VI) In the same fashion as in finite automata, consider deterministic versions of GJFAs with the newly defined jumping modes.

4.2 Multi-Parallel Jumping Finite Automata

This section proposes a modification of jumping finite automata—*n-parallel jumping finite automata*, originated in Kocman and Meduna [2016]. This modification presents a concept where the input is divided into several arbitrary parts and these parts are then separately processed with distinct synchronized heads. A quite similar concept was thoroughly studied in terms of formal grammars, where several nonterminals are being synchronously rewritten at once; for example, simple matrix grammars (see Ibarra [1970]) and n-parallel grammars (see Rosebrugh and Wood [1975]; Wood [1977, 1973]; Rosebrugh and Wood [1973, 1974]). However, to the best of our knowledge, no such research was done in terms of automata, where n heads synchronously read from distinct parts on the single tape. When this concept is combined with the mechanics of jumping finite automata, each part can be read discontinuously, but the overall order between parts is preserved; such an automaton then can handle additional languages (e.g., $\{a\}^*\{b\}^*$). Therefore, this modification represents the combined model of discontinuous and continuous reading.

The unrestricted version of jumping finite automata accepts a quite unique language family which initially had no known counterparts in grammars until jumping grammars were introduced (see Křivka and Meduna [2015]). Therefore, we have decided to base our initial research mainly on the restricted version of these automata which use only right jumps. Note that restricted jumping finite automata define the same language family as classical finite automata. However, when such a restriction is combined with the previously described concept, we get a model which is very similar to n-parallel grammars. These automata utilize the jumping only during the initialization, when the heads jump to their start positions. After that, all heads read their parts of the input continuously in a left-to-right way. We compare these automata with n-parallel right-linear grammars and show that these models actually represent the same language families.

Prerequisites

n-parallel right-linear grammars were introduced and deeply studied in Wood [1973, 1975, 1977]; Rosebrugh and Wood [1973, 1974, 1975]. In order to state some results about n-parallel jumping finite automata, we need to formally define so-called n-parallel right-linear grammars (see Rosebrugh and Wood [1973, 1975]; Wood [1973, 1975]).

Definition 4.3 For $n \geq 1$, an *n-parallel right-linear grammar* (n-PRLG) is an $(n+3)$-tuple

$$G = \big(N_1, \ldots, N_n, \Delta, S, P\big)$$

where N_i, $1 \leq i \leq n$, are pairwise disjoint *nonterminal alphabets*, Δ is a *terminal alphabet*, $S \notin N$ is an *initial symbol*, where $N = N_1 \cup \cdots \cup N_n$, and P is a finite set of *rules* that contains these three kinds of rules

1. $S \rightarrow X_1 \cdots X_n$, $\quad X_i \in N_i$, $1 \leq i \leq n$;
2. $X \rightarrow wY$, $\quad X, Y \in N_i$ for some i, $1 \leq i \leq n$, $w \in \Delta^*$;
3. $X \rightarrow w$, $\quad X \in N$, $w \in \Delta^*$.

For $x, y \in (N \cup \Delta \cup \{S\})^*$,

$$x \Rightarrow_G y$$

if and only if

1. either $x = S$ and $S \rightarrow y \in P$,
2. or $x = y_1X_1 \cdots y_nX_n$, $y = y_1x_1 \cdots y_nx_n$, where $y_i \in \Delta^*$, $x_i \in \Delta^*N \cup \Delta^*$, $X_i \in N_i$, and $X_i \rightarrow x_i \in P$, $1 \leq i \leq n$.

Let $x, y \in (N \cup \Delta \cup \{S\})^*$ and $\ell > 0$. Then, $x \Rightarrow_G^\ell y$ if and only if there exists a sequence

$$x_0 \Rightarrow_G x_1 \Rightarrow_G \cdots \Rightarrow_G x_\ell$$

where $x_0 = x$, $x_\ell = y$. As usual, $x \Rightarrow_G^+ y$ if and only if there exists $\ell > 0$ such that $x \Rightarrow_G^\ell y$, and $x \Rightarrow_G^* y$ if and only if $x = y$ or $x \Rightarrow_G^+ y$.

The *language* of G is defined as

$$L(G) = \big\{w \in \Delta^* \mid S \Rightarrow_G^+ w\big\}$$

A language $K \subseteq \Delta^*$ is an *n-parallel right-linear language* if there is an n-PRLG G such that $K = L(G)$. The family of n-parallel right-linear languages is denoted by n-**PRL**.

Definitions

In this section, we define a modification of jumping finite automata—n-parallel jumping finite automata—which read input strings discontinuously with multiple synchronized heads. Moreover, we also define a more restricted mode for these automata which uses only the right jumps.

Definition 4.4 For $n \geq 1$, an *n-parallel general jumping finite automaton* (n-PGJFA) is a quintuple

$$M = (Q, \Delta, R, S, F)$$

where Q is a finite set of states, Δ is an input alphabet, $Q \cap \Delta = \emptyset$, $R \subseteq Q \times \Delta^* \times Q$ is finite, $S \subseteq Q^n$ is a set of start state strings, and $F \subseteq Q$ is a set of final states. Members of R are referred to as rules of M and instead of $(p, y, q) \in R$, we write $py \rightarrow q \in R$.

A *configuration* of M is any string in $\Delta^* Q \Delta^*$. Let X denote the set of all configurations over M. The binary jumping relation, symbolically denoted by $\curvearrowright$, over X, is defined as follows. Let $x, z, x', z' \in \Delta^*$ such that $xz = x'z'$ and $py \rightarrow q \in R$; then, M makes a *jump* from $xpyz$ to $x'qz'$, symbolically written as

$$xpyz \curvearrowright x'qz'$$

Let \$ be a special symbol, $\$ \notin (Q \cup \Delta)$. An *n-configuration* of M is any string in $(X\{\$\})^n$. Let ${}_nX$ denote the set of all n-configurations over M. The binary n-jumping relation, symbolically denoted by ${}_n\curvearrowright$, over ${}_nX$, is defined as follows. Let $\zeta_1\$ \cdots \zeta_n\$, \vartheta_1\$ \cdots \vartheta_n\$ \in {}_nX$, so $\zeta_i, \vartheta_i \in X$, $1 \leq i \leq n$; then, M makes an *n-jump* from $\zeta_1\$ \cdots \zeta_n\$$ to $\vartheta_1\$ \cdots \vartheta_n\$$, symbolically written as

$$\zeta_1\$ \cdots \zeta_n\$ \ {}_n\curvearrowright \ \vartheta_1\$ \cdots \vartheta_n\$$$

if and only if $\zeta_i \curvearrowright \vartheta_i$ for all $1 \leq i \leq n$. In the standard manner, we extend ${}_n\curvearrowright$ to ${}_n\curvearrowright^m$, where $m \geq 0$. Let ${}_n\curvearrowright^+$ and ${}_n\curvearrowright^*$ denote the transitive closure of ${}_n\curvearrowright$ and transitive-reflexive closure of ${}_n\curvearrowright$, respectively.

The language accepted by M, denoted by $L(M, n)$, is defined as

$$\begin{aligned} L(M, n) = \{u_1v_1 \cdots u_nv_n \mid\ & u_1s_1v_1\$ \cdots u_ns_nv_n\$ \ {}_n\curvearrowright^* \ f_1\$ \cdots f_n\$, \\ & u_i, v_i \in \Delta^*,\ s_1 \cdots s_n \in S,\ f_i \in F,\ 1 \leq i \leq n\}. \end{aligned}$$

Let $w \in \Delta^*$. We say that M accepts w if and only if $w \in L(M, n)$. M rejects w if and only if $w \in \Delta^* - L(M, n)$.

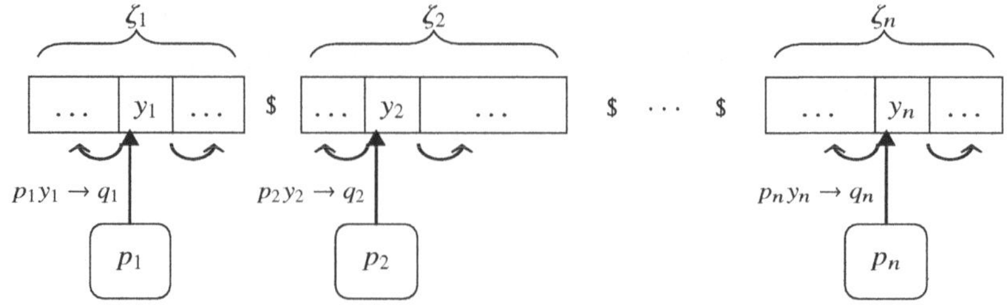

Fig. 4.5 n-PGJFA.

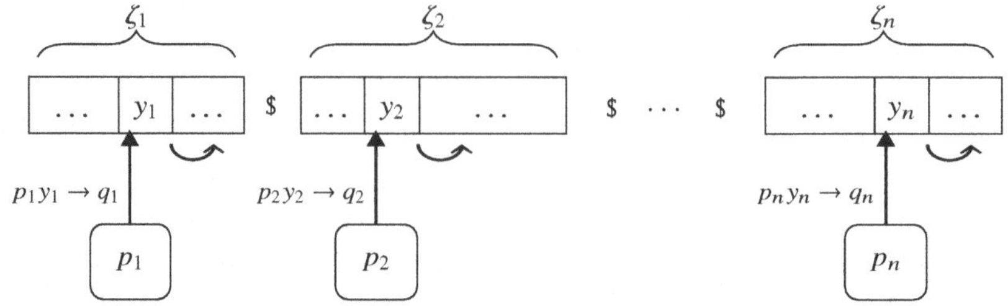

Fig. 4.6 n-PGJFA using right n-jumps.

Definition 4.5 For $n \geq 1$, let $M = (Q, \Delta, R, S, F)$ be an n-PGJFA, and let X denote the set of all configurations over M. The binary right jumping relation, symbolically denoted by ${}_r\curvearrowright$, over X, is defined as follows. Let $w, x, y, z \in \Delta^*$, and $py \rightarrow q \in R$; then, M makes a *right jump* from $wpyxz$ to $wxqz$, symbolically written as

$$wpyxz \ {}_r\curvearrowright \ wxqz$$

Let ${}_nX$ denote the set of all n-configurations over M. The binary right n-jumping relation, symbolically denoted by ${}_{n-r}\curvearrowright$, over ${}_nX$, is defined as follows. Let $\zeta_1\$\cdots\zeta_n\$, \vartheta_1\$\cdots\ \vartheta_n\$ \in {}_nX$, so $\zeta_i, \vartheta_i \in X$, $1 \leq i \leq n$; then, M makes a *right n-jump* from $\zeta_1\$\cdots\zeta_n\$$ to $\vartheta_1\$\cdots\vartheta_n\$$, symbolically written as

$$\zeta_1\$\cdots\zeta_n\$ \ {}_{n-r}\curvearrowright \ \vartheta_1\$\cdots\vartheta_n\$$$

if and only if $\zeta_i \ {}_r\curvearrowright \vartheta_i$ for all $1 \leq i \leq n$.

We extend ${}_{n-r}\curvearrowright$ to ${}_{n-r}\curvearrowright^m$, ${}_{n-r}\curvearrowright^+$, and ${}_{n-r}\curvearrowright^*$, where $m \geq 0$, by analogy with extending the corresponding notations for ${}_n\curvearrowright$. Let $L(M, n{-}r)$ denote the language accepted by M using only right n-jumps.

Let $\mathbf{PGJFA}_{\blacklozenge n}$ and $\mathbf{PGJFA}_{\blacktriangleright n}$ denote the language families accepted by n-PGJFAs and n-PGJFAs using only right n-jumps, respectively. These two kinds of models are illustrated in Figures 4.5 and 4.6.

Examples

To demonstrate the behavior of these automata, we present two simple examples.

Example 4.9 Consider the 2-PGJFA

$$M = (\{s, r, p, q\}, \Delta, R, \{sr\}, \{s, r\})$$

where $\Delta = \{a, b, c, d\}$ and R consists of the rules

$$sa \rightarrow p, \quad pb \rightarrow s, \quad rc \rightarrow q, \quad qd \rightarrow r$$

Starting from sr, M has to read some a and b with the first head and some c and d with the second head, entering again the start (and also the final) states sr. If we work with the unrestricted jumps, both heads can read the symbols in an arbitrary order. However, if we work with the right jumps, both heads must read all symbols in their original order; otherwise, the automaton will eventually get stuck. Therefore, the accepted languages are

$$L(M, 2) = \{uv \mid u \in \{a, b\}^*,\ v \in \{c, d\}^*,\ \text{occur}(u, a) = \text{occur}(u, b) = \text{occur}(v, c) = \text{occur}(v, d)\}$$

$$L(M, 2\text{-}r) = \{(ab)^n(cd)^n \mid n \geq 0\}$$

Example 4.10 Consider the 2-PGJFA

$$M = (\{s, r, t\}, \Delta, R, \{ss\}, \{s\})$$

where $\Delta = \{a, b, c\}$ and R consists of the rules

$$sa \rightarrow r, \quad rb \rightarrow t, \quad tc \rightarrow s$$

Starting from ss, M has to read some a, b, and c with both heads, entering again the start (and also the final) states ss. Therefore, the accepted languages are

$$L(M, 2) = \{uv \mid u, v \in \{a, b, c\}^*,\ \text{occur}(u, a) = \text{occur}(u, b) = \text{occur}(u, c) = \text{occur}(v, a) = \text{occur}(v, b) = \text{occur}(v, c)\}$$

$$L(M, 2\text{-}r) = \{uu \mid u \in \{abc\}^*\}$$

It can be easily shown that the languages accepted with unrestricted n-jumps in Examples 4.9 and 4.10 cannot be defined by any original jumping finite automata. In the case of languages accepted with right n-jumps, Example 4.9 defines a linear language, but Example 4.10 defines only a regular language.

Unrestricted n-Jumping Relation

This section gives a basic characterization of the language families accepted by n-PGJFAs with unrestricted n-jumps. Most notably, we show that n-PGJFAs with unrestricted n-jumps define an infinite hierarchy of language families.

Theorem 4.29 $\mathbf{PGJFA}_{\blacklozenge 1} = \mathbf{GJFA}$.

Proof The definition of the binary jumping relation is identical between GJFAs (see Section 3.1) and n-PGJFAs (see Definition 4.4). Consequently, if $n = 1$, both models transit between configurations in the same way, and they also require the same conditions for accepting configurations. Therefore, the only difference is in their initial configurations since GJFAs have a single start state, but 1-PGJFAs have a set of start states. Nonetheless, we can convert any 1-PGJFA $M = (Q, \Delta, R, S, F)$ into the equivalent 1-PGJFA $N = (Q', \Delta, R', \{s\}, F)$ such that $s \notin (Q \cup \Delta)$, $Q' = Q \cup \{s\}$, and $R' = R \cup \{s \rightarrow s' \mid s' \in S\}$. Then, the conversions between GJFAs and 1-PGJFAs are trivial. □

Lemma 4.15 *For all $n \geq 1$, there is an n-PGJFA $M = (Q, \Delta, R, S, F)$ such that $\Delta = \{a_1, \ldots, a_n\}$ and $L(M, n) = \{a_1\}^* \cdots \{a_n\}^*$.*

Proof For any $n \geq 1$, define the n-PGJFA $M = (Q, \Delta, R, S, F)$, where $Q = \{s_1, \ldots, s_n\}$, $\Delta = \{a_1, \ldots, a_n\}$, $R = \{s_i a_i \rightarrow s_i,\ s_i \rightarrow s_i \mid 1 \geq i \geq n\}$, $S = \{s_1 \cdots s_n\}$, and $F = Q$. Observe that each head handles a different symbol and that it can read zero or one occurrence of this symbol in each step. Therefore, the accepted language is clearly $L(M, n) = \{a_1\}^* \cdots \{a_n\}^*$. □

Lemma 4.16 *For all $n \geq 1$ and $m > n$, there is no n-PGJFA $M = (Q, \Delta, R, S, F)$ such that $\Delta = \{a_1, \ldots, a_m\}$ and $L(M, n) = \{a_1\}^* \cdots \{a_m\}^*$.*

Proof (*by contradition*) We extend the reasoning from Lemma 3.3 that shows that there is no GJFA that accepts $\{a\}^*\{b\}^*$. For the sake of contradiction, assume that, for some $n \geq 1$ and $m > n$, there is a n-PGJFA $M = (Q, \Delta, R, S, F)$ such that $\Delta = \{a_1, \ldots, a_m\}$ and $L(M, n) = \{a_1\}^* \cdots \{a_m\}^*$. Then, some of the heads of M must handle at least two types of symbols. Assume any $w_1 uvw_2 \in L(M, n)$ such that uv is a whole part read with one head, uv contains at least two types of symbols, v is read in a single step, $|u| \geq 1$, and $|v| \geq 1$. Clearly, for any $n \geq 1$ and $m > n$, there has to exist some $w_1 uvw_2 \in L(M, n)$ that satisfy these conditions. Due to the behavior of the unrestricted n-jumps, it must then also hold that $w_1 vuw_2 \in L(M, n)$; however, $w_1 vuw_2 \notin \{a_1\}^* \cdots \{a_m\}^*$. That is a contradiction with the assumption that $L(M, n) = \{a_1\}^* \cdots \{a_m\}^*$. Therefore, there is no n-PGJFA $M = (Q, \Delta, R, S, F)$ such that $n \geq 1$, $m > n$, $\Delta = \{a_1, \ldots, a_m\}$, and $L(M, n) = \{a_1\}^* \cdots \{a_m\}^*$. □

Theorem 4.30 *For all $n \geq 1$,* $\mathbf{PGJFA}_{\blacklozenge n} \subset \mathbf{PGJFA}_{\blacklozenge (n+1)}$.

Proof First, we show that, for all $n \geq 1$, $\mathbf{PGJFA}_{\blacklozenge n} \subseteq \mathbf{PGJFA}_{\blacklozenge (n+1)}$. For any n-PGJFA $M = (Q, \Delta, R, S, F)$ we can construct the $(n{+}1)$-PGJFA $N = (Q', \Delta, R', S', F')$ such that $f \notin (Q \cup \Delta)$, $Q' = Q \cup \{f\}$, $R' = R \cup \{f \rightarrow f\}$, $S' = \{wf \mid w \in S\}$, $F' = F \cup \{f\}$. It is not hard to see that $L(M, n) = L(N, n+1)$. Second, for all $n \geq 1$, $\mathbf{PGJFA}_{\blacklozenge(n+1)} \not\subseteq \mathbf{PGJFA}_{\blacklozenge n}$ follows directly from Lemmas 4.15 and 4.16. □

With Theorems 4.29 and 4.30, we can easily derive the following additional characterization of the language families accepted by n-PGJFAs with unrestricted n-jumps.

Theorem 4.31 *For all* $n \geq 1$, $\mathbf{FIN} \subset \mathbf{PGJFA}_{\blacklozenge n}$.

Proof This theorem directly follows from **FIN** ⊂ **GJFA** (see Theorem 3.8). □

Theorem 4.32 *For all* $n \geq 1$, $\mathbf{PGJFA}_{\blacklozenge n} \not\subseteq \mathbf{REG}$ *and* $\mathbf{PGJFA}_{\blacklozenge n} \not\subseteq \mathbf{CF}$.

Proof This theorem directly follows from the fact that there is a GJFA $M = (Q, \Delta, R, s, F)$ such that $\Delta = \{a, b, c\}$ and $L(M) = \{w \in \Delta^* \mid \text{occur}(w, a) = \text{occur}(w, b) = \text{occur}(w, c)\}$ which is a well-known non-context-free language (see Example 3.1). □

Theorem 4.33 *For all* $n \geq 1$, $\mathbf{PGJFA}_{\blacklozenge n} \subset \mathbf{CS}$.

Proof The jumps of GJFAs can be simulated by linear bounded automata (see Theorem 3.11), and the same also holds for the n-jumps of n-PGJFAs. Thus, for all $n \geq 1$, $\mathbf{PGJFA}_{\blacklozenge n} \subseteq \mathbf{CS}$. From Lemma 4.16, for all $n \geq 1$, $\mathbf{CS} - \mathbf{PGJFA}_{\blacklozenge n} \neq \emptyset$. □

Right n-Jumping Relation

This section gives a detailed characterization of the language families accepted by n-PGJFA with right n-jumps. First, we prove that n-PGJFAs with right n-jumps and n-PRLGs define the same language families.

Lemma 4.17 *For every n-PRLG* $G = (N_1, \ldots, N_n, \Delta, S_1, P)$*, there is an n-PGJFA* $M = (Q, \Delta, R, S_2, F)$ *using only right n-jumps such that* $L(M, n\text{-}r) = L(G)$.

Proof Let $G = (N_1, \ldots, N_n, \Delta, S_1, P)$ be an n-PRLG. Without loss of generality, assume that $f \notin (N_1 \cup \cdots \cup N_n \cup \Delta)$. Keep the same n and define the n-PGJFA

$$M = (\{f\} \cup N_1 \cup \cdots \cup N_n, \Delta, R, S_2, \{f\}),$$

where R and S_2 are constructed in the following way:

(1) For each rule of the form $S_1 \rightarrow X_1 \cdots X_n$, $X_i \in N_i$, $1 \leq i \leq n$, in P, add the start state string $X_1 \cdots X_n$ to S_2.
(2) For each rule of the form $X \rightarrow aY$, $X, Y \in N_i$, for some i, $1 \leq i \leq n$, $a \in \Delta^*$, in P, add the rule $Xa \rightarrow Y$ to R.
(3) For each rule of the form $X \rightarrow a$, $X \in N_i$, for some i, $1 \leq i \leq n$, $a \in \Delta^*$, in P, add the rule $Xa \rightarrow f$ to R.

Observe that the constructed n-PGJFA M with right n-jumps simulates the n-PRLG G in such a way that its heads read symbols in the same fashion as the nonterminals of G generate them.

Any sentence $w \in L(G)$ can be divided into $w = u_1 \cdots u_n$, where u_i represents the part of the sentence which can be generated from the nonterminal X_i of a rule $S_1 \rightarrow X_1 \cdots X_n$, $X_i \in N_i$, $1 \le i \le n$. In the same way, M can start from an n-configuration $X_1u_1\$ \cdots X_nu_n\$$, where the heads with the states X_i have to read u_i. Therefore the part (1), where we convert the rules $S_1 \rightarrow X_1 \cdots X_n$ into the start state strings, and the selection of a start state string thus covers the first derivation step of the grammar.

Any consecutive non-final derivation step of the grammar then rewrites all n nonterminals in the sentential form with the rules of the form $X \rightarrow aY$, $X, Y \in N_i$, for some i, $1 \le i \le n$, $a \in \Delta^*$. Therefore the part (2), where we convert the grammar rules $X \rightarrow aY$ into the automaton rules $Xa \rightarrow Y$. The automaton M always works with all its heads simultaneously, and thus the equivalent effect of these steps should be obvious.

In the last derivation step of the grammar, every nonterminal is rewritten with a rule of the form $X \rightarrow a$, $X \in N_i$, for some i, $1 \le i \le n$, $a \in \Delta^*$. We can simulate the same behavior in the automaton if we end up in a final state from which there are no ongoing rules. Therefore the part (3), where we convert the grammar rules $X \rightarrow a$ into the automaton rules $Xa \rightarrow f$, where f is the sole final state. All heads of the automaton must also end up in this final state simultaneously, or the automaton will get stuck; there are no ongoing rules from f, and all heads must make a move during every step.

The automaton M can also start from an n-configuration where the input is divided into such parts that they cannot be generated from the nonterminals X_i of the rules $S_1 \rightarrow X_1 \cdots X_n$, $X_i \in N_i$, $1 \le i \le n$. However, such an attempt will eventually get the automaton stuck because M simulates only the derivation steps of the grammar.□

Lemma 4.18 *For every n-PGJFA $M = (Q, \Delta, R, S_2, F)$ using only right n-jumps, there is an n-PRLG $G = (N_1, \dots, N_n, \Delta, S_1, P)$ such that $L(G) = L(M, n{-}r)$.*

Proof Let $M = (Q, \Delta, R, S_2, F)$ be an n-PGJFA with right n-jumps. Keep the same n and define the n-PRLG

$$G = (N_1, \dots, N_n, \Delta, S_1, P),$$

where $N_1, \dots, N_n$, and P are constructed in the following way:

(1) For each state $p \in Q$,
add the nonterminal p_i to N_i for all $1 \le i \le n$.

(2) For each start state string $p_1 \cdots p_n \in S_2$, $p_i \in Q$, $1 \le i \le n$,
add the start rule $S_1 \rightarrow p_{1_1} \cdots p_{n_n}$ to P.

(3) For each rule $py \rightarrow q \in R$, $p, q \in Q$, $y \in \Delta^*$,
add the rule $p_i \rightarrow yq_i$ to P for all $1 \le i \le n$.

(4) For each state $p \in F$,
add the rule $p_i \rightarrow \varepsilon$ to P for all $1 \le i \le n$.

Observe that the constructed n-PRLG G simulates the n-PGJFA M with right n-jumps in such a way that its nonterminals generate terminals in the same fashion as the heads of M read them.

The definition of n-PRLGs requires that $N_1, \ldots, N_n$ are mutually disjoint nonterminal alphabets. However, the states of n-PGJFAs do not have such a restriction. Therefore, we use a new index in all converted occurrences of states; this creates a separate item for each nonterminal position. The index is represented by i and is used in all conversion steps.

Any sentence $w \in L(M, n{-}r)$ can be divided into $w = u_1 \cdots u_n$, where u_i represents the part of the sentence which can be accepted by the head of M with a start state p_i from a start n-configuration $p_1u_1\$ \cdots p_nu_n\$$, where $p_1 \cdots p_n \in S_2$, $1 \leq i \leq n$. In the grammar, we can simulate the start n-configurations with the rules $S_1 \rightarrow p_{1_1} \cdots p_{n_n}$, where the nonterminals p_{i_i} must be able to generate u_i. Therefore the part (2), where we convert the start state strings into the rules.

During every step of the automaton all heads simultaneously make a move. Likewise, during every non-initial step of the grammar all non-terminals are simultaneously rewritten. Therefore the part (3), where we convert the automaton rules $py \rightarrow q$ into the grammar rules $p_i \rightarrow yq_i$. The equivalent effect of these steps should be obvious.

The automaton can successfully end if all its heads are in the final states. We can simulate this situation in the grammar if we rewrite every nonterminal to ε. Therefore the part (4), where we create new erasing rules for all final states. These rules can be used only once during the last derivation step of the grammar; otherwise, the generation process of the grammar will get stuck. □

Theorem 4.34 $\mathbf{PGJFA}_{\blacktriangleright n} = n\text{-}\mathbf{PRL}$.

Proof n-**PRL** $\subseteq$ $\mathbf{PGJFA}_{\blacktriangleright n}$ follows from Lemma 4.17. $\mathbf{PGJFA}_{\blacktriangleright n} \subseteq n$-**PRL** follows from Lemma 4.18. □

With Theorem 4.34 we can easily derive the following additional characterization of the language families accepted by n-PGJFAs using only right n-jumps.

Theorem 4.35 *For all* $n \geq 1$, $\mathbf{PGJFA}_{\blacktriangleright n} \subset \mathbf{PGJFA}_{\blacktriangleright (n+1)}$.

Proof This theorem directly follows from n-**PRL** $\subset$ $(n{+}1)$-**PRL** (see Rosebrugh and Wood [1975]). □

Theorem 4.36 *For all* $n \geq 1$, $\mathbf{PGJFA}_{\blacktriangleright n}$ *is closed under union, finite substitution, homomorphism, reflection, and intersection with a regular set.*

Proof This theorem directly follows from the same results for n-**PRL** (see Rosebrugh and Wood [1975]). □

Theorem 4.37 *For all* $n \geq 2$, $\mathbf{PGJFA}_{\blacktriangleright n}$ *is not closed under intersection or complement.*

Proof This theorem directly follows from the same results for n-**PRL** (see Rosebrugh and Wood [1975]). □

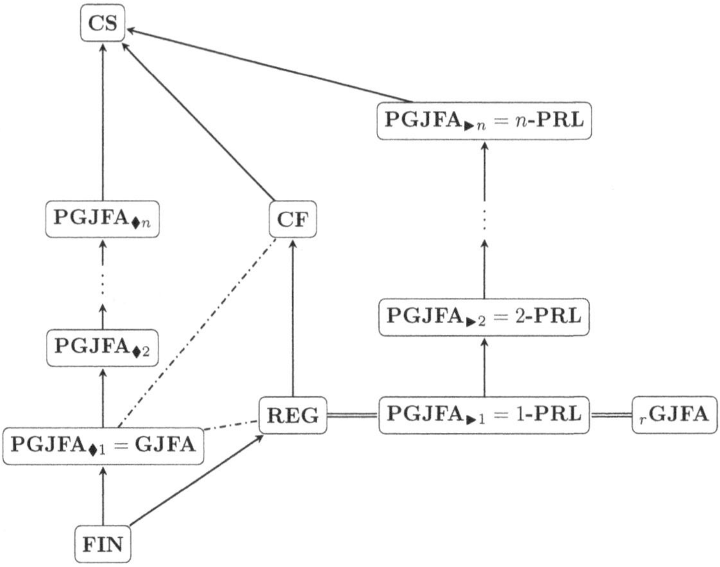

Fig. 4.7 $\mathbf{PGJFA}_{\blacktriangleright n}$ related to other language families.

Theorem 4.38 $\mathbf{PGJFA}_{\blacktriangleright 1} = {}_r\mathbf{GJFA} = \mathbf{REG}$.

Proof This theorem directly follows from $1\text{-}\mathbf{PRL} = \mathbf{REG}$ (see Rosebrugh and Wood [1975]) and from ${}_r\mathbf{GJFA} = \mathbf{REG}$ (see Theorem 3.33). □

Theorem 4.39 $\mathbf{PGJFA}_{\blacktriangleright 2} \subset \mathbf{CF}$.

Proof This theorem directly follows from $2\text{-}\mathbf{PRL} \subset \mathbf{CF}$ (see Rosebrugh and Wood [1975]). □

Theorem 4.40 $\mathbf{PGJFA}_{\blacktriangleright n} \subset \mathbf{CS}$ *and there exist non-context-free languages in* $\mathbf{PGJFA}_{\blacktriangleright n}$ *for all* $n \geq 3$.

Proof This theorem directly follows from the same results for $n\text{-}\mathbf{PRL}$ (see Rosebrugh and Wood [1975]). □

Figure 4.7 displays the mutual relationships between the language families resulting from n-PGJFAs with unrestricted n-jumps as well as n-PGJFAs with right n-jumps; **FIN**, **REG**, **CF**, and **CS** are included, too.

Concluding Remarks

The presented results show that the concept of the parallel jumping has a positive effect on the model of jumping finite automata. The most significant part of these results is the fact that every additional head always increases the power of these automata, and this is true for both the unrestricted and right n-jumping relation. Therefore, this creates two infinite hierarchies of language families. Next, due to the very simple conversions and similar concepts, we can see n-parallel general jumping finite automata using only right n-jumps as a direct counterpart to n-parallel right-linear grammars. There are already other automata with the same power as n-parallel right-linear grammars (e.g., self-regulating finite automata, see Meduna and Masopust [2007]); however, they use considerably different mechanisms, and the conversions between models are not straightforward. Therefore, they would hardly qualify as a direct counterpart. Furthermore, with a little bit of tweaking, we could easily adjust our model so that it coincides with other well-known grammars that synchronously rewrite several nonterminals at once, e.g., right-linear simple matrix grammars (see Ibarra [1970]). On the other hand, considering n-parallel general jumping finite automata with unrestricted n-jumps, due to their unconventional behavior we were not able to find a fitting counterpart for them in grammars. It is possible that no such counterpart exists, and it would need to be introduced; as it was with general jumping finite automata and their counterpart in the form of jumping grammars (see Křivka and Meduna [2015]).

Finally, we propose some suggestions for further investigation.

(I) In this section, we have considered only the situation where all heads keep their own state and always work synchronously together. Investigate other options, where, e.g., all heads follow a single state, not all heads have to make a move during the n-jump, or only one head can make a move during the n-jump.

(II) Consider other grammars that rewrite several nonterminals at once for which there is no direct counterpart in the form of an automaton model. Can we use the concept of the parallel jumping to introduce such a model?

(III) Study closure and decidability properties for n-parallel general jumping finite automata with unrestricted n-jumps.

4.3 Jumping Watson–Crick Finite Automata

In this section, we concetrate our principal attention to special variants of WKFAs with two simultaneously working heads that process their input strings in a non-continuous manner. Specifically, we explore jumping Watson–Crick finite automata, introduced in Mahalingam et al. [2019], which represent a straightforward application of jumping computation in terms of WKFAs, discussed in Section 2.2.3.

Recall that in many respects, WKFAs resemble classical FAs, but their tapes always carry double-stranded (DS) sequences of symbols from an alphabet, Δ. At the beginning, both strands necessarily satisfy a symmetric complementarity relation, ρ. Formally, the notion of a WKFA is defined as a sextuple $M = (Q, \Delta, \rho, R, s, F)$, where Q, Δ, s, and F have the same meaning as in the definition of an FA (see

Section 2.2.1); apart from these components, however, ρ is a symmetric relation on Δ, and R is a finite set of rules of the form

$$p\binom{u}{v} \to q$$

where $p, q \in Q$ and $u, v \in \Delta^*$ or in the DS notation $\binom{u}{v} \in \binom{V^*}{V^*}$.

Now, we give an intuitive insight into the way M works. M has a single tape containing a DS string on which M works from left to right by performing computational steps according to rules from R. During a step, M independently reads both strands. Initially, on its tape, M has a DS string with both strands satifying the complementarity defined by ρ, and it starts working on its tape from s with its both heads at the leftmost position. If starting from this initial configuration, M can make a sequence of computational steps so it completely reads both strands and ends up in a final state, the input DS string is accepted. It is worth pointing out that the complementarity is verified only in the initial configuration; during the rest of computation, it is not.

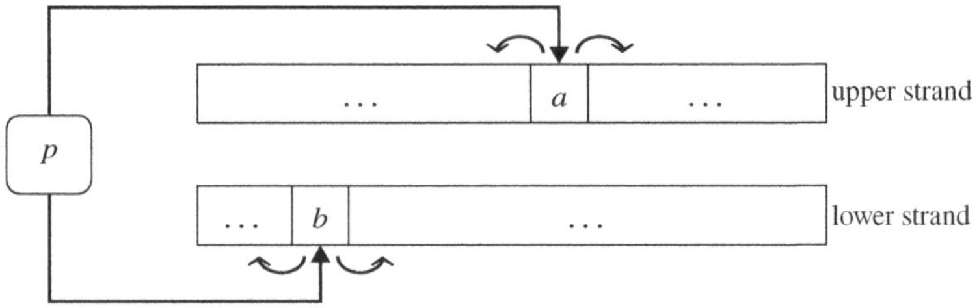

Fig. 4.8 JWKFA.

It is worth making a note about the notation concerning Watson–Crick models. As opposed to our specification of M given above, many studies describe M as $M = (\Delta, \rho, Q, s, F, R)$ instead of $M = (Q, \Delta, \rho, R, s, F)$. We use the latter in order to uniformly specify automata throughout the present book as a whole.

The jumping version of WKFAs explored in the present section works similarly to the way sketched above except that the read heads are placed at any positions in the initial configuration, and after performing a computational step, either head can jump at any position in its strand (see Figure 4.8).

Note that jumping WKFAs fall into the category (PA.1) of parallelism in finite automata (see page 65).

Definitions and Examples

Now, we formally define jumping Watson–Crick finite automata.

Definition 4.6 A *jumping Watson–Crick finite automaton* (JWKFA) is a sextuple $M = (Q, \Delta, \rho, R, s, F)$, where Q, Δ, ρ, s, and F are the same as in WKFA (see Definition 2.6), $\Delta \cap Q = \emptyset$, and

$$R \subseteq Q \times \binom{\Delta^*}{\Delta^*} \times Q$$

is a finite sef of rules. For better readability, a rule is written in the form

$$p\binom{y_1}{y_2} \to q$$

where $p, q \in Q$ and $\binom{y_1}{y_2} \in \binom{V^*}{V^*}$.

A *configuration* of JWKFA M is a string from $\binom{\Delta^*}{\Delta^*}Q\binom{\Delta^*}{\Delta^*}$. For $\binom{x_1y_1z_1}{x_2y_2z_2}, \binom{x_1'z_1'}{x_2'z_2'} \in \mathrm{WK}_\rho(\Delta)$ and $p, q \in Q$, we write

$$\binom{x_1}{x_2}p\binom{y_1}{y_2}\binom{z_1}{z_2} {}_{WK}\curvearrowright \binom{x_1'}{x_2'}q\binom{z_1'}{z_2'}$$

if and only if $p\binom{y_1}{y_2} \to q \in R$ and $\binom{x_1z_1}{x_2z_2} = \binom{x_1'z_1'}{x_2'z_2'}$.

In the standard manner, let us extend ${}_{WK}\curvearrowright$ to ${}_{WK}\curvearrowright^n$, where $n \geq 0$; then, based on ${}_{WK}\curvearrowright^n$, let us define ${}_{WK}\curvearrowright^+$ and ${}_{WK}\curvearrowright^*$. The accepted language, denoted by $L(M)$, is defined as

$$L(M) = \left\{uv \mid \binom{u}{u'}s\binom{v}{v'} {}_{WK}\curvearrowright f, \text{ where } f \in F, u, v, u', v' \in \Delta^*, \begin{bmatrix}uv\\u'v'\end{bmatrix} \in \mathrm{WK}_\rho(\Delta)\right\}$$

The family of languages accepted by JWKFAs is denoted by **JWK**.

To demonstrate the behavior of the automata, we present a few simple examples.

Example 4.11 Let a JWKFA $M = (\{s, q, f\}, \{a, b, c\}, \rho, R, s, \{f\})$, where ρ is the identity relation and R consists of

$$\left\{s\binom{ab}{\varepsilon} \to s,\ s\binom{\varepsilon}{bc} \to q,\ q\binom{\varepsilon}{bc} \to q,\right.$$
$$\left. q\binom{c}{a} \to f,\ f\binom{c}{a} \to f\right\}.$$

Using the rules of M, we illustrate the acceptance of DS string $\begin{bmatrix}aabbcc\\aabbcc\end{bmatrix}$:

$$\binom{a}{aabbcc}s\binom{abbcc}{\varepsilon} {}_{WK}\curvearrowright \binom{\varepsilon}{aabbcc}s\binom{abcc}{\varepsilon} {}_{WK}\curvearrowright \binom{cc}{aabb}s\binom{\varepsilon}{bcc} {}_{WK}\curvearrowright$$

$$\binom{cc}{aa}q\binom{\varepsilon}{bc} {}_{WK}\curvearrowright \binom{aabc}{a}q\binom{cc}{abccc} {}_{WK}\curvearrowright \binom{aabcc}{aa}f\binom{c}{abccc} {}_{WK}\curvearrowright f$$

From R, the upper strand in state s checks that the same amount of as precedes all bs. Then, the rules applied in the lower strand handle the check of the same amount of bs and cs. In addition, these same rules check that bs occurs before cs. Altogether, the language accepted by M is $L(M) = \{a^nb^nc^n \mid n \geq 1\}^+$ which is non-context-free language.

As an exercise, observe that modeling just $\{a^nb^nc^n \mid n \geq 1\}$ without the positive iteration as in Example 4.11 is problematic or even impossible (see Lemma 4.21).

Example 4.12 Let a JWKFA $M = (\{s,p,q,r,t\},\{a,b,c\},\rho,R,s,\{s,p,q,r,t\})$, where ρ is the identity relation and R consists of

$$\{s\binom{a}{\varepsilon} \to p,\ p\binom{b}{\varepsilon} \to q,\ q\binom{c}{\varepsilon} \to s,$$
$$s\binom{\varepsilon}{a} \to r,\ r\binom{\varepsilon}{b} \to t,\ t\binom{\varepsilon}{c} \to s\}.$$

Obviously, the language accepted by M is $L(M) = \{w \in \{a,b,c\}^* \mid \text{occur}(w,a) = \text{occur}(w,b) = \text{occur}(w,c)\}$ which is another non-context-free language.

Variants of JWKFA Models

By analogy with the variants of WKFAs (see Definition 2.7), based on the form of rules, we define the corresponding variants of JWKFAs.

Definition 4.7 A JWKFA $M = (Q,\Delta,\rho,R,s,F)$ is

(i) *stateless*, if $Q = F = \{s\}$;
(ii) *all-final*, if $Q = F$;
(iii) *simple*, if $(p,\binom{v_1}{v_2},q) \in R$ implies $v_1 = \varepsilon$ or $v_2 = \varepsilon$;
(iv) 1-*limited*, if $(p,\binom{v_1}{v_2},q) \in R$ implies $|v_1v_2| = 1$.

The families of languages accepted by stateless, all-final, simple, and 1-limited JWKFAs are denoted by **NJWK**, **FJWK**, **SJWK**, and **1JWK**, respectively.

Some of these restrictions, if it makes sense, can be pairwise combined to get four language families **F1JWK**, **N1JWK**, **FSJWK**, and **NSJWK**.

Example 4.13 To demonstrate a restricted variant introduced in the previous definition, consider a simple JWKFA $M = (\{s,p,f\},\{a,b\},\rho,R,s,\{s,f\})$, where ρ is the identity relation and R consists of

$$\{s\binom{ab}{\varepsilon} \to s,\ s\binom{\varepsilon}{ba} \to s,\ s\binom{\varepsilon}{a} \to p,\ p\binom{\varepsilon}{b} \to f\}$$

The language accepted by M, $L(M) = \{ab\}^*$. Note that the second rule helps to maintain that in any strand ab cannot be inserted in the middle of another substring ab.

Reconsider the automaton from Example 4.12. Observe that it represents, in fact, a 1-limited variant of JWKFAs, thus illustrating (iv) in Definition 4.7.

Another example shows that even without states (the set of state is a singleton), it is possible to model a language with the strings containing the same numbers of three different symbols.

Example 4.14 Consider a stateless JWKFA $M = (\{p\},\{a,b,c\},\rho,R,p,\{p\})$. Note that $Q = \{p\}$, the start state p, and $F = Q$ are constants, so these are omitted from the definition sometimes.

$$R = \{p\binom{a}{b} \to p,\ p\binom{b}{c} \to p,\ p\binom{\varepsilon}{a} \to p,\ p\binom{c}{\varepsilon} \to p\}$$

The language accepted by M coincides with that from Example 4.12—$L(M) = \{w \in \{a,b,c\}^* \mid \text{occur}(w,a) = \text{occur}(w,b) = \text{occur}(w,c)\}$.

Consider a similar language, which is, however, based upon a simpler condition; for instance, take $L_{ab} = \{w \in \{a,b\}^* \mid \text{occur}(w,a) = \text{occur}(w,b)\}$. Notice that even for a simpler language like this, the construction of a JWKFA that accepts it represents a non-trivial task.

Results and Properties

In this subsection, we recall main results and properties of JWKFAs and their variants.

Lemma 4.19 (Mahalingam et al. [2019]) $\mathbf{GJFA} \subset \mathbf{SJWK}$ *and* $\mathbf{JFA} \subseteq \mathbf{1JWK}$

Proof (sketch) Without loss of generality, assume an ε-free GJFA $M = (Q_M, \Delta, R_M, s, F)$ (see Theorem 3.2). We construct an equivalent simple JWKFA $N = (Q_N, \Delta, \rho, R_N, s, F)$, where ρ is the identity relation on Δ.

For every labeled rule $i: \ pw \rightarrow q$ from R_M, we add the following two rules into R_N (with assumption that $q_i \notin Q_M$ and q_i is a new state in Q_N):

$$p\binom{w}{\varepsilon} \rightarrow q_i \quad \text{and} \quad q_i\binom{\varepsilon}{w} \rightarrow q$$

Set $Q_N = Q_M \cup \{q_i \mid i \text{ is a label of } r \in R_M\}$. It is easy to demonstrate that $L(M, \curvearrowright) = L(N)$, so $\mathbf{GJFA} \subseteq \mathbf{SJWK}$. Next, let $L = \{ab\}^*$. By Lemma 3.4, $L \notin \mathbf{GJFA}$, and by Example 4.13, $L \in \mathbf{SJWK}$, so $\mathbf{GJFA} \subset \mathbf{SJWK}$.

In analogy, we get $\mathbf{JFA} \subseteq \mathbf{1JWK}$. □

Similarly to Theorem 3.5, we have the relation to permutation even for JWKFAs.

Lemma 4.20 (Mahalingam et al. [2019]) *If* $M = (Q, \Delta, \rho, R, s, F)$ *is a JWKFA with rules from* R *of the form* $p\binom{x}{y} \rightarrow q$ *such that* $|x| \leq 1$ *and* $|y| \leq 1$*, then* $L(M) = \text{perm}(L(M))$.

Corollary 4.1 *The following are true:*

(i) If $L \in \mathbf{1JWK}$*, then* $L = \text{perm}(L)$.
(ii) $\{ab\} \notin \mathbf{1JWK}$.

Using anologous technique to the proof of Lemma 3.3, we get the following result.

Lemma 4.21 (Mahalingam et al. [2019]) $\{a\}^*\{b\}^* \notin \mathbf{JWK}$

In addition, observe that by Theorem 2.2, $\mathbf{REG} \subset \mathbf{WK}$, so regular language $\{a\}^*\{b\}^* \in \mathbf{WK}$. On the other hand, by Lemma 4.21, $\{a\}^*\{b\}^* \notin \mathbf{JWK}$, so $\mathbf{WK} \not\subseteq \mathbf{JWK}$. Further, by Example 4.13 and $\mathbf{REG} \subset \mathbf{WK}$, $\{ab\}^* \in \mathbf{WK} \cap \mathbf{JWK}$.

Lemma 4.22 (Mahalingam et al. [2019]) FIN ⊂ SJWK

Proof (sketch) Let $K \in$ **FIN** contain $n \geq 0$ strings. When described using a simple JWKFA M, for each $w_i \in K$, $1 \leq i \leq n$, two rules are constructed of the form

$$s\binom{w_i}{\varepsilon} \to q_i \quad \text{and} \quad q_i\binom{\varepsilon}{w_i} \to f$$

such that s is a start state and f the only final state of M. Obviously, $L(M) = K$. Therefore, **FIN** ⊆ **SJWK**. An infinite non-context-free language accepted by a simple JWKFA in Example 4.12 proves the strictness of the inclusion, so **FIN** ⊂ **SJWK**. □

Similarly to the construction in the proof of Lemma 4.22, we can demonstrate that **FIN** ⊂ **FJWK**. In details, we make $Q = F$ and ignore ε in the inspiring construction.

In what follows, we explore some relations between variants of JWKFAs.

Lemma 4.23 (Mahalingam et al. [2019]) N1JWK ⊂ NSJWK

Proof (sketch) By Definition 4.7, **N1JWK** ⊆ **NSJWK**. Consider a stateless JWKFA M with $Q = F = \{s\}$, $\Delta = \{a, b\}$, the identity relation ρ, and R containing two rules

$$s\binom{ab}{\varepsilon} \to s \quad \text{and} \quad s\binom{\varepsilon}{ab} \to s$$

Obviously, M accepts semi-Dyck language D_1 over {a,b} (see Example 2.9). By (i) in Corollary 4.1, it is required that not only $\{ab\}$ but also $\{ba\}$ belongs to D_1 which is a contradiction, so $D_1 \notin$ **N1JWK**. Therefore, **N1JWK** ⊂ **NSJWK**. □

Based on the same argument as in the previous proof, we can show that

(i) **F1JWK** ⊂ **FSJWK**
(ii) **NSJWK** ⊂ **FSJWK**
(iii) **N1JWK** ⊂ **F1JWK**
(iv) **N1JWK** ⊂ **FSJWK**

Further, by Lemma 4.22 and (ii) in Corollary 4.1, **1JWK** ⊂ **SJWK**. Finally, using D_1 from the proof of Lemma 4.23 and (i) in Corollary 4.1, we show that **NSJWK** **F1JWK** are incomparable.

Conclusion

Key results comparing the accepting power of different variants of jumping WK automata are summarized in Figure 4.9.

The results of closure properties of various **JWK** families are given in Table 4.1, where + marks closure, – marks non-closure, and ? marks open problem. These results are proved in Mahalingam et al. [2019, 2020]; Mishra et al. [2021c].

As observed in this and the previous sections of this chapter, there are many ways we can apply the jumping computation in parallel and/or multi-tape finite automata.

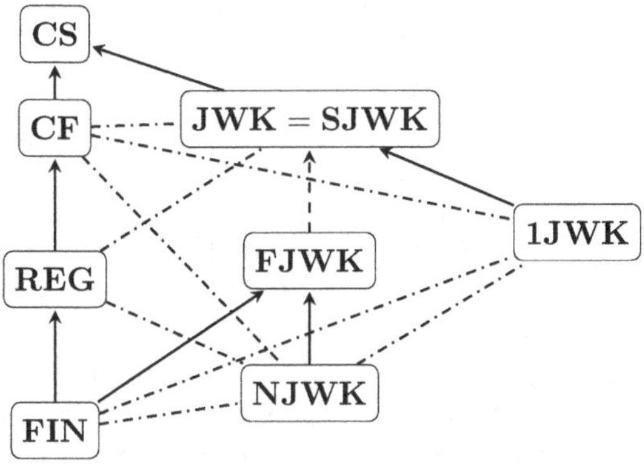

Fig. 4.9 **JWK** and its language family relationships given in Mahalingam et al. [2019, 2020].

	JWK	NJWK	FJWK	SJWK	1JWK	F1JWK	N1JWK	FSJWK	NSJWK
concatenation	−	−	−	−	−	−	−	−	−
union	+	−	+	+	+	+	−	+	−
complement	−	−	−	−	?	−	−	−	−
intersection	?	?	?	?	?	?	+	?	?
Kleene star	?	+	?	?	−	−	+	?	+
homomorphism	?	−	?	?	−	−	−	?	−

Table 4.1 Closure properties of **JWK** families.

4.4 Jumping 5′ → 3′ Watson–Crick Finite Automata

To extend the study of application of jumping computation in DNA computing, this section investigates alternative variant of Watson–Crick finite automata (WKFAs) in combination with general jumping finite automata (GJFAs).

Recall that the DNA strands are oriented, consist of four different nucleotides, and have a 5′ end and a 3′ end. Whenever a two-stranded DNA is considered, the two strands are oriented in the opposite way, and the nucleotides at the same position of the two strands must be in Watson–Crick (WK) complementarity relation, that is, Adenine appears with Thymine on the other strand, and Cytosine appears with Guanine on the other strand. As described in Section 2.2.3, WKFAs represent biology-inspired models that can be used to formally process DNA strands. In essence, a WKFA also works just like a classical finite automaton (FA) except it uses a WK tape (i.e., double-stranded tape), and it has a separate head for each of the two strands in the tape. Therefore, this is a group of models that always naturally use two heads. The classical version of a WKFA processes the input tape quite conventionally: each head works separately on its own strand of the tape, and both heads read the input in the traditional symbol-by-symbol left-to-right way.

$5' \to 3'$ Sensing Watson–Crick Automaton

More recently, new variants of the WKFA model were introduced that process the input in non-conventional ways. In a $5' \to 3'$ *Watson–Crick finite automaton* ($5' \to 3'$ WKFA; see Nagy [2008, 2010, 2013, 2020]), both heads read their specific strand in the biochemical $5'$ to $3'$ direction. From a computing point of view, this means that they read the DS string in opposite directions. Furthermore, a $5' \to 3'$ WKFA is *sensing* if the heads sense that they are meeting each other, and the processing of the input ends if for each pair of the sequence one of the letters is read. The sensing $5' \to 3'$ WKFAs generally accept the family of linear languages. This concept is also studied further in several follow-up papers that explore alternative definitions and combinations with different mechanics (see Nagy and Kovács [2019]; Nagy and Otto [2019, 2020]; Nagy and Parchami [2020]; Nagy et al. [2017]; Parchami and Nagy [2018]).

Even though these two groups significantly differ in their original definitions, their newer models sometimes work in a very similar way. Both concepts are also not mutually exclusive in a single formal model. This section defines *jumping* $5' \to 3'$ *Watson–Crick finite automaton*—a combined model of GJFAs and sensing $5' \to 3'$ WKFAs—and studies their characteristics. We primarily investigate the accepting power of the model and also the effects of common restrictions on the model.

To recall the notion of WKFA discussed in Section 2.2.3, a WKFA is $M = (Q, \Delta, \rho, \delta, q_0, F)$, where Q, Δ, q_0, and F are the same as in FAs, $\rho \subseteq \Delta \times \Delta$ is a symmetric relation (of complementarity), and the mapping $\delta\colon (Q \times \binom{\Delta^*}{\Delta^*}) \to 2^Q$ is a transition function such that $\delta(q, \binom{w_1}{w_2}) \neq \emptyset$ only for finitely many triples $(q, w_1, w_2) \in Q \times \Delta^* \times \Delta^*$.

The elementary difference between FAs and WKFAs, besides the doubled tape, is the number of heads. WKFAs scan each of the two strands of the tape separately with a unique head. In classical WKFAs, the heads scan both strands from left to right, and the processing of the input sequence ends when all complementary pairs of the DS string are read with both heads. The language accepted by M is $L(M) = \{w_1 \in \Delta^* \mid s\left[\begin{smallmatrix} w_1 \\ w_2 \end{smallmatrix}\right] \vDash^* \left[\begin{smallmatrix} w_1 \\ w_2 \end{smallmatrix}\right] f,\, f \in F,\, \left[\begin{smallmatrix} w_1 \\ w_2 \end{smallmatrix}\right] \in \mathrm{WK}_\rho(\Delta)\}$.

Let us recall the most important restricted variants of WKFAs usually studied in the literature (see Definition 2.7):

- stateless (**N**): if $Q = F = \{q_0\}$;
- all-final (**F**): if $Q = F$;
- simple (**S**): at most one head moves in a rewriting step;
- 1-limited (**1**): exactly one symbol is being read in a rewriting step.

By combining these constraints, we identify additional variants such as **NS**, **FS**, **N1**, and **F1** WKFAs.

In $5' \to 3'$ *WKFAs* (see Nagy [2008, 2010, 2013]; Nagy et al. [2017]), both heads start from the biochemical $5'$ end of the appropriate strand. Physically/mathematically and from a computing point of view, they read the DS string in opposite directions, while biochemically they go in the same direction. A $5' \to 3'$ WKFA is *sensing* if the heads sense that they are meeting (i.e., they are close enough to meet in the next step or there is a possibility to read strings at overlapping positions). In sensing 5′ → 3′ WKFAs, the processing of the input sequence ends when for each pair of the sequence precisely one of the letters is read. Since the original WK complementarity (in biology) is not only symmetric but also a one-to-one relation, we consider the input sequence to be fully processed, and thus the automaton makes a decision on the acceptance. Actually, it is a very natural assumption/restriction for most of the 5′ → 3′ WK automata models that ρ defines a bijection on Δ.

Definition 4.8 In WKFAs, the state transition δ is usually a mapping of the form $(Q \times \binom{\Delta^*}{\Delta^*}) \rightarrow 2^Q$. To help define an extended state transition δ' for sensing 5′ → 3′ WKFAs, in the transition $q' \in \delta(q, \binom{w_1}{w_2})$, we call $r_l = |w_1|$ and $r_r = |w_2|$ the left and right *radius* of the transition (they are the lengths of the strings that the heads will read from *left to right* and from *right to left* in this step, respectively). The value $r = r_l + r_r$ is the radius of the transition. Since $\delta(q, \binom{w_1}{w_2})$ is nonempty only for finitely many triples (q, w_1, w_2), there is a transition (maybe more) with the maximal radius for a given automaton. We extend δ to δ' with a sensing condition in the following way: Let $r_{\max}$ be the maximal radius among all rules. Then, let $\delta' : (Q \times \binom{V^*}{V^*} \times D) \rightarrow 2^Q$, where D is the *sensing distance set* $\{-\infty, 0, 1, \ldots, r_{\max}, +\infty\}$. This set gives the distance of the two heads between 0 and $r_{\max}$, $+\infty$ when the heads are further than $r_{\max}$, or $-\infty$ when the heads are after their meeting point. Trivially, this automaton is finite, and D can be used only to control the sensing (i.e., the appropriate meeting of the heads). To describe the work of the automata, we use the concept of configuration. A configuration $\binom{w_1}{w_2}(q, s)\binom{w_1'}{w_2'}$ consists of the state q, the current sensing distance s, and the input $\begin{bmatrix} w_1 w_1' \\ w_2 w_2' \end{bmatrix} \in \mathrm{WK}_\rho(V)$ in such a way that the first head (on the upper strand) has already processed the part w_1, while the second head (on the lower strand) has already processed w_2'. A step of the sensing 5′ → 3′ WKFA, according to the state transition function δ', can be of the following two types:

(1) Normal steps: $\binom{w_1}{w_2 y}(q, +\infty)\binom{x w_1'}{w_2'} \Rightarrow \binom{w_1 x}{w_2}(q', s)\binom{w_1'}{y w_2'}$,
for $w_1, w_2, w_1', w_2', x, y \in V^*$ with $|w_2 y| - |w_1| > r_{\max}$, $q, q' \in Q$,
if $\begin{bmatrix} w_1 x w_1' \\ w_2 y w_2' \end{bmatrix} \in \mathrm{WK}_\rho(V)$ and $q' \in \delta'(q, \binom{x}{y}, +\infty)$,

$$\text{and } s = \begin{cases} |w_2| - |w_1 x| & \text{if } |w_2| - |w_1 x| \leq r_{\max}; \\ +\infty & \text{in other cases.} \end{cases}$$

(2) Sensing steps: $\binom{w_1}{w_2 y}(q, s)\binom{x w_1'}{w_2'} \Rightarrow \binom{w_1 x}{w_2}(q', s')\binom{w_1'}{y w_2'}$,
for $w_1, w_2, w_1', w_2', x, y \in V^*$ and $s \in \{0, 1, \ldots, r_{\max}\}$ with $s = |w_2 y| - |w_1|$,
if $\begin{bmatrix} w_1 x w_1' \\ w_2 y w_2' \end{bmatrix} \in \mathrm{WK}_\rho(V)$ and $q' \in \delta'(q, \binom{x}{y}, s)$,

$$\text{and } s' = \begin{cases} s - |x| - |y| & \text{if } s - |x| - |y| \geq 0; \\ -\infty & \text{in other cases.} \end{cases}$$

Note that there are no possible steps for the sensing distance $-\infty$. In the standard manner, let us extend $\Rightarrow$ to $\Rightarrow^n$, where $n \geq 0$; then, based on $\Rightarrow^n$, let us define $\Rightarrow^+$ and $\Rightarrow^*$. The set of all accepted double-stranded strings from $\mathrm{WK}_\rho(V)$, denoted by $LM(M)$, can be defined by the final accepting configurations that can be reached from the initial one: A double-stranded string $\begin{bmatrix} w_1 \\ w_2 \end{bmatrix} \in \mathrm{WK}_\rho(V)$ is accepted by a sensing $5' \rightarrow 3'$ WKFA M if and only if $\binom{\varepsilon}{w_2}(q_0, s_0)\binom{w_1}{\varepsilon} \Rightarrow^* \begin{bmatrix} w_1' \\ w_2' \end{bmatrix}(q_f, 0)\begin{bmatrix} w_1'' \\ w_2'' \end{bmatrix}$, for $q_f \in F$, where $\begin{bmatrix} w_1' \\ w_2' \end{bmatrix}\begin{bmatrix} w_1'' \\ w_2'' \end{bmatrix} = \begin{bmatrix} w_1 \\ w_2 \end{bmatrix}$ with the proper value of s_0 (it is $+\infty$ if $|w_1| > r_{\max}$, elsewhere it is $|w_1|$). Then, the language accepted by M, denoted $L(M)$, is defined as $L(M) = \uparrow_V (LM(M))$.

Lastly, we briefly mention other closely related $5' \rightarrow 3'$ WK automata models. Besides the sensing version, the papers Nagy [2008, 2010, 2013] also define the *full-reading sensing version*. The formal definition remains almost identical; however, the automaton continues with the reading after the heads meet, and both heads have to read their strand completely from the $5'$ end to the $3'$ end. Therefore, this model actually defines the remaining steps for the sensing distance $-\infty$. The resulting behavior then combines some properties of classical WKFAs and sensing $5' \rightarrow 3'$ WKFAs. It can be easily seen that the full-reading sensing version is generally stronger than the sensing version. And finally, the paper by Nagy et al. [2017] introduces a new version of sensing $5' \rightarrow 3'$ WKFAs without the sensing distance. It shows that it is not strictly necessary to know the precise sensing distance and that we can obtain the same power even if we are able to recognize only the actual meeting event of heads. Nonetheless, this result does not hold in general if we consider restricted variants of these models.

Definitions

Considering the previously described sensing $5' \rightarrow 3'$ WKFAs and full-reading sensing $5' \rightarrow 3'$ WKFAs, there is quite a large gap between their behaviors. On the one hand, sensing $5' \rightarrow 3'$ WKFAs deliberately read only one of the letters from each complementary pair of the input sequence. However, this also limits the movement of their heads because they can read their strands only until they meet. On the other hand, the definition of full-reading sensing $5' \rightarrow 3'$ WKFAs allows both heads to traverse their strands completely. Nonetheless, this also means that all complementary pairs of the input sequence are again read twice (as in classical WKFAs). If we consider other formal models, we can see that GJFAs utilize a mechanism that allows heads to skip (jump over) symbols. Furthermore, the recently introduced double-jumping modes already behave very similarly to $5' \rightarrow 3'$ WKFAs. Due to this natural fit, it is our intention to fill and explore this gap by introducing the jumping mechanism into sensing $5' \rightarrow 3'$ WKFAs. We want both heads to be able to traverse their strands completely, but we also want to read only one of the letters from each complementary pair of the input sequence. For visual illustration, see the scheme in Figure 4.10.

From a theoretical perspective, the study of such a model is also beneficial for the further understanding of the jumping mechanism. In Section 3.1, it was clearly established that the general behavior of jumping finite automata models is highly nondeterministic. This can be problematic when we try to create viable parsing algorithms based on these models (see Fernau et al. [2017]). Therefore, there is an

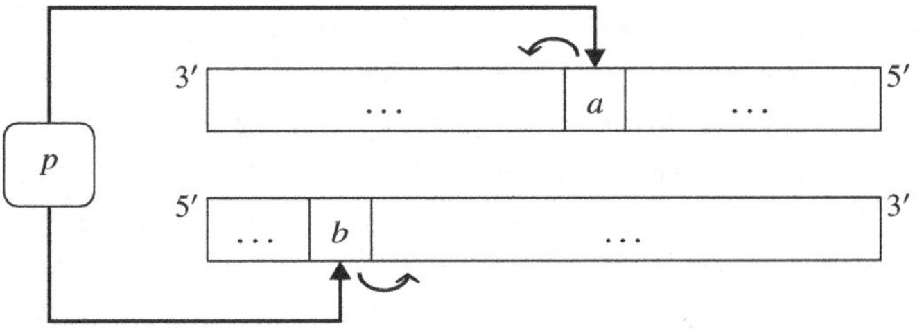

Fig. 4.10 A jumping 5′ → 3′ WKFA.

interest to study variants of jumping finite automata with more streamlined behavior. Indeed, there are already one-way jumping finite automata with fully deterministic behavior introduced in Chigahara et al. [2016] (see Section 3.2). Nonetheless, another option is to only limit the amount of possibilities of how the heads of the automaton can jump.

With a simple direct approach, it is possible to fit the jumping mechanism straightforwardly into the original definition of sensing 5′ → 3′ WKFAs, investigated in Kocman et al. [2022]. Note that we are now tracking only the meeting event of the heads as it was introduced in Nagy et al. [2017] and not the original precise sensing distance from Nagy [2008, 2010, 2013].

Definition 4.9 A *sensing 5′ → 3′ Watson–Crick finite automaton with jumping feature* (sensing 5′ → 3′ WKFA with jumping feature, for short) is a sextuple $M = (Q, \Delta, \rho, \delta, q_0, F)$, where Q, Δ, ρ, q_0, and F are the same as in WKFAs, $\Delta \cap \{\#\} = \emptyset$, $\delta\colon (Q \times \binom{\Delta^*}{\Delta^*} \times D) \to 2^Q$, where $D = \{\oplus, \ominus\}$ indicates the mutual position of heads, and $\delta(q, \binom{w_1}{w_2}, s) \neq \emptyset$ only for finitely many quadruples $(q, w_1, w_2, s) \in Q \times \Delta^* \times \Delta^* \times D$. We denote the head as ►-head or ◄-head if it reads from left to right or from right to left, respectively. We use the symbol $\oplus$ if the ►-head is on the input tape positioned before the ◄-head; otherwise, we use the symbol $\ominus$. A configuration $\binom{w_1}{w_2}(q, s)\binom{w_1'}{w_2'}$ has the same structure as in sensing 5′ → 3′ WKFAs; however, s indicates only the mutual position of heads, and a partially processed input $\binom{w_1 w_1'}{w_2 w_2'}$ may not satisfy the complementarity ρ. A step of the automaton can be of the following two types: Let $w_1', w_2, x, y, u, v \in \Delta^*$ and $w_1, w_2' \in (\Delta \cup \{\#\})^*$.

(1) Reading steps: $\binom{w_1}{w_2 y}(q, s)\binom{x w_1'}{w_2'} \curvearrowright \binom{w_1 \{\#\}^{|x|}}{w_2}(q', s')\binom{w_1'}{\{\#\}^{|y|} w_2'}$, where $q' \in \delta(q, \binom{x}{y}, s)$, and s' is either $\oplus$ if $|w_2| > |w_1 x|$ or $\ominus$ in other cases.

(2) Jumping steps: $\binom{w_1}{w_2 v}(q, s)\binom{u w_1'}{w_2'} \curvearrowright \binom{w_1 u}{w_2}(q, s')\binom{w_1'}{v w_2'}$, where s' is either $\oplus$ if $|w_2| > |w_1 u|$ or $\ominus$ in other cases.

Note that the jumping steps are an integral and inseparable part of the behavior of the automaton, and thus they are not affected by the state transition function. In the standard manner, let us extend $\curvearrowright$ to $\curvearrowright^n$, where $n \geq 0$; then, based on $\curvearrowright^n$, let us define $\curvearrowright^+$ and $\curvearrowright^*$. The set of all accepted double-stranded strings from $\mathrm{WK}_\rho(\Delta)$, denoted by $LM(M)$, can be defined by the final accepting configurations that can be reached from the initial one: A double-stranded string $\left[\begin{smallmatrix} w_1 \\ w_2 \end{smallmatrix}\right] \in WK_\rho(\Delta)$ is accepted by a sensing $5' \to 3'$ WKFA with jumping feature M if and only if $\left(\begin{smallmatrix} \varepsilon \\ w_2 \end{smallmatrix}\right)(q_0, \oplus)\left(\begin{smallmatrix} w_1 \\ \varepsilon \end{smallmatrix}\right) \curvearrowright^* \left(\begin{smallmatrix} w_1' \\ \varepsilon \end{smallmatrix}\right)(q_f, \ominus)\left(\begin{smallmatrix} \varepsilon \\ w_2' \end{smallmatrix}\right)$, for $q_f \in F$, where $w_1' = a_1 a_2 \cdots a_m$, $w_2' = b_1 b_2 \cdots b_m$, $a_i, b_i \in (\Delta \cup \{\#\})$, and either $a_i = \#$ and $b_i \in \Delta$, or $a_i \in \Delta$ and $b_i = \#$, for all $i = 1, \dots, m$, $m = |w_1|$. The language accepted by M, denoted $L(M)$, is defined as $L(M) = \uparrow_\Delta (LM(M))$.

From a practical point of view, however, this definition is not ideal. The automaton can easily end up in a configuration that cannot yield accepting results, and the correct positions of auxiliary symbols # need to be checked separately at the end of the process. Therefore, we present a modified definition that has the jumping mechanism more integrated into its structure. We are also using a simplification for complementary pairs and treat them as single letters; such a change has no effect on the accepting power, and this form of input is more natural for formal language theory.

Definition 4.10 A *jumping $5' \to 3'$ Watson–Crick finite automaton* (jumping $5' \to 3'$ WKFA, for short) is a quintuple $M = (Q, \Delta, \delta, q_0, F)$, where Q, Δ, q_0, and F are the same as in WKFAs, $\Delta \cap \{\#\} = \emptyset$, $\delta\colon (Q \times \Delta^* \times \Delta^* \times D) \to 2^Q$, where $D = \{\oplus, \ominus\}$ indicates the mutual position of heads, and $\delta(q, w_1, w_2, s) \neq \emptyset$ only for finitely many quadruples $(q, w_1, w_2, s) \in Q \times \Delta^* \times \Delta^* \times D$. A configuration (q, s, w_1, w_2, w_3) consists of the state $q \in Q$, the mutual position of heads $s \in D$, and the three unprocessed portions of the input tape: (a) before the first head (w_1), (b) between the heads (w_2), and (c) after the second head (w_3). A step of the automaton can be of the following four types: Let $x, y, u, v, w_2 \in \Delta^*$ and $w_1, w_3 \in (\Delta \cup \{\#\})^*$.

(1) $\oplus$-reading: $(q, \oplus, w_1, x w_2 y, w_3) \curvearrowright (q', s, w_1\{\#\}^{|x|}, w_2, \{\#\}^{|y|} w_3)$, where $q' \in \delta(q, x, y, \oplus)$, and s is either $\oplus$ if $|w_2| > 0$ or $\ominus$ in other cases.
(2) $\ominus$-reading: $(q, \ominus, w_1 y, \varepsilon, x w_3) \curvearrowright (q', \ominus, w_1, \varepsilon, w_3)$, where $q' \in \delta(q, x, y, \ominus)$.
(3) $\oplus$-jumping: $(q, \oplus, w_1, u w_2 v, w_3) \curvearrowright (q, s, w_1 u, w_2, v w_3)$, where s is either $\oplus$ if $|w_2| > 0$ or $\ominus$ in other cases.
(4) $\ominus$-jumping: $(q, \ominus, w_1\{\#\}^*, \varepsilon, \{\#\}^* w_3) \curvearrowright (q, \ominus, w_1, \varepsilon, w_3)$.

In the standard manner, let us extend $\curvearrowright$ to $\curvearrowright^n$, where $n \geq 0$; then, based on $\curvearrowright^n$, let us define $\curvearrowright^+$ and $\curvearrowright^*$. The accepted language, denoted by $L(M)$, can be defined by the final accepting configurations that can be reached from the initial one: A string w is accepted by a jumping $5' \to 3'$ WKFA M if and only if $(q_0, \oplus, \varepsilon, w, \varepsilon) \curvearrowright^* (q_f, \ominus, \varepsilon, \varepsilon, \varepsilon)$, for $q_f \in F$.

Even though the structure of this modified definition is considerably different from Definition 4.9, it is not very difficult to show that both models indeed accept the same family of languages.

Lemma 4.24 *For every sensing $5' \to 3'$ WKFA with jumping feature M, there is a jumping $5' \to 3'$ WKFA N such that $L(M) = L(N)$.*

Proof Consider any sensing $5' \to 3'$ WKFA with jumping feature $M = (Q, \Delta, \rho, \delta, q_0, F)$. In [Kuske and Weigel, 2004, Theorem 4], it was shown that any classical WKFA $M' = (Q', \Delta', \rho', \delta', q_0', F')$ can be converted into the classical

WKFA $M'' = (\Delta', \rho'', Q', q_0', F', \delta'')$ such that $\rho'' = \{(a,a) \mid a \in \Delta'\}$ and $L(M') = L(M'')$. The new transition function δ'' is constructed in the following way: For each $q' \in \delta'(q, \binom{u}{v})$ and $\left[\begin{smallmatrix} w \\ v \end{smallmatrix}\right] \in \mathrm{WK}_{\rho'}(\Delta')$, where $q, q' \in Q'$ and $u, v, w \in \Delta'^*$, let $q' \in \delta''(q, \binom{u}{w})$. A similar approach also works for sensing $5' \to 3'$ WKFAs. Thus, without loss of generality, assume that ρ in M is an identity relation. Now, let us define the jumping $5' \to 3'$ WKFA $N = (Q, \Delta, \delta', q_0, F)$, where $\delta'(q, w_1, w_2, s) = \delta(q, \binom{w_1}{w_2}, s)$ for all $q \in Q$, $w_1, w_2 \in \Delta^*$, and $s \in \{\oplus, \ominus\}$.

Now, we show that M and N accept the same language. We say that a current configuration of M is *potentially valid* if M can still potentially reach some accepting configuration $\binom{w_1'}{\varepsilon}(q_f, \ominus)\binom{\varepsilon}{w_2'}$, $q_f \in F$, where $w_1' = a_1 a_2 \cdots a_n$, $w_2' = b_1 b_2 \cdots b_n$, $a_i, b_i \in (\Delta \cup \{\#\})$, and either $a_i = \#$ and $b_i \in \Delta$, or $a_i \in \Delta$ and $b_i = \#$, for all $i = 1, \ldots, n$, $n = |w_1'|$. Observe that the condition regarding #'s can be checked continuously and individually for each pair $\binom{a_i}{b_i}$ that was already passed by both heads. The following description thus considers only the configurations of M that are still potentially valid.

Let us explore how M can be simulated with N. The accepting process of M can be divided into three distinct stages:

(1) Before the heads meet (the mutual position of heads remains $\oplus$): The reading steps of M clearly correspond with the $\oplus$-reading steps of N—the processed positions are marked with # in both models. Likewise, the jumping steps of M clearly correspond with the $\oplus$-jumping steps of N—the passed positions are left unchanged for the other head in both models.

(2) The meeting point of heads (when the mutual position changes from $\oplus$ to $\ominus$): The same steps as in (1) are still applicable. The difference is that in M the heads can cross each other, but in N the heads must meet each other precisely. However, the crossing situations in M that lead to potentially valid configurations are quite limited. Assume that the heads of M cross each other, the $\blacktriangleright$-head reads/skips u and the $\blacktriangleleft$-head reads/skips v, then:

   (a) If $|u| > 1$ and $|v| > 1$, the resulting configuration cannot be potentially valid since some pair $\binom{a_i}{b_i}$ was either read or skipped by both heads.

   (b) If $|u| > 1$ and $|v| = 0$: Considering a reading step, all symbols from u that are read after the meeting point must be skipped by the $\blacktriangleleft$-head. However, since jumping steps can occur arbitrarily, there is also an alternative sequence of steps in M where the heads precisely meet, the $\blacktriangleleft$-head jumps afterward, and the same configuration is reached. Moreover, any jumping step can be replaced with several shorter jumping steps.

   (c) If $|u| = 0$ and $|v| > 1$, the situation is analogous to (b).

   Thus, N does not need to cover these crossing situations.

(3) After the heads meet (the mutual position of heads is $\ominus$): To keep the current configuration potentially valid, M can use reading steps only on positions that were not yet read. Correspondingly, N can use $\ominus$-reading steps on positions that do not contain #. Also, M can effectively use jumping steps only on positions that were already read. Correspondingly, N can use $\ominus$-jumping steps on positions that contain #.

From the previous description, it is also clear that N cannot accept additional inputs that are not accepted by M since it follows identical state transitions, and the steps behave correspondingly between models. Thus, $L(N) = L(M)$.

A rigorous version of this proof is rather lengthy but straightforward, so we left it to the reader. □

Lemma 4.25 *For every jumping* $5' \to 3'$ *WKFA* M*, there is a sensing* $5' \to 3'$ *WKFA with jumping feature* N *such that* $L(M) = L(N)$.

Proof Consider any jumping $5' \to 3'$ WKFA $M = (\Delta, Q, q_0, F, \delta)$. Define the sensing $5' \to 3'$ WKFA with jumping feature $N = (\Delta, \rho, Q, q_0, F, \delta')$, where $\rho = \{(a, a) \mid a \in \Delta\}$ and $\delta'(q, \binom{w_1}{w_2}, s) = \delta(q, w_1, w_2, s)$ for all $q \in Q$, $w_1, w_2 \in \Delta^*$, and $s \in \{\oplus, \ominus\}$.

To show that M and N accept the same language, we can follow the reasoning described in the proof of Lemma 4.24. The simulation of M with N is trivial since any $\oplus$/$\ominus$-reading/jumping step of M can be easily simulated with a reading/jumping step of N. Moreover, for the simulated steps, it is guaranteed that the condition regarding #'s holds. Finally, N is clearly not able to accept additional inputs that are not accepted by M. Thus, $L(N) = L(M)$. □

Proposition 4.1 *The models of Definitions 4.9 and 4.10 accept the same family of languages.*

Proof This proposition follows directly from Lemmas 4.24 and 4.25. □

Hereafter, we primarily use Definition 4.10.

Examples

To demonstrate the behavior of the automata, we present a few simple examples.

Example 4.15 Let us recall that $L = \{w \in \{a, b\}^* \mid \text{occur}(w, a) = \text{occur}(w, b)\}$ is a well-known nonlinear context-free language. We show that, even though the jumping directions in the model are quite restricted, we are able to accept such a language. Consider the following jumping $5' \to 3'$ WKFA

$$M = (\{a, b\}, \{s\}, s, \{s\}, \delta)$$

with the state transition function δ: $\delta(s, a, b, \oplus) = \{s\}$ and $\delta(s, a, b, \ominus) = \{s\}$. Starting from s, M can either utilize the jumping or read simultaneously with both heads (the ▸-head reads a and the ◂-head reads b), and it always stays in the sole state s. Now, consider the inputs $aaabbb$ and $baabba$. The former can be accepted by using three $\oplus$-readings and one $\ominus$-jumping:

$$(s, \oplus, \varepsilon, aaabbb, \varepsilon) \curvearrowright (s, \oplus, \#, aabb, \#) \curvearrowright (s, \oplus, \#\#, ab, \#\#) \curvearrowright$$
$$(s, \ominus, \#\#\#, \varepsilon, \#\#\#) \curvearrowright (s, \ominus, \varepsilon, \varepsilon, \varepsilon).$$

The latter input is more complex and can be accepted by using one ⊕-jumping, two ⊕-readings, one ⊖-jumping, and one ⊖-reading:

$$(s, \oplus, \varepsilon, baabba, \varepsilon) \curvearrowright (s, \oplus, b, aabb, a) \curvearrowright (s, \oplus, b\#, ab, \#a) \curvearrowright$$
$$(s, \ominus, b\#\#, \varepsilon, \#\#a) \curvearrowright (s, \ominus, b, \varepsilon, a) \curvearrowright (s, \ominus, \varepsilon, \varepsilon, \varepsilon).$$

It is not hard to see that, by combining different types of steps, we can accept any input containing the same number of a's and b's, and thus $L(M) = L$.

Example 4.16 Consider the following jumping 5′ → 3′ WKFA

$$M = (\{a, b\}, \{s\}, s, \{s\}, \delta)$$

with the state transition function δ: $\delta(s, a, b, \oplus) = \{s\}$. Observe that this is almost identical to Example 4.15; however, we cannot use the ⊖-reading anymore. Consequently, we also cannot effectively use the ⊕-jumping because there is no way to process remaining symbols afterward. As a result, the accepted language changes to $L(M) = \{a^n b^n \mid n \geq 0\}$.

Lastly, we give a more complex example that uses all parts of the model.

Example 4.17 Consider the following jumping 5′ → 3′ WKFA

$$M = (\{a, b, c\}, \{s_0, s_1, s_2\}, s_0, \{s_0\}, \delta)$$

with δ: $\delta(s_0, a, b, \oplus) = \{s_1\}$, $\delta(s_1, \varepsilon, b, \oplus) = \{s_0\}$, $\delta(s_0, c, c, \ominus) = \{s_2\}$, and $\delta(s_2, \varepsilon, c, \ominus) = \{s_0\}$. We can divide the accepting process of M into two stages. First, before the heads meet, the automaton ensures that for every a on the left-hand side there are two b's on the right-hand side; other symbols are skipped with the jumps. Second, after the heads meet, the automaton checks if the part before the meeting point has double the number of c's as the part after the meeting point. Thus, $L(M) = \{w_1 w_2 \mid w_1 \in \{a, c\}^*,\ w_2 \in \{b, c\}^*,\ 2 \cdot \text{occur}(w_1, a) = \text{occur}(w_2, b), \text{occur}(w_1, c) = 2 \cdot \text{occur}(w_2, c)\}$.

General Results

These results cover the general behavior of jumping 5′ → 3′ WKFAs without any additional restrictions on the model. Let **Sen5′→3′WK**, **J5′→3′WK**, **GJFA**, and **JFA** denote the language families accepted by sensing 5′ → 3′ WKFAs, jumping 5′ → 3′ WKFA, GJFAs, and JFAs, respectively.

Considering previous results on other models that use the jumping mechanism (see Meduna and Zemek [2012, 2014]; Křivka and Meduna [2015]; Kocman et al. [2016, 2018]), it is a common characteristic that they define language families that are incomparable with the classical families of regular, linear, and context-free languages. On the other hand, sensing 5′ → 3′ WKFAs (see Nagy [2008, 2010,

2013]; Nagy et al. [2017]) are closely related to the family of linear languages. First, we show that the new model is able to accept all linear languages and that its accepting power goes even beyond the family of linear languages.

Lemma 4.26 *For every sensing* $5' \rightarrow 3'$ *WKFA* M_1, *there is a jumping* $5' \rightarrow 3'$ *WKFA* M_2 *such that* $L(M_1) = L(M_2)$.

Proof This can be proven by construction. Consider any sensing $5' \rightarrow 3'$ WKFA M_1. A direct conversion would be complicated; however, let us recall that **LIN** = **Sen5′→3′WK** (see [Nagy, 2013, Theorem 2]). Consider a linear grammar $G = (\Sigma, \Delta, P, S)$ with $N = \Sigma - \Delta$ such that $L(G) = L(M_1)$. We can construct the jumping $5' \rightarrow 3'$ WKFA M_2 such that $L(M_2) = L(G)$. Assume that $q_f \notin \Sigma$. Define $M_2 = (N \cup \{q_f\}, \Delta, \delta, S, \{q_f\})$, where $B \in \delta(A, u, v, \oplus)$ if $A \rightarrow uBv \in P$ and $q_f \in \delta(A, u, \varepsilon, \oplus)$ if $A \rightarrow u \in P$ $(A, B \in N, u, v \in \Delta^*)$.

From the definition of jumping $5' \rightarrow 3'$ WKFA, the $\oplus$-reading steps will always look like this: $(q, \oplus, w_1, uw_2v, w_3) \curvearrowright (q', s, w_1\{\#\}^{|u|}, w_2, \{\#\}^{|v|}w_3)$, where $q' \in \delta(q, u, v, \oplus)$, $w_2 \in \Delta^*$, $w_1, w_3 \in (\Delta \cup \{\#\})^*$, and s is either $\oplus$ if $|w_2| > 0$ or $\ominus$ in other cases. In M_2, there are no possible $\ominus$-reading steps. The $\oplus$-jumping can be potentially used to skip some symbols before the heads meet; nonetheless, this leads to the configuration (q, s, w_1, w_2, w_3) where $\text{symbols}(w_1w_3) \cap \Delta \neq \emptyset$. Since without $\ominus$-reading steps there is no way to read symbols of Δ in w_1 and w_3, such a configuration cannot yield an accepting result. Consequently, starting from $(S, \oplus, \varepsilon, w, \varepsilon)$ where $w \in \Delta^*$, it can be easily seen that if M_2 accepts w, it reads all symbols of w in the same fashion as G generates them; the remaining #'s can be erased with the $\ominus$-jumping afterward. Moreover, the heads of M_2 can meet each other with the accepting state q_f if and only if G can finish the generation process with a rule $A \rightarrow u$. Thus, $L(M_2) = L(G) = L(M_1)$. □

Theorem 4.41 LIN = Sen5′→3′WK ⊂ J5′→3′WK.

Proof **Sen5′→3′WK** ⊆ **J5′→3′WK** follows from Lemma 4.26. **LIN** = **Sen5′→3′WK** was proven in Nagy [2013]. **J5′→3′WK** ⊈ **LIN** follows from Example 4.15. □

The next two characteristics follow from the previous results.

Theorem 4.42 *Jumping* $5' \rightarrow 3'$ *WKFAs that do not use* $\ominus$*-reading steps accept linear languages.*

Proof Consider any jumping $5' \rightarrow 3'$ WKFA $M = (Q, \Delta, \delta, q_0, F)$ that has no possible $\ominus$-reading steps. Following the reasoning from the proof of Lemma 4.26, if there are no possible $\ominus$-reading steps, the $\oplus$-jumping cannot be effectively used, and we can construct a linear grammar that generates strings in the same fashion as M reads them. Define the linear grammar $G = (Q \cup \Delta, \Delta, R, q_0)$, where R is constructed in the following way: (1) For each $p \in \delta(q, u, v, \oplus)$, add $q \rightarrow upv$ to R. (2) For each $f \in F$, add $f \rightarrow \varepsilon$ to R. Clearly, $L(G) = L(M)$. □

Proposition 4.2 *The language family accepted by double-jumping finite automata that perform right-left and left-right jumps (see Section 4.1, SEL language, see Definition 4.2) is strictly included in* **J5′→3′WK**.

Proof First, Theorem 4.6 shows that jumping finite automata that perform right-left and left-right jumps accept the same family of languages. Second, Theorem 4.2 shows that this family is strictly included in **LIN**. Finally, Theorem 4.41 shows that **LIN** is strictly included in **J5′→3′WK**. □

Even though jumping $5' \to 3'$ WKFAs are able to accept some nonlinear languages, the jumping directions of their heads are quite restricted compared to GJFAs. Consequently, there are some languages accepted by jumping $5' \to 3'$ WKFAs and GJFAs that cannot be accepted with the other model. To formally prove these results, we need to introduce the concept of the debt of a configuration in jumping $5' \to 3'$ WKFAs. First, we start with the formal definition of a reachable state.

Definition 4.11 Let $M = (Q, \Delta, \delta, q_0, F)$ be a jumping $5' \to 3'$ WKFA. Assuming some states $q, q' \in Q$ and a mutual position of heads $s \in \{\oplus, \ominus\}$, we say that q' is *reachable* from q and s if there exists a configuration (q, s, w_1, w_2, w_3) such that $(q, s, w_1, w_2, w_3) \curvearrowright^* (q', s', w'_1, w'_2, w'_3)$ in M, $s' \in \{\oplus, \ominus\}$, $w_1, w_2, w_3, w'_1, w'_2, w'_3 \in (\Delta \cup \{\#\})^*$.

Next, we show that for any computation C that takes a jumping $5' \to 3'$ WKFA M from a starting configuration to a configuration from which a final state is reachable, there exists $w' \in L(M)$ such that w' can be fully processed with the same sequence of reading steps as in C and a limited number of additional steps. Note that jumping steps in C are unimportant for the result since jumping steps can occur arbitrarily and they do not process any symbols of the input.

Lemma 4.27 *For each jumping $5' \to 3'$ WKFA $M = (Q, \Delta, \delta, q_0, F)$ there exists a constant k such that the following holds. Let $q \in Q$ and $s \in \{\oplus, \ominus\}$ such that $f \in F$ is reachable from q and s. For every computation C that takes M from $(q_0, \oplus, \varepsilon, w, \varepsilon)$ to (q, s, w_1, w_2, w_3), $w \in \Delta^*$, $w_1, w_2, w_3 \in (\Delta \cup \{\#\})^*$, there exists $w' \in L(M)$ such that M starting with w' can reach q and $s' \in \{\oplus, \ominus\}$ by using the same sequence of $\oplus/\ominus$-reading steps as in C and the rest of w' can be processed with a limited number of additional steps bounded by k.*

Proof First, if f is reachable from q and s, then there exists a sequence of pairs $\mathcal{P} = (p_0, s_0) \cdots (p_n, s_n)$, for some $n \geq 0$, where

- $p_i \in Q$, $s_i \in \{\oplus, \ominus\}$, for all $i = 0, \ldots, n$,
- $p_0 = q$, $s_0 = s$ or $s_0 = \ominus$, $p_n = f$, $s_n = \ominus$,
- for all $i = 0, \ldots, n-1$ it holds: $p_{i+1} \in \delta(p_i, x_i, y_i, s_i)$, $x_i, y_i \in \Delta^*$,
- for all $i = 0, \ldots, n-1$ it holds: $s_{i+1} = s_i$ or $s_{i+1} = \ominus$, and
- $(p_i, s_i) = (p_j, s_j)$ implies $i = j$, $i, j = 0, \ldots, n$ (all pairs are unique).

This sequence is finite, and its maximum length is bounded by $k' = 2 \cdot \mathrm{card}(Q)$.

Second, let us represent a $\oplus/\ominus$-reading step as a quintuple (q', x, y, s'', q'') according to $q'' \in \delta(q', x, y, s'')$, $q', q'' \in Q$, $x, y \in \Delta^*$, $s'' \in \{\oplus, \ominus\}$. From the computation C we extract a sequence of $\oplus/\ominus$-reading steps $\mathcal{S}$. From the sequence of pairs $\mathcal{P}$ we can easily derive a sequence of $\oplus/\ominus$-reading steps $\mathcal{S}'$ that follows the state transitions of $\mathcal{P}$. Let $\mathcal{S}'' = \mathcal{S}\mathcal{S}'$. We split $\mathcal{S}''$ into two parts $\mathcal{S}'' = \mathcal{S}''_\oplus \mathcal{S}''_\ominus$ such that $\mathcal{S}''_\oplus = (p'_0, a_0, b_0, \oplus, q'_0) \cdots (p'_n, a_n, b_n, \oplus, q'_n)$ and

$\mathcal{S}''_{\ominus} = (p''_0, c_0, d_0, \ominus, q''_0) \cdots (p''_m, c_m, d_m, \ominus, q''_m)$, where $n, m \geq 0$, $i = 0, \ldots, n$, $j = 0, \ldots, m$, $p'_i, q'_i, p''_j, q''_j \in Q$, $a_i, b_i, c_j, d_j \in \Delta^*$.

Third, we consider input $w' = a_0 \cdots a_n d_m \cdots d_0 c_0 \cdots c_m b_n \cdots b_0$. It is not hard to construct a computation C' of M from $\mathcal{S}''_{\oplus}$, one $\oplus$-jumping step, $\mathcal{S}''_{\ominus}$, and one $\ominus$-jumping step such that $(q_0, \oplus, \varepsilon, a_0 \cdots a_n d_m \cdots d_0 c_0 \cdots c_m b_n \cdots b_0, \varepsilon) \curvearrowright^* (q', s''', \{\#\}^{|a_0 \cdots a_n|}, d_m \cdots d_0 c_0 \cdots c_m, \{\#\}^{|b_n \cdots b_0|}) \curvearrowright (q', \ominus, \{\#\}^{|a_0 \cdots a_n|} d_m \cdots d_0, \varepsilon, c_0 \cdots c_m \{\#\}^{|b_n \cdots b_0|}) \curvearrowright^* (f, \ominus, \{\#\}^{|a_0 \cdots a_n|}, \varepsilon, \{\#\}^{|b_n \cdots b_0|}) \curvearrowright (f, \ominus, \varepsilon, \varepsilon, \varepsilon)$, $q' \in Q$, $s''' \in \{\oplus, \ominus\}$. Thus, $w' \in L(M)$ and there exists $k \leq k'$ for M that bounds the number of additional steps. □

Next, based on known M and $L(M)$, we can define the debt of a configuration of M. If we follow a computation of M on an input w, we can easily determine the Parikh vector o of symbols already processed from w in a current configuration γ. Additionally, with the known $L(M)$, we can determine Parikh vectors for all $w' \in L(M)$. The debt of the configuration γ represents the minimum number of symbols that have to be added to o so that o matches the Parikh vector of some $w' \in L(M)$. Note that we use ∞ to cover situations when no match is possible.

Definition 4.12 Let $M = (Q, \Delta, \delta, q_0, F)$ be a jumping $5' \rightarrow 3'$ WKFA, where $\Delta = \{a_1, \ldots, a_n\}$, and let $w \in \Delta^*$. We define the Parikh vector $o = (o_1, \ldots, o_n)$ of processed (read) symbols from w in a configuration $\gamma = (q, s, w_1, w_2, w_3)$ of M reached from an initial configuration $(q_0, \oplus, \varepsilon, w, \varepsilon)$ of M as $o = \psi_\Delta(w) - \psi_\Delta(w_1 w_2 w_3)$, $q \in Q$, $s \in \{\oplus, \ominus\}$, $w \in \Delta^*$, $w_1, w_2, w_3 \in (\Delta \cup \{\#\})^*$. Using the Parikh mapping of $L(M)$, we define $\Delta(o) = \{\sum_{i=1}^{n}(m_i - o_i) \mid (m_1, \ldots, m_n) \in \psi_\Delta(L(M)),\ m_i \geq o_i,\ 1 \leq i \leq n\} \cup \{\infty\}$. Finally, we define the *debt* of the configuration γ of M as $\min \Delta(o)$.

And finally, we can combine Lemma 4.27 and Definition 4.12 to show that each jumping $5' \rightarrow 3'$ WKFA M has to accept all $w \in L(M)$ over configurations with some bounded debt.

Lemma 4.28 *Let L be a language, and let $M = (Q, \Delta, \delta, q_0, F)$ be a jumping $5' \rightarrow 3'$ WKFA. If $L(M) = L$, there exists a constant k for M such that M accepts all $w \in L$ using only configurations that have their debt bounded by k.*

Proof (*by contradition*) Assume, for the sake of contradiction, that there is no constant k for M such that M accepts all $w \in L$ using only configurations that have their debt bounded by k. Then, M can accept some $w \in L$ over a configuration for which the debt cannot be bounded by any k. Let $\Delta = \{a_1, \ldots, a_n\}$. Consider any configuration γ of M reached from an initial configuration $(q_0, \oplus, \varepsilon, w, \varepsilon)$ of M. Let $o = (o_1, \ldots, o_n)$ be the Parikh vector of processed symbols from w in γ. First, assume that γ contains a state $q \in Q$ with a mutual position of heads $s \in \{\oplus, \ominus\}$ from which a final state $f \in F$ is reachable. Then, due to Lemma 4.27, there is $w' \in L(M)$ such that $\psi_\Delta(w') = (m_1, \ldots, m_n)$, $m_i \geq o_i$, $1 \leq i \leq n$, and $|w'| \leq \sum_{i=1}^{n}(o_i) + k'$, where k' is some constant for M. According to Definition 4.12, $w' \in L(M)$ implies $\min \Delta(o) \leq k'$. Second, assume that γ contains a state q with a mutual position of heads s from which no final state f is reachable. Then, by Definitions 4.10 and 4.11, there is no computation that takes M from γ to a final accepting configuration. Thus, when M accepts w, it must be done over configurations with the debt $\leq k'$. However, that is a contradiction with the assumption that M can accept some $w \in L$ over a configuration for which the debt cannot be bounded by any k. □

Observe that the debt alone does not depend on the order of symbols in the strings of $L(M)$, e.g., $\psi_\Delta(\{(abc)^n \mid n \geq 0\}) = \psi_\Delta(\{a^n b^n c^n \mid n \geq 0\})$, for $\Delta = \{a, b, c\}$. However, when the debt is combined with the computational possibilities of M on an input w, we can show that a language L cannot be accepted by M if there is no constant k for M such that all $w \in L$ can be fully processed over configurations of M with the debt bounded by k.

Lemma 4.29 *There is no jumping 5′ → 3′ WKFA M such that $L(M) = \{a^n b^n c^n \mid n \geq 0\}$.*

Proof *Basic idea.* Considering any sufficiently large constant k, we show that M cannot process all symbols of $a^{10k} b^{10k} c^{10k}$ using only configurations that have their debt bounded by k.

Formal proof (by contradition). Let $L = \{a^n b^n c^n \mid n \geq 0\}$, and let $M = (\Delta, Q, q_0, F, \delta)$ be a jumping 5′ → 3′ WKFA such that $L(M) = L$. Due to Lemma 4.28, there must exist a constant k for M such that M accepts all $w \in L$ using only configurations that have their debt bounded by k. (Observe that if Lemma 4.28 holds for some constant k', it also holds for all $k'' > k'$.) Let $k_{\min} = \max\{|uv| \mid \delta(q, u, v, s) \neq \emptyset,\ q \in Q,\ u, v \in \Delta^*,\ s \in \{\oplus, \ominus\}\}$. Consider any k for M such that $k > k_{\min}$. Due to the structure of L, we can represent the debt of the configuration of M as $\langle d_a, d_b, d_c\rangle$, where d_a, d_b, d_c is the minimum number of symbols a, b, c that M must yet to read to get the balanced number of processed symbols. (For illustration, an initial configuration of M has the debt $\langle 0, 0, 0\rangle$. When M reads a, the following configuration has the debt $\langle 0, 1, 1\rangle$ because at least one b and one c have yet to be read to keep the number of processed symbols balanced.) When $(q_0, \oplus, \varepsilon, w, \varepsilon) \curvearrowright^* (q_f, \ominus, \varepsilon, \varepsilon, \varepsilon)$ in M, $q_f \in F$, for all traversed configurations must hold $d_a + d_b + d_c \leq k$. Let $w = a^{10k} b^{10k} c^{10k}$.

First, we explore the maximum number of symbols that M can read from w before the heads meet. Starting from the initial configuration $(q_0, \oplus, \varepsilon, w, \varepsilon)$ with the debt $\langle 0, 0, 0\rangle$ and until the mutual position $\ominus$ is reached, M can use $\oplus$-reading steps to process symbols and $\oplus$-jumping steps to skip symbols. Consider different reading strategies that try to process the maximum number of symbols from $a^{10k} b^{10k} c^{10k}$ before the heads meet. There are three distinct places where the heads of M can meet:

(A) Assume that the heads meet inside the segment of a's:
  (1) M can process (with multiple steps) a^k and c^k until it reaches the debt $\langle 0, k, 0\rangle$. Then, M has to start read b's.
  (2) M can read l symbols together in one step (balanced number of a's, b's, and c's) while keeping the debt $\langle 0, k, 0\rangle$, $l < k$. Nonetheless, the ◀-head ends up in the segment of b's.
  (3) M can process a^k and b^{2k} until it reaches the debt $\langle 0, 0, k\rangle$. Clearly, there is no way how to read additional c's.

No further reading is possible, and this strategy can process $5k + l$ symbols.

(B) Assume that the heads meet inside the segment of c's. Then, this is just a mirror case of (A), and this strategy can process $5k + l$ symbols.

(C) Assume that the heads meet inside the segment of b's. Observe that in (A) and (B) the heads can meet on the border of a's and b's or b's and c's. There are no additional possibilities when both heads read b's since the debt is limited by the letters that were already skipped by one of the heads. Thus, this strategy can process $5k + l$ symbols as well.

Consequently, before the heads meet, M can process no more than $5k + l$ symbols.

Second, when the heads meet, $a^{>4k}b^{>4k}c^{>4k}$ has yet to be processed. The heads are next to each other, and M can use $\ominus$-reading steps to process symbols and $\ominus$-jumping steps to remove the auxiliary #'s. Consider different reading strategies that try to process the maximum number of symbols after the heads meet. There are several distinct places where the heads of M can be positioned:

(A) Assume that the heads are between a's and b's. It is possible to start with a debt up to k. Consider the debt $\langle 0, k, 0\rangle$. M can process a^k and b^{2k} until it reaches the debt $\langle 0, 0, k\rangle$. Since there is $b^{>4k}$, it is not possible to reach c's. Clearly, it is not possible to select a different debt that would yield a better result. Thus, this strategy can process $3k$ symbols.

(B) Assume that the heads are between b's and c's. Then, this is just a mirror case of (A), and this strategy can process $3k$ symbols.

(C) Assume that the heads are in the middle of b's with the debt $\langle 0, k, 0\rangle$. M can process $b^{\frac{3}{2}k}$ until it reaches $\langle \frac{1}{2}k, 0, \frac{1}{2}k\rangle$. It is not possible to reach neither a's nor c's. Thus, this strategy can process $\frac{3}{2}k$ symbols.

(D) Any other position of heads can be seen as a slightly modified case of (A), (B), or (C). Since neither of these cases is able to reach all three types of symbols, they can process only up to $3k$ symbols.

Consequently, after the heads meet, M can process no more than $3k$ symbols.

Finally, we can see that M is not able to process more than $8k + l$ symbols from $w = a^{10k}b^{10k}c^{10k}$ when the debt of configurations of M is bounded by k. Since, for any k, $w \in L$ and w contains $30k$ symbols, there is no constant k for M such that M accepts all $w \in L$ using only configurations that have their debt bounded by k. But that is a contradiction with the assumption that there is a jumping $5' \to 3'$ WKFA M such that $L(M) = \{a^n b^n c^n \mid n \geq 0\}$. □

Lemma 4.30 *There is no jumping $5' \to 3'$ WKFA M such that $L(M) = \{w \in \{a, b, c\}^* \mid \text{occur}(w, a) = \text{occur}(w, b) = \text{occur}(w, c)\}$.*

Proof Let $N = (Q, \Delta, \delta, q_0, F)$ be a jumping $5' \to 3'$ WKFA, $L = \{w \in \{a, b, c\}^* \mid \text{occur}(w, a) = \text{occur}(w, b) = \text{occur}(w, c)\}$, and $K = \{a^n b^n c^n \mid n \geq 0\}$. Let w be an input of the form $\{a\}^*\{b\}^*\{c\}^*$. Let γ be a configuration of N reached from an initial configuration $(q_0, \oplus, \varepsilon, w, \varepsilon)$ of N. Let o be the Parikh vector of processed symbols from w in γ. Observe that, for any configuration γ, the debt of the configuration $\min \Delta(o)$ is similar for $L(N) = L$ and $L(N) = K$ since it only depends on o and the quantities of symbols in the strings of the language $L(N)$. Consequently, the proof that there is no such M is analogous to the proof of Lemma 4.29. □

Proposition 4.3 J5′→3′WK *is incomparable with* **GJFA** *and* **JFA**.

Proof The language $\{w \in \{a, b\}^* \mid \text{occur}(w, a) = \text{occur}(w, b)\}$ from Example 4.15 and the language $\{w \in \{a, b, c\}^* \mid \text{occur}(w, a) = \text{occur}(w, b) = \text{occur}(w, c)\}$ from Lemma 4.30 are accepted with (general) jumping finite automata (see Example 3.1). The language $\{a^n b^n \mid n \geq 0\}$ from Example 4.16 is not accepted with (general) jumping finite automata because by Lemma 3.3 even simpler language $\{a\}^*\{b\}^* \notin$ **GJFA**. □

The last group of results compares the accepting power of jumping 5′ → 3′ WKFAs with the families of context-sensitive and context-free languages.

Theorem 4.43 J5′→3′WK ⊂ CS.

Proof Clearly, the use of two heads and the jumping behavior can be simulated by linear bounded automata, so **J5′→3′WK** ⊆ **CS**. From Lemma 4.29, **CS** − **J5′→3′WK** ≠ ∅. □

Lemma 4.31 *There are some non-context-free languages accepted by jumping* 5′ → 3′ *WKFAs.*

Proof *(by contradition)* Consider the following jumping 5′ → 3′ WKFA

$$M = (\{s\}, \{a, b, c, d\}, \delta, s, \{s\})$$

with the state transition function δ: $\delta(s, a, c, \oplus) = \{s\}$ and $\delta(s, d, b, \ominus) = \{s\}$. The accepting process has two stages. First, before the heads meet, the automaton reads the same number of a's and c's. Second, after the heads meet, the automaton reads the same number of d's and b's. Thus, $L(M) = \{w_1 w_2 \mid w_1 \in \{a, b\}^*,\ w_2 \in \{c, d\}^*,\ \text{occur}(w_1, a) = \text{occur}(w_2, c),\ \text{occur}(w_1, b) = \text{occur}(w_2, d)\}$.

For the sake of contradiction, assume that $L(M)$ is a context-free language. The family of context-free languages is closed under intersection with regular sets. Let $K = L(M) \cap \{a\}^*\{b\}^*\{c\}^*\{d\}^*$. Clearly, there are some strings in $L(M)$ that satisfy this forced order of symbols. Furthermore, they all have the proper correlated numbers of these symbols. Consequently, $K = \{a^n b^m c^n d^m \mid n, m \geq 0\}$. However, K is a well-known non-context-free language (see [Rozenberg and Salomaa, 1997b, Chapter 3.1]). That is a contradiction with the assumption that $L(M)$ is a context-free language. Therefore, $L(M)$ is a non-context-free language. □

Lemma 4.32 *There is no jumping* 5′ → 3′ *WKFA* M *such that* $L(M) = \{a^n b^n c^m d^m \mid n, m \geq 0\}$.

Proof *Basic idea.* We follow the proof structure of Lemma 4.29. Considering any sufficiently large constant k, we show that M cannot process all symbols of $a^{10k} b^{10k} c^{10k} d^{10k}$ using only configurations that have their debt bounded by k.

Formal proof (by contradition). Let $L = \{a^n b^n c^m d^m \mid n, m \geq 0\}$, and let $M = (\Delta, Q, q_0, F, \delta)$ be a jumping 5′ → 3′ WKFA such that $L(M) = L$. Due to Lemma 4.28, there must exist a constant k for M such that M accepts all $w \in L$ using only configurations that have their debt bounded by k. Let $k_{\min} = \max\{|uv| \mid \delta(q, u, v, s) \neq \emptyset,\ q \in Q,\ u, v \in \Delta^*,\ s \in \{\oplus, \ominus\}\}$. Consider any k for M such that $k > k_{\min}$. Let $w = a^{10k}b^{10k}c^{10k}d^{10k}$.

We follow a computation of M from an initial configuration $\sigma = (q_0, \oplus, \varepsilon, w, \varepsilon)$. First, we explore the limits of how many symbols M can read with $\ominus$-reading steps. Let γ be the first configuration of the computation of M with the mutual position of heads $\ominus$ reached from σ. Consider the maximum number of b's that the ◂-head can read with $\ominus$-reading steps starting from γ. Since a's are in front of b's and since a's are linked with b's, this number must be limited. The configuration γ can have the debt of at most k b's, the debt can reach at most k a's, and only one step can read both types of symbols together. Thus, the maximum number of b's that the ◂-head can read with $\ominus$-reading steps starting from γ is less than $3k$. In the same manner, the maximum number of c's that the ▸-head can read with $\ominus$-reading steps starting from γ is less than $3k$.

Second, we explore the limits of how many symbols M can read with $\oplus$-reading steps. Consider the maximum number of a's and b's that the ▸-head can read on its own with $\oplus$-reading steps starting from γ. The configuration σ has no debt, the debt can reach at most k b's, only one step can read both types of symbols together, and then the debt can reach at most k a's. Thus, the maximum number of a's and b's that the ◂-head can read on its own with $\oplus$-reading steps starting from γ is less than $4k$. In the same manner, the maximum number of c's and d's that the ◂-head can read on its own with $\oplus$-reading steps starting from γ is less than $4k$. Due to the previous limits with $\ominus$-reading steps, in a successful computation, the ▸-head cannot jump over all remaining b's and the ◂-head cannot jump over all remaining c's. Thus, the heads cannot meet in a configuration that can yield a successful computation.

Finally, we can see that M is not able to accept $w = a^{10k}b^{10k}c^{10k}d^{10k}$ when the debt of configurations of M is bounded by k. Since, for any k, $w \in L$, there is no constant k for M such that M accepts all $w \in L$ using only configurations that have their debt bounded by k. But that is a contradiction with the assumption that there is a jumping $5' \rightarrow 3'$ WKFA M such that $L(M) = \{a^n b^n c^m d^m \mid n, m \geq 0\}$. □

Theorem 4.44 **J5′→3′WK** *and* **CF** *are incomparable.*

Proof **J5′→3′WK** $\not\subseteq$ **CF** follows from Lemma 4.31. **CF** $\not\subseteq$ **J5′→3′WK** follows from Lemma 4.32. Lastly, **LIN** $\subset$ **J5′→3′WK** and **LIN** $\subset$ **CF**. □

Results on Restricted Variants

In this section, we compare the accepting power of unrestricted and restricted variants of jumping $5' \rightarrow 3'$ WKFAs. This section considers the same standard restrictions as they are defined for WKFAs (see Definition 2.7). Since these restrictions regulate only the state control and reading steps of the automaton, the jumping is not affected in any way. Let **J5′→3′WK** denote the language family accepted by jumping $5' \rightarrow 3'$

WKFAs. We are using prefixes **N**, **F**, **S**, **1**, **NS**, **FS**, **N1**, and **F1** to specify the restricted variants of jumping $5' \to 3'$ WKFAs and appropriate language families.

In Section 3.1, it was shown that the use of the jumping mechanism can have an unusual impact on the expressive power of the model when we restrict the state control of the model. In the case of classical finite automata, it makes no difference if the steps of the automaton read single symbols or longer strings. Nonetheless, in the case of jumping finite automata, this change has a large impact on the expressive power of the model. Moreover, most of the standard restrictions studied in WKFAs were not yet considered together with the jumping mechanism. Therefore, it is our intention to thoroughly explore the impact of these restrictions on the accepting power of jumping $5' \to 3'$ WKFAs and compare it with the similar results on sensing $5' \to 3'$ WKFAs.

In the field of DNA computing, the empty string/sequence usually does not belong to any language because it does not refer to a molecule. This section is not so strict and thus considers the empty string as a possible valid input. Let $\mathbf{FIN}_{\varepsilon\text{-inc}}$ denote finite languages which contain the empty string. Nonetheless, the following proofs are deliberately based on more complex inputs to mitigate the impact of the empty string on the results. Moreover, we distinguish between **FIN** and $\mathbf{FIN}_{\varepsilon\text{-inc}}$, when the difference is unavoidable.

Note that there are some inherent inclusions between language families based on the application of restrictions on the model. Additionally, several other basic relationships can be established directly from the definitions of the restrictions:

Lemma 4.33 *The following relationships hold: (i)* $\mathbf{N\ J5'{\to}3'WK} \subseteq \mathbf{F\ J5'{\to}3'WK}$*; (ii)* $\mathbf{1\ J5'{\to}3'WK} \subseteq \mathbf{S\ J5'{\to}3'WK}$*; (iii)* $\mathbf{F1\ J5'{\to}3'WK} \subseteq \mathbf{FS\ J5'{\to}3'WK}$*; (iv)* $\mathbf{N1\ J5'{\to}3'WK} \subseteq \mathbf{NS\ J5'{\to}3'WK}$*; (v)* $\mathbf{NS\ J5'{\to}3'WK} \subseteq \mathbf{FS\ J5'{\to}3'WK}$*; (vi)* $\mathbf{N1\ J5'{\to}3'WK} \subseteq \mathbf{F1\ J5'{\to}3'WK}$.

Proof These results follow directly from the definitions since the stateless restriction (**N**) is a special case of the all-final restriction (**F**) and the 1-limited restriction (**1**) is a special case of the simple restriction (**S**). □

On the simple restriction

Theorem 4.45 $\mathbf{S\ J5'{\to}3'WK} = \mathbf{J5'{\to}3'WK}$.

Proof *Basic idea.* Any general reading step can be replaced with at most two simple reading steps and a new auxiliary state that together accomplish the same action.
Formal proof. Consider any jumping $5' \to 3'$ WKFA $M = (Q_1, \Delta, \delta_1, q_0, F)$. We can construct the **S** jumping $5' \to 3'$ WKFA N such that $L(N) = L(M)$. Define $N = (Q_2, \Delta, \delta_2, q_0, F)$, where Q_2 and δ_2 are created in the following way: Let $q \in Q_1$, $x, y \in \Delta^*$, and $s \in \{\oplus, \ominus\}$.

(1) Set $Q_2 = Q_1$.
(2) For each $\delta_1(q, x, y, s) \neq \emptyset$ where $|x| = 0$ or $|y| = 0$,
let $\delta_2(q, x, y, s) = \delta_1(q, x, y, s)$.

(3) For each $\delta_1(q, x, y, s) \neq \emptyset$ where $|x| > 0$ and $|y| > 0$, add a new unique state p to Q_2 and let $p \in \delta_2(q, x, \varepsilon, s)$ and $\delta_2(p, \varepsilon, y, s) = \delta_1(q, x, y, s)$.

It is clear that all original transitions that did not satisfy the simple restriction were transformed into the new suitable transitions.

Now we show that this change has no effect on the accepted language. Let $w \in L(M)$ be accepted by an accepting computation γ of M. There is a computation γ' of N corresponding to γ of M. We can construct γ' from γ in the following way:

(A) If there is $(q, \oplus, w_1, xw_2y, w_3) \curvearrowright (q', s, w_1\{\#\}^{|x|}, w_2, \{\#\}^{|y|}, w_3)$ in γ, where $x, y \in \Delta^+$, $w_1, w_2, w_3 \in (\Delta \cup \{\#\})^*$, $q, q' \in Q_1$, $s \in \{\oplus, \ominus\}$, we replace it in γ' with $(q, \oplus, w_1, xw_2y, w_3) \curvearrowright (p, \oplus, w_1\{\#\}^{|x|}, w_2y, w_3) \curvearrowright (q', s, w_1\{\#\}^{|x|}, w_2, \{\#\}^{|y|}w_3)$, where p is the new state introduced for $\delta_1(q, x, y, \oplus)$ in step (3).

(B) If there is $(q, \ominus, w_1y, \varepsilon, xw_3) \curvearrowright (q', \ominus, w_1, \varepsilon, w_3)$ in γ, where $x, y \in \Delta^+$, $w_1, w_3 \in (\Delta \cup \{\#\})^*$, $q, q' \in Q_1$, we replace it in γ' with $(q, \ominus, w_1y, \varepsilon, xw_3) \curvearrowright (p, \ominus, w_1y, \varepsilon, w_3) \curvearrowright (q', \ominus, w_1, \varepsilon, w_3)$, where p is the new state introduced for $\delta_1(q, x, y, \ominus)$ in step (3).

(C) We keep other steps of the computation without changes.

Clearly, γ' is an accepting computation of N and $w \in L(N)$. Thus, $L(M) \subseteq L(N)$.

Let $w \in L(N)$ be accepted by an accepting computation γ of N. Clearly, any sequence of consecutive $\oplus$/$\ominus$-jumping steps can be replaced with a single $\oplus$/$\ominus$-jumping step, and it is also possible to utilize empty jumping steps that do not move the heads. Thus, without loss of generality, assume that γ does not contain sequences of consecutive $\oplus$/$\ominus$-jumping steps and that every reading step in γ is followed by a jumping step. There is a computation γ' of M corresponding to γ of N. We can construct γ' from γ in the following way:

(A) If there is $(q, \oplus, w_1, xuw_2yv, w_3) \curvearrowright (p, \oplus, w_1\{\#\}^{|x|}, uw_2yv, w_3) \curvearrowright (p, \oplus, w_1\{\#\}^{|x|}u, w_2y, vw_3) \curvearrowright (q', s, w_1\{\#\}^{|x|}u, w_2, \{\#\}^{|y|}vw_3)$ in γ, where $x, y \in \Delta^+$, $u, v \in \Delta^*$, $w_1, w_2, w_3 \in (\Delta \cup \{\#\})^*$, $q, q' \in Q_1$, $s \in \{\oplus, \ominus\}$, and p is the new state introduced for $\delta_1(q, x, y, \oplus)$ in step (3), we replace these steps in γ' with $(q, \oplus, w_1, xuw_2yv, w_3) \curvearrowright (q, \oplus, w_1, xuw_2y, vw_3) \curvearrowright (q', s', w_1\{\#\}^{|x|}, uw_2, \{\#\}^{|y|}vw_3) \curvearrowright (q', s, w_1\{\#\}^{|x|}u, w_2, \{\#\}^{|y|}vw_3)$, where $s' \in \{\oplus, \ominus\}$ according to the definition of $\oplus$-reading steps. Observe that, due to the unique p, it is clear that $q' \in \delta_1(q, x, y, \oplus)$ in M.

(B) If there is $(q, \ominus, w_1y\{\#\}^v, \varepsilon, x\{\#\}^u w_3) \curvearrowright (p, \ominus, w_1y\{\#\}^v, \varepsilon, \{\#\}^u w_3) \curvearrowright (p, \ominus, w_1y, \varepsilon, w_3) \curvearrowright (q', \ominus, w_1, \varepsilon, w_3)$ in γ, where $x, y \in \Delta^+$, $u, v \geq 0$, $w_1, w_3 \in (\Delta \cup \{\#\})^*$, $q, q' \in Q_1$, and p is the new state introduced for $\delta_1(q, x, y, \ominus)$ in step (3), we replace these steps in γ' with $(q, \ominus, w_1y\{\#\}^v, \varepsilon, x\{\#\}^u w_3) \curvearrowright (q, \ominus, w_1y, \varepsilon, x\{\#\}^u w_3) \curvearrowright (q', \ominus, w_1, \varepsilon, \{\#\}^u w_3) \curvearrowright (q', \ominus, w_1, \varepsilon, w_3)$.

(C) We keep other steps of the computation without changes.

Clearly, γ' is an accepting computation of M and $w \in L(M)$. Thus, $L(N) \subseteq L(M)$. Consequently, $L(N) = L(M)$. $\square$

On the 1-limited restriction

Example 4.18 Consider the following jumping $5' \to 3'$ WKFA $M = (\{s, f\}, \{a, b, c\}, \delta, s, \{f\})$ with the state transition function δ:

$$\delta(s, a, b, \oplus) = \{s\}, \quad \delta(f, a, b, \oplus) = \{f\}, \quad \delta(f, a, b, \ominus) = \{f\},$$
$$\delta(s, cc, \varepsilon, \oplus) = \{f\}, \quad \delta(s, \varepsilon, cc, \oplus) = \{f\}.$$

The first three transitions mimic the behavior of Example 4.15. The other two transitions ensure that the input is accepted only if it also contains precisely one substring cc. Therefore, $L(M) = \{w_1 cc w_2 \mid w_1, w_2 \in \{a, b\}^*, \text{occur}(w_1 w_2, a) = \text{occur}(w_1 w_2, b)\}$.

Lemma 4.34 *Let $M = (Q, \Delta, \delta, q_0, F)$ be a* **1** *jumping $5' \to 3'$ WKFA M, and let $w \in L(M)$ be accepted by an accepting computation γ of M. Let us represent the $\oplus$-reading step of M that follows $\delta(q, u, v, \oplus)$, $q \in Q$, $u, v \in (\Delta \cup \{\varepsilon\})$, as a quadruple $(u, v, \varepsilon, \varepsilon)$ and the $\ominus$-reading step of M that follows $\delta(q, u', v', \ominus)$, $q \in Q$, $u', v' \in (\Delta \cup \{\varepsilon\})$, as a quadruple $(\varepsilon, \varepsilon, u', v')$. Then, we can represent the reading steps of γ as a sequence $(u_1, v_1, u'_1, v'_1) \cdots (u_n, v_n, u'_n, v'_n)$, $i = 1, \dots, n$, $n \geq 1$. Let $w_{\blacktriangleright\oplus} = u_1 \cdots u_n$, $w_{\blacktriangleright\ominus} = u'_1 \cdots u'_n$, $w_{\blacktriangleleft\oplus} = v_n \cdots v_1$, $w_{\blacktriangleleft\ominus} = v'_n \cdots v'_1$. It holds that $xy \in L(M)$ for all $x \in ш(w_{\blacktriangleright\oplus}, w_{\blacktriangleleft\ominus})$ and $y \in ш(w_{\blacktriangleleft\oplus}, w_{\blacktriangleright\ominus})$.*

Proof Since M satisfies the 1-limited restriction, exactly one symbol is always being read with a reading step. Therefore, for all i, only one of u_i, v_i, u'_i, v'_i is nonempty, and it contains one symbol. When M follows an accepting computation and a head of M jumps over a symbol with a $\oplus$-jumping step, such a symbol is read later with the other head of M with a $\ominus$-reading step. Since jumping steps can occur arbitrarily between reading steps and since they do not depend on the current state of M, it follows that every xy, where x is a shuffle of $w_{\blacktriangleright\oplus}$ and $w_{\blacktriangleleft\ominus}$ and y is a shuffle of $w_{\blacktriangleleft\oplus}$ and $w_{\blacktriangleright\ominus}$, has to belong to $L(M)$. □

Lemma 4.35 *There is no* **1** *jumping $5' \to 3'$ WKFA M such that $L(M) = \{w_1 cc w_2 \mid w_1, w_2 \in \{a, b\}^*, \text{occur}(w_1 w_2, a) = \text{occur}(w_1 w_2, b)\}$.*

Proof *Basic idea.* We follow the proof structure of Lemma 4.29. Considering any sufficiently large constant k, we show that M cannot process all symbols of $a^{3k} b^{3k} cc b^{3k} a^{3k}$ using only configurations that have their debt bounded by k.
Formal proof (by contradition). Let $L = \{w_1 cc w_2 \mid w_1, w_2 \in \{a, b\}^*, \text{occur}(w_1 w_2, a) = \text{occur}(w_1 w_2, b)\}$, and let $M = (\Delta, Q, q_0, F, \delta)$ be a **1** jumping $5' \to 3'$ WKFA such that $L(M) = L$. Due to Lemma 4.28, there must exist a constant k for M such that M accepts all $w \in L$ using only configurations that have their debt bounded by k. Consider any k for M such that $k \geq 2$. Let $w = a^{3k} b^{3k} cc b^{3k} a^{3k}$.

Consider restrictions on how M can accept w so that it does not also accept any $w' \notin L$. Due to Lemma 4.34, to ensure that both c's are always next to each other, some parts of $w_{\blacktriangleright\oplus}, w_{\blacktriangleright\ominus}, w_{\blacktriangleleft\oplus}, w_{\blacktriangleleft\ominus}$ must remain empty.

Consider cases where two or three parts remain empty. To ensure the proper position of c's, only one head can read or only $\oplus$-reading or only $\ominus$-reading steps can be used. Note that the debt of an initial configuration of M is always 2 since at least cc has to be processed before an input can be successfully accepted. First, M cannot accept w with only one head because in this case jumping steps cannot be effectively used, the debt of the configuration of M reaches k after $k - 2$ reading steps, and no further reading is possible. Second, the situation is similar for M using only $\oplus$-reading steps. Third, for M using only $\ominus$-reading steps, the heads can meet between a's and b's and process up to $7k + 2$ symbols from w, but M is clearly still not able to process the whole w.

If only one part remains empty, the appropriate opposite part for the shuffle must contain both c's. Let us assume that $w_{\blacktriangleleft\ominus}$ remains empty. Consequently, $w_{\blacktriangleright\oplus}$ must contain at least $a^{3k}b^{3k}cc$. Consider possibilities how the $\blacktriangleright$-head can process $a^{3k}b^{3k}cc$ from w with $\oplus$-reading-steps. To process more than $k - 2$ symbols a with the $\blacktriangleright$-head, both heads has to cooperate. Let us assume that M first reads $k - 2$ times a with the $\blacktriangleleft$-head. Then, the $\blacktriangleleft$-head jumps to b's on the right-hand side of w, and the heads can start cooperate. The $\blacktriangleleft$-head reads b, the $\blacktriangleright$-head reads a, and this can be repeated $3k$ times. Now, the $\blacktriangleright$-head still has to process $b^{3k}cc$. Since there is the debt of $k - 2$ symbols b created with the initial readings of the $\blacktriangleleft$-head, the $\blacktriangleright$-head can read $2k - 4$ times b before the debt of the configuration of M reaches k. The $\blacktriangleright$-head still has to process $b^{k+4}cc$, but the debt cannot be compensated with the $\blacktriangleleft$-head any further. Consequently, the $\blacktriangleright$-head cannot process $a^{3k}b^{3k}cc$ from w with $\oplus$-reading-steps. The proof strategy and results are analogous for the other cases where $w_{\blacktriangleright\ominus}$, $w_{\blacktriangleleft\oplus}$, or $w_{\blacktriangleleft\ominus}$ remains empty.

Finally, we can see that M is not able to accept $w = a^{3k}b^{3k}ccb^{3k}a^{3k}$ when the debt of configurations of M is bounded by k. Since, for any k, $w \in L$, there is no constant k for M such that M accepts all $w \in L$ using only configurations that have their debt bounded by k. But that is a contradiction with the assumption that there is a **1** jumping $5' \to 3'$ WKFA M such that $L(M) = \{w_1ccw_2 \mid w_1, w_2 \in \{a, b\}^*, \text{occur}(w_1w_2, a) = \text{occur}(w_1w_2, b)\}$. □

Theorem 4.46 1 J5′→3′WK ⊂ J5′→3′WK.

Proof This theorem follows directly from Example 4.18 and Lemma 4.35. □

Example 4.19 Consider the following **1** jumping $5' \to 3'$ WKFA $M = (\{s, p\}, \{a, b\}, \delta, s, \{s\})$ with the state transition function δ:

$$\delta(s, a, \varepsilon, \oplus) = \{p\}, \quad \delta(p, \varepsilon, b, \oplus) = \{s\},$$
$$\delta(s, a, \varepsilon, \ominus) = \{p\}, \quad \delta(p, \varepsilon, b, \ominus) = \{s\}.$$

It is not hard to see that the resulting behavior is similar to Example 4.15. The automaton now reads a's and b's with separate steps and uses one auxiliary state that is not final. Consequently, $L(M) = \{w \in \{a, b\}^* \mid \text{occur}(w, a) = \text{occur}(w, b)\}$.

Lemma 4.36 *For every linear grammar G, there is a* **1** *jumping* $5' \to 3'$ *WKFA M such that $L(G) = L(M)$.*

Proof Consider any linear grammar $G = (\Sigma, \Delta, P, S)$ with $N = \Sigma - \Delta$. Every linear grammar has an equivalent grammar with rules in the form: (1) $S \to \varepsilon$, (2) $A \to aB$, (3) $A \to Ba$, (4) $A \to a$, where $A \in N$, $B \in (N - \{S\})$, and $a \in \Delta$. Without loss of generality, assume that G satisfies this special form of rules and $q_f \notin \Sigma$. Define the **1** jumping 5′ → 3′ WKFA $M = (N \cup \{q_f\}, \Delta, \delta, S, F)$, where F and δ are constructed in the following way:

(1) Set $F = \{q_f\}$. If $S \to \varepsilon \in P$, add S to F.
(2) For each $A \to aB \in P$, add B to $\delta(A, a, \varepsilon, \oplus)$.
(3) For each $A \to Ba \in P$, add B to $\delta(A, \varepsilon, a, \oplus)$.
(4) For each $A \to a \in P$, add q_f to $\delta(A, a, \varepsilon, \oplus)$.

Following the same reasoning as in Lemma 4.26, $L(M) = L(G)$. □

Theorem 4.47 LIN ⊂ 1 J5′→3′WK.

Proof This theorem follows directly from Example 4.19 and Lemma 4.36. □

On the all-final restriction

Lemma 4.37 *There is no* **F** *jumping 5′ → 3′ WKFA M such that* $L(M) = \{ca^ncb^nc \mid n \geq 0\} \cup \{\varepsilon\}$.

Proof *(by contradition)* Assume, for the sake of contradiction, that there is an **F** jumping 5′ → 3′ WKFA $M = (Q, \Delta, \delta, q_0, F)$ such that $L(M) = \{ca^ncb^nc \mid n \geq 0\} \cup \{\varepsilon\}$. Since M satisfies the all-final restriction, all states are final. Therefore, if in the first nonempty reading step the ►-head reads u and the ◄-head reads v, then uv or vu belongs to $L(M)$. Let $k_{\min} = \max\{|uv| \mid \delta(q, u, v, s) \neq \emptyset,\ q \in Q,\ u, v \in \Delta^*,\ s \in \{\oplus, \ominus\}\}$. Consider any k such that $k > k_{\min}$. Let $w = ca^kcb^kc$. It is not hard to see that for any first nonempty reading step on w (which reads u and v) it must hold that $\mathrm{occur}(uv, c) \leq 2$. However, for all $w' \in (L(M) - \{\varepsilon\})$ it holds that $\mathrm{occur}(w', c) = 3$. Therefore, if M accepts w, it also accepts $uv \notin L(M)$ or $vu \notin L(M)$. But that is a contradiction with the assumption that M exists. □

Theorem 4.48 F J5′→3′WK ⊂ J5′→3′WK.

Proof This theorem follows directly from Theorem 4.41 and Lemma 4.37. □

Proposition 4.4 F J5′→3′WK *and* **LIN** *are incomparable.*

Proof **LIN** ⊄ **F J5′→3′WK** follows from Lemma 4.37. **F J5′→3′WK** ⊄ **LIN** follows from Example 4.15. Lastly, **F J5′→3′WK** and **LIN** contain the language $\{a\}^*$. □

Lemma 4.38 *For every* $L \in$ **F J5′→3′WK** *it holds that* $\varepsilon \in L$.

Proof Consider any **F** jumping 5′ → 3′ WKFA $M = (Q, \Delta, \delta, q_0, F)$. Since $Q = F$, q_0 is a final state and $(q_0, \oplus, \varepsilon, \varepsilon, \varepsilon) \curvearrowright (q_0, \ominus, \varepsilon, \varepsilon, \varepsilon)$ can be done with a $\oplus$-jumping step; thus, $\varepsilon \in L(M)$. □

Proposition 4.5 **F J5′→3′WK** *and* **FIN** *are incomparable.*

Proof **FIN** $\not\subseteq$ **F J5′→3′WK** follows from Lemma 4.38. **F J5′→3′WK** $\not\subseteq$ **FIN** follows from Example 4.15. Lastly, it is trivial to construct an **F** jumping $5' \to 3'$ WKFA with two states that accepts the finite language $\{\varepsilon, a\}$. □

Theorem 4.49 **FIN**$_{\varepsilon\text{-}inc} \subset$ **F J5′→3′WK.**

Proof Consider any alphabet Δ and $L = \{x_1, \ldots, x_n\} \in$ **FIN**$_{\varepsilon\text{-inc}}$ such that $x_i \in \Delta^*$, $i = 1, \ldots, n$, $n \geq 1$. Define the **F** jumping $5' \to 3'$ WKFA $M = (\{q_0, q_f\}, \Delta, \delta, q_0, \{q_0, q_f\})$, where δ is constructed in the following way: For each $x \in L$, set $\delta(q_0, x, \varepsilon, \oplus) = \{q_f\}$. It is clear that $L(M) = L$. Thus, **FIN**$_{\varepsilon\text{-inc}} \subseteq$ **F J5′→3′WK**. **F J5′→3′WK** $\not\subseteq$ **FIN**$_{\varepsilon\text{-inc}}$ follows from Example 4.15. □

Example 4.20 Consider the following **F** (in fact, even **N**) jumping $5' \to 3'$ WKFA $M = (\{s\}, \{a, b, c\}, \delta, s, \{s\})$ with the state transition function δ:

$$\delta(s, a, b, \oplus) = \{s\}, \quad \delta(s, a, b, \ominus) = \{s\},$$
$$\delta(s, cc, \varepsilon, \oplus) = \{s\}, \quad \delta(s, \varepsilon, cc, \oplus) = \{s\}.$$

This is a modification of Examples 4.15 and 4.18. The first two transitions ensure that M can accept any input containing the same number of a's and b's. The other two transitions ensure that the accepted inputs can also contain an arbitrary number of substrings cc. Therefore, $L(M) = \{w \in \{a, b, cc\}^* \mid \text{occur}(w, a) = \text{occur}(w, b)\}$.

Proposition 4.6 **F J5′→3′WK** *and* **1 J5′→3′WK** *are incomparable.*

Proof First, **1 J5′→3′WK** $\not\subseteq$ **F J5′→3′WK** follows from Theorem 4.47 and Lemma 4.37. Second, let L be the language $L(M)$ from Example 4.20. The proof by contradiction from Lemma 4.35 can be modified in a straightforward way so that it shows that there is no **1** jumping $5' \to 3'$ WKFA M such that $L(M) = L$. Therefore, **F J5′→3′WK** $\not\subseteq$ **1 J5′→3′WK**. Lastly, both families contain $\{a\}^*$. □

On the stateless restriction

Lemma 4.39 *There is no* **N** *jumping* $5' \to 3'$ *WKFA* $M = (\{q_0\}, \Delta, \delta, q_0, \{q_0\})$ *such that* $L(M) \in$ **FIN** *and* $L(M) \neq \{\varepsilon\}$.

Proof First, due to Lemma 4.38, $L(M)$ must always contain ε. Second, by contradiction, assume that there is a **N** jumping $5' \to 3'$ WKFA M_2 such that $L(M_2) \in$ **FIN** and $L(M_2)$ contains a nonempty string. Since there is only one state, any $\oplus/\ominus$-reading step can be repeated arbitrarily many times. Therefore, if in the first nonempty reading step the ▸-head reads u and the ◂-head reads v, then $u^i v^i$ or $v^i u^i$ belongs to $L(M_2)$ for all $i \geq 1$. Thus, if M_2 accepts a nonempty string, $L(M_2) \notin$ **FIN**. But that is a contradiction with the assumption that M_2 exists. Consequently, if $L(M) \in$ **FIN**, $L(M) = \{\varepsilon\}$. □

Theorem 4.50 N J5′→3′WK ⊂ F J5′→3′WK.

Proof From Lemma 4.33, **N J5′→3′WK** ⊆ **F J5′→3′WK**. **F J5′→3′WK** ⊈ **N J5′→3′WK** follows from Theorem 4.49 and Lemma 4.39. □

Proposition 4.7 N J5′→3′WK *is incomparable with* **LIN**, **FIN**, *and* **FIN**$_{\varepsilon\text{-}inc}$.

Proof **LIN**, **FIN**, **FIN**$_{\varepsilon\text{-inc}}$ ⊈ **N J5′→3′WK** follows from Lemma 4.39. **N J5′→3′WK** ⊈ **LIN**, **FIN**, **FIN**$_{\varepsilon\text{-inc}}$ follows from Example 4.15. Next, **N J5′→3′WK** and **LIN** contain the language $\{a\}^*$. Finally, there is the sole language $\{\varepsilon\}$ that **N J5′→3′WK** shares with **FIN** and **FIN**$_{\varepsilon\text{-inc}}$. □

Proposition 4.8 N J5′→3′WK *and* **1 J5′→3′WK** *are incomparable.*

Proof First, **1 J5′→3′WK** ⊈ **N J5′→3′WK** follows from Theorem 4.47 and Lemma 4.39. Second, **N J5′→3′WK** ⊈ **1 J5′→3′WK** follows from Example 4.20 and the proof of Proposition 4.6. Lastly, both families contain the language $\{a\}^*$. □

On the combined restrictions

Proposition 4.9 FS J5′→3′WK ⊂ F J5′→3′WK.

Proof Let $L = \{cca^n cc \mid n \geq 0\} \cup \{\varepsilon\}$. It is trivial to construct an **F** jumping 5′ → 3′ WKFA that accepts L. However, there is no **FS** jumping 5′ → 3′ WKFA that accepts L. By contradiction. Assume that there is an **FS** jumping 5′ → 3′ WKFA M such that $L(M) = L$. Using the basic premise of Lemma 4.37, all c's has to be read with the first nonempty reading step. Nonetheless, a single head cannot read all c's in one step if they are arbitrarily far away from each other—a contradiction with the assumption that M exists. □

Theorem 4.51 FIN$_{\varepsilon\text{-}inc}$ **⊂ FS J5′→3′WK.**

Proof **FS J5′→3′WK** ⊈ **FIN**$_{\varepsilon\text{-inc}}$ follows from $\{a\}^* \in$ **FS J5′→3′WK**. The rest of the proof is analogous to Theorem 4.49. □

Example 4.21 Consider the following **FS** jumping 5′ → 3′ WKFA $M = (\{s, p\}, \{a, b, c\}, \delta, s, \{s, p\})$ with the state transition function δ:

$$\begin{aligned} \delta(s, a, \varepsilon, \oplus) &= \{p\}, & \delta(p, \varepsilon, b, \oplus) &= \{s\}, \\ \delta(s, a, \varepsilon, \ominus) &= \{p\}, & \delta(p, \varepsilon, b, \ominus) &= \{s\}, \\ \delta(s, cc, \varepsilon, \oplus) &= \{s\}, & \delta(s, \varepsilon, cc, \oplus) &= \{s\}, \\ \delta(p, cc, \varepsilon, \oplus) &= \{p\}, & \delta(p, \varepsilon, cc, \oplus) &= \{p\}. \end{aligned}$$

As a result, $L(M) = \{w \in \{a, b, cc\}^* \mid \text{occur}(w, a) = \text{occur}(w, b) \text{ or } \text{occur}(w, a) = \text{occur}(w, b) + 1\}$.
This automaton is just a combination of previous approaches from Examples 4.19 and 4.20. Note that $L(M)$ resembles the resulting language of Example 4.20.

Proposition 4.10 **FS J5′→3′WK** *and* **1 J5′→3′WK** *are incomparable.*

Proof First, **1 J5′→3′WK** $\not\subseteq$ **FS J5′→3′WK** follows from the language in the proof of Proposition 4.9. Second, let L be the language $L(M)$ from Example 4.21. The proof by contradiction from Lemma 4.35 can be modified in a straightforward way so that it shows that there is no **1** jumping $5' \rightarrow 3'$ WKFA M such that $L(M) = L$. Therefore, **FS J5′→3′WK** $\not\subseteq$ **1 J5′→3′WK**. Lastly, **FS J5′→3′WK** and **1 J5′→3′WK** contain the language $\{a\}^*$. □

Proposition 4.11 **F1 J5′→3′WK** $\subset$ **FS J5′→3′WK***.*

Proof From Lemma 4.33, **F1 J5′→3′WK** $\subseteq$ **FS J5′→3′WK**. It is trivial to construct an **FS** jumping $5' \rightarrow 3'$ WKFA that accepts $\{aa\}^*$. However, there cannot be an **F1** jumping $5' \rightarrow 3'$ WKFA that accepts only even-length inputs. □

Proposition 4.12 **F1 J5′→3′WK** *and* **LIN** *are incomparable.*

Proof **LIN** $\not\subseteq$ **F1 J5′→3′WK** follows from $\{aa\}^* \in$ **LIN**. Considering Example 4.21, there is an **F1** jumping $5' \rightarrow 3'$ WKFA M such that $L(M) = \{w \in \{a, b\}^* \mid \text{occur}(w, a) = \text{occur}(w, b) \text{ or } \text{occur}(w, a) = \text{occur}(w, b) + 1\}$. Clearly, $L(M)$ is not a linear language. Lastly, **F1 J5′→3′WK** and **LIN** contain the language $\{a\}^*$. □

Corollary 4.2 **F1 J5′→3′WK** $\subset$ **1 J5′→3′WK***.*

Theorem 4.52 **NS J5′→3′WK** $\subset$ **REG***.*

Proof **NS J5′→3′WK** $\subseteq$ **REG** can be proven by construction. We show that for any **NS** jumping $5' \rightarrow 3'$ WKFA we can construct a finite automaton that accepts the same language. Consider any **NS** jumping $5' \rightarrow 3'$ WKFA $M = (\{q_0\}, \Delta, \delta, q_0, \{q_0\})$. The following claims hold:

Claim A Any $w \in L(M)$ can be expressed in the following special form $w = x_1 y_1' \cdots x_n y_n' x_1' y_1 \cdots x_m' y_m$, where $x_i, y_i', x_j', y_j \in \Delta^*$, for all $i = 1, \dots, n$ and $j = 1, \dots, m$, for some $n, m \geq 1$, and for all x_i, y_i', x_j', y_j hold:

(i) either $x_i = \varepsilon$ or $\delta(q_0, x_i, \varepsilon, \oplus) = \{q_0\}$,
(ii) either $y_j = \varepsilon$ or $\delta(q_0, \varepsilon, y_j, \oplus) = \{q_0\}$,
(iii) either $x_j' = \varepsilon$ or $\delta(q_0, x_j', \varepsilon, \ominus) = \{q_0\}$,
(iv) either $y_i' = \varepsilon$ or $\delta(q_0, \varepsilon, y_i', \ominus) = \{q_0\}$. □

Proof (Claim A) Due to the restrictions, parts (i), (ii), (iii), and (iv) cover all possible types of state transitions. The accepted input can be always divided into two parts, depending on the position where the heads of M meet each other during the processing of this input. The first part $x_1 y_1' \cdots x_n y_n'$ is a combination of $\oplus$-readings with the ►-head and $\ominus$-readings with the ◄-head. Likewise, the second part $x_1' y_1 \cdots x_m' y_m$ is a combination of $\ominus$-readings with the ►-head and $\oplus$-readings with the ◄-head. To get the uncertain reading order forced by the jumping steps, we also allow each part x_i, y_i', x_j', y_j to be empty. Therefore, all $w \in L(M)$ have to be able to satisfy this special form. □

Claim B Any $w \in \Delta^*$ that can be expressed in the previous special form belongs to $L(M)$. □

Proof (Claim B) Considering the restrictions, M has only one state, and only one head can read in a step. Therefore, if there is a possible reading step, it can be used arbitrarily many times. Furthermore, the possible reading steps can change only when the heads meet each other. Also, since each head reads separately, there cannot be any dependence between the first and second part of the input in the special form. Consequently, any $w \in \Delta^*$ that can be expressed in the form from Claim 1 has to belong to $L(M)$. □

Considering both claims, it is easy to construct a finite automaton that accepts all inputs of this special form. **REG** $\not\subseteq$ **NS J5′→3′WK** follows from Lemma 4.39. □

Proposition 4.13 N1 J5′→3′WK ⊂ NS J5′→3′WK.

Proof This proof is analogous to that of Proposition 4.11. □

Proposition 4.14 *The following relationships hold:*

(*i*) **NS J5′→3′WK ⊂ N J5′→3′WK**
(*ii*) **NS J5′→3′WK ⊂ FS J5′→3′WK**
(*iii*) **N1 J5′→3′WK ⊂ F1 J5′→3′WK**

Proof Examples 4.15 and 4.21 and Proposition 4.12 show that **N J5′→3′WK**, **FS J5′→3′WK**, and **F1 J5′→3′WK** contain some non-regular languages. Considering Lemma 4.33 and Theorem 4.52, all three proposed relationships directly follow. □

Proposition 4.15 FS J5′→3′WK *and* **N J5′→3′WK** *are incomparable.*

Proof (*by contradition*) First, **FS J5′→3′WK** $\not\subseteq$ **N J5′→3′WK** follows from Lemma 4.39 and Theorem 4.51. Second, let $L = \{a^n b^n \mid n \geq 0\}$. It is trivial to construct an **N** jumping 5′ → 3′ WKFA that accepts L. However, there is no **FS** jumping 5′ → 3′ WKFA that accepts L. For the sake of contradiction, assume that there is an **FS** jumping 5′ → 3′ WKFA $M = (Q, \Delta, \delta, q_0, F)$ such that $L(M) = L$. Due to the restrictions, if a head of M reads u in a step, it must hold that $\text{occur}(u, a) = \text{occur}(u, b)$. Otherwise, there would be $w' \in L(M)$ such that $\text{occur}(w', a) \neq \text{occur}(w', b)$. Let $k_{\min} = \max\{|v_1 v_2| \mid \delta(q, v_1, v_2, s) \neq \emptyset,\ q \in Q,\ v_1, v_2 \in \Delta^*,\ s \in \{\oplus, \ominus\}\}$. Consider any k such that $k > k_{\min}$. Let $w = a^{2k} b^{2k}$. Clearly, when M processes w, each head can read u such that $\text{occur}(u, a) = \text{occur}(u, b)$ no more than once. However, these balanced steps can thus process only less than $2k$ symbols. Consequently, if M accepts w, it also accepts some $w' \notin L$—a contradiction with the assumption that M exists. Therefore, **N J5′→3′WK** $\not\subseteq$ **FS J5′→3′WK**. Lastly, **FS J5′→3′WK** and **N J5′→3′WK** contain the language $\{a\}^*$. □

Proposition 4.16 F1 J5′→3′WK *and* **NS J5′→3′WK** *are incomparable.*

Proof First, **F1 J5′→3′WK** $\not\subseteq$ **NS J5′→3′WK** follows from Lemma 4.39 and $\{\varepsilon, a\} \in$ **F1 J5′→3′WK**. Second, **NS J5′→3′WK** $\not\subseteq$ **F1 J5′→3′WK** follows from $\{aa\}^* \in$ **NS J5′→3′WK**. Lastly, both families contain the language $\{a\}^*$. □

Proposition 4.17 **REG** *is incomparable with* **F J5′→3′WK**, **N J5′→3′WK**, **FS J5′→3′WK**, *and* **F1 J5′→3′WK**.

Proof First, Examples 4.15 and 4.21 and Proposition 4.12 show that **F J5′→3′WK**, **N J5′→3′WK**, **FS J5′→3′WK**, and **F1 J5′→3′WK** contain some non-regular languages. Second, let $L = \{ca^ncb^mc \mid n, m \geq 0\} \cup \{\varepsilon\}$. L is clearly a regular language. Considering the proof of Lemma 4.37 and the previous results, we can easily see that **F J5′→3′WK**, **N J5′→3′WK**, **FS J5′→3′WK**, and **F1 J5′→3′WK** cannot contain L. Lastly, all families contain the language $\{a\}^*$. □

Proposition 4.18 **FIN** *is incomparable with* **FS J5′→3′WK**, **F1 J5′→3′WK**, **NS J5′→3′WK**, *and* **N1 J5′→3′WK**.

Proof Considering previous results. First, **FS J5′→3′WK**, **F1 J5′→3′WK**, **NS J5′→3′WK**, and **N1 J5′→3′WK** cannot contain $\emptyset$. Second, **FS J5′→3′WK**, **F1 J5′→3′WK**, **NS J5′→3′WK**, and **N1 J5′→3′WK** contain $\{a\}^*$. Lastly, all families contain $\{\varepsilon\}$. □

Proposition 4.19 $\mathbf{FIN}_{\varepsilon\text{-}inc}$ *is incomparable with* **F1 J5′→3′WK**, **NS J5′→3′WK**, *and* **N1 J5′→3′WK**.

Proof Considering previous results. First, **F1 J5′→3′WK**, **NS J5′→3′WK**, and **N1 J5′→3′WK** cannot contain $\{\varepsilon, aa\}$. Second, **F1 J5′→3′WK**, **NS J5′→3′WK**, and **N1 J5′→3′WK** contain $\{a\}^*$. Lastly, all families contain $\{\varepsilon\}$. □

All the obtained results comparing the accepting power of different variants of jumping $5' \to 3'$ WKFAs are summarized in Figure 4.11.

Conclusion

The results clearly show that, with the addition of the jumping mechanism into the model, the accepting power has been increased above sensing $5' \to 3'$ WKFA. The model is now able to accept some nonlinear and even some non-context-free languages. On the other hand, the jumping movement of the heads is restricted compared to jumping finite automata, and this limits its capabilities to accept languages that require a more sophisticated discontinuous information processing. Considering the comparison with full-reading sensing $5' \to 3'$ WKFAs, the results are not yet clear and further research is required. However, we know that there are some languages, like $\{a^nb^nc^n \mid n \geq 0\}$, that cannot be accepted by jumping $5' \to 3'$ WKFAs and that are accepted by full-reading sensing $5' \to 3'$ WKFAs (see Nagy [2008, 2010, 2013]).

If we compare the hierarchies of language families related to the restricted variants of jumping $5' \to 3'$ WKFAs and sensing $5' \to 3'$ WKFAs (see Nagy [2010, 2013]; Nagy et al. [2017]), there are several noticeable remarks. Most importantly, the 1-limited restriction (**1**) has a negative impact on the accepting power, which is

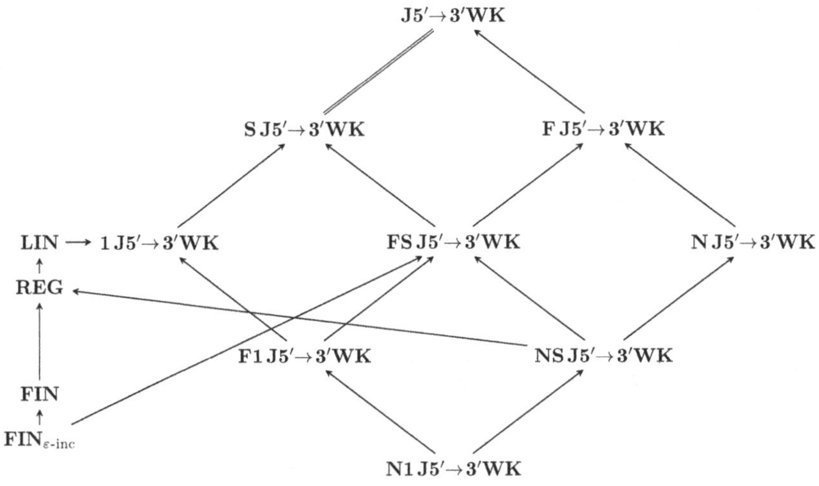

Fig. 4.11 **J5′→3′WK** and its language family relationships (in this figure, any two families are incomparable unless explicitly diagrammed otherwise).

usually not the case in sensing 5′ → 3′ WKFAs. Secondly, when several restrictions are combined together, the hierarchy structure resembles the alternative structure of sensing 5′ → 3′ WKFAs without the sensing distance from Nagy et al. [2017]. Lastly, almost all restricted variants, with the exception of **NS** and **N1**, are still able to accept some nonlinear languages, which cannot be accepted by any variants of sensing 5′ → 3′ WKFAs.

The reader may notice that the ⊖-jumping can be used only in situations where it is forced by the current configuration. Jumping finite automata usually immediately erase symbols from the configuration and do not use the auxiliary symbol #. It is thus a question for future research whether we can safely remove this part from the model and keep the accepting power intact.

Finally, let us note that Section 4.3 has introduced a less restrictive combination of jumping finite automata and classical WKFAs. Compared to jumping 5′ → 3′ WKFAs, both JWKFA heads jump freely over the input tape while all symbols on both input tape strands have to be processed. This approach generates a very different behavior compared to sensing 5′ → 3′ WKFAs, which resembles the original behavior of GJFAs in many respects.

Part III
Jumping Grammars

As a whole, the theory of computation makes use of incredibly many different language-defining models. Nevertheless, despite their huge diversity and quantity, in terms of the way they work, all these models can be classified into two fundamental categories—automata, which accept languages, and grammars, which generate them. The theory of jumping computation is no exception. While the previous part of this book has been devoted to jumping automata, the present part covers jumping grammars as the fundamental grammatical models that work in a discontinuous or, to put it in the terminology of the present monograph, jumping way.

This part consists of Chapters 5 through 7. Chapter 5 studies the jumping generation of language by classical grammars, which work in a strictly sequential way. Then, Chapter 6 discusses the same topic in terms of grammars that work in semi-parallel. Finally, Chapter 7 explores the jumping generation of language by pure sequential and parallel grammars, which have only terminals.

Chapter 5
Sequential Jumping Grammars

This three-section chapter is organized as follows. Section 5.1 gives an introduction into its subject. Section 5.2 recalls all the definitions that are needed and illustrates them by examples. Then, Section 5.3 presents fundamental results as well as open problems concerning jumping grammars.

5.1 Introduction

To start with, recall the notion of a classical grammar (see Section 2.3), G, which represents a language-generating rewriting system based upon an alphabet of symbols and a finite set of production rules or, simply, rules. The alphabet of symbols is divided into two disjoint subalphabets—the alphabet of terminal symbols and the alphabet of nonterminal symbols. Each production rule represents a pair of the form (x, y), where x and y are strings over the alphabet of G. Customarily, (x, y) is written as $x \rightarrow y$, where x and y are referred to as the left-hand side and the right-hand side of $x \rightarrow y$. Starting from a special start nonterminal symbol, G repeatedly rewrites strings according to its rules until it obtains a sentence—that is, a string that solely consists of terminal symbols; the set of all sentences represents the language generated by the grammar. During every rewriting step of this generating process, G always applies a single rule, so it represents a grammatical model that works strictly sequentially.

To see the similarity as well as the difference between the classical grammatical concept and its jumping version, take a closer look at a single rewriting step in G. Classically, G rewrites a string z according to $x \rightarrow y$ in the following three-phase way:

(1) selects an occurrence of x in z;
(2) erases it;
(3) inserts y precisely at the position of this erasure.

More briefly and formally, let $z = uxv$, where u and v are strings; by using $x \to y$, G rewrites uxv as uyv.

Introduced in Křivka and Meduna [2015], the notion of a *jumping grammar*—the central subject of this chapter—is conceptualized just like that of a classical grammar, and it works sequentially, too; however, it rewrites strings in a different way. More precisely, consider G as a jumping grammar. Let z and $x \to y$ have the same meaning as above. G rewrites a string z according to $x \to y$ in the following way:

(j1) it performs (1) and (2), then
(j2) it inserts y anywhere in uv.

Therefore, during (j2), G can jump over a portion of the rewritten string in either direction and inserts y there. Formally, by using $x \to y$, G rewrites ucv as udv, where u, v, w, c, d are strings such that either (i) $c = xw$ and $d = wy$ or (ii) $c = wx$ and $d = yw$. Otherwise, it coincides with the standard notion of a grammar.

To illustrate the difference between classical and jumping versions of grammars, consider any sentential form occurring in any derivation made by a context-free grammar G. Let A be the leftmost nonterminal in this sentential form. If G represents a classical non-jumping context-free grammar, it can never modify the terminal prefix preceding A throughout the rest of this derivation. However, if G is a jumping context-free grammar, it can perform this modification by inserting the right-hand side of a rule into this prefix.

The fundamental purpose of this chapter is to give an essential body of rigorous knowledge concerning jumping grammars. Since the determination of the power of language-defining devices has always fulfilled perhaps the most important role in formal language theory, it focuses its coverage on this topic. Regarding the general versions of jumping grammars, it demonstrates that they are as powerful as the classical unrestricted grammars. As there exist many important special versions of the unrestricted grammars, defined in Section 2.3, the present chapter discusses their jumping counterparts as well. It studies the jumping versions of context-free grammars and their special cases, including regular grammars, right-linear grammars, linear grammars, and context-free grammars of finite index. Surprisingly, all of them have a different power than their classical counterparts. The chapter also compares the generative power of jumping grammars with the accepting power of jumping finite automata, covered in Part II. More specifically, it demonstrates that regular jumping grammars are as powerful as these automata.

Although applications are systematically covered later in this book (Chapter 9), we can make some preliminary remarks and suggestions concerning the expected future to jumping grammars. It should be clear by now that jumping grammars primarily serve as grammatical models that allow us to explore information processing performed in a discontinuous way adequately and rigorously. Consequently, applications of these grammars are expected in any scientific area involving this kind of information processing, ranging from applied mathematics through computational linguistics and compiler writing up to data mining and biology-related informatics. Taking into account the way these grammars are conceptualized, we see that they are particularly useful and applicable under the circumstances that primarily concern the number of occurrences of various symbols or substrings rather than their mutual context. To give a more specific insight into possible applications of this kind in terms of bioinformatics, consider DNA computing, whose significance is indisputable in computer science at present. Recall that DNA is a molecule encoding genetic information by a repetition of four basic units called nucleotides—namely, guanine, adenine, thymine, and cytosine, denoted by letters G, A, T, and C, respectively. In terms of formal language theory, a DNA sequence is described as a string over $\{G, A, T, C\}$; for instance,

$$GGGGAGTGGGATTGGGAGAGGGGTTTGCCCCGCTCCC$$

Suppose that a DNA-computing-related investigation needs to study all the strings that contain the same number of Cs and Gs and the same number of As and Ts; for instance, $CGGCATCCGGTA$ is a proper string, but $CGCACCGGTA$ is not. Consider the jumping right-linear grammar containing rules

$$1 \to C2, 2 \to G1, 1 \to 3, 3 \to A4, 4 \to T3, 3 \to \varepsilon$$

where 1 through 4 are nonterminal symbols with 1 being the start nonterminal, and G, A, T, and C are terminal symbols. As is obvious, this grammar generates the language consisting of all the strings satisfying the above-stated requirements. Therefore, as we can see, jumping grammars may fulfill a useful role in studies related to DNA computing in the future, and we return to this topic in Chapter 9 in greater detail.

5.2 Definitions and Examples

Now, we introduce four modes of derivation relations, three of which represent jumping derivation steps. We also briefly recall some terminology, such as the notion of a phrase-structure grammar, introduced earlier in this book (see Section 2.3).

Definition 5.1 Let $G = (\Sigma, \Delta, P, S)$ be a PSG. We introduce four *modes of derivation steps* as derivation relations over Σ^*—namely, ${}_s\Rightarrow$, ${}_{lj}\Rightarrow$, ${}_{rj}\Rightarrow$, and ${}_j\Rightarrow$.

Let $u, v \in \Sigma^*$. We define the four derivation relations as follows:

(i) $u \ {}_s\Rightarrow v$ in G iff there exist $x \to y \in P$ and $w, z \in \Sigma^*$ such that $u = wxz$ and $v = wyz$;

(ii) $u \ {}_{lj}\Rightarrow v$ in G iff there exist $x \to y \in P$ and $w, t, z \in \Sigma^*$ such that $u = wtxz$ and $v = wytz$;

(iii) $u \ {}_{rj}\Rightarrow v$ in G iff there exist $x \to y \in P$ and $w, t, z \in \Sigma^*$ such that $u = wxtz$ and $v = wtyz$;

(iv) $u \ {}_j\Rightarrow v$ in G iff $u \ {}_{lj}\Rightarrow v$ or $u \ {}_{rj}\Rightarrow v$ in G.

Let ${}_h\Rightarrow$ be one of the four derivation relations (i) through (iv) over Σ^*; in other words, h equals s, lj, rj, or j. As usual, for every $n \geq 0$, the nth power of ${}_h\Rightarrow$ is denoted by ${}_h\Rightarrow^n$. The transitive-reflexive closure and the transitive closure of ${}_h\Rightarrow$ are denoted by ${}_h\Rightarrow^*$ and ${}_h\Rightarrow^+$, respectively.

Example 5.1 Consider the following RG

$$G = (\{A, B, C, a, b, c\}, \Delta = \{a, b, c\}, P, A)$$

where $P = \{A \to aB,\ B \to bC,\ C \to cA,\ C \to c\}$. Observe that

$$L(G, {}_s\Rightarrow) = \{abc\}\{abc\}^*, \text{ but}$$

$$L(G, {}_j\Rightarrow) = \{w \in \Delta^* \mid \text{occur}(w, a) = \text{occur}(w, b) = \text{occur}(w, c)\}$$

Notice that although $L(G, {}_s\Rightarrow)$ is regular, $L(G, {}_j\Rightarrow) \in \mathbf{CS}$ is a well-known non-context-free language.

Example 5.2 Consider the following CSG $G = (\{S, A, B, a, b\}, \{a, b\}, P, S)$ containing the following rules:

$$\begin{aligned} S &\to aABb \\ S &\to ab \\ AB &\to AABB \\ aA &\to aa \\ Bb &\to bb \end{aligned}$$

Trivially, $L(G, {}_s\Rightarrow) = \{a^n b^n \mid n \geq 1\}$. Using ${}_j\Rightarrow$, we can make the following derivation sequence (the rewritten substring is underlined):

$$\underline{S}\ {}_j\Rightarrow a\underline{AB}b\ {}_j\Rightarrow aAAB\underline{Bb}\ {}_j\Rightarrow \underline{aA}ABbb\ {}_j\Rightarrow a\underline{aA}Bbb\ {}_j\Rightarrow a\underline{Bb}baa\ {}_j\Rightarrow abbbaa$$

Notice that $L(G, {}_s\Rightarrow)$ is context-free, but we cannot generate this language by any CFG, CSG or even MONG in jumping derivation mode.

Example 5.3 Consider the language of all well-written arithmetic expressions with parentheses (,) and [,] (see semi-Dyck language D_2 in Example 2.9). Eliminate everything but the parentheses in this language to obtain the language $L(G, {}_s\Rightarrow)$ defined by the CFG $G = (\Sigma = \{E, (,), [,]\}, \Delta = \{(,), [,]\}, \{E \to (E)E,\ E \to [E]E,\ E \to \varepsilon\}, E)$. G is not of a finite index (see [Salomaa, 1973, Example 10.1 on page 210]). Consider the jumping RLG $H = (\Sigma, \Delta, P_H, E)$, where P_H contains

$$\begin{aligned} E &\to ()E \\ E &\to []E \\ E &\to \varepsilon \end{aligned}$$

Since H is a RLG, there is at most one occurrence of E in any sentential form derived from E in H, so H is of index 1. Next, we sketch a proof that $L(G, {}_s\Rightarrow) = L(H, {}_j\Rightarrow)$. As is obvious, $\{\varepsilon, (), []\} \subseteq L(G, {}_s\Rightarrow) \cap L(H, {}_j\Rightarrow)$. Consider

$$\alpha E \beta \ {}_s\Rightarrow \alpha(E)E\beta \, [E \rightarrow (E)E] \ {}_s\Rightarrow^* \alpha(\gamma)\delta\beta$$

in G with $\gamma \neq \varepsilon$. H can simulate this derivation as follows

$$\alpha E \beta \ {}_j\Rightarrow \alpha()E\beta \ {}_j\Rightarrow^* \alpha()\delta' E \delta'' \beta \ {}_j\Rightarrow \alpha(xE)\delta\beta \ {}_j\Rightarrow^* \alpha(\gamma)\delta\beta$$

where $\delta = \delta'\delta''$, $x \in \{(), []\}$, and $\alpha, \beta, \gamma, \delta \in \Sigma^*$. For $\gamma = \varepsilon$, we modify the previous jumping derivation so we make a jumping derivation step from $\alpha()\delta' E \delta'' \beta$ to $\alpha()\delta\beta$ by $E \rightarrow \varepsilon$ in H. We deal with $E \rightarrow [E]E$ analogically, so $L(G, {}_s\Rightarrow) \subseteq L(H, {}_j\Rightarrow)$. Since $L(G, {}_s\Rightarrow)$ contains all proper strings with the three types of parentheses, to prove $L(H, {}_j\Rightarrow) \subseteq L(G, {}_s\Rightarrow)$, we have to show that H cannot generate an improper string of parentheses. As each non-erasing rule of H inserts both left and right parentheses in the sentential form at once, the numbers of parentheses are always correctly balanced. In addition, in H we cannot generate an improper mixture of two kinds of parentheses, such as $([)]$, or an improper parenthesis order, such as $)($, so $L(G, {}_s\Rightarrow) = L(H, {}_j\Rightarrow)$.

5.3 Results

This section primarily investigates the generative power of jumping grammars. First, it compares the generative power of jumping grammars with the accepting power of jumping finite automata. More specifically, it demonstrates that regular jumping grammars are as powerful as jumping finite automata. Regarding grammars, the general versions of jumping grammars are as powerful as classical phrase-structure grammars. As there exist many important special versions of these classical grammars, we discuss their jumping counterparts in the present section as well. It studies the jumping versions of context-free grammars and their special cases, including regular grammars, right-linear grammars, and linear grammars. Surprisingly, all of them have a different power than their classical counterparts. In its conclusion, this section formulates several open problems and suggests future investigation areas.

Lemma 5.1 $\{a\}^*\{b\}^* \notin$ **JMON**.

Proof Assume that there exists a MONG $G = (\Sigma, \Delta, P, S)$ such that $L(G, {}_j\Rightarrow) = \{a\}^*\{b\}^*$. Let $p\colon\ x \rightarrow y \in P$ be the last applied rule during a derivation $S \ {}_j\Rightarrow^+ w$, where $w \in L(G, {}_j\Rightarrow)$; that is, $S \ {}_j\Rightarrow^* uxv \ {}_j\Rightarrow w \, [p]$, where $u, v, w \in \Delta^*$ and $y \in \{a\}^+ \cup \{b\}^+ \cup \{a\}^+\{b\}^+$. In addition, assume that the sentential form uxv is longer than x such that $uv \in \{a\}^+\{b\}^+$.

(i) If y contains at least one symbol b, the last jumping derivation step can place y at the beginning of the sentence and create a string from

$$\{a,b\}^*\{b\}\{a,b\}^*\{a\}\{a,b\}^*$$

that does not belong to $\{a\}^*\{b\}^*$.

(ii) By analogy, if y contains at least one symbol a, the last jumping derivation step can place y at the end of the sentence and, therefore, place at least one a behind some bs.

This is a contradiction, so there is no MONG that generates the regular language $\{a\}^*\{b\}^*$ using ${}_j\Rightarrow$. □

We reopen a discussion related to Lemma 5.1 at the end of of this section.

Corollary 5.1 *The following pairs of language families are incomparable but not disjoint:*

(i) **REG** *and* **JMON***;*
(ii) **CF** *and* **JMON***;*
(iii) **REG** *and* **JREG***;*
(iv) **CF** *and* **JREG**.

Proof Since **REG** ⊂ **CF**, it is sufficient to prove that **REG** − **JMON**, **JREG** − **CF**, and **REG** ∩ **JREG** are nonempty. By Lemma 5.1,

$$\{a\}^*\{b\}^* \in \mathbf{REG} - \mathbf{JMON}.$$

In Example 5.1, we define a jumping RG that generates a non-context-free language that belongs to **JREG** − **CF**. Observe that regular language $\{a\}^*$ belongs to **JREG**, so **REG** ∩ **JREG** is nonempty. □

As even some very simple regular language such as $\{a\}^+\{b\}^+$ cannot be generated by jumping derivation in CSGs or even MONGs, we pinpoint the following open problem and state a theorem comparing these families with context-sensitive languages.

Open Problem Is **JCS** ⊆ **JMON** proper? □

Theorem 5.1 **JMON** ⊂ **CS**.

Proof To see that **JMON** ⊆ **CS**, we demonstrate how to transform any jumping MONG, $G = (\Sigma_G, \Delta, P_G, S)$, to a MONG, $H = (\Sigma_H, \Delta, P_H, S)$, such that $L(G, {}_j\Rightarrow) = L(H, {}_s\Rightarrow)$. Set $\Sigma_H = N_H \cup \Delta$ and $N_H = N_G \cup \{\bar{X} \mid X \in \Sigma_G\}$. Let π be the homomorphism from Σ_G^* to Σ_H^* defined by $\pi(X) = \bar{X}$ for all $X \in \Sigma_G$. Set $P_H = P_1 \cup P_2$, where

$$P_1 = \bigcup_{\alpha \to \beta \in P_G} \{\alpha \to \pi(\beta), \pi(\beta) \to \beta\}$$

and

$$P_2 = \bigcup_{\alpha \to \beta \in P_G} \{X\pi(\beta) \to \pi(\beta)X, \pi(\beta)X \to X\pi(\beta) \mid X \in \Sigma_G\}$$

As is obvious, $L(G, {}_j\Rightarrow) = L(H, {}_s\Rightarrow)$. Clearly, $\{a\}^*\{b\}^* \in \mathbf{CS}$. Thus, by Lemma 5.1, $\mathbf{CS} - \mathbf{JMON} \neq \emptyset$, so this theorem holds. □

Relationships between the Language Families Resulting from Various Jumping Grammars

We establish several relationships between the language families generated by jumping versions of grammars defined earlier in this section.

Theorem 5.2 JRL = JLIN = JCFfin.

Proof Since **JRL** ⊆ **JLIN** ⊆ **JCFfin** follows from the definitions, it suffices to proof that **JCFfin** ⊆ **JRL**.

Construction. Let Σ and Δ be an alphabet and an alphabet of terminals, respectively. Set $N = \Sigma - \Delta$. Let $\eta: \Sigma \to N \cup \{\varepsilon\}$ be the homomorphism such that $\eta(X) = X$ if $X \in N$; otherwise, $\eta(X) = \varepsilon$. Let $\tau: \Sigma \to \Delta \cup \{\varepsilon\}$ be the homomorphism such that $\tau(X) = X$ if $X \in \Delta$; otherwise, $\eta(X) = \varepsilon$. As usual, extend η and τ to strings of symbols.

For every CFG $G = (\Sigma_G, \Delta, P_G, S)$ and index $k \geq 1$, we construct a RLG $H = (\Sigma_H, \Delta, P_H, \langle S \rangle)$ such that $L(G, {}_j\Rightarrow_k) = L(H, {}_j\Rightarrow)$. Set

$$\Sigma_H = \{\langle x \rangle \mid x \in \bigcup_{i=1}^{k} (\Sigma_G - \Delta)^i\} \cup \Delta$$

and set

$$P_H = \{\langle \alpha A \beta \rangle \to \tau(x)\langle \gamma \rangle \mid A \to x \in P_G, \alpha, \beta \in N^*, \gamma = \alpha\beta\eta(x), 1 \leq |\gamma| \leq k\}$$
$$\cup \{\langle A \rangle \to x \mid A \to x \in P_G, x \in \Delta^*\}$$

Basic Idea. CFG G working with index k means that every sentential form contains at most k nonterminal symbols. In jumping derivation mode, the position of a nonterminal symbol does not matter for context-free rewriting. Together with the finiteness of N, we can store the list of nonterminals using just one nonterminal from constructed $\Sigma_H - \Delta$ in the simulating RLG.

For every jumping derivation step $\gamma A \delta \ {}_j\Rightarrow_k \gamma' x \delta'$ by $A \to x$ in G, there is a simulating jumping derivation step $\tau(\bar{\gamma})\langle \eta(\gamma A \delta) \rangle \tau(\bar{\delta}) \ {}_j\Rightarrow \tau(\bar{\gamma}')\tau(x)\langle \eta(\gamma \delta x) \rangle \tau(\bar{\delta}')$ in H, where $\gamma\delta = \gamma'\delta' = \bar{\gamma}\bar{\delta} = \bar{\gamma}'\bar{\delta}'$. The last simulating step of jumping application of $A \to w$ with $w \in \Delta^*$ replaces the only nonterminal of the form $\langle A \rangle$ by w that can be placed anywhere in the string. □

Consider the finite index restriction in the family **JCFfin** in Theorem 5.2. Dropping this restriction gives rise to the question, whether the inclusion **JCFfin** $\subseteq$ **JCF** is proper that was proved in Madejski [2016].

Theorem 5.3 ([Madejski, 2016, Theorem 3.10])

$$\mathbf{JCFfin} \subset \mathbf{JCF}.$$

Indeed, from a broader perspective, an investigation of finite-index-based restrictions placed upon various jumping grammars and their effect on the resulting generative power represents a challenging open problem area as illustrated by Example 5.3.

Theorem 5.4 $\mathbf{JCF}^{-\varepsilon} = \mathbf{JCF}$.

Proof It is straightforward to establish this theorem by analogy with the same statement reformulated in terms of ordinary CFGs, which work based on ${}_s\Rightarrow$ (see [Meduna, 2000, Theorem 5.1.3.2.4 on page 328]). □

Lemma 5.2 $\mathbf{RE} \subseteq \mathbf{JRE}$.

Proof *Construction.* For every PSG $G = (\Sigma_G, \Delta, P_G, S_G)$, we construct another PSG $H = (\Sigma_H = \Sigma_G \cup \{S_H, \$, \#, \lfloor, \rfloor\}, \Delta, P_H, S_H)$ such that $L(G, {}_s\Rightarrow) = L(H, {}_j\Rightarrow)$. $S_H, \$, \#, \lfloor$, and $\rfloor$ are new nonterminal symbols in H. Set

$$P_H = \{S_H \rightarrow \#S_G, \# \rightarrow \lfloor\$, \lfloor\rfloor \rightarrow \#, \# \rightarrow \varepsilon\}$$

$$\cup\{\$\alpha \rightarrow \rfloor\beta \mid \alpha \rightarrow \beta \in P_G\}$$

Basic Idea. Nonterminal # has at most one occurrence in the sentential form. # is generated by the initial rule $S_H \rightarrow \#S_G$. This symbol participates in the beginning and end of every simulation of the application of a rule from P_G. Each simulation consists of several jumping derivation steps:

(i) # is expanded to a string of two nonterminals—marker of a position ($\lfloor$), where the rule is applied in the sentential form, and auxiliary symbol ($) presented as a left context symbol in the left-hand side of every simulated rule from P_G.
(ii) For each $x \rightarrow y$ from P_G, $\$x \rightarrow \rfloor y$ is applied in H. To be able to finish the simulation properly, the right-hand side ($\rfloor y$) of applied rule has to be placed right next to the marker symbol $\lfloor$; otherwise, we cannot generate a sentence.
(iii) The end of the simulation (rule $\lfloor\rfloor \rightarrow \#$) checks that the jumping derivation was applied like in terms of ${}_s\Rightarrow$.
(iv) In the end, # is removed to finish the generation of a string of terminal symbols.

Claim A Let y be a sentential form of H; that is, $S_H\ {}_j\Rightarrow^* y$. For every $X \in \{\#, \$, \lfloor, \rfloor, S_H\}$, $\mathrm{occur}(y, X) \leq 1$. □

Proof (Claim A) The claim follows from the rules in P_H (see the construction in the proof of Lemma 5.2). Note that occur$(y, \{\#, \$, \lfloor, \rfloor, S_H\}) \leq 2$ and in addition, if symbol # occurs in y then occur$(y, \{\$, \lfloor, \rfloor, S_H\}) = 0$. □

Define the homomorphism $h\colon \Sigma_H^* \to \Sigma_G^*$ as $h(X) = X$ for all $X \in \Sigma_G$, $h(S_H) = S_G$, and $h(Y) = \varepsilon$ for all $Y \in \{\$, \#, \lfloor, \rfloor\}$.

Claim B If $S_G\ {}_s\!\Rightarrow^m w$ in G, where $w \in \Delta^*$ and $m \geq 0$, then $S_H\ {}_j\!\Rightarrow^* w$ in H. □

Proof (Claim B) First, we prove by induction on $m \geq 0$ that for every $S_G\ {}_s\!\Rightarrow^m x$ in G with $x \in \Sigma_G^*$, there is $S_H\ {}_j\!\Rightarrow^* x'$ in H such that $h(x') = x$.

Basis. For $S_G\ {}_s\!\Rightarrow^0 S_G$ in G, there is $S_H\ {}_j\!\Rightarrow \#S_G$ in H.

Induction Hypothesis. Suppose there exists $k \geq 0$ such that $S_G\ {}_s\!\Rightarrow^m x$ in G implies that $S_H\ {}_j\!\Rightarrow^* x'$ in H, where $h(x') = x$, for all $0 \leq m \leq k$.

Induction Step. Assume that $S_G\ {}_s\!\Rightarrow^k y\ {}_s\!\Rightarrow x$ in G. By the induction hypothesis, $S_H\ {}_j\!\Rightarrow^* y'$ in H with $h(y') = y$.

The derivation step $y\ {}_s\!\Rightarrow x$ in G is simulated by an application of three jumping rules from P_H in H to get $y'\ {}_j\!\Rightarrow^3 x'$ with $h(x') = x$ as follows.

$$\begin{aligned} y' = u'\#v'\ &{}_j\!\Rightarrow u''\lfloor\$\alpha v''\ \ [\# \to \lfloor\$] \\ &{}_j\!\Rightarrow u''\lfloor\rfloor\beta v''\ \ [\lfloor\rfloor \to \#] \\ &{}_j\!\Rightarrow u'''\#v'''\ \ \ [\# \to \varepsilon]\ = x' \end{aligned}$$

where $u'v' = u''\alpha v''$ and $u''\beta v'' = u'''v'''$.

In case $x \in \Delta^*$, there is one additional jumping derivation step during the simulation that erases the only occurrence of #-symbol (see Claim A) by rule $\# \to \varepsilon$.

Note that $h(x)$ for $x \in \Delta^*$ is the identity. Therefore, in case $x \in \Delta^*$ the induction proves the claim. □

Claim C If $S_H\ {}_j\!\Rightarrow^m w$ in H, for some $m \geq 0$, where $w \in \Delta^*$, then $S_G\ {}_s\!\Rightarrow^* w$ in G.□

Proof (Claim C) To prove this claim, first, we prove by induction on $m \geq 0$ that for every $S_H\ {}_j\!\Rightarrow^m x$ in H with $x \in \Sigma_H^*$ such that there exists a jumping derivation $x\ {}_j\!\Rightarrow^* w$, where $w \in \Delta^*$, then $S_G\ {}_s\!\Rightarrow^* x'$ in G such that $h(x) = x'$.

Basis. For $m = 0$, when we have $S_H\ {}_j\!\Rightarrow^0 S_H\ {}_j\!\Rightarrow^* w$ in H, then there is $S_G\ {}_s\!\Rightarrow^0 S_G$ in G such that $h(S_H) = S_G$. Furthermore, for $m = 1$, we have $S_H\ {}_j\!\Rightarrow^1 \#S_G\ {}_j\!\Rightarrow^* w$ in H, then again there is $S_G\ {}_s\!\Rightarrow^0 S_G$ in G such that $h(\#S_G) = S_G$, so the basis holds.

Induction Hypothesis. Suppose there exists $k \geq 1$ such that $S_H\ {}_j\!\Rightarrow^m x\ {}_j\!\Rightarrow^* w$ in H implies that $S_G\ {}_s\!\Rightarrow^* x'$ in G, where $h(x) = x'$, for all $1 \leq m \leq k$.

Induction Step. Assume that $S_H\ {}_j\!\Rightarrow^k y\ {}_j\!\Rightarrow x\ {}_j\!\Rightarrow^* w$ in H with $w \in \Delta^*$. By the induction hypothesis, $S_G\ {}_s\!\Rightarrow^* y'$ in G such that $h(y) = y'$. Let $u, v \in \Sigma_G^*$ and $\bar{u}, \bar{v} \in \Sigma_H^*$. Let us examine the following possibilities of $y\ {}_j\!\Rightarrow x$ in H:

(i) $y = u\#v \;_j\!\Rightarrow \bar{u}\lfloor\$\bar{v} = x$ in H such that $uv = \bar{u}\bar{v}$: Simply, $y' = uv \;_s\!\Rightarrow^0 uv$ in G and by Claim A $h(\bar{u}\lfloor\$\bar{v}) = h(\bar{u}\bar{v}) = h(uv) = uv$.
(ii) $u\lfloor\$\alpha v \;_j\!\Rightarrow \bar{u}\rfloor\beta\bar{v}$ in H by rule $\$\alpha \rightarrow \rfloor\beta$ such that $uv = \bar{u}\bar{v}$: In fact, to be able to rewrite $\lfloor$, the symbol $\lfloor$ needs $\rfloor$ as its right neighbor, so $u = \bar{u}$ and $v = \bar{v}$ in this jumping derivation step; otherwise, the jumping derivation is prevented from generating a string of terminals. According to rule $\alpha \rightarrow \beta$, $u\alpha v \;_s\!\Rightarrow u\beta v$ in G and $h(\bar{u}\rfloor\beta\bar{v}) = u\beta v$.
(iii) $u\lfloor\,\rfloor v \;_j\!\Rightarrow \bar{u}\#\bar{v}$ in H such that $uv = \bar{u}\bar{v}$: In G, $uv \;_s\!\Rightarrow^0 uv$ and $h(\bar{u}\#\bar{v}) = h(\bar{u}\bar{v}) = h(uv) = uv$.
(iv) $u\#v \;_j\!\Rightarrow uv$ in H by $\# \rightarrow \varepsilon$: Trivially, $uv \;_s\!\Rightarrow^0 uv$ in G and $h(uv) = uv$. □

If $x \in \Delta^*$, then the induction proves the claim. □

This closes the proof of Lemma 5.2.

Theorem 5.5 JRE = RE.

Proof By the Turing-Church thesis, **JRE** $\subseteq$ **RE**. The opposite inclusion holds by Lemma 5.2 that is proved in details by Claim B and Claim C. □

Properties of Jumping Derivations

We demonstrate that the order of nonterminals in a sentential form of jumping CFGs is irrelevant. Then, in this section, we study the semilinearity of language families generated by various jumping grammars.

As a generalization of the proof of Theorem 5.2, we give the following lemma demonstrating that the order in which nonterminals occur in sentential forms is irrelevant in jumping derivation mode based on context-free rules in terms of generative power.

Lemma 5.3 *Let η and τ be the homomorphisms from the proof of Theorem 5.2 and $X \in \{RG, RLG, LG, CFG\}$. For every X $G = (\Sigma, \Delta, P, S)$ with $N = \Sigma - \Delta$, if $S \;_j\!\Rightarrow^* \gamma \;_j\!\Rightarrow^m w$ in G, $m \geq 0$, $\gamma \in \Sigma^*$, $w \in \Delta^*$, then for every $\delta \in \Sigma^*$ such that $\tau(\gamma) = \tau(\delta)$ and $\eta(\delta) \in \mathrm{perm}(\eta(\gamma))$, there is $\delta \;_j\!\Rightarrow^* w$ in G.*

Proof We prove this lemma by induction on $m \geq 0$.

Basis. Let $m = 0$. That is, $S \;_j\!\Rightarrow^* \gamma \;_j\!\Rightarrow^0 w$ in G, so $\gamma = w$. By $\tau(\delta) = \tau(\gamma)$, we have $\gamma = w = \delta$, so $\delta \;_j\!\Rightarrow^0 w$ in G.

Induction Hypothesis. Assume that there exists $k \geq 0$ such that the lemma holds for all $0 \leq m \leq k$.

Induction Step. Assume that $S \;_j\!\Rightarrow^* \gamma \;_j\!\Rightarrow \gamma' \, [A \rightarrow x] \;_j\!\Rightarrow^k w$ in G with $k \geq 0$. Observe that $\tau(\delta) = \tau(\gamma)$ and $\eta(\delta) \in \mathrm{perm}(\eta(\gamma))$. By the above-mentioned assumption, $|\eta(\gamma)| \geq 1$—that is $|\eta(\delta)| \geq 1$. Thus, the jumping derivation $\delta \;_j\!\Rightarrow^* w$

in G can be written as $\delta\ {}_j\!\Rightarrow \delta'\ [A \rightarrow x]\ {}_j\!\Rightarrow^* w$. Since all the rules in G are context-free, the position of A in δ and its context is irrelevant, and the occurrence of A in δ is guaranteed by the lemma precondition. During the application of $A \rightarrow x$, (1) an occurrence of A is found in δ, (2) removed, and (3) the right-hand side of the rule, x, is inserted anywhere in δ instead of A without preserving the position of the rewritten A. Assume x is inserted into δ' so that $\tau(\delta') = \tau(\gamma')$. We also preserve that $\eta(\delta') \in \text{perm}(\eta(\gamma'))$; therefore, the lemma holds.

Notice that even if there is no derivation $S\ {}_j\!\Rightarrow^* \delta$ in G, the lemma holds.

Note that based on the proof of Lemma 5.3, we can turn any jumping version of a CFG to an equivalent jumping CFG satisfying a modified Greibach normal form, in which each rule is of the form $A \rightarrow \alpha\beta$, where $\alpha \in \Delta^*, \beta \in N^*$. Observe that $\alpha \notin \Delta$. Consider, for instance, a context-free rule p with $\alpha = a_1 \cdots a_n$. By an application of p during a derivation of a string of terminals w, we arrange that a_1 appears somewhere in front of a_n in w. In other words, from Theorem 3.5 and Corollary 3.2 together with Theorem 5.8, it follows that for any language L, $L \in$ **JREG** implies $L = \text{perm}(L)$, which means that the order of all terminals in $w \in L$ is utterly irrelevant.

Corollary 5.2 *Let $X \in \{RG, RLG, LG, CFG\}$. For every X G, $S\ {}_j\!\Rightarrow^* \gamma\ {}_j\!\Rightarrow^* w$ in G implies an existence of a derivation of the following form*

$$S\ {}_j\!\Rightarrow^* \alpha\beta\ {}_j\!\Rightarrow^* w \text{ in } G$$

where $\alpha = \tau(\gamma)$, $\beta \in \text{perm}(\eta(\gamma))$, S is the start nonterminal, and w is a string of terminals.

Lemma 5.4 **JREG**, **JRL**, **JLIN**, *and* **JCF** *are semilinear.*

Proof By Parikh's Theorem (see [Harrison, 1978, Theorem 6.9.2 on page 228]), for each context-free language $L \subseteq \Sigma^*$, $\psi_\Sigma(L)$ is semilinear. Let G be a CFG such that $L(G, {}_s\!\Rightarrow) = L$. From the definition of ${}_j\!\Rightarrow$ and CFG it follows that $\psi_\Sigma(L(G, {}_s\!\Rightarrow)) = \psi_\Sigma(L(G, {}_j\!\Rightarrow))$, so $\psi_\Sigma(L(G, {}_j\!\Rightarrow))$ is semilinear as well. □

Recall that the family of context-sensitive languages is not semilinear (for instance, from [Dassow and Păun, 1989, Example 2.3.1 and Theorem 2.3.1], it follows that $\{a^{2^n} \mid n \geq 0\} \in$ **CS**, but it is not a semilinear language). By no means, this result rules out that **JCS** or **JMON** are semilinear. There is, however, another kind of results concerning multiset grammars (see Kudlek et al. [2000]) saying that a context-sensitive multiset grammar generates a non-semilinear language. The multiset grammars work with Parikh vector of a sentential form so the order of symbols in the sentential form is irrelevant. Then, all permutations of terminal strings generated by the grammar belong to the generated language.

Instead of the full definition of multiset grammars (see Kudlek et al. [2000]), based on notions from the theory of macrosets, we introduce *multiset derivation mode* concerning the classical string formal language theory.

Definition 5.2 Let $G = (\Sigma, \Delta, P, S)$ be a PSG and $u, v \in \Sigma^*$; then, $u\ {}_m\!\Rightarrow v\ [x \to y]$ in G iff there exist $x \to y \in P$ and $t, t', z, z' \in \Sigma^*$ such that $txt' \in \mathrm{perm}(u)$, $zyz' \in \mathrm{perm}(v)$, and $tt' \in \mathrm{perm}(zz')$.

Lemma 5.5 *Let G be a PSG; then, $w \in L(G, {}_m\!\Rightarrow)$ implies that* $\mathrm{perm}(w) \subseteq L(G, {}_m\!\Rightarrow)$.

Proof Consider Definition 5.2 with v representing every permutation of v in every $u\ {}_m\!\Rightarrow v$ in G to see that this lemma holds true. □

Let the family of languages generated by a MONG using ${}_m\!\Rightarrow$ be denoted by **mMON**. Recall that **mMON** is not semilinear (see Kudlek et al. [2000]). As every context-sensitive multiset grammar can be transformed into a CSG that generates the same language under jumping derivation mode, we establish the following theorem.

Theorem 5.6 JCS *is not semilinear. Neither is* **JMON**.

Proof Recall that **mMON** contains non-semilinear languages (see [Kudlek et al., 2000, Theorem 1]). Thus, to prove Theorem 5.6, we only need to prove that **mMON** $\subseteq$ **JCS** because **JCS** $\subseteq$ **JMON** follows from Definition 5.1.

Construction. For every MONG $G = (\Sigma_G, \Delta, P_G, S)$, we next construct a CSG $H = (\Sigma_H, \Delta, P_H, S)$ such that $L(G, {}_m\!\Rightarrow) = L(H, {}_j\!\Rightarrow)$. Let $N_G = \Sigma_G - \Delta$ and h be the homomorphism $h\colon \Sigma_G^* \to \Sigma_H^*$ defined as $h(X) = X$ for all $X \in N_G$ and $h(a) = \langle a \rangle$ for all $a \in \Delta$. First, set $\Sigma_H = \Sigma_G \cup N_t \cup N_{cs}$, where $N_t = \{\langle a \rangle \mid a \in \Delta\}$ and $N_{cs} = \{{}_pX \mid X \in N_G \cup N_t,\ p \in P_G \text{ with } |\mathrm{lhs}(p)| > 1\}$. For every $p \in P_G$ with $|\mathrm{lhs}(p)| > 1$, let $g_p\colon (N_G \cup N_t)^* \to N_{cs}^*$ be the homomorphism defined as $g_p(X) = {}_pX$ for all $X \in N_G \cup N_t$. Set $P_t = \{\langle a \rangle \to a \mid a \in \Delta\}$, $P_{cf} = \{A \to h(x) \mid A \to x \in P_G,\ A \in \Sigma_G - \Delta \text{ and } x \in \Sigma_G^*\}$, and $P_{cs} = \emptyset$. For every rule $p\colon X_1X_2\cdots X_n \to Y_1Y_2\cdots Y_m \in P_G$ with $2 \le n \le m$, where $X_i, Y_{i'} \in \Sigma_G$, $1 \le i \le n$, and $1 \le i' \le m$, add these $2n$ new rules with labels $p_1, p_2, \ldots, p_{2n}$

$$
\begin{aligned}
p_1\colon&\quad h(X_1X_2\cdots X_n) \to g_p(h(X_1))h(X_2\cdots X_n)\\
p_2\colon&\quad g_p(h(X_1))h(X_2\cdots X_n) \to g_p(h(X_1X_2))h(X_3\cdots X_n)\\
&\quad\vdots\\
p_n\colon&\quad g_p(h(X_1X_2\cdots X_{n-1}))h(X_n) \to g_p(h(X_1X_2\cdots X_{n-1}X_n))\\
p_{n+1}\colon&\quad g_p(h(X_1X_2\cdots X_n)) \to h(Y_1)g_p(h(X_2\cdots X_n))\\
p_{n+2}\colon&\quad h(Y_1)g_p(h(X_2\cdots X_n)) \to h(Y_1Y_2)g_p(h(X_3\cdots X_n))\\
&\quad\vdots\\
p_{2n}\colon&\quad h(Y_1Y_2\cdots Y_{n-1})g_p(h(X_n)) \to h(Y_1Y_2\cdots Y_{n-1}Y_nY_{n+1}\cdots Y_m)
\end{aligned}
$$

into P_{cs}. Set $P_c = \{A \to A \mid A \in \Sigma_H - \Delta\}$. Finally, set $P_H = P_{cf} \cup P_t \cup P_c \cup P_{cs}$.

Basic Idea. There are two essential differences between multiset derivation mode of a MONG and jumping derivation mode of a CSG.

(I) While a MONG rewrites a string at once in a single derivation step, a CSG rewrites only a single nonterminal that occurs within a given context during a single derivation step.

(II) In the multiset derivation mode, the mutual neighborhood of the rewritten symbols is completely irrelevant—that is, G applies any rule without any restriction placed upon the mutual adjacency of the rewritten symbols in the multiset derivation mode (see Definition 5.2). To put this in a different way, G rewrites any permutation of the required context in this way.

In the construction of the jumping CSG H, which simulates the multiset MONG G, we arrange (II) as follows.

(II.a) In H, the only rules generating terminals belong to P_t. By using homomorphism h, in every other rule, each terminal a is changed to the corresponding nonterminal $\langle a \rangle$.

(II.b) In P_c, there are rules that can rearrange the order of all nonterminals arbitrarily in any sentential form of H. Thus, considering (II.a), just like in G, no context restriction placed upon the mutual adjacency of rewritten symbols occurs in H. Indeed, H only requires the occurrence of the symbols from $h(\text{lhs}(p))$ during the simulation of an application of $p \in P_G$.

In order to arrange (I), an application of a monotonous context-sensitive rule $p\colon X_1X_2 \cdots X_n \to Y_1Y_2 \cdots Y_m \in P_G$, $2 \leq n \leq m$ in $u \;{}_m\!\Rightarrow v\; [p]$ in G is simulated in H by the following two phases.

(i) First, H verifies that a sentential form u contains all symbols from $h(\text{lhs}(p))$ and marks them by subscript p for the consecutive rewriting. Therefore, to finish the simulation of the application of p, H has to use rules created based on p during the construction of P_{cs} since no other rules from P_H rewrite symbols ${}_pX$, $X \in N_G \cup N_t$.

$$
\begin{array}{llll}
u \;{}_j\!\Rightarrow^* & \alpha_0\, X'_1 X'_2 \cdots X'_n\, \beta_0\, [\rho_0] & {}_j\!\Rightarrow & u_1\, [p_1] \\
{}_j\!\Rightarrow^* & \alpha_1\, {}_pX'_1 X'_2 \cdots X'_n\, \beta_1\, [\rho_1] & {}_j\!\Rightarrow & u_2\, [p_2] \\
{}_j\!\Rightarrow^* & \alpha_2\, {}_pX'_1\, {}_pX'_2 \cdots X'_n\, \beta_2\, [\rho_2] & {}_j\!\Rightarrow & u_3\, [p_3] \\
\vdots & & & \\
{}_j\!\Rightarrow^* & \alpha_{n-1}\, {}_pX'_1\, {}_pX'_2 \cdots {}_pX'_{n-1} X'_n\, \beta_{n-1}\, [\rho_{n-1}] & {}_j\!\Rightarrow & u_n\, [p_n]
\end{array}
$$

where $\rho_i \in P_c^*$ for $0 \leq i < n$ and $X'_\ell = h(X_\ell)$ for $1 \leq \ell \leq n$.

(ii) Then, by performing $u_n \;{}_j\!\Rightarrow^* v$, H simulates the application of p in G.

$$
\begin{array}{llll}
u_n \;{}_j\!\Rightarrow^* & \alpha_n\, {}_pX'_1\, {}_pX'_2 \cdots {}_pX'_n\, \beta_n\, [\rho_n] & {}_j\!\Rightarrow & u_{n+1}\, [p_{n+1}] \\
{}_j\!\Rightarrow^* & \alpha_{n+1}\, Y'_1\, {}_pX'_2 \cdots {}_pX'_n\, \beta_{n+1}\, [\rho_{n+1}] & {}_j\!\Rightarrow & u_{n+2}\, [p_{n+2}] \\
\vdots & & & \\
{}_j\!\Rightarrow^* & \alpha_{2n-1}\, Y'_1 Y'_2 \cdots Y'_{n-1}\, {}_pX'_n\, \beta_{2n-1}\, [\rho_{2n-1}] & {}_j\!\Rightarrow & u_{2n}\, [p_{2n}] \\
= & \alpha_{2n}\, Y'_1 Y'_2 \cdots Y'_m\, \beta_{2n} & {}_j\!\Rightarrow^* & v\, [\rho_{2n}]
\end{array}
$$

□

where $\rho_i \in P_c^*$ for $n \leq i \leq 2n$, $X'_\ell = h(X_\ell)$ for $1 \leq \ell \leq n$, and $Y'_k = h(Y_k)$ for $1 \leq k \leq m$.

The simulation of application of rules of P_G is repeated using rules from $P_c \cup P_{cf} \cup P_{cs}$ in H until a multiset derivation of a string of terminals in G is simulated. (In fact, we can simultaneously simulate more than one application of a rule from P_G if there is no interference in H.)

Then, in the final phase of the entire simulation, each nonterminal $\langle a \rangle$ is replaced with terminal a by using rules from P_t. To be precise, the rules of P_t can be applied even sooner, but symbols rewritten by these rules can be no longer rewritten by rules from $P_c \cup P_{cf} \cup P_{cs}$ in H.

To formally prove that $L(G, {}_m\Rightarrow) = L(H, {}_j\Rightarrow)$, we establish the following claims.

Claim A Every $w \in L(H, {}_j\Rightarrow)$ can be generated by a derivation of the form

$$S \;{}_j\Rightarrow^* w' \;{}_j\Rightarrow^* w \text{ in } H \text{ such that } w' = h(w) \text{ and } w \in \Delta^*$$

Proof (Claim A) In the construction given in the proof of Theorem 5.6, we introduce P_{cf} and P_{cs} such that for every $p \in P_H - P_t$, $\text{rhs}(p) \in (\Sigma_H - \Delta)^*$. In $S \;{}_j\Rightarrow^* w'$, we apply rules only from $P_H - P_t$ so $w' \in N_t^*$, and no terminal symbol occurs in any sentential form in $S \;{}_j\Rightarrow^* w'$. Then, by rules from P_t, we generate w such that $w = h(w')$. □

Claim B If $w \in L(H, {}_j\Rightarrow)$, then $\text{perm}(w) \subseteq L(H, {}_j\Rightarrow)$. □

Proof (Claim B) Let $w \in \Delta^*$. Assume that w is generated in H as described in Claim A—that is, $S \;{}_j\Rightarrow^* w' \;{}_j\Rightarrow^* w$ such that $w' = h(w)$. Since rules from P_t rewrite nonterminals in w' in a one-by-one way in the jumping derivation mode, we have $w' \;{}_j\Rightarrow^* w''$ in H for every $w'' \in \text{perm}(w)$. □

Claim C If $S \;{}_m\Rightarrow^\ell v$ in G for some $\ell \geq 0$, then $S \;{}_j\Rightarrow^* v'$ in H such that $v' \in \text{perm}(h(v))$. □

Proof (Claim C) We prove this claim by induction on $\ell \geq 0$.

Basis. Let $\ell = 0$. That is, $S \;{}_m\Rightarrow^0 S$ in G, so $S \;{}_j\Rightarrow^0 S$ in G. By $h(S) = S$, $S \in \text{perm}(h(S))$.

Induction Hypothesis. Assume that the claim holds for all $0 \leq \ell \leq k$, for some $k \geq 0$.

Induction Step. Take any $S \;{}_m\Rightarrow^{k+1} v$. Express $S \;{}_m\Rightarrow^{k+1} v$ as

$$S \;{}_m\Rightarrow^k u \;{}_m\Rightarrow v\; [p: x \to y]$$

in G. By the induction hypothesis, $S \;{}_j\Rightarrow^* u'$ in H such that $u' \in \text{perm}(h(u))$. According to the form of monotonous rule $p: x \to y \in P_G$, there are the following two cases, (i) and (ii), concerning $u \;{}_m\Rightarrow v$ in G to examine.

(i) $|x| = 1$: Let $x = A$. By the induction hypothesis, $\text{occur}(u, A) \geq 1$ implies $\text{occur}(u', A) \geq 1$. By the construction according to p, we have $p': A \to h(y) \in P_{cf}$. Assume $u = u_1 A u_2 \;{}_m\Rightarrow v$ in G with $u_1 y u_2 \in \text{perm}(v)$. Then, $u' = u_1' A u_2' \;{}_j\Rightarrow u_3' h(y) u_4'\; [p'] = v'$ in H, where $u_1' u_2' = u_3' u_4'$, so $v' \in \text{perm}(h(v))$.

(ii) $|x| \geq 2$: Let $x = X_1X_2\cdots X_n$, $y = Y_1Y_2\cdots Y_m$, where $|x| = n \leq m = |y|$, $X_i \in \Sigma_G$, $1 \leq i \leq n$, but $x \notin \Delta^*$, $Y_{i'} \in \Sigma_G$, $1 \leq i' \leq m$. By construction of P_{cs}, we have $p_1, p_2, \ldots, p_{2n} \in P_H$. If p can be applied in G, then, by the induction hypothesis, $\text{occur}(u, X_i) = \text{occur}(u', \{h(X_i)\})$ for $1 \leq i \leq n$. To simulate the application of p in H, first, apply rules from P_c to yield $u' {}_j\!\Rightarrow^* u'_1 h(X_1X_2\cdots X_n)u'_2$. Next, consecutively apply $p_1, p_2, \ldots, p_{2n}$ so $u'_1 h(X_1X_2\cdots X_n)u'_2 {}_j\!\Rightarrow^* u'_3 h(Y_1Y_2\cdots Y_m)u'_4 = v'$ with $u'_1u'_2 = u'_3u'_4$ and $v' \in \text{perm}(h(v))$. □

By Claim C with $v = w$ and $w \in \Delta^*$, for every $S {}_m\!\Rightarrow^* w$ in G, there is a derivation $S {}_j\!\Rightarrow^* w''$ in H such that $w'' \in \text{perm}(h(w))$. By Claim A, there is a jumping derivation in H from w'' to w' such that $w' \in \Delta^*$ and $w' \in \text{perm}(w)$. Therefore, by Lemma 5.5 and Claim B, if $w \in L(G, {}_m\!\Rightarrow)$, then $\text{perm}(w) \subseteq L(H, {}_j\!\Rightarrow)$, so $L(G, {}_m\!\Rightarrow) \subseteq L(H, {}_j\!\Rightarrow)$.

Claim D If $S {}_j\!\Rightarrow^\ell v {}_j\!\Rightarrow^* \bar{v}$ in H for some $\ell \geq 0$, then $S {}_m\!\Rightarrow^* v'$ in G such that $\bar{v} \in \text{perm}(h(v'))$. □

Proof (Claim D) We prove this claim by induction on $\ell \geq 0$.

Basis. Let $\ell = 0$. Express $S {}_j\!\Rightarrow^0 S {}_j\!\Rightarrow^* S$ as $S {}_j\!\Rightarrow^0 S {}_j\!\Rightarrow^0 S$ in H; therefore, $S {}_m\!\Rightarrow^0 S$ in G. By $h(S) = S$, $S \in \text{perm}(h(S))$.

Induction Hypothesis. Assume that the claim holds for all $0 \leq \ell \leq k$, for some $k \geq 0$.

Induction Step. Take any $S {}_j\!\Rightarrow^{k+1} v {}_j\!\Rightarrow^* \bar{v}$. Express $S {}_j\!\Rightarrow^{k+1} v {}_j\!\Rightarrow^* \bar{v}$ as

$$S {}_j\!\Rightarrow^k u {}_j\!\Rightarrow v\, [q\colon x \to y] {}_j\!\Rightarrow^* \bar{v}$$

in H. Without any loss of generality, assume that $q \in P_H - P_t$ so $u, v \in (\Sigma_H - \Delta)^*$ (see Claim A). If $q \in P_{cf} \cup P_{cs}$, then p denotes the rule from P_G that implied the addition of q into P_{cf} or P_{cs} during the construction in the proof of Theorem 5.6. Without any loss of generality and with respect to p from P_G, assume that there is no simulation of another context-sensitive rule from P_G in progress in H so $\text{occur}(u_1u_2, N_{cs}) = \text{occur}(v_1v_2, N_{cs}) = 0$, where $u = u_1xu_2$ and $v = v_1yv_2$. By the induction hypothesis, $S {}_j\!\Rightarrow^* u {}_j\!\Rightarrow^* \bar{u}$ in H implies $S {}_m\!\Rightarrow^* u'$ in G such that $\bar{u} \in \text{perm}(h(u'))$. Now, we study several cases based on the form of q:

(i) $q \in P_c$ and $x = y = A$: Then, in a jumping derivation $u {}_j\!\Rightarrow v\, [q] {}_j\!\Rightarrow^0 \bar{v}$ in H, $u = u_1Au_2$ and $v = v_1Av_2$, where $u_1u_2 = v_1v_2$, so $v = \bar{v} \in \text{perm}(u)$. By the induction hypothesis, with $u {}_j\!\Rightarrow^0 \bar{u}$ in H so $u = \bar{u}$, there is a derivation $S {}_m\!\Rightarrow^* u'$ in G such that $u \in \text{perm}(h(u'))$. Together with $\bar{v} \in \text{perm}(u)$, there is also a derivation $S {}_m\!\Rightarrow^* u' {}_m\!\Rightarrow^0 v'$ in G with $\bar{v} \in \text{perm}(h(v'))$.
(ii) $q \in P_{cf}$ and $x = A$: Then, $u = u_1Au_2$ and $v = v_1yv_2$ with $u_1u_2 = v_1v_2$ and $v {}_j\!\Rightarrow^0 \bar{v}$ in H, so $v = \bar{v}$. By the induction hypothesis, with $u {}_j\!\Rightarrow^0 \bar{u}$ in H so $u = \bar{u}$, there is $S {}_m\!\Rightarrow^* u'$ in G with $u \in \text{perm}(h(u'))$ and we can write $u' = u'_1Au'_2$. By the construction, $p\colon A \to y \in P_G$, so together with the induction hypothesis we have $S {}_m\!\Rightarrow^* u'_1Au'_2 {}_m\!\Rightarrow v'\, [p]$ in G, where $v' \in \text{perm}(u'_1yu'_2)$, so $\bar{v} \in \text{perm}(h(v'))$.

(iii) $q = p_i \in P_{cs}$, where $1 \le i \le 2n$ and $n = |\,\mathrm{lhs}(p)|$: Express $S\ {}_j\!\Rightarrow^k u\ {}_j\!\Rightarrow v\ {}_j\!\Rightarrow^* \bar{v}$ in H as

$$S\ {}_j\!\Rightarrow^{k-i+1} \tilde{u}\ {}_j\!\Rightarrow^{i-1} u\,[\tilde{\rho}]\ {}_j\!\Rightarrow v\,[p_i]\ {}_j\!\Rightarrow^* \alpha_{2n} h(Y_1Y_2\cdots Y_m)\beta_{2n}\,[\bar{\rho}] = \bar{v}$$

in H. By the construction of P_{cs} according to p and by the induction hypothesis, $\tilde{\rho} = p_1 \cdots p_{i-1}$ and $\bar{\rho} = p_{i+1} \cdots p_{2n}$. By the induction hypothesis, $S\ {}_m\!\Rightarrow^* \tilde{u}'$ in G such that $\tilde{u} \in \mathrm{perm}(h(\tilde{u}'))$. Then, by the application of $p \in P_G$, we have $S\ {}_m\!\Rightarrow^* \tilde{u}'\ {}_m\!\Rightarrow v'$ such that $\bar{v} \in \mathrm{perm}(h(v'))$.

In (iii), there are three subcases of $u\ {}_j\!\Rightarrow v$ with $u_1u_2 = v_1v_2$ in H:

(iii.a) $1 \le i \le n$: Then, $u = u_1 g_p(h(X_1 \cdots X_{i-1}))h(X_iX_{i+1} \cdots X_n)u_2$ and $v = v_1 g_p(h(X_1 \cdots X_{i-1}X_i))h(X_{i+1} \cdots X_n)v_2$.

(iii.b) $n < i < 2n$ and $i' = i - n$: Then, $u = u_1 h(Y_1 \cdots Y_{i'-1}) g_p(h(X_{i'}X_{i'+1} \cdots X_n))u_2$ and $v = v_1 h(Y_1 \cdots Y_{i'}) g_p(h(X_{i'+1} \cdots X_n))v_2$.

(iii.c) $i = 2n$: Then, $u = u_1 h(Y_1 \cdots Y_{n-1}) g_p(h(X_n))u_2$ and $v = v_1 h(Y_1 \cdots Y_{n-1}Y_n \cdots Y_m)v_2$.

Therefore, the claim holds for $k + 1$ as well. □

Assume $v \in N_t^*$ in Claim D so $v' \in \Delta^*$. Based on Claim A, without any loss of generality, we can assume that all rules from P_t are applied in the end of a derivation of $w \in \Delta^*$ in H. Specifically, $S\ {}_j\!\Rightarrow^* v\,[\rho_v]\ {}_j\!\Rightarrow^* w\,[\rho_w]$ in H, where $\rho_v \in (P_H - P_t)^*$, $\rho_w \in P_t^*$, and $v = h(w)$. By Claim D, we have $S\ {}_m\!\Rightarrow^* v'$ in G with $v \in \mathrm{perm}(h(v'))$. Recall that $v \in N_t^*$ and $v' \in \Delta^*$. Therefore, $S\ {}_m\!\Rightarrow^* v'$ in G and $w \in \mathrm{perm}(v')$.

Next, by Claim B, $w \in L(H, {}_j\!\Rightarrow)$ implies $\mathrm{perm}(w) \subseteq L(H, {}_j\!\Rightarrow)$. By the previous paragraph and Lemma 5.5, for w, we generate $\mathrm{perm}(w)$ in G included in $L(G, {}_m\!\Rightarrow)$, that is, $L(H, {}_j\!\Rightarrow) \subseteq L(G, {}_m\!\Rightarrow)$.

This closes the proof of Theorem 5.6. □

Concerning the semilinearity of language families defined by jumping grammars under investigation, the following corollary sums up all important properties established in this section.

Corollary 5.3 JREG, JRL, JLIN, JCF *are semilinear, and* **JCS, JMON, JRE** *are not semilinear.*

Proof For **JRE**, the non-semilinearity follows from the well-known facts that **CS** is not semilinear (see [Dassow and Păun, 1989, Example 2.3.1 and Theorem 2.3.1]) and **CS** $\subset$ **RE** and from Theorem 5.5. The rest follows from Lemma 5.4 and Theorem 5.6. □

Corollary 5.4 JCF $\subset$ **JCS.**

Proof Obviously, by Definition 5.1, **JCF** $\subseteq$ **JCS**. By Corollary 5.3, **JCS** contains a non-semilinear language that does not belong to **JCF**. □

Relationships Between Jumping Automata and Jumping Grammars

Next, we demonstrate that the generative power of regular and right-linear jumping grammars is the same as accepting power of jumping finite automata and general jumping finite automata, respectively. Consequently, the following equivalence and the previous results in this chapter imply several additional properties of languages that are generated by regular and right-linear jumping grammars such as closure properties and decidability.

Lemma 5.6 GJFA $\subseteq$ JRL.

Proof *Construction.* For every GJFA $M = (Q, \Delta, R, s, F)$, we construct a RLG $G = (Q \cup \Delta \cup \{S\}, \Delta, P', S)$, where S is a new nonterminal, $S \notin Q \cup \Delta$, such that $L(M, \curvearrowright) = L(G, {}_j\Rightarrow)$. Set $P' = \{S \rightarrow f \mid f \in F\} \cup \{q \rightarrow xp \mid px \rightarrow q \in R\} \cup \{q \rightarrow x \mid sx \rightarrow q \in R\}$.

Basic Idea. The principle of the conversion is analogical to the conversion from classical lazy finite automata to equivalent RLGs with sequential derivation mode (see Section 2.6.2 in Wood [1987] and Theorem 4.1 in Salomaa [1973]).

The states of M are used as nonterminals in G. In addition, we introduce new start nonterminal S in G. The input symbols Δ are terminal symbols in G.

During the simulation of M in G there is always exactly one nonterminal symbol in the sentential form until the last jumping derivation step that produces the string of terminal symbols. If there is a sequence of jumping moves $usv \curvearrowright^* ypxy' \curvearrowright zqz'z'' \curvearrowright^* f$ in M, then G simulates it by jumping derivation

$$S \;{}_j\Rightarrow f \;{}_j\Rightarrow^* zz'qz'' \;{}_j\Rightarrow yxpy' \;{}_j\Rightarrow^* w,$$

where $yy' = zz'z''$ and $w = uv$. Firstly, S is nondeterministically rewritten to some f in G to simulate the entrance to the corresponding accepting final state of M. Then, for each rule $px \rightarrow q$ in M that processes substring x in the input string, there is x generated by the corresponding rule of the form $q \rightarrow xp$ in G. As the last jumping derivation step in G, we simulate the first jumping move of M from the start state s by rewriting the only nonterminal in the sentential form of G to a string of terminals and the simulation of M by G is completed.

Lemma 5.7 JRL $\subseteq$ GJFA.

Proof *Construction.* For every RLG $G = (\Sigma, \Delta, P', S)$, we construct a GJFA $M = (N \cup \{\sigma\}, \Delta, R, \sigma, \{S\})$, where σ is a new start state, $\sigma \notin \Sigma$ and $N = \Sigma - \Delta$, such that $L(G, {}_j\Rightarrow) = L(M, \curvearrowright)$. Set $R = \{Bx \rightarrow A \mid A \rightarrow xB \in P', A, B \in N, x \in \Delta^*\} \cup \{\sigma x \rightarrow A \mid A \rightarrow x \in P', x \in \Delta^*\}$.

Basic Idea. In the simulation of G in M we use nonterminals N as states, new state σ as the start state, and terminals Δ corresponds to input symbols of M. In addition, the start nonterminal of G corresponds to the only final state of M. Every application of a rule from P' in G is simulated by a move according to the corresponding rule from R constructed above. If there is a jumping derivation $S\ {}_j\!\Rightarrow^* yy'Ay''\ {}_j\!\Rightarrow zxBz'\ {}_j\!\Rightarrow^* w$ in G, then M simulates it by jumping moves $u\sigma v \curvearrowright^* zBxz' \curvearrowright yAy'y'' \curvearrowright^* S$, where $yy'y'' = zz'$ and $w = uv$. □

Theorem 5.7 GJFA = JRL.

Proof This theorem holds by Lemmas 5.6 and 5.7. □

In the following theorem, consider jumping finite automata that process only one input symbol in one move. We state their equivalence with jumping RGs.

Theorem 5.8 JFA = JREG.

Proof Prove this statement by analogy with the proof of Theorem 5.7. □

Figure 5.1 summarizes the achieved results on the generative and accepting power of jumping grammars and automata.

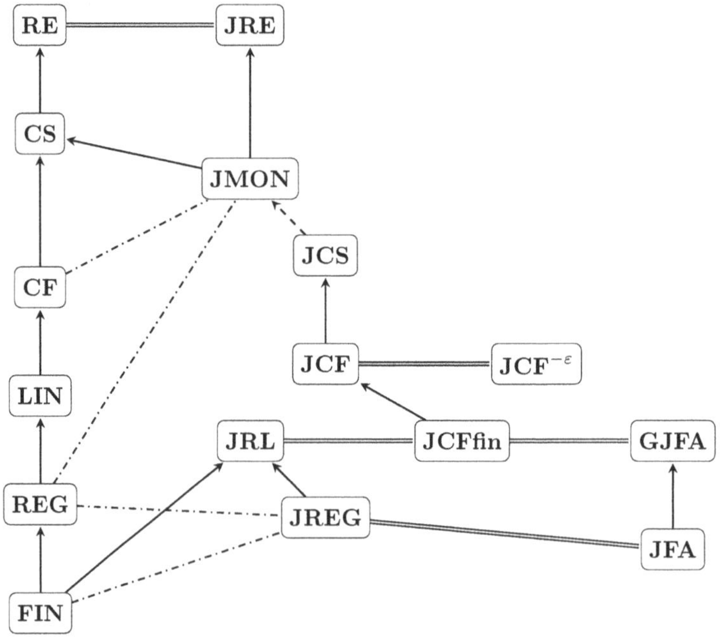

Fig. 5.1 Language families defined by jumping grammars and automata in relationships to the Chomsky hierarchy.

Future Investigation

We close this chapter by proposing several future investigation areas concerning jumping grammars. Some of them relate to specific open questions pointed out earlier in this chapter; next, we formulate them from broader viewpoint.

I. *Other Types of Grammars*. The present chapter has concentrated its attention on the language families resulting from classical grammars, such as the grammars underlying the Chomsky hierarchy (see Chomsky [1959]). Apart from them, however, the formal language theory has introduced many other types of grammars, ranging from regulated grammars (see Dassow and Păun [1989]; Meduna and Zemek [2014]) through WK grammars (see Mohamad Zulkufli et al. [2016]), parallel grammars (see Greibach and Hopcroft [1969]; Siromoney and Krithivasan [1974]), and pure grammars (see Gabrielian [1970]) up to grammar systems (see Csuhaj-Varju et al. [1994]). Naturally, their jumping versions are also worth to be studied as demonstrated in the following two chapters.

II. *Left and Right Jumping Mode*. Considering the left and right jumps introduced in Definition 5.1, study them in terms of classical types of grammars. Later in Section 3.1, this book gives an introduction to discussion of left and right jumping derivation modes in terms of automata.

III. *Closure Properties*. Several results and some open problems concerning closure properties follow from Section 5.3. Additionally, study closure properties of language families generated in a jumping way. Specifically, investigate these properties in terms of CFGs, CSGs, and MONGs.

IV. *Alternative Definition of Jumping Mode with Context*. Assume context-sensitive rules (CSG) of the following form

$$\alpha A\beta \to \alpha\gamma\beta, \text{ where } A \in N, \alpha, \beta, \gamma \in \Sigma^*, \gamma \neq \varepsilon.$$

There are three interesting ways of defining a jumping derivation step:

IV.a Using the previous definition (see Definition 5.1) of jumping derivation; that is, find $\alpha A\beta$ in the current sentential form $u\alpha A\beta v$, remove $\alpha A\beta$, and place $\alpha\gamma\beta$ anywhere in uv. For instance,

$$aAbc \ {}_j\!\Rightarrow caxb \ [aAb \to axb]$$

IV.b Do not move the context of the rewritten nonterminal; that is, find A with left context α and right context β, remove this A from the current sentential form, and place γ in the new sentential form, such that string γ will be again in the context of both α and β (but it can be different occurrence of α and β). For instance,

$$aAbab \ {}_{j'}\!\Rightarrow abaxb \ [aAb \to axb]$$

IV.c Similarly to (b), in the third variant we do not move the context of the rewritten nonterminal either and, in addition, γ has to be placed between the same occurrence of α and β. As a consequence, context-sensitive rules are applied sequentially even in this jumping derivation mode. For instance,

$$aAbab \ {}_{j''}\!\Rightarrow axbab \ [aAb \rightarrow axb]$$

Notice that this derivation mode influences only the application of context-free rules (i.e., $\alpha = \beta = \varepsilon$).

Example 5.4 Example 5.2 shows a CSG that generates $\{a^n b^n \mid n \geq 1\}$ when the alternative jumping derivation mode ${}_{j'}\!\Rightarrow$ for CSGs is used. In context of Lemma 5.1, the alternative jumping derivation mode (b) can increase the generative power of jumping CSGs (a). In fact, it is an open question whether the language family generated by CSGs with ${}_{j'}\!\Rightarrow$ mode is strictly included in the language family generated by MONGs with ${}_{j'}\!\Rightarrow$ mode.

V. *Relationship with Formal Macroset Theory*. Recently, formal language theory has introduced various rewriting devices that generate different objects than classical formal languages. Specifically, in this way, Formal Macroset Theory has investigated the generation of macrosets—that is, sets of multisets over alphabets. Notice that some of its results resemble results achieved in the present study (c.f., for instance, Theorem 1 in Kudlek et al. [2000] and Theorems 5.2 and 5.3 above). Explain this resemblance mathematically.

Chapter 6
Parallel Jumping Grammars

This chapter consists of three sections. Section 6.1 gives an introduction into parallel versions of jumping grammars. Section 6.2 presents all the definitions needed. Finally, Section 6.3 presents all the fundamental results about parallel jumping grammars.

6.1 Introduction

All the grammars discussed in the previous chapter work strictly sequentially in the sense that they apply a single rule during every derivation step. Considering the current universal trend of performing computation in parallel, it is more than natural and desirable to modify the grammatical computational models so that they also work in parallel, and this is precisely what the present chapter is devoted to. Out of all the sequential grammars, this chapter selects context-free grammars for this modification because these grammars and their variants represent perhaps the most significant grammatical model from a theoretical as well as practical standpoint; for instance, these grammars are by far the most widely accepted specification tool for the syntactic structure of programming language as clearly demonstrated by an examination of any programming high-level language manual. In other words, the present chapter, based on Meduna and Soukup [2017a], studies jumping versions of parallelly modified context-free grammars, referred to as scattered context grammars, which can simultaneously apply several rules during a single derivation step.

To give a more detailed insight into the key motivation and reason for introducing and investigating jumping versions of scattered context grammars, let us take a closer look at a more specific kind of information processing in a discontinuous way. Consider a process p that deals with information i. Typically, during a single computational step, p (1) reads n pieces of information, x_1 through x_n, in i, (2) erases them, (3) generates n new pieces of information, y_1 through y_n, and (4) inserts them into i possibly at different positions than the original occurrence of x_1 through x_n, which was erased. To explore computation like this systematically and rigorously, the present chapter introduces and discusses jumping versions of scattered context grammars, which represent suitable grammatical models of computation like this.

To see this suitability, recall that the notion of a scattered context grammar G represents a language-generating rewriting system based upon an alphabet of symbols and a finite set of rules (see Greibach and Hopcroft [1969]). The alphabet of symbols is divided into two disjoint subalphabets—the alphabet of terminal symbols and the alphabet of nonterminal symbols. In G, a rule r is of the form

$$(A_1, A_2, \ldots, A_n) \rightarrow (x_1, x_2, \ldots, x_n)$$

for some positive integer n. On the left-hand side of r, the As are nonterminals. On the right-hand side, the xs are strings. G can apply r to any string u of the form

$$u = u_0 A_1 u_1 \ldots u_{n-1} A_n u_n$$

where us are any strings. Notice that A_1 through A_n are scattered throughout u, but they occur in the order prescribed by the left-hand side of r. In essence, G applies r to u so

(1) it deletes $A_1, A_2, \ldots, A_n$ in u, after which
(2) it inserts $x_1, x_2, \ldots, x_n$ into the string resulting from the deletion (1).

By this application, G makes a derivation step from u to a string v of the form

$$v = v_0 x_1 v_1 \ldots v_{n-1} x_n v_n$$

Notice that $x_1, x_2, \ldots, x_n$ are inserted in the order prescribed by the right-hand side of r. However, they are inserted in a scattered way—that is, between the inserted xs, some substrings vs occur.

To formalize the above-described computation, consisting of phases (1) through (4), the present section introduces and studies the following nine jumping derivation modes of the standard application:

(1) Mode 1 requires that $u_i = v_i$ for all $i = 0, \ldots, n$ in the above-described derivation step.
(2) Mode 2 obtains v from u as follows:
   (2.a) $A_1, A_2, \ldots, A_n$ are deleted;
   (2.b) x_1 through x_n are inserted between u_0 and u_n.
(3) Mode 3 obtains v from u so it changes u by performing (3.a) through (3.c), described next:
   (3.a) $A_1, A_2, \ldots, A_n$ are deleted;
   (3.b) x_1 and x_n are inserted into u_0 and u_n, respectively;
   (3.c) x_2 through x_{n-1} are inserted between the newly inserted x_1 and x_n.
(4) In Mode 4, the derivation from u to v is performed by the following steps:
   (4.a) $A_1, A_2, \ldots, A_n$ are deleted;

(4.b) a central u_i is nondeterministically chosen, for some $0 \leq i \leq n$;
(4.c) x_i and x_{i+1} are inserted into u_i;
(4.d) x_j is inserted between u_j and u_{j+1}, for all $j < i$;
(4.e) x_k is inserted between u_{k-2} and u_{k-1}, for all $k > i + 1$.

(5) In Mode 5, v is obtained from u by (5.a) through (5.e), given next:

(5.a) $A_1, A_2, \ldots, A_n$ are deleted;
(5.b) a central u_i is nondeterministically chosen, for some $0 \leq i \leq n$;
(5.c) x_1 and x_n are inserted into u_0 and u_n, respectively;
(5.d) x_j is inserted between u_{j-2} and u_{j-1}, for all $1 < j \leq i$;
(5.e) x_k is inserted between u_k and u_{k+1}, for all $i + 1 \leq k < n$.

(6) Mode 6 derives v from u applying the next steps:

(6.a) $A_1, A_2, \ldots, A_n$ are deleted;
(6.b) a central u_i is nondeterministically chosen, for some $0 \leq i \leq n$;
(6.c) x_j is inserted between u_j and u_{j+1}, for all $j < i$;
(6.d) x_k is inserted between u_{k-2} and u_{k-1}, for all $k > i + 1$.

(7) Mode 7 obtains v from u performing the steps stated below:

(7.a) $A_1, A_2, \ldots, A_n$ are deleted;
(7.b) a central u_i is nondeterministically chosen, for some $0 \leq i \leq n$;
(7.c) x_j is inserted between u_{j-2} and u_{j-1}, for all $1 < j \leq i$;
(7.d) x_k is inserted between u_k and u_{k+1}, for all $i + 1 \leq k < n$.

(8) In Mode 8, v is produced from u by following the given steps:

(8.a) $A_1, A_2, \ldots, A_n$ are deleted;
(8.b) x_1 and x_n are inserted into u_1 and u_{n-1}, respectively;
(8.c) x_i is inserted into $u_{i-1}u_i$, for all $1 < i < n$, to the right of x_{i-1} and to the left of x_{i+1}.

(9) Mode 9 derives v from u by the next procedure:

(9.a) $A_1, A_2, \ldots, A_n$ are deleted;
(9.b) x_1 and x_n are inserted into u_0 and u_n, respectively;
(9.c) x_i is inserted into $u_{i-1}u_i$, for all $1 < i < n$, to the right of x_{i-1} and to the left of x_{i+1}.

As is obvious, all these jumping derivation modes reflect and formalize the above-described four-phase computation performed in a discontinuous way more adequately than their standard counterpart. Consequently, applications of these grammars are expected in any scientific area involving this kind of computation, ranging from applied mathematics through computational linguistics and compiler writing up to data mining and bioinformatics.

6.2 Definitions

First, recall a parallel language generation represented by the notion of a scattered context grammar (introduced in Greibach and Hopcroft [1969]) that modifies a context-free grammar such that it can simultaneously apply several rules during a single derivation step while keeping the rest of the rewritten string unchanged.

Definition 6.1 A *scattered context grammar* (SCG) is a quadruple

$$G = (\Sigma, \Delta, P, S); \quad N = \Sigma - \Delta$$

where

- Σ is a *total alphabet*;
- $\Delta \subset \Sigma$ an alphabet of *terminals*;
- $P \subseteq \bigcup_{m=1}^{\infty} N^m \times (\Sigma^*)^m$ is a finite set of *rules* of the form

$$(A_1, A_2, \ldots, A_n) \rightarrow (x_1, x_2, \ldots, x_n)$$

  where $A_i \in N$, and $x_i \in \Sigma^*$, for $1 \leq i \leq n$, for some $n \geq 1$;
- $S \in \Sigma - \Delta$ is the *start symbol*;
- N is an alphabet of *nonterminals*.

If

$$u = u_1 A_1 \ldots u_n A_n u_{n+1}$$
$$v = u_1 x_1 \ldots u_n x_n u_{n+1}$$

and $p = (A_1, \ldots, A_n) \rightarrow (x_1, \ldots, x_n) \in P$, where $u_i \in \Sigma^*$, for all i, $1 \leq i \leq n+1$, then G makes a *derivation step* from u to v according to p, symbolically written as

$$u \Rightarrow_G v\ [p]$$

or, simply, $u \Rightarrow_G v$. Set

$$\text{lhs}(p) = A_1 \ldots A_n$$
$$\text{rhs}(p) = x_1 \ldots x_n.$$

If $n \geq 2$, p is said to be a *context-sensitive rule* while for $n = 1$, p is said to be *context-free*. Define $\Rightarrow_G^k$, $\Rightarrow_G^*$, and $\Rightarrow_G^+$ in the standard way. The *language* of G is denoted by $L(G)$ and defined as

$$L(G) = \{w \in \Delta^* \mid S \Rightarrow_G^* w\}$$

A language L is a *scattered context language* if there exists a scattered context grammar G such that $L = L(G)$.

Definition 6.2 A *propagating scattered context grammar* is a scattered context grammar

$$G = (\Sigma, \Delta, P, S)$$

in which every $(A_1, \ldots, A_n) \to (x_1, \ldots, x_n) \in R$ satisfies $|x_i| \geq 1$, for all i, $1 \leq i \leq n$. A *propagating scattered context language* is the language generated by a propagating SCG.

In the following example, we illustrate how SCG works.

Example 6.1 Consider the non-context-free language $L = \{a^n b^n c^n \mid n \geq 1\}$. This language can be generated by the SCG

$$G = \big(\{S, A, a, b, c\}, \{a, b, c\}, P, S\big)$$

where

$$\begin{aligned} P = \big\{&(S) \to (aAbAcA), \\ &(A, A, A) \to (aA, bA, cA), \\ &(A, A, A) \to (\varepsilon, \varepsilon, \varepsilon)\big\} \end{aligned}$$

For example, the sentence $aabbcc$ is generated by G as follows:

$$S \Rightarrow_G aAbAcA \Rightarrow_G aaAbbAccA \Rightarrow_G aabbcc$$

Notice, however, that L can be also generated by the propagating SCG

$$G' = \big(\{S, A, a, b, c\}, \{a, b, c\}, P', S\big)$$

where

$$\begin{aligned} P' = \big\{&(S) \to (AAA), \\ &(A, A, A) \to (aA, bA, cA), \\ &(A, A, A) \to (a, b, c)\big\} \end{aligned}$$

To find a detailed overview of many results about SCGs, see Meduna and Techet [2010]. The investigation of SCGs is still a vivid topic in the theory of formal languages as indicated in Csuhaj-Varjú and Vaszil [2010]; Křoustek et al. [2011]; and Křivka and Meduna [2021] with some very interesting results.

In the rest of this section, we formally define nine derivation modes (1) through (9), sketched in the previous introductory section.

Definition 6.3 Let $G = (\Sigma, \Delta, P, S)$ be an SCG, and let ϱ be a relation over Σ^*. Set

$$L(G, \varrho) = \{x \mid x \in \Delta^*, S \, \varrho^* \, x\}$$

$L(G, \varrho)$ is said to be the *language that G generates by* ϱ. Set

$$\mathbf{JSC}_\varrho = \{L(G, \varrho) \mid G \text{ is an SCG}\}$$

$\mathbf{JSC}_\varrho$ is said to be *the language family that SCGs generate by* ϱ.

Definition 6.4 Let $G = (\Sigma, \Delta, P, S)$ be an SCG. Next, we rigorously define the following direct derivation relations ${}_1\Rightarrow$ through ${}_9\Rightarrow$ over Σ^*, intuitively sketched in the previous introductory section.

First, let $(A) \rightarrow (x) \in P$ and $u = w_1 A w_2 \in \Sigma^*$. Then,

$$w_1 A w_2 \ {}_i\!\Rightarrow w_1 x w_2, \text{ for } i = 1, \ldots, 9$$

Second, let $(A_1, A_2, \ldots, A_n) \rightarrow (x_1, x_2, \ldots, x_n) \in P$, $u = u_0 A_1 u_1 \ldots A_n u_n$, and $u_0 u_1 \ldots u_n = v_0 v_1 \ldots v_n$, where $u_i, v_i \in \Sigma^*$, $0 \leq i \leq n$, for some $n \geq 2$. Then,

(1) $u_0 A_1 u_1 A_2 u_2 \ldots A_n u_n \ {}_1\!\Rightarrow u_0 x_1 u_1 x_2 v_2 \ldots x_n u_n$;
(2) $u_0 A_1 u_1 A_2 u_2 \ldots A_n u_n \ {}_2\!\Rightarrow v_0 x_1 v_1 x_2 v_2 \ldots x_n v_n$, where $u_0 z_1 = v_0$, $z_2 u_n = v_n$;
(3) $u_0 A_1 u_1 A_2 u_2 \ldots A_n u_n \ {}_3\!\Rightarrow v_0 x_1 v_1 x_2 v_2 \ldots x_n v_n$, where $u_0 = v_0 z_1$, $u_n = z_2 v_n$;
(4) $u_0 A_1 u_1 A_2 u_2 \ldots u_{i-1} A_i u_i A_{i+1} u_{i+1} \ldots u_{n-1} A_n u_n \ {}_4\!\Rightarrow$
$u_0 u_1 x_1 u_2 x_2 \ldots u_{i-1} x_{i-1} u_{i_1} x_i u_{i_2} x_{i+1} u_{i_3} x_{i+2} u_{i+1} \ldots x_n u_{n-1} u_n$, where $u_i = u_{i_1} u_{i_2} u_{i_3}$;
(5) $u_0 A_1 u_1 A_2 \ldots u_{i-1} A_{i-1} u_i A_i u_{i+1} \ldots A_n u_n \ {}_5\!\Rightarrow$
$u_{0_1} x_1 u_{0_2} x_2 u_1 \ldots x_{i-1} u_{i-1} u_i u_{i+1} x_i \ldots u_{n_1} x_n u_{n_2}$,
where $u_0 = u_{0_1} u_{0_2}$, $u_n = u_{n_1} u_{n_2}$;
(6) $u_0 A_1 u_1 A_2 u_2 \ldots u_{i-1} A_i u_i A_{i+1} u_{i+1} \ldots u_{n-1} A_n u_n \ {}_6\!\Rightarrow$
$u_0 u_1 x_1 u_2 x_2 \ldots u_{i-1} x_{i-1} u_i x_{i+2} u_{i+1} \ldots x_n u_{n-1} u_n$;
(7) $u_0 A_1 u_1 A_2 \ldots u_{i-1} A_i u_i A_{i+1} u_{i+1} \ldots A_n u_n \ {}_7\!\Rightarrow$
$u_0 x_2 u_1 \ldots x_i u_{i-1} u_i u_{i+1} x_{i+1} \ldots u_n$;
(8) $u_0 A_1 u_1 A_2 u_2 \ldots A_n u_n \ {}_8\!\Rightarrow v_0 x_1 v_1 x_2 v_2 \ldots x_n v_n$, where $u_0 z_1 = v_0$, $z_2 u_n = v_n$, $|u_0 u_1 \ldots u_{j-1}| \leq |v_0 v_1 \ldots v_j|$, $|u_{j+1} \ldots u_n| \leq |v_j v_{j+1} \ldots v_n|$, $0 < j < n$;
(9) $u_0 A_1 u_1 A_2 u_2 \ldots A_n u_n \ {}_9\!\Rightarrow v_0 x_1 v_1 x_2 v_2 \ldots x_n v_n$, where $u_0 = v_0 z_1$, $u_n = z_2 v_n$, $|u_0 u_1 \ldots u_{j-1}| \leq |v_0 v_1 \ldots v_j|$, $|u_{j+1} \ldots u_n| \leq |v_j v_{j+1} \ldots v_n|$,
$0 < j < n$.

We close this section by illustrating the above-introduced notation in Definition 6.3. Let $G = (\Sigma, \Delta, P, S)$ be an SCG; then, $L(G, {}_5\!\Rightarrow) = \{x \mid x \in \Delta^*, S \ {}_5\!\Rightarrow^* x\}$ and $\mathbf{JSC}_{5\Rightarrow} = \{L(G, {}_5\!\Rightarrow) \mid G \text{ is an SCG}\}$. To give another example, $\mathbf{JSC}_{1\Rightarrow}$ denotes the family of all scattered context languages.

6.3 Results

This section demonstrates that SCGs working under any of the derivation modes defined in the previous section are computationally complete—that is, they characterize the family of recursively enumerable languages. In addition, in its conclusion, it formulates several open problems.

Let us recall Theorem 2.9 that fulfills an important role in the proofs throughout this section. Theorem 2.9 states that every $L \in \mathbf{RE}$ can be expressed as a homomorphism of the intersection of two context-free languages.

Jumping Derivation Mode 1

${}_1\!\Rightarrow$ represents, in fact, the ordinary scattered context derivation mode.

Definition 6.5 Let $G = (\Sigma, \Delta, P, S)$ be an SCG. Let $u_0A_1u_1 \dots A_nu_n \in \Sigma^*$ and $(A_1,A_2,\dots,A_n) \to (x_1,x_2,\dots,x_n) \in P$, for $n \geq 1$. Then,

$$u_0A_1u_1A_2u_2 \dots A_nu_n \ {}_1\!\Rightarrow u_0x_1u_1x_2v_2 \dots x_nu_n$$

Example 6.2 Let $G = (\Sigma, \Delta, P, S)$ be an SCG, where $\Sigma = \{S, S', S'', S''', A, B, C$ $A', B', C', a, b, c\}$, $\Delta = \{a, b, c\}$, and P contains the following rules:

(i) $(S) \to (aSA)$	(vii) $(S', C) \to (cS', C')$
(ii) $(S) \to (bSB)$	(viii) $(S', S'') \to (\varepsilon, S''')$
(iii) $(S) \to (cSC)$	(ix) $(S''', A') \to (S''', a)$
(iv) $(S) \to (S'S'')$	(x) $(S''', B') \to (S''', b)$
(v) $(S', A) \to (aS', A')$	(xi) $(S''', C') \to (S''', c)$
(vi) $(S', B) \to (bS', B')$	(xii) $(S''' \to \varepsilon)$

Consider ${}_1\!\Rightarrow$. Then, the derivation of G is as follows.

First, G generates any string $w \in \Delta^*$ to the left of S and its reversal in capital letters to the right of S with linear rules. Then, it replaces S with $S'S''$. Next, while nondeterministically rewriting nonterminal symbols to the right of S'' to their prime versions, it generates the sequence of terminals in the same order to the left of S', which we denote w'. Since all the symbols to the right of S' must be rewritten, the sequence of symbols generated to the left of S' must have the same composition of symbols. Otherwise, no terminal string can be generated, so the derivation is blocked. Thereafter, S' is erased, and S'' is rewritten to S'''. Finally, the prime versions of symbols to the right of S''' are rewritten to the terminal string denoted w''. Consequently,

$$L(G, {}_1\!\Rightarrow) = \{x \in \Delta^* \mid x = ww'w'', w = \text{reversal}(w''), w' \text{ is any permutation of } w\}$$

For instance, the string $abccabcba$ is generated by G in the following way:

$$\begin{aligned} S \ {}_1\!\Rightarrow aSA \ {}_1\!\Rightarrow abSBA \ {}_1\!\Rightarrow abcSCBA \ {}_1\!\Rightarrow abcS'S''CBA \ {}_1\!\Rightarrow abccS'S''C'BA \\ {}_1\!\Rightarrow abccaS'S''C'BA' \ {}_1\!\Rightarrow abccabS'S''C'B'A' \ {}_1\!\Rightarrow abccabS'''C'B'A' \\ {}_1\!\Rightarrow abccabS'''cB'A' \ {}_1\!\Rightarrow abccabS'''cbA' \ {}_1\!\Rightarrow abccabS'''cba \ {}_1\!\Rightarrow abccabcba \end{aligned}$$

Next, we prove that SCGs working under ${}_1\!\Rightarrow$ characterize **RE**.

Theorem 6.1 (Fernau and Meduna [2003]) $\mathbf{JSC}_{{}_1\Rightarrow} = \mathbf{RE}$.

Proof As is obvious, any SCG G can be turned to a Turing machine M so M accepts $L(G, {}_1\!\Rightarrow)$. Thus, $\mathbf{JSC}_{{}_1\Rightarrow} \subseteq \mathbf{RE}$. Therefore, we only need to prove $\mathbf{RE} \subseteq \mathbf{JSC}_{{}_1\Rightarrow}$.

Let $L \in \mathbf{RE}$. Express $L = h(L_1 \cap L_2)$, where h, L_1, and L_2 have the same meaning as in Theorem 2.9. Since L_2 is context-free, so is reversal(L_2) (see page 419 in Wood [1987]). Thus, there are context-free grammars G_1 and G_2 that generate L_1 and reversal(L_2), respectively. More precisely, let $G_i = (\Sigma_i, \Delta, P_i, S_i)$ for $i = 1, 2$. Let $\Delta = \{a_1, \dots, a_n\}$ and 0, 1, \$, $S \notin \Sigma_1 \cup \Sigma_2$ be the new symbols. Without any loss of generality, assume that $\Sigma_1 \cap \Sigma_2 = \emptyset$. Define the new morphisms

(I) $c : a_i \mapsto 10^i1$;

(II) $C_1 : \Sigma_1 \cup \Delta \to \Sigma_1 \cup \Delta^*\{0,1\}^*$,
$\begin{cases} A \mapsto A, & A \in \Sigma_1 - \Delta, \\ a \mapsto f(a), & a \in \Delta; \end{cases}$

(III) $C_2 : \Sigma_2 \cup \Delta \to \Sigma_2 \cup \{0,1\}^*$,
$\begin{cases} A \mapsto A, & A \in \Sigma_2 - \Delta, \\ a \mapsto c(a), & a \in \Delta; \end{cases}$

(IV) $f : a_i \mapsto h(a_i)c(a_i)$;

(V) $t : \Delta \cup \{0,1,\$\} \to \Delta \cup \{\varepsilon\}$,
$\begin{cases} a \mapsto a, & a \in \Delta, \\ A \mapsto \varepsilon, & A \notin \Delta; \end{cases}$

(VI) $t' : \Delta \cup \{0,1,\$\} \to \{0,1,\varepsilon\}$,
$\begin{cases} a \mapsto a, & a \in \{0,1\}, \\ A \mapsto \varepsilon, & A \notin \{0,1\}. \end{cases}$

Finally, let $G = (\Sigma, \Delta, P, S)$ be SCG, with $\Sigma = \Sigma_1 \cup \Sigma_2 \cup \{S, 0, 1, \$\}$ and P containing the rules

(1) $(S) \to (\$S_1 1111 S_2\$)$;
(2) $(A) \to (C_i(w))$, for all $A \to w \in P_i$, where $i = 1, 2$;
(3) $(\$, a, a, \$) \to (\varepsilon, \$, \$, \varepsilon)$, for $a = 0, 1$;
(4) $(\$) \to (\varepsilon)$.

Claim A $L(G, {}_1\Rightarrow) = L$. □

Proof (Claim A) *Basic idea.* First, the starting rule (1) is applied. The starting nonterminals S_1 and S_2 are inserted into the current sentential form. Then, by using the rules from (2), G simulates derivations of both G_1 and G_2 and generates the sentential form $w = \$w_1 1111 w_2\$$.

Suppose $S \;{}_1\Rightarrow^* w$, where symbols$(w) \cap (N_1 \cup N_2) = \emptyset$. Recall, N_1 and N_2 denote the nonterminal alphabets of G_1 and G_2, respectively. If $t'(w_1) = \text{reversal}(w_2)$, then $t(w_1) = h(v)$, where $v \in L_1 \cap L_2$ and $h(v) \in L$. In other words, w represents a successful derivation of both G_1 and G_2, where both grammars have generated the same sentence v; therefore, G must generate the sentence $h(v)$.

The rules from (3) serve to check, whether the simulated grammars have generated the identical strings. Binary codings of the generated strings are erased while checking the equality. Always the leftmost and the rightmost symbols are erased; otherwise, some symbol is skipped. If the codings do not match, some 0 or 1 cannot be erased and no terminal string can be generated.

Finally, the symbols \$ are erased with rule (4). If G_1 and G_2 generated the same sentence and both codings were successfully erased, G has generated the terminal sentence $h(v) \in L$. □

Claim A implies $\mathbf{RE} \subseteq \mathbf{JSC}_{{}_1\Rightarrow}$. Thus, Theorem 6.1 holds. □

For brevity, we make use of some terminology introduced in the proof of Theorem 6.1 throughout the rest of this section. That is, each of the upcoming proofs given in Section 6.3 introduces its own new notions; apart from them, however, it also uses the notions introduced in the proof of Theorem 6.1 without repeating their definitions therefrom.

Jumping Derivation Mode 2

Definition 6.6 Let $G = (\Sigma, \Delta, P, S)$ be an SCG. Let $u = u_0A_1u_1 \dots A_nu_n \in \Sigma^*$ and $(A_1,A_2,\dots,A_n) \to (x_1,x_2,\dots,x_n) \in P$, for $n \geq 1$. Then,

$$u_0A_1u_1A_2u_2 \dots A_nu_n \;{}_2\!\Rightarrow v_0x_1v_1x_2v_2 \dots x_nv_n$$

where $u_0u_1 \dots u_n = v_0v_1 \dots v_n$, $u_0z_1 = v_0$ and $z_2u_n = v_n$, $z_1, z_2 \in \Sigma^*$.

Informally, by using $(A_1,A_2,\dots,A_n) \to (x_1,x_2,\dots,x_n) \in P$, G obtains $v = v_0x_1v_1x_2v_2 \dots x_nv_n$ from $u = u_0A_1u_1A_2u_2 \dots A_nu_n$ in ${}_2\!\Rightarrow$ as follows:

(1) $A_1, A_2, \dots, A_n$ are deleted;
(2) x_1 through x_n are inserted between u_0 and u_n.

Notice, the mutual order of inserted right-hand-side strings must be always preserved.

Example 6.3 Consider SCG defined in Example 6.2 and ${}_2\!\Rightarrow$. Context-free rules act in the same way as in ${}_1\!\Rightarrow$ unlike context-sensitive rules. Let us focus on the differences.

First, G generates the sentential form $wS'S''\overline{w}$, where $w \in \Delta^*$ and $\overline{w}$ is the reversal of w in capital letters, with context-free derivations. Then, the nonterminals to the right of S' are rewritten to their prime versions and possibly randomly shifted closer to S', which may arbitrarily change their order. Additionally, the sequence of terminals in the same order is generated to the left of S', which we denote w'. S' may be also shifted; however, in such case it appears to the right of S'', and future application of rule (viii) is excluded and no terminal string can be generated. Since all the symbols to the right of S' must be rewritten, the sequence generated to the left of S' must have the same composition of symbols. Next, S' is erased and S'' is rewritten to S''' at once, which ensures their mutual order is preserved. If any prime symbol occurs to the left of S''', it cannot be erased and the derivation is blocked. Finally, the prime versions of symbols to the right of S''' are rewritten to the terminal string denoted w'', which also enables random disordering. Consequently,

$$L(G, {}_2\!\Rightarrow) = \{x \in \Delta^* \mid x = ww'w'', w', w'' \text{ are any permutations of } w\}$$

For example, the string $abcacbbac$ is generated by G in the following way:

$$\begin{aligned} S &{}_2\!\Rightarrow aSA \;{}_2\!\Rightarrow abSBA \;{}_2\!\Rightarrow abcSCBA \;{}_2\!\Rightarrow abcS'S''CBA \;{}_2\!\Rightarrow abcaS'S''A'CB \\ &{}_2\!\Rightarrow abcacS'S''A'C'B \;{}_2\!\Rightarrow abcacbS'S''B'A'C' \;{}_2\!\Rightarrow abcacbS'''B'A'C' \\ &{}_2\!\Rightarrow abcacbS'''B'A'c \;{}_2\!\Rightarrow abcacbS'''bA'c \;{}_2\!\Rightarrow abcacbS'''bac \;{}_2\!\Rightarrow abcacbbac \end{aligned}$$

Theorem 6.2 $\mathbf{JSC}_{{}_2\Rightarrow} = \mathbf{RE}$.

Proof Clearly $\mathbf{JSC}_{{}_2\Rightarrow} \subseteq \mathbf{RE}$, so we only need to prove $\mathbf{RE} \subseteq \mathbf{JSC}_{{}_2\Rightarrow}$.

Let $G = (\Sigma, \Delta, P, S)$ be the SCG constructed in the proof of Theorem 6.1. First, we modify G to a new SCG G' so $L(G, {}_1\!\Rightarrow) = L(G', {}_1\!\Rightarrow)$. Then, we prove $L(G', {}_2\!\Rightarrow) = L(G', {}_1\!\Rightarrow)$.

Construction. Set

$$N = \{\lceil, \rceil, \lfloor, \rfloor, |, X, \underline{X}, \overline{X}, \overline{\underline{X}}, Y, \underline{Y}, \overline{Y}, \overline{\underline{Y}}\}$$

where $\Sigma \cap N = \emptyset$. Define the new morphisms

(I) $\overline{C}_1 : \Sigma_1 \cup \Delta \to \Sigma_1 \cup \Delta^*\{0, 1\}^*$,
$\begin{cases} A \mapsto A, & A \in \Sigma_1 - \Delta, \\ a \mapsto \lceil f(a) \rceil \,|, & a \in \Delta; \end{cases}$

(II) $\overline{C}_2 : \Sigma_2 \cup \Delta \to \Sigma_2 \cup (N \cup \{0, 1\})^*$,
$\begin{cases} A \mapsto A, & A \in \Sigma_2 - \Delta, \\ a \mapsto \,| \lceil c(a) \rceil, & a \in \Delta; \end{cases}$

(III) $b : \Delta \cup \{0, 1, \$\} \cup N \to \{0, 1, \varepsilon\}$,
$\begin{cases} A \mapsto A, & A \in \{0, 1\}, \\ A \mapsto \varepsilon, & A \notin \{0, 1\}; \end{cases}$

(IV) $\overline{t'} : \Delta \cup \{0, 1, \$\} \cup N \to \{0, 1, \$, \varepsilon\} \cup N$,
$\begin{cases} A \mapsto A, & A \in \{\$\} \cup N, \\ A \mapsto t'(A), & A \notin \{\$\} \cup N. \end{cases}$

Let $G' = (\Sigma', \Delta, P', S)$ be SCG, with $\Sigma' = \Sigma \cup N$ and P' containing

(1) $(S) \to (\rceil X \$ S_1 \lceil 11 \,||\, 11 \rceil S_2 \$ Y \lceil)$;
(2) $(A) \to (\overline{C}_i(w))$ for $A \to w \in P_i$, where $i = 1, 2$;
(3) $(\rceil, X, \lceil) \to (\rfloor, \overline{\underline{X}}, \rfloor)$, $(\rceil, Y, \lceil) \to (\lfloor, \overline{\underline{Y}}, \lfloor)$;
(4) $(\rfloor, \overline{\underline{X}}, \rfloor) \to (\rfloor, \overline{\overline{X}}, \rfloor)$, $(\lfloor, \overline{\underline{Y}}, \lfloor) \to (\lfloor, \overline{\overline{Y}}, \lfloor)$;
(5) $(\$, 0, \overline{X}, \overline{Y}, 0, \$) \to (\varepsilon, \$, \overline{\underline{X}}, \overline{\underline{Y}}, \$, \varepsilon)$;
(6) $(\$, \overline{X}, \overline{Y}, \$) \to (\varepsilon, \overline{X}\$, \$\overline{Y}, \varepsilon)$;
(7) $(\rfloor, \overline{X}, \$, \rfloor, \lfloor, \$, \overline{Y}, \lfloor) \to (\varepsilon, \varepsilon, \varepsilon, \underline{X}\$, \$\underline{Y}, \varepsilon, \varepsilon, \varepsilon)$;
(8) $(\underline{X}, 1, 1, |, |, 1, 1, \underline{Y}) \to (\varepsilon, \varepsilon, \varepsilon, X, Y, \varepsilon, \varepsilon, \varepsilon)$;
(9) $(\$) \to (\varepsilon)$, $(X) \to (\varepsilon)$, $(Y) \to (\varepsilon)$.

Notice that X and Y hold the current state of computation and force the context-sensitive rules to be used in the following order:

(a) after applying rules from (3), only rules from (4) may be applied;
(b) after applying rules from (4), only rule (5) or rule (6) may be applied;
(c) after applying rule (5), only rules from (4) may be applied;
(d) after applying rule (6), only rule (7) may be applied;
(e) after applying rule (7), only rule (8) may be applied;
(f) after applying rule (8), only rules from (3) may be applied.

Claim A $L(G', {}_1\!\Rightarrow) = L(G, {}_1\!\Rightarrow)$. □

Proof (Claim A) The context-free rules from (1) and (2) of G' correspond one-to-one to the rules constructed in (1) and (2) of G, only the codings of terminals contain additional symbols. Thus, for every derivation in G

$$S \;{}_1\!\Rightarrow^* \$v_1 1111 v_2 \$ = v$$

where v is generated by using rules from (1) and (2) constructed in G and $\text{symbols}(v) \cap (N_1 \cup N_2) = \emptyset$, there is

$$S \;{}_1\!\Rightarrow^* \rceil X\$w_1\lceil 11 \mid\mid 11\rceil w_2\$Y\lceil = w$$

in G' generated by rules from (1) and (2), where $b(w_1) = t'(v_1)$, $b(w_2) = v_2$. This also holds vice versa. Since such a sentential form represents a successful derivation of both G_1 and G_2, without any loss of generality, we can consider it in every successful derivation of either G, or G'. Additionally, in G

$$v \;{}_1\!\Rightarrow^* v', v' \in \Delta^*$$

if and only if $t'(v_1) = \text{reversal}(v_2)$. Note, $v' = t(v)$. Therefore, we have to prove

$$w \;{}_1\!\Rightarrow^* w', w' \in \Delta^*$$

if and only if $\overline{t'}(w_1) = \text{reversal}(w_2)$. Then, $v' = w'$.

Claim B In G', for

$$S \;{}_1\!\Rightarrow^* \rceil X\$w_1\lceil 11 \mid\mid 11\rceil w_2\$Y\lceil = w, \text{symbols}(w) \cap (N_1 \cup N_2) = \emptyset$$

where w is generated by using rules from (1) and (2),

$$w \;{}_1\!\Rightarrow^* w'$$

where $w' \in \Delta^*$ if and only if $\overline{t'}(w_1) = \text{reversal}(w_2)$. □

For the sake of readability, in the next proof we omit all symbols from Δ in w_1—that is, we consider only nonterminal symbols, which are to be erased.

Proof (Claim B) *If.* Suppose $w_1 = \text{reversal}(w_2)$, then $w \;{}_1\!\Rightarrow^* \varepsilon$. From the construction of G', $w_1 = (\lceil 10^{i_1}1\rceil \mid)(\lceil 10^{i_2}1\rceil \mid) \dots (\lceil 10^{i_n}1\rceil \mid)$, where $i_j \in \{1, \dots, \text{card}(\Delta)\}$, $1 \leq j \leq n$, $n \geq 0$. Consider two cases—(I) $n = 0$ and (II) $n \geq 1$.

(I) If $n = 0$, $w = \rceil X\$\lceil 11 \mid\mid 11\rceil\$Y\lceil$. Then, by using rules from (3) and (4), rules (7) and (8), and four times rules from (9), we obtain

$$\begin{aligned}
&\rceil X\$\lceil 11 \mid\mid 11\rceil\$Y\lceil \;{}_1\!\Rightarrow \rfloor\underline{\underline{\overline{X}}}\$\rfloor 11 \mid\mid 11\rceil\$Y\lceil \;{}_1\!\Rightarrow \\
&\rfloor\underline{\underline{\overline{X}}}\$\rfloor 11 \mid\mid 11\lfloor\$\underline{\underline{\overline{Y}}}\lfloor \;{}_1\!\Rightarrow \rfloor\overline{X}\$\rfloor 11 \mid\mid 11\lfloor\$\underline{\overline{Y}}\lfloor \;{}_1\!\Rightarrow \\
&\rfloor\overline{X}\$\rfloor 11 \mid\mid 11\lfloor\$\overline{Y}\lfloor \;{}_1\!\Rightarrow \underline{X}\$11 \mid\mid 11\$\underline{Y} \quad {}_1\!\Rightarrow \\
&\$XY\$ \;{}_1\!\Rightarrow XY\$ \;{}_1\!\Rightarrow Y\$ \;{}_1\!\Rightarrow \$ \;{}_1\!\Rightarrow \varepsilon
\end{aligned}$$

and the claim holds.

(II) Let $n \geq 1$,

$$\begin{aligned}
w &= \rceil X\$\lceil 10^{i'}1\rceil \mid (\lceil 10^{i_m}1\rceil \mid)^k \lceil 11 \mid\mid 11\rceil (\mid \lceil 10^{j_{m'}}1\rceil)^k \mid \lceil 10^{j'}1\rceil\$Y\lceil \\
&= \rceil X\$\lceil 10^{i'}1\rceil \mid u \mid \lceil 10^{j'}1\rceil\$Y\lceil
\end{aligned}$$

where $k \geq 0$, $m, m' \in \{1, \dots, k\}$, $i', i_m, j', j_{m'} \in \{1, \dots, \text{card}(\Delta)\}$. Sequentially using rules from (3) and rules from (4) and rule (7) we obtain the derivation

$$\begin{array}{l} \rceil X\$\lceil 10^{i'}1\rceil \mid u \mid \lceil 10^{j'}1\rceil\$Y\lceil {}_1\Rightarrow \rfloor\overline{\underline{X}}\$\rfloor 10^{i'}1\rceil \mid u \mid \lceil 10^{j'}1\rceil\$Y\lceil {}_1\Rightarrow \\ \rfloor\overline{\underline{\underline{X}}}\$\rfloor 10^{i'}1\rceil \mid u \mid \lceil 10^{j'}1\lfloor\$\overline{\underline{\underline{Y}}}\lfloor {}_1\Rightarrow \rfloor\overline{\overline{X}}\$\rfloor 10^{i'}1\rceil \mid u \mid \lceil 10^{j'}1\lfloor\$\overline{\underline{Y}}\lfloor {}_1\Rightarrow \\ \rfloor\overline{\overline{X}}\$\rfloor 10^{i'}1\rceil \mid u \mid \lceil 10^{j'}1\lfloor\$\overline{\overline{Y}}\lfloor {}_1\Rightarrow \underline{X}\$10^{i'}1\rceil \mid u \mid \lceil 10^{j'}1\$\underline{Y} \end{array}$$

Next, we prove

$$w' = \underline{X}\$10^{i'}1\rceil \mid (\lceil 10^{i_m}1\rceil \mid)^k\lceil 11 \mid\mid 11\rceil(\mid \lceil 10^{j_{m'}}1\rceil)^k \mid \lceil 10^{j'}1\$\underline{Y} {}_1\Rightarrow^* \varepsilon$$

by induction on $k \geq 0$.

Basis. Let $k = 0$. Then,

$$w' = \underline{X}\$10^{i'}1\rceil \mid \lceil 11 \mid\mid 11\rceil \mid \lceil 10^{j'}1\$\underline{Y}$$

By using the rule produced in (8) and twice rules from (3) G' performs

$$\begin{array}{ll} \underline{X}\$10^{i'}1\rceil \mid \lceil 11 \mid\mid 11\rceil \mid \lceil 10^{j'}1\$\underline{Y} & {}_1\Rightarrow \$0^{i'}\rceil X\lceil 11 \mid\mid 11\rceil Y\lceil 0^{j'}\$ \\ {}_1\Rightarrow \$0^{i'}\rfloor\overline{\underline{X}}\rfloor 11 \mid\mid 11\rceil Y\lceil 0^{j'}\$ & {}_1\Rightarrow \$0^{i'}\rfloor\overline{\underline{X}}\rfloor 11 \mid\mid 11\lfloor\overline{\underline{Y}}\lfloor 0^{j'}\$ \end{array}$$

Since $i' = j'$, both sequences of 0s are simultaneously erased by repeatedly using both rules from (4) and the rule from (5). Observe that

$$\$0^{i'}\rfloor\overline{\underline{X}}\rfloor 11 \mid\mid 11\lfloor\overline{\underline{Y}}\lfloor 0^{j'}\$ {}_1\Rightarrow^* \$\rfloor\overline{X}\rfloor 11 \mid\mid 11\lfloor\overline{Y}\lfloor\$$$

Finally, by applying rules from (4), (6), (7), (8), and (9), we finish the derivation as

$$\begin{array}{c} \$\rfloor\overline{X}\rfloor 11 \mid\mid 11\lfloor\overline{Y}\lfloor\$ {}_1\Rightarrow \rfloor\overline{X}\$\rfloor 11 \mid\mid 11\lfloor\$\overline{Y}\lfloor {}_1\Rightarrow \\ \underline{X}\$11 \mid\mid 11\$\underline{Y} {}_1\Rightarrow \$XY\$ {}_1\Rightarrow^* \varepsilon \end{array}$$

and the basis holds.

Induction Hypothesis. Suppose there exists $k \geq 0$ such that

$$w' = \underline{X}\$10^{i'}1\rceil \mid (\lceil 10^{i_m}1\rceil \mid)^l\lceil 11 \mid\mid 11\rceil(\mid \lceil 10^{j_{m'}}1\rceil)^l \mid \lceil 10^{j'}1\$\underline{Y} {}_1\Rightarrow^* \varepsilon$$

where $m, m' \in \{1, \dots, l\}$, $i', i_m, j', j_{m'} \in \{1, \dots, \text{card}(\Delta)\}$, for all $0 \leq l \leq k$.

Induction Step. Consider any

$$w' = \underline{X}\$10^{i'}1\rceil \mid (\lceil 10^{i_m}1\rceil \mid)^{k+1}\lceil 11 \mid\mid 11\rceil(\mid \lceil 10^{j_{m'}}1\rceil)^{k+1} \mid \lceil 10^{j'}1\$\underline{Y}$$

where $m, m' \in \{1, \dots, k+1\}$, $i', i_m, j', j_{m'} \in \{1, \dots, \text{card}(\Delta)\}$. Since $k+1 \geq 1$

$$\begin{array}{l} w' = \underline{X}\$10^{i'}1\rceil \mid \lceil 10^{i''}1\rceil \mid u \mid \lceil 10^{j''}1\rceil \mid \lceil 10^{j'}1\$\underline{Y} \\ u \ = (\lceil 10^{i_m}1\rceil \mid)^k\lceil 11 \mid\mid 11\rceil(\mid \lceil 10^{j_{m'}}1\rceil)^k \end{array}$$

By using rule (8) and both rules from (3) G' performs

$$\begin{aligned}
&\underline{X}\$10^{i'}1\rceil \mid \lceil 10^{i''}1\rceil \mid u \mid \lceil 10^{j''}1\rceil \mid \lceil 10^{j'}1\$\underline{Y} && {}_1\Rightarrow\\
&\$0^{i'}\rceil X\lceil 10^{i''}1\rceil \mid u \mid \lceil 10^{j''}1\rceil Y\lceil 0^{j'}\$ && {}_1\Rightarrow\\
&\$0^{i'}\rfloor\underline{\overline{X}}\rfloor 10^{i''}1\rceil \mid u \mid \lceil 10^{j''}1\rceil Y\lceil 0^{j'}\$ && {}_1\Rightarrow\\
&\$0^{i'}\rfloor\underline{\overline{X}}\rfloor 10^{i''}1\rceil \mid u \mid \lceil 10^{j''}1\lfloor\underline{\overline{Y}}\lfloor 0^{j'}\$
\end{aligned}$$

Since $i' = j'$, the prefix of 0s and the suffix of 0s are simultaneously erased by repeatedly using rules from (4) and rule (5).

$$\$0^{i'}\rfloor\underline{\overline{X}}\rfloor 10^{i''}1\rceil \mid u \mid \lceil 10^{j''}1\lfloor\underline{\overline{Y}}\lfloor 0^{j'}\$ \;{}_1\Rightarrow^* \; \$\rfloor\overline{X}\rfloor 10^{i''}1\rceil \mid u \mid \lceil 10^{j''}1\lfloor\overline{Y}\lfloor\$$$

Finally, G' uses the rule (6) and the rule (7)

$$\begin{gathered}
\$\rfloor\overline{X}\rfloor 10^{i''}1\rceil \mid u \mid \lceil 10^{j''}1\lfloor\overline{Y}\lfloor\$ \;{}_1\Rightarrow\; \rfloor\overline{X}\$\rfloor 10^{i''}1\rceil \mid u \mid \lceil 10^{j''}1\lfloor\$\overline{Y}\lfloor \;{}_1\Rightarrow\\
\underline{X}\$10^{i''}1\rceil \mid u \mid \lceil 10^{j''}1\$\underline{Y} = w''
\end{gathered}$$

where

$$w'' = \underline{X}\$10^{i''}1\rceil \mid (\lceil 10^{i_m}1\rceil \mid)^k\lceil 11 \mid\mid 11\rceil(\mid \lceil 10^{j_{m'}}1\rceil)^k \mid \lceil 10^{j''}1\$\underline{Y}$$

By the induction hypothesis, $w''\,{}_1\Rightarrow^* \varepsilon$, which completes the proof.

Only if. Suppose that $w_1 \neq \text{reversal}(w_2)$, then there is no w' satisfying $w\;{}_1\Rightarrow^* w'$ and $w' = \varepsilon$.

From the construction of G', there is no rule shifting the left \$ to the left and no rule shifting the right \$ to the right. Since rule (5) is the only one erasing 0s and these 0s must occur between two \$s, if there is any 0, which is not between the two \$s, it is unable to be erased. Moreover, an application of rule (5) moves the left \$ on the previous position of erased left 0; if it is not the leftmost, the derivation is blocked. It is symmetric on the right. A similar situation is regarding 1s, X, and Y. Thus, for the sentential form w, if 0 or 1 is the rightmost or the leftmost symbol of w, no terminal string can be generated.

Since $w_1 \neq \text{reversal}(w_2)$, the codings of terminal strings generated by G_1 and G_2 are different. Then, there is a and a', where $w_1 = vau$, $w_2 = u'a'v$, and $a \neq a'$. Observe that always the outermost 0 or 1 is erased; otherwise, the derivation is blocked. Suppose the derivation correctly erases both strings v, so a and a' are the outermost symbols. The derivation can continue in the following two ways:

(I) Suppose the outermost 0s are erased before the outermost 1s. Then, rule (5) is used, which requires $\overline{X}$ and $\overline{Y}$ between the previous positions of 0s. However, there is 1, a or a', which is not between X and Y.

(II) Suppose the outermost 1s are erased before the outermost 0s. Then, rule (8) is used, which requires $\underline{X}$ and $\underline{Y}$ in the current sentential form. The symbols $\underline{X}$ and $\underline{Y}$ are produced by rule (7), which requires X and \$ between two symbols $\rfloor$ and Y and \$ between two symbols $\lfloor$. Suppose w' is the current sentential form. Since w_1 or reversal(w_2) is of the form

$$\ldots \ulcorner 10^{i_0}1\urcorner \mid \ulcorner 10^{i_1}1\urcorner \mid \ulcorner 10^{i_2}1\urcorner \mid \ldots$$

where $i_0, i_1, i_2 \in \{1, \ldots, \text{card}(\Delta)\}$, there is 0 as the leftmost or rightmost symbol of w' and $X\$$ and $\$Y$ occurs between $\rfloor$s and $\lfloor$s, respectively. However, this 0 is obviously not between the two \$ and remains permanently in the sentential form.

We showed that G' can generate the terminal string from the sentential form w if and only if $\overline{t'}(w_1) = \text{reversal}(w_2)$, so the claim holds. □

We proved that for any $w \in \Delta^*$, $S\ {}_1\!\Rightarrow^*\ w$ in G if and only if $S\ {}_1\!\Rightarrow^*\ w$ in G', and Claim A holds. □

Let us turn to ${}_2\!\Rightarrow$.

Claim C $L(G', {}_2\!\Rightarrow) = L(G', {}_1\!\Rightarrow)$. □

Proof (Claim C) In ${}_2\!\Rightarrow$, applications of context-free rules progress in the same way as in ${}_1\!\Rightarrow$. While using context-sensitive rules inserted right-hand-side strings can be nondeterministically scattered between the previous positions of the leftmost and rightmost affected nonterminals, only their order is preserved. We show that we can control this by the construction of G'.

Recall the observations made at the beginning of the proof of Claim A. Since the behavior of context-free rules remains unchanged in terms of ${}_2\!\Rightarrow$, these still hold true. It remains to prove that Claim B also holds in ${}_2\!\Rightarrow$.

In a special case, ${}_2\!\Rightarrow$ behave exactly as ${}_1\!\Rightarrow$, hence definitely $L(G', {}_1\!\Rightarrow) \subseteq L(G', {}_2\!\Rightarrow)$. We prove

$$w \notin L(G', {}_1\!\Rightarrow) \Rightarrow w \notin L(G', {}_2\!\Rightarrow)$$

Therefore, to complete the proof of Claim C, we establish the following claim:

Claim D In G', for

$$S\ {}_1\!\Rightarrow^*\ \urcorner X\$w_1\ulcorner 11 \mid\mid 11\urcorner w_2\$Y\ulcorner = w, \text{symbols}(w) \cap (N_1 \cup N_2) = \emptyset$$

where w is generated only by using rules from (1) and (2), and $\overline{t'}(w_1) \neq \text{reversal}(w_2)$, there is no w', where

$$w\ {}_1\!\Rightarrow^*\ w', w' \in \Delta^*$$

For the sake of readability, in the next proof we omit all symbols from Δ in w_1—we consider only nonterminal symbols, which are to be erased.

Proof (Claim D) Suppose any w, where

$$S\ {}_1\!\Rightarrow^*\ w = \urcorner X\$w_1\ulcorner 11 \mid\mid 11\urcorner w_2\$Y\ulcorner$$

in G' and w is generated by using rules from (1) and (2), $\text{symbols}(w) \cap (N_1 \cup N_2) = \emptyset$, and $w_1 \neq \text{reversal}(w_2)$.

From the construction of G', there is no rule shifting the left \$ to the left and no rule shifting the right \$ to the right. Neither ${}_2\Rightarrow$ can do this. Since the rule (5) is the only one erasing 0s, and these 0s must be between two \$s, if there is any 0, which is not between the two \$s, it cannot be erased. A similar situation is regarding 1s, X, and Y. Thus, for the sentential form w, if 0 or 1 is the outermost symbol of w, no terminal string can be generated.

Consider two cases (I) $w_1 = \varepsilon$ or $w_2 = \varepsilon$ and (II) $w_1 \neq \varepsilon$ and $w_2 \neq \varepsilon$.

(I) Suppose the condition does not apply. Without any loss of generality, suppose $w_1 = \varepsilon$. Since $w_1 \neq \text{reversal}(w_2)$, $w_2 \neq \varepsilon$. Then,

$$w = \rceil X\$\lceil 11 \mid\mid 11\rceil(\mid \lceil 10^{i_m}1\rceil)^k \mid \lceil 10^{i'}1\rceil\$Y\lceil$$

where $k \geq 0$, $m \in \{1, \dots, k\}$, $i_m, i' \in \{1, \dots, \text{card}(\Delta)\}$.

First, the rules from (3) and (9) are the only applicable rules; however, application of a rule from (9) would block the derivation, so we do not consider it. While rewriting X, the leftmost $\rceil$ is rewritten. Unless the leftmost $\lceil$ is chosen, it becomes unpaired and, thus, cannot be erased. It is symmetric with Y. After the application of rules from (3), rules from (4) become applicable. The positions of the symbols \$ must be preserved for future use of rule (7). Then, the only way of continuing a successful derivation is

$$\begin{array}{l}
\rceil X\$\lceil 11 \mid\mid 11\rceil(\mid \lceil 10^{i_m}1\rceil)^k \mid \lceil 10^{i'}1\rceil\$Y\lceil\ {}_2\Rightarrow \\
\rfloor\underline{\underline{\overline{X}}}\$\rfloor 11 \mid\mid 11\rceil(\mid \lceil 10^{i_m}1\rceil)^k \mid \lceil 10^{i'}1\rceil\$Y\lceil\ {}_2\Rightarrow \\
\rfloor\underline{\overline{\overline{X}}}\$\rfloor 11 \mid\mid 11\rceil(\mid \lceil 10^{i_m}1\rceil)^k \mid \lceil 10^{i'}1\lfloor\$\underline{\underline{\overline{Y}}}\lfloor\ {}_2\Rightarrow \\
\rfloor\overline{\overline{X}}\$\rfloor 11 \mid\mid 11\rceil(\mid \lceil 10^{i_m}1\rceil)^k \mid \lceil 10^{i'}1\lfloor\$\underline{\overline{\overline{Y}}}\lfloor\ {}_2\Rightarrow \\
\rfloor\overline{X}\$\rfloor 11 \mid\mid 11\rceil(\mid \lceil 10^{i_m}1\rceil)^k \mid \lceil 10^{i'}1\lfloor\$\overline{Y}\lfloor
\end{array}$$

Notice that if neighboring nonterminals are rewritten, ${}_2\Rightarrow$ do not shift any symbol.

Next, rule (7) is the only applicable rule, which shifts $\underline{X}$, $\underline{Y}$, and \$s inside into the current sentential form. However, if any shift is performed, there is a symbol 1 as the outermost symbol, which is obviously unable to be erased. Thus,

$$\begin{array}{l}
\rfloor\overline{X}\$\rfloor 11 \mid\mid 11\rceil(\mid \lceil 10^{i_m}1\rceil)^k \mid \lceil 10^{i'}1\lfloor\$\overline{Y}\lfloor {}_2\Rightarrow \\
\underline{X}\$11 \mid\mid 11\rceil(\mid \lceil 10^{i_m}1\rceil)^k \mid \lceil 10^{i'}1\$\underline{Y} = w'
\end{array}$$

Next, consider two cases depending on k.

(I.i) Suppose $k = 0$. Then,

$$w' = \underline{X}\$11 \mid\mid 11\rceil \mid \lceil 10^{i'}1\$\underline{Y}$$

Since $i' > 0$, rule (5) must be used. It requires presence of $\overline{X}$ and $\overline{Y}$ in the current sentential form. These can be obtained only by application of rule (8) and both rules from (3) and (4). However, it must rewrite two pairs of $\rceil, \lceil$, but there is only one remaining. Therefore, there are i' symbols 0, which cannot be erased, and no terminal string can be generated.

(I.ii) Suppose $k > 0$. Then, w' is of the form

$$\underline{X}\$11 \mid\mid 11\rceil \mid \lceil u\rceil \mid \lceil 10^{i'}1\$\underline{Y}$$

Rule (8) is the only one applicable. It rewrites $\underline{X}$ to X, $\underline{Y}$ to Y and puts them potentially anywhere into the current sentential form. However, the rules from (3), which are the only rules containing X and Y on the left-hand side, require X and Y to be situated between $\rceil$ and $\lceil$.

$$\underline{X}\$11 \mid\mid 11\rceil \mid \lceil u\rceil \mid \lceil 10^{i'}1\$\underline{Y} \;{}_2\!\Rightarrow\; \$11 \mid\mid 11\rceil X\lceil u\rceil Y\lceil 0^{i'}\$$$

Without any loss of generality, we omit other possibilities of erasing the symbols $\mid$ or 1, because the derivation would be blocked in the same way. Since there is no 0 to the left of X, the future application of rule (5) is excluded, and the rightmost sequence of 0s is obviously skipped and cannot be erased any more.

(II) Suppose the condition applies. Then,

$$\begin{aligned} w &= \rceil X\$\lceil 10^{i}1\rceil \mid (\lceil 10^{j_m}1\rceil \mid)^{k}\lceil 11 \mid\mid 11\rceil(\mid \lceil 10^{j_{m'}}1\rceil)^{k'} \mid \lceil 10^{i'}1\rceil\$Y\lceil \\ &= \rceil X\$\lceil 10^{i}1\rceil \mid \lceil u\rceil \mid \lceil 10^{i'}1\rceil\$Y\lceil \end{aligned}$$

where $k, k' \geq 0$, $m \in \{1, \ldots, k\}$, $m' \in \{1, \ldots, k'\}$, $i_m, i'_m, j, j' \in \{1, \ldots, \mathrm{card}(\Delta)\}$.

First, the situation is completely the same as in (I), the only possibly non-blocking derivation consists of application of both rules from (3) and (4) followed by application of rule (7). No left-hand-side string may be shifted during the application of these rules or the derivation is blocked.

$$\begin{aligned} &\rceil X\$\lceil 10^{i}1\rceil \mid \lceil u\rceil \mid \lceil 10^{i'}1\rceil\$Y\lceil \;{}_2\!\Rightarrow\; \rfloor\overline{\underline{\underline{X}}}\$\rfloor 10^{i}1\rceil \mid \lceil u\rceil \mid \lceil 10^{i'}1\rceil\$Y\lceil \;{}_2\!\Rightarrow \\ &\rfloor\overline{\underline{\underline{X}}}\$\rfloor 10^{i}1\rceil \mid \lceil u\rceil \mid \lceil 10^{i'}1\lfloor\$\overline{\underline{\underline{Y}}}\lfloor \;{}_2\!\Rightarrow\; \rfloor\overline{X}\$\rfloor 10^{i}1\rceil \mid \lceil u\rceil \mid \lceil 10^{i'}1\lfloor\$\overline{\underline{Y}}\lfloor \;{}_2\!\Rightarrow \\ &\rfloor\overline{X}\$\rfloor 10^{i}1\rceil \mid \lceil u\rceil \mid \lceil 10^{i'}1\lfloor\$\overline{Y}\lfloor \;{}_2\!\Rightarrow\; \underline{X}\$10^{i}1\rceil \mid \lceil u\rceil \mid \lceil 10^{i'}1\$\underline{Y} \end{aligned}$$

Next, rule (8) is the only applicable rule, which erases four symbols 1, two $\mid$, rewrites $\underline{X}$ to X and $\underline{Y}$ to Y, and inserts them possibly anywhere into the current sentential form. However, X must be inserted between $\rceil$ and $\lceil$; otherwise, no rule from (3) is applicable, and X remains permanently in the sentential form. Unless the leftmost pair of $\rceil$ and $\lceil$ is chosen, there are skipped symbols 1 remaining to the left of X. Rules (6) and (7) ensure the derivation is blocked, if X is shifted to the right. Additionally, the only way to erase 1s is rule (8), but these 1s must be to the right of X. Thus, the skipped symbols 1 cannot be erased. Therefore, the pair of $\rceil$ and $\lceil$ is the leftmost or the derivation is blocked. Moreover, the two erased 1s are also the leftmost or they cannot be erased in the future, and the same holds for the left erased symbol $|$. A similar situation is regarding Y. Then,

$$\underline{X}\$10^{i}1\rceil \mid \lceil u\rceil \mid \lceil 10^{i'}1\$\underline{Y} \;{}_2\!\Rightarrow\; \$0^{i}\rceil X\lceil u\rceil Y\lceil 0^{i'}\$$$

and by using the rules from(3) and repeatedly rules from (4) and (5) both outermost sequences of 0s can be erased, if $i = i'$. Additionally, rules from (4) ensure that X and Y are never shifted. If there is any 0 skipped, it cannot be erased and the derivation is blocked.

$$\$0^{i}\rceil X\lceil u\rceil Y\lceil 0^{i'}\$ \;{}_2\!\Rightarrow^*\; \$0^{i}\rfloor\underline{\overline{X}}\rfloor u\lfloor\underline{\overline{Y}}\lfloor 0^{i'}\$ \;{}_2\!\Rightarrow^*\; \$\rfloor\overline{X}\rfloor u\lfloor\overline{Y}\lfloor\$$$

Finally, by rules (6) and (7) both terminal codings can be completely erased and $\underline{X}$, $\underline{Y}$, and two \$ are the outermost symbols, if no symbol is skipped.

$$\$\rfloor\overline{X}\rfloor u\lfloor\overline{Y}\lfloor\$ \;{}_2\!\Rightarrow\; \rfloor\underline{X}\$\rfloor u\lfloor\$\underline{Y}\lfloor \;{}_2\!\Rightarrow\; \underline{X}\$u\$\underline{Y}$$

Since $w_1 \neq w_2$, $w_1 = vau$ and $w_2 = u'a'v$, where $a \neq a'$ are the outermost non-identical terminal codings. Derivation can always erase vs, as it was described, or be blocked before. Without any loss of generality, we have to consider two cases:

(II.i) Suppose $au = \varepsilon$. Then, $u'a' \neq \varepsilon$ and the situation is the same as in (I), no terminal string can be generated and the derivation is blocked.

(II.ii) Suppose $au \neq \varepsilon$, $u'a' \neq \varepsilon$. If the derivation is not blocked before, it may generate the sentential form

$$\$0^{i}\rceil X\lceil u\rceil Y\lceil 0^{i'}\$$$

where $10^{i}1 = a$, $10^{i'}1 = a'$. Then, $i \neq i'$ and while simultaneously erasing the sequences of 0s of both codings, one is erased before the second one. Rule (5) becomes inapplicable, and there is no way not to skip the remaining part of the second sequence of 0s. The derivation is blocked.

We covered all possibilities and showed that there is no way to generate terminal string $w' \notin L(G', {}_1\!\Rightarrow)$, and the claim holds. □

Since $S \;{}_1\!\Rightarrow^*\; w$, $w \in \Delta^*$ if and only if $S \;{}_2\!\Rightarrow^*\; w$, Claim C holds. □

We proved that $L(G', {}_2\!\Rightarrow) = L(G', {}_1\!\Rightarrow)$, $L(G', {}_1\!\Rightarrow) = L(G, {}_1\!\Rightarrow)$, and $L(G, {}_1\!\Rightarrow) = L$, then $L(G', {}_2\!\Rightarrow) = L$, so the proof of Theorem 6.2 is completed. □

Jumping Derivation Mode 3

Definition 6.7 Let $G = (\Sigma, \Delta, P, S)$ be an SCG. Let $u = u_0 A_1 u_1 \dots A_n u_n \in \Sigma^*$ and $(A_1,A_2,\dots,A_n) \rightarrow (x_1,x_2,\dots,x_n) \in P$, for $n \geq 1$. Then,

$$u_0 A_1 u_1 A_2 u_2 \dots A_n u_n \;{}_3\!\Rightarrow v_0 x_1 v_1 x_2 v_2 \dots x_n v_n$$

where $u_0 u_1 \dots u_n = v_0 v_1 \dots v_n$, $u_0 = v_0 z_1$ and $u_n = z_2 v_n$, $z_1, z_2 \in \Sigma^*$.

Informally, G obtains $v = v_0 x_1 v_1 x_2 v_2 \dots x_n v_n$ from $u = u_0 A_1 u_1 A_2 u_2 \dots A_n u_n$ by $(A_1,A_2,\dots,A_n) \rightarrow (x_1,x_2,\dots,x_n) \in P$ in terms of ${}_3\!\Rightarrow$ as follows:

(1) $A_1, A_2, \dots, A_n$ are deleted;
(2) x_1 and x_n are inserted into u_0 and u_n, respectively;
(3) x_2 through x_{n-1} are inserted between the newly inserted x_1 and x_n.

Example 6.4 Let $G = (\Sigma, \Delta, P, S)$, where $\Sigma = \{S, A, \$, a, b\}$, $\Delta = \{a, b\}$, be an SCG with P containing the following rules:

(i) $(S) \rightarrow (A\$)$	(iv) $(A) \rightarrow (\varepsilon)$
(ii) $(A) \rightarrow (aAb)$	(v) $(\$) \rightarrow (\varepsilon)$
(iii) $(A, \$) \rightarrow (A, \$)$	

Consider G uses ${}_3\!\Rightarrow$. Notice that context-free rules are not influenced by ${}_3\!\Rightarrow$.
After applying starting rule (i), G generates $\{a\}^n\{b\}^n$, where $n \geq 0$, by using rule (ii) or finishes the derivation with rules (iv) and (v). However, at any time during the derivation rule (iii) can be applied. It inserts or erases nothing, but it potentially shifts A to the left. Notice, the symbol \$ is always the rightmost and, thus, cannot be shifted. Then,

$$L(G, {}_3\!\Rightarrow) = \big\{x \in \Delta^* \mid x = \varepsilon \text{ or } x = uvwb^n, uw = a^n, n \geq 0, \\ \text{and } v \text{ is defined recursively as } x\big\}$$

For example, the string $aaaababbabbb$ is generated by G in the following way:

$$\begin{aligned} S \;{}_3\!\Rightarrow A\$ \;{}_3\!\Rightarrow aAb\$ \;{}_3\!\Rightarrow aaAbb\$ \;{}_3\!\Rightarrow aaaAbbb\$ \;{}_3\!\Rightarrow aaAabbb\$ \\ {}_3\!\Rightarrow aaaAbabbb\$ \;{}_3\!\Rightarrow aaaaAbbabbb\$ \;{}_3\!\Rightarrow aaaAabbabbb\$ \\ {}_3\!\Rightarrow aaaaAbabbabbb\$ \;{}_3\!\Rightarrow aaaababbabbb\$ \;{}_3\!\Rightarrow aaaababbabbb \end{aligned}$$

Theorem 6.3 $\mathbf{JSC}_{3\Rightarrow} = \mathbf{RE}$.

Proof Clearly $\mathbf{JSC}_{3\Rightarrow} \subseteq \mathbf{RE}$, so we only need to prove $\mathbf{RE} \subseteq \mathbf{JSC}_{3\Rightarrow}$.
Let $G = (\Sigma, \Delta, P, S)$ be the SCG constructed in the proof of Theorem 6.1. Next, we modify G to a new SCG G' satisfying $L(G, {}_1\!\Rightarrow) = L(G', {}_1\!\Rightarrow)$. Finally, we prove $L(G', {}_3\!\Rightarrow) = L(G', {}_1\!\Rightarrow)$.

Construction. Let $G' = (\Sigma, \Delta, P', S)$ be SCG with P' containing

(1) $(S) \to (S_1 11\$\$11 S_2)$;
(2) $(A) \to (C_i(w))$ for $A \to w \in P_i$, where $i = 1, 2$;
(3) $(a, \$, \$, a) \to (\$, \varepsilon, \varepsilon, \$)$, for $a = 0, 1$;
(4) $(\$) \to (\varepsilon)$.

We establish the proof of Theorem 6.3 by demonstrating the following two claims.

Claim A $L(G', {}_1\!\Rightarrow) = L(G, {}_1\!\Rightarrow)$. □

Proof (Claim A) G' is closely related to G, only rule (1) and the rules from (3) are slightly modified. As a result the correspondence of the sentences generated by the simulated G_1, G_2, respectively, is not checked in the direction from the outermost to the central symbols but from the central to the outermost symbols. Again, if the current two symbols do not match, these symbols cannot be erased and the derivation is blocked. □

Claim B $L(G', {}_3\!\Rightarrow) = L(G', {}_1\!\Rightarrow)$. □

Proof (Claim B) Without any loss of generality, we can suppose rule (1) and rules from (2) are used only before the first usage of a rule from (3). The context-free rules work unchanged with ${}_3\!\Rightarrow$. Then, for every derivation

$$S \;{}_1\!\Rightarrow^* w = w_1 11\$\$11 w_2$$

generated only by rule (1) and rules from (2), where $\text{symbols}(w) \cap (N_1 \cup N_2) = \emptyset$, there is the identical derivation

$$S \;{}_3\!\Rightarrow^* w$$

and vice versa. Since

$$w \;{}_1\!\Rightarrow^* w', w' \in \Delta^*$$

if and only if $t'(w_1) = \text{reversal}(w_2)$, we can complete the proof of the previous claim by the following one.

Claim C Let the sentential form w be generated only by rule (1) and rules from (2). Without any loss of generality, suppose $\text{symbols}(w) \cap (N_1 \cup N_2) = \emptyset$. Consider

$$S \;{}_3\!\Rightarrow^* w = w_1 11\$\$11 w_2$$

Then, $w \;{}_3\!\Rightarrow^* w'$, where $w' \in \Delta^*$ if and only if $t'(w_1) = \text{reversal}(w_2)$. □

For better readability, in the next proof we omit all symbols of w_1 from Δ—we consider only nonterminal symbols, which are to be erased.

Basic idea. The rules from (3) are the only ones with 0s and 1s on their left-hand sides. These symbols are simultaneously erasing to the left and to the right of \$s checking the equality. While proceeding from the center to the edges, when there is any symbol skipped, which is remaining between \$s, there is no way, how to erase it, and no terminal string can be generated.

Consider ${}_3\Rightarrow$. Even when the symbols are erasing one after another from the center to the left and right, ${}_3\Rightarrow$ can potentially shift the left \$ to the left and the right \$ to the right skipping some symbols. Also in this case the symbols between \$s cannot be erased anymore.

Proof (Claim C) *If.* Recall

$$w = 10^{m_1}110^{m_2}1 \dots 10^{m_l}111\$\$1110^{m_l}1 \dots 10^{m_2}110^{m_1}1$$

Suppose the check works properly not skipping any symbol. Then,

$$w \ {}_3\Rightarrow^* \ w' = \$\$$$

and twice applying rule (4) the derivation finishes.
Only if. If $w_1 \neq \text{reversal}(w_2)$, though the check works properly,

$$w \ {}_1\Rightarrow^* \ w' = w_1' x\$\$x' w_2'$$

and $x, x' \in \{0, 1\}$, $x \neq x'$. Continuing the check with application of the rules from (3) will definitely skip x or x'. Consequently, no terminal string can be generated.
We showed that G' can generate the terminal string from the sentential form w if and only if $t'(w_1) = \text{reversal}(w_2)$, and the claim holds. □

Since $S \ {}_1\Rightarrow^* \ w$, $w \in \Delta^*$ if and only if $S \ {}_3\Rightarrow^* \ w$, Claim B holds. □

We proved that $L(G, {}_1\Rightarrow) = L$, $L(G', {}_1\Rightarrow) = L(G, {}_1\Rightarrow)$, $L(G', {}_3\Rightarrow) = L(G', {}_1\Rightarrow)$; therefore, $L(G', {}_3\Rightarrow) = L$ holds. Thus, the proof of Theorem 6.3 is completed. □

Jumping Derivation Mode 4

Definition 6.8 Let $G = (\Sigma, \Delta, P, S)$ be an SCG. Let $uAv \in \Sigma^*$ and $(A) \to (x) \in P$. Then, $uAv \ {}_4\Rightarrow \ uxv$. Let $u = u_0A_1u_1 \dots A_nu_n \in \Sigma^*$ and $(A_1, A_2, \dots, A_n) \to (x_1, x_2, \dots, x_n) \in P$, for $n \geq 2$. Then,

$$u_0A_1u_1A_2u_2 \dots u_{i-1}A_iu_iA_{i+1}u_{i+1} \dots u_{n-1}A_nu_n \ {}_4\Rightarrow$$
$$u_0u_1x_1u_2x_2 \dots u_{i-1}x_{i-1}u_{i_1}x_iu_{i_2}x_{i+1}u_{i_3}x_{i+2}u_{i+1} \dots x_nu_{n-1}u_n$$

where $u_i = u_{i_1}u_{i_2}u_{i_3}$.

Informally, $v = u_0u_1x_1u_2x_2 \dots u_{i-1}x_{i-1}u_{i_1}x_iu_{i_2}x_{i+1}u_{i_3}x_{i+2}u_{i+1} \dots x_nu_{n-1}u_n$ is obtained from $u = u_0A_1u_1A_2u_2 \dots u_{i-1}A_iu_iA_{i+1}u_{i+1} \dots u_{n-1}A_nu_n$ in G by $(A_1, A_2, \dots, A_n) \to (x_1, x_2, \dots, x_n) \in P$ in ${}_4\Rightarrow$ as follows:

(1) $A_1, A_2, \dots, A_n$ are deleted;
(2) a central u_i is nondeterministically chosen, for some $i \in \{0, \dots, n\}$;
(3) x_i and x_{i+1} are inserted into u_i;

(4) x_j is inserted between u_j and u_{j+1}, for all $j < i$;
(5) x_k is inserted between u_{k-2} and u_{k-1}, for all $k > i + 1$.

Example 6.5 Let $G = (\Sigma, \Delta, P, S)$, where $\Sigma = \{S, A, B, C, \$, a, b, c, d\}$, $\Delta = \{a, b, c, d\}$, be an SCG with P containing the following rules:

(i) $(S) \to (AB\$\$BA)$	(iv) $(A, B, B, A) \to (A, C, C, A)$
(ii) $(A) \to (aAb)$	(v) $(\$, C, C, \$) \to (\varepsilon, \varepsilon, \varepsilon, \varepsilon)$
(iii) $(B) \to (cBd)$	(vi) $(A) \to (\varepsilon)$

Consider G uses ${}_4\Rightarrow$. Then, every context-sensitive rule is applied in the following way. First, all affected nonterminals are erased. Next, some position of the current sentential form called center is nondeterministically chosen. Finaly, the corresponding right-hand sides of the selected rule are inserted each at the original place of the neighboring erased nonterminal closer to the center. The central right-hand-side strings are randomly put closer to the chosen central position. In this example, we show how to control the choice.

First, rule (i) rewrites S to $AB\$\$BA$. Then, G uses rules (ii) and (iii) generating a sentential form

$$a^{n_1}Ab^{n_1}c^{n_2}Bd^{n_2}\$\$c^{n_3}Bd^{n_3}a^{n_4}Ab^{n_4}$$

where $n_i \geq 0$, for $i \in \{1, 2, 3, 4\}$. If rule (vi) is used, derivation is blocked. Next, G uses the context-sensitive rule (iv), which may act in several different ways. In any case, it inserts two Cs into the current sentential form and the only possibility to erase them is rule (v). However, thereby we force rule (iv) to choose the center for interchanging nonterminals between Bs and moreover to insert Cs between the two symbols \$. Finally, G continues by using rule (ii) and eventually finishes twice rule (vi). Consequently,

$$L(G, {}_4\Rightarrow) = \big\{x \in \Delta^* \mid x = a^{n_1}b^{n_1}c^{n_2}a^{n_3}b^{n_3}d^{n_2}c^{n_4}a^{n_5}b^{n_5}d^{n_4}a^{n_6}b^{n_6}, \\ n_i \geq 0, i \in \{1, 2, 3, 4, 5, 6\}\big\}$$

Then, the string $aabbcabdccddab$ is generated by G in the following way:

$$S \;{}_4\Rightarrow AB\$\$BA \;{}_4\Rightarrow aAbB\$\$BA \;{}_4\Rightarrow aaAbbB\$\$BA \;{}_4\Rightarrow aaAbbcBd\$\$BA \\ {}_4\Rightarrow aaAbbcBd\$\$cBdA \;{}_4\Rightarrow aaAbbcBd\$\$ccBddA \;{}_4\Rightarrow aaAbbcBd\$\$ccBddaAb \\ {}_4\Rightarrow aabbcAd\$CC\$ccAddab \;{}_4\Rightarrow aabbcAdccAddab \;{}_4\Rightarrow aabbcaAbdccAddab \\ {}_4\Rightarrow aabbcabdccAddab \;{}_4\Rightarrow aabbcabdccddab$$

Theorem 6.4 $\mathbf{JSC}_{4\Rightarrow} = \mathbf{RE}$.

Proof As is obvious, $\mathbf{JSC}_{4\Rightarrow} \subseteq \mathbf{RE}$, so we only prove $\mathbf{RE} \subseteq \mathbf{JSC}_{4\Rightarrow}$.

Let $G = (\Sigma, \Delta, P, S)$ be the SCG constructed in the proof of Theorem 6.1. Next, we modify G to a new SCG G' so $L(G, {}_1\Rightarrow) = L(G', {}_4\Rightarrow)$.

Construction. Introduce five new symbols—D,E,F,$|$, and $\top$. Set $N = \{D, E, F, |, \top\}$. Let $G' = (\Sigma', \Delta, P', S)$ be SCG, with $\Sigma' = \Sigma \cup N$ and P' containing the rules

(1) $(S) \to (F\$S_1 11|E|11S_2\$F)$;
(2) $(A) \to (C_i(w))$ for $A \to w \in P_i$, where $i = 1, 2$;
(3) $(F) \to (FF)$;
(4) $(\$, a, a, \$) \to (\varepsilon, D, D, \varepsilon)$, for $a = 0, 1$;
(5) $(F, D, |, |, D, F) \to (\$, \varepsilon, \top, \top, \varepsilon, \$)$;
(6) $(\top, E, \top) \to (\varepsilon, |E|, \varepsilon)$;
(7) $(\$) \to (\varepsilon)$, $(E) \to (\varepsilon)$, $(|) \to (\varepsilon)$.

Claim A $L(G, {}_1\Rightarrow) = L(G', {}_4\Rightarrow)$. □

Proof (Claim A) The behavior of context-free rules remains unchanged under ${}_4\Rightarrow$. Since the rules of G' simulating the derivations of G_1 and G_2 are identical to the ones of G simulating both grammars, for every derivation of G

$$S \ {}_1\Rightarrow^* \ \$w_1 1111 w_2\$ = w$$

where w is generated only by using rule (1) and rules from (2) constructed in G and symbols$(w) \cap (N_1 \cup N_2) = \emptyset$, there is

$$S \ {}_4\Rightarrow^* \ F\$w_1 11|E|11w_2\$\#\#F = w'$$

in G', generated by the corresponding rule (1) and rules from (2) produced in G', and vice versa. Without any loss of generality, we can consider such a sentential form in every successful derivation. Additionally, in G

$$w \ {}_1\Rightarrow^* \ v, v \in \Delta^*$$

if and only if $t'(w_1) = \text{reversal}(w_2)$; then $v = t(w)$. Therefore, we have to prove

$$w' \ {}_4\Rightarrow^* \ v', v' \in \Delta^*$$

if and only if $t'(w_1) = \text{reversal}(w_2)$. Then, obviously $v' = v$ and we can complete the proof by the following claim.

Claim B In G', for

$$S \ {}_4\Rightarrow^* \ w = F^{i_1}\$w_1 11|E|11w_2\$\#\#F^{i_2}, \ \text{symbols}(w) \cap (N_1 \cup N_2) = \emptyset$$

where w is generated only by using the rule (1) and rules from (2),

$$w \ {}_4\Rightarrow^* \ w'$$

where $w' \in \Delta^*$ if and only if $t'(w_1) = \text{reversal}(w_2)$, for some $i_1, i_2 \geq 0$. □

The new rule (3) potentially arbitrarily multiplies the number of Fs to the left and right. Then, Fs from both sequences are simultaneously erasing by using rule (5). Thus, without any loss of generality, suppose $i_1 = i_2$ equal the number of future usages of rule (5).

For the sake of readability, in the next proof, in w_1, we omit all symbols from Δ—we consider only nonterminal symbols, which are to be erased.

Proof (Claim B) *If.* Suppose $w_1 = \text{reversal}(w_2)$, then $w\ {}_4\Rightarrow^*\ \varepsilon$. We prove this by the induction on the length of w_1,w_2, where $|w_1| = |w_2| = k$.

Basis. Let $k = 0$. Then, $w = FF\$11|E|11\$FF$. Except for the rules from (7), a rule from (4) is the only applicable. The center for interchanging the right-hand-side strings must be chosen between the two rewritten 1s and additionally inserted Ds must remain on the different sides of the central string $|E|$. Moreover, if any 1 stays outside the two Ds, it cannot be erased, so

$$FF\$11|E|11\$FF\ {}_4\Rightarrow\ FFD1|E|1DFF$$

Next, rule (5) rewrites Ds back to \$s, erases Fs, and changes |s to $\top$s. The center must be chosen between the two |s and inserted $\top$s may not be shifted; otherwise, they appear on the same side of E and rule (6) is inapplicable. It secures the former usage of rules from (4) was as expected, so

$$FFD1|E|1DFF\ {}_4\Rightarrow\ F\$1\top E\top 1\$F$$

By rule (6) the symbols $\top$ may be rewritten back to |s. No left-hand-side string may be shifted during the application of the rule and the choice of the central position has no influence, because the neighboring symbols are rewritten. It secures the former usage of rule (5) was as expected; therefore,

$$F\$1\top E\top 1\$F\ {}_4\Rightarrow\ F\$1|E|1\$F$$

Then, the same sequence of rules with the same restrictions can be used again to erase remaining 1s and the check is finished by rules from (7) as

$$F\$1|E|1\$F\ {}_4\Rightarrow\ FD|E|DF\ {}_4\Rightarrow\ \$\top E\top\$\ {}_4\Rightarrow\ \$|E|\$\ {}_4\Rightarrow^*\ \varepsilon$$

and the basis holds.

Induction Hypothesis. Suppose there exists $k \geq 0$ such that the claim holds for all $0 \leq m \leq k$, where

$$w = F^{i_1}\$w_1 11|E|11w_2\$F^{i_2},\ |w_1| = |w_2| = m$$

Induction Step. Consider G' generating w with

$$w = F^{i_1}\$w_1 11|E|11w_2\$F^{i_2}$$

where $|w_1| = |w_2| = k + 1$, $w_1 = \text{reversal}(w_2) = aw'_1$, and $a \in \{0, 1\}$. Except for the rules from (7), a rule from (4) is the only applicable one. The center for interchanging of the right-hand-side strings must be chosen between the two rewritten 0s or 1s and additionally inserted Ds must remain on the different sides of the central string $|E|$.

Moreover, the outermost 0s or 1s must be rewritten, and Ds may not be shifted between the new outermost ones; otherwise, they cannot be erased.

$$F^{i_1}\$w_1 11|E|11w_2\$F^{i_2}\ {}_4\Rightarrow F^{i_1}Dw'_1 11|E|11w'_2DF^{i_2}$$

Next, rule (5) rewrites Ds back to \$s, erases Fs, and changes |s to ⊤s. The center must be chosen between the two |s and inserted ⊤s may not be shifted; otherwise, they appear on the same side of E and rule (6) is inapplicable. It secures the former usage of a rule from (4) was as expected.

$$F^{i_1}Dw'_1 11|E|11w'_2DF^{i_2}\ {}_4\Rightarrow F^{i'_1}\$w'_1 11\top E\top 11w'_2\$F^{i'_2}$$

By rule (6) the symbols ⊤ may be rewritten back to |s. No left-hand-side string may be shifted during the application of the rule, and the position of the chosen center has no influence, because the neighboring symbols are rewritten. It secures the former usage of rule (5) was as expected.

$$F^{i'_1}\$w'_1 11\top E\top 11w'_2\$F^{i'_2}\ {}_4\Rightarrow F^{i'_1}\$w'_1 11|E|11w'_2\$F^{i'_2} = w'$$

By the induction hypothesis, $w'\ {}_4\Rightarrow^* \varepsilon$, which completes the proof.

Only if. Suppose $w_1 \neq \text{reversal}(w_2)$; there is no w', where $w\ {}_4\Rightarrow^*\ w'$ and $w' = \varepsilon$.

Since $w_1 \neq \text{reversal}(w_2)$, $w_1 = vau$, $w_2 = u'a'v$, and $a \neq a'$. Suppose both vs are correctly erased, and no symbol is skipped producing the sentential form

$$F^{i_1}\$au11|E|11u'a'\$F^{i_2}$$

Next, rules from (4) can be applied to erase outermost 0s or 1s. However, then, there is 0 or 1 outside inserted Ds and, thus, unable to be erased, which completes the proof.

We showed that G' can generate the terminal string from the sentential form w if and only if $t'(w_1) = \text{reversal}(w_2)$, and the claim holds. □

We proved that for some $w \in \Delta^*$, $S\ {}_1\Rightarrow^*\ w$ in G if and only if $S\ {}_4\Rightarrow^*\ w$ in G', and the claim holds. □

Since $L(G,\ {}_1\Rightarrow) = L(G',\ {}_4\Rightarrow) = L$, the proof of Theorem 6.4 is completed. □

Jumping Derivation Mode 5

Definition 6.9 Let $G = (\Sigma, \Delta, P, S)$ be an SCG. Let $uAv \in \Sigma^*$ and $(A) \rightarrow (x) \in P$. Then, $uAv\ {}_5\Rightarrow\ uxv$. Let $u = u_0A_1u_1 \ldots A_nu_n \in \Sigma^*$ and $(A_1, A_2, \ldots, A_n) \rightarrow (x_1, x_2, \ldots, x_n) \in P$, for $n \geq 2$. Then,

$$u_0A_1u_1A_2 \ldots u_{i-1}A_{i-1}u_iA_iu_{i+1} \ldots A_nu_n\ {}_5\Rightarrow$$
$$u_{0_1}x_1u_{0_2}x_2u_1 \ldots x_{i-1}u_{i-1}u_iu_{i+1}x_i \ldots u_{n_1}x_nu_{n_2}$$

where $u_0 = u_{0_1}u_{0_2}$, $u_n = u_{n_1}u_{n_2}$.

Informally, G obtains $u_{0_1}x_1u_{0_2}x_2u_1 \dots x_{i-1}u_{i-1}u_iu_{i+1}x_i \dots u_{n_1}x_nu_{n_2}$ from u_0A_1 $u_1A_2 \dots\ u_{i-1}A_{i-1}u_iA_iu_{i+1} \dots A_nu_n$ by $(A_1,A_2,\dots,A_n) \to (x_1,x_2,\dots,x_n) \in P$ in ${}_5\Rightarrow$ as follows:

(1) $A_1, A_2, \dots, A_n$ are deleted;
(2) a central u_i is nondeterministically chosen, for some $i \in \{0, \dots, n\}$;
(3) x_1 and x_n are inserted into u_0 and u_n, respectively;
(4) x_j is inserted between u_{j-2} and u_{j-1}, for all $1 < j \leq i$;
(5) x_k is inserted between u_k and u_{k+1}, for all $i + 1 \leq k < n$.

Example 6.6 Let $G = (\Sigma, \Delta, P, S)$, where $\Sigma = \{S, A, B, \$, a, b\}$, $\Delta = \{a, b\}$, be an SCG with P containing the following rules:

(i) $(S) \to (\$AA\$)$
(ii) $(A) \to (aAb)$
(iii) $(A, A) \to (B, B)$
(iv) $(B, \$, \$, B) \to (A, \varepsilon, \varepsilon, A)$
(v) $(A) \to (\varepsilon)$

Recall Example 6.5. ${}_4\Rightarrow$ interchanges the positions of nonterminals influenced by context-sensitive rules in the direction from the outer ones to the central ones. Opposed to ${}_4\Rightarrow$, ${}_5\Rightarrow$ interchanges nonterminals in the direction from a nondeterministically chosen center. In the present example, we show one possibility to control the choice.

Consider G uses ${}_5\Rightarrow$. First, rule (i) rewrites S to $\$AA\$$. Then, G uses rule (ii) generating the sentential form

$$\$a^mAb^ma^nAb^n\$$$

where $m, n \geq 0$. If rule (v) is used, derivation is blocked, because there is no way to erase the symbols \$. Next, G uses the context-sensitive rule (iii), which nondeterministically chooses a center and nondeterministically shifts Bs from the previous positions of As in the direction from this center. However, for the future application of rule (iv) the chosen center must lie between As, and moreover Bs must be inserted as the leftmost and the rightmost symbols of the current sentential form. The subsequent usage of rule (iv) preserves As as the leftmost and the rightmost symbols independently of the effect of ${}_5\Rightarrow$. Finally, G continues by using rule (ii) and eventually finishes twice rule (v). If rule (iii) is used again, there is no possibility to erase inserted Bs. Consequently,

$$L(G, {}_5\Rightarrow) = \left\{x \in \Delta^* \mid x = a^kb^ka^lb^la^mb^ma^nb^n, k, l, m, n \geq 0\right\}$$

Then, the string $aabbabaaabbb$ is generated by G in the following way:

$$\begin{gathered} S\ {}_5\Rightarrow\ \$AA\$\ {}_5\Rightarrow\ \$aAbA\$\ {}_5\Rightarrow\ \$aaAbbA\$\ {}_5\Rightarrow\ \$aaAbbaAb\$ \\ {}_5\Rightarrow\ B\$aabbab\$B\ {}_5\Rightarrow\ AaabbabA\ {}_5\Rightarrow\ AaabbabaAb\ {}_5\Rightarrow\ AaabbabaaAbb \\ {}_5\Rightarrow\ AaabbabaaaAbbb\ {}_5\Rightarrow\ aabbabaaaAbbb\ {}_5\Rightarrow\ aabbabaaabbb \end{gathered}$$

Theorem 6.5 $\mathbf{JSC}_{5\Rightarrow} = \mathbf{RE}$.

Proof As is obvious, $\mathbf{JSC}_{5\Rightarrow} \subseteq \mathbf{RE}$, so we only prove $\mathbf{RE} \subseteq \mathbf{JSC}_{5\Rightarrow}$.

Let $G = (\Sigma, \Delta, P, S)$ be the SCG constructed in the proof of Theorem 6.1. Next, we modify G to a new SCG G' so $L(G, {}_1\Rightarrow) = L(G', {}_5\Rightarrow)$.

Construction. Introduce four new symbols—D,E,F, and $\circ$. Set $N = \{D,E,F,\circ\}$. Let $G' = (\Sigma', \Delta, P', S)$ be SCG, with $\Sigma' = \Sigma \cup N$ and P' containing the rules

(1) $(S) \rightarrow (\$S_1 1111 S_2\$ \circ E \circ F)$;
(2) $(A) \rightarrow (C_i(w))$ for $A \rightarrow w \in P_i$, where $i = 1, 2$;
(3) $(F) \rightarrow (FF)$;
(4) $(\$, a, a, \$, E, F) \rightarrow (\varepsilon, \varepsilon, \$, \$, \varepsilon, D)$, for $a = 0, 1$;
(5) $(\circ, D, \circ) \rightarrow (\varepsilon, \circ E \circ, \varepsilon)$;
(6) $(\$) \rightarrow (\varepsilon)$, $(E) \rightarrow (\varepsilon)$, $(\circ) \rightarrow (\varepsilon)$.

Claim A $L(G, {}_1\Rightarrow) = L(G', {}_5\Rightarrow)$. □

Proof (Claim A) Context-free rules are not influenced by ${}_5\Rightarrow$. Rule (3) must generate precisely as many Fs as the number of applications of rules from (4). Context-sensitive rules of G' correspond to context-sensitive rules of G, except for the special rule (5). We show that the construction of G' forces context-sensitive rules to work exactly in the same way as the rules of G do.

Every application of a rule from (4) must be followed by the application of rule (5) to rewrite D back to E, which requires the symbol D between two $\circ$s. It ensures the previous usage of context-sensitive rule selected the center to the right of the rightmost affected nonterminal, and all right-hand-side strings changed their positions with the more left ones. The leftmost right-hand-side string is then shifted randomly to the left, but it is always ε. ${}_5\Rightarrow$ has no influence on rule (5).

From the construction of G', it works exactly in the same way as G does. □

$L(G, {}_1\Rightarrow) = L(G', {}_5\Rightarrow)$ and $L(G, {}_1\Rightarrow) = L$; therefore, $L(G', {}_5\Rightarrow) = L$. Thus, the proof of Theorem 6.5 is completed. □

Jumping Derivation Mode 6

Definition 6.10 Let $G = (\Sigma, \Delta, P, S)$ be an SCG. Let $uAv \in \Sigma^*$ and $(A) \rightarrow (x) \in P$. Then, $uAv \;{}_6\Rightarrow\; uxv$. Let $u = u_0 A_1 u_1 \ldots A_n u_n \in \Sigma^*$ and $(A_1,A_2,\ldots,A_n) \rightarrow (x_1,x_2,\ldots,x_n) \in P$, for $n \geq 2$. Then,

$$u_0 A_1 u_1 A_2 u_2 \ldots u_{i-1} A_i u_i A_{i+1} u_{i+1} \ldots u_{n-1} A_n u_n \;{}_6\Rightarrow$$
$$u_0 u_1 x_1 u_2 x_2 \ldots u_{i-1} x_{i-1} u_i x_{i+2} u_{i+1} \ldots x_n u_{n-1} u_n$$

Informally, G obtains $u_0 u_1 x_1 u_2 x_2 \ldots u_{i-1} x_{i-1} u_i x_{i+2} u_{i+1} \ldots x_n u_{n-1} u_n$ from $u_0 A_1 u_1 A_2 u_2 \ldots u_{i-1} A_i u_i A_{i+1} u_{i+1} \ldots u_{n-1} A_n u_n$ by using $(A_1,A_2,\ldots,A_n) \rightarrow (x_1,x_2,\ldots,x_n) \in P$ in ${}_6\Rightarrow$ as follows:

(1) $A_1, A_2, \ldots, A_n$ are deleted;
(2) a central u_i is nondeterministically chosen, for some $i \in \{0, \ldots, n\}$;
(3) x_j is inserted between u_j and u_{j+1}, for all $j < i$;
(4) x_k is inserted between u_{k-2} and u_{k-1}, for all $k > i + 1$.

Example 6.7 Let $G = (\Sigma, \Delta, P, S)$, where $\Sigma = \{S, A, B, a, b\}$, $\Delta = \{a, b\}$, be an SCG with P containing the following rules:

(i) $(S) \to (ABBA)$	(iii) $(A, B, B, A) \to (AB, B, B, BA)$
(ii) $(A) \to (aAb)$	(iv) $(A, B, B, A) \to (\varepsilon, B, B, \varepsilon)$

Consider G uses ${}_6\Rightarrow$. ${}_6\Rightarrow$ interchanges nonterminals similarly as ${}_4\Rightarrow$ does in Example 6.5; however, the central nonterminals are removed. This property can be used to eliminate nondeterminism of choosing of the center, which we demonstrate next.

Rules (i) and (ii) are context-free, not affected by ${}_6\Rightarrow$. First the starting rule (i) rewrites S to $ABBA$. Then, G uses rule (ii) generating the sentential form

$$a^m Ab^m BBa^n Ab^n$$

where $m, n \geq 0$. Next, G uses the context-sensitive rule (iii) or (iv). Notice, there is no rule erasing Bs; thus, in both cases the center of interchanging of nonterminals must be chosen between the two Bs. Otherwise, in both cases there is exactly one A remaining, thus the only applicable rule is rule (ii), which is context-free and not erasing. Therefore, G uses rule (iii) generating the sentential form

$$a^m b^m ABBAa^n b^n$$

and continues by using rule (ii) or it uses rule (iv) and finishes the derivation.

Subsequently, the language G generates is

$$L(G, {}_6\Rightarrow) = \left\{x \in \Delta^* \mid x = a^{n_1} b^{n_1} a^{n_2} b^{n_2} \ldots a^{n_{2k}} b^{n_{2k}}, k, n_i \geq 0, 1 \leq i \leq 2k\right\}$$

Then, the string $aabbabaabbab$ is generated by G in the following way:

$$\begin{gathered} S \;{}_6\Rightarrow ABBA \;{}_6\Rightarrow aAbBBA \;{}_6\Rightarrow aaAbbBBA \;{}_6\Rightarrow aaAbbBBaAb \\ {}_6\Rightarrow aabbABBAab \;{}_6\Rightarrow aabbaAbBBAab \;{}_6\Rightarrow aabbaAbBBaAbab \\ {}_6\Rightarrow aabbaAbBBaaAbbab \;{}_6\Rightarrow aabbabaabbab \end{gathered}$$

Theorem 6.6 $\mathbf{JSC}_{6\Rightarrow} = \mathbf{RE}$.

Proof Clearly, $\mathbf{JSC}_{6\Rightarrow} \subseteq \mathbf{RE}$. Next, we prove $\mathbf{RE} \subseteq \mathbf{JSC}_{6\Rightarrow}$.

Let $G = (\Sigma, \Delta, P, S)$ be the SCG constructed in the proof of Theorem 6.1. Next, we modify G to a new SCG G' so $L(G, {}_1\Rightarrow) = L(G', {}_6\Rightarrow)$.

Construction. Introduce two new symbols—E and F. Let $G' = (\Sigma', \Delta, P', S)$ be SCG, with $\Sigma' = \Sigma \cup \{E, F\}$ and P' containing the rules

(1) $(S) \to (F\$S_1 1111S_2\$)$;
(2) $(A) \to (C_i(w))$ for $A \to w \in P_i$, where $i = 1, 2$;
(3) $(F) \to (FF)$;
(4) $(F, \$, a, a, \$) \to (E, E, \varepsilon, \$, \$)$, for $a = 0, 1$;
(5) $(\$) \to (\varepsilon)$.

Claim A $L(G, {}_1\Rightarrow) = L(G', {}_6\Rightarrow)$. □

Proof (Claim A) Context-free rules are not influenced by ${}_6\Rightarrow$. Context-sensitive rules of G' closely correspond to context-sensitive rules of G. The new symbols are used to force modified rules to act in the same way as sample ones do. The symbols F are first multiplied and then consumed by context-sensitive rules, so their number must equal the number of usages of these rules. The new symbols E are essential. E never appears on the left-hand side of any rule; thus, whenever it is inserted into the sentential form, no terminal string can be generated. Therefore, the center is always chosen between two Es, which are basically never inserted, and other right-hand-side strings are then inserted deterministically.

G' with ${}_6\Rightarrow$ works in the same way as G with ${}_1\Rightarrow$ does. □

$L(G, {}_1\Rightarrow) = L(G', {}_6\Rightarrow)$, hence $L(G', {}_6\Rightarrow) = L$. Thus, the proof of Theorem 6.6 is completed. □

Jumping Derivation Mode 7

Definition 6.11 Let $G = (\Sigma, \Delta, P, S)$ be an SCG. Let $(A) \to (x) \in P$ and $uAv \in \Sigma^*$. Then, $uAv\ {}_7\Rightarrow uxv$. Let $u = u_0A_1u_1 \dots A_nu_n \in \Sigma^*$ and $(A_1,A_2,\dots,A_n) \to (x_1,x_2,\dots,x_n) \in P$, for $n \geq 2$. Then,

$$u_0A_1u_1A_2 \dots u_{i-1}A_iu_iA_{i+1}u_{i+1} \dots A_nu_n\ {}_7\Rightarrow$$
$$u_0x_2u_1 \dots x_iu_{i-1}u_iu_{i+1}x_{i+1} \dots u_n$$

Informally, by using the rule $(A_1,A_2,\dots,A_n) \to (x_1,x_2,\dots,x_n) \in P$, G obtains $u_0x_2u_1 \dots x_iu_{i-1}u_iu_{i+1}x_{i+1} \dots u_n$ from $u_0A_1u_1A_2 \dots u_{i-1}A_iu_iA_{i+1}u_{i+1} \dots A_nu_n$ in ${}_7\Rightarrow$ as follows:

(1) $A_1, A_2, \dots, A_n$ are deleted;
(2) a central u_i is nondeterministically chosen, for some $i \in \{0 \dots, n\}$;
(3) x_j is inserted between u_{j-2} and u_{j-1}, for all $1 < j \leq i$;
(4) x_k is inserted between u_k and u_{k+1}, for all $i + 1 \leq k < n$.

Example 6.8 Let $G = (\Sigma, \Delta, P, S)$, where $\Sigma = \{S, A, B, C, \$, a, b, c\}$, $\Delta = \{a, b, c\}$, be an SCG with P containing the following rules:

(i) $(S) \to (ABC\$)$	(v) $(A, B, C) \to (A, B, C)$
(ii) $(A) \to (aAa)$	(vi) $(A, B) \to (A, B)$
(iii) $(B) \to (bBb)$	(vii) $(A, \$) \to (\varepsilon, \varepsilon)$
(iv) $(C) \to (cCc)$	

Consider G uses ${}_7\Rightarrow$. ${}_7\Rightarrow$ interchanges nonterminals in the direction from the nondeterministically chosen center and erases the outermost nonterminals. In this example, we show that we may force the center to lie outside the part of a sentential form between the affected nonterminals.

The derivation starts by using the starting rule (i) and continues by using rules (ii) through (iv) generating the sentential form

$$a^m A a^m b^n B b^n c^l C c^l \$$$

where $m, n, l \geq 0$. Next, G uses the context-sensitive rule (v) choosing the center to the left of A erasing C. If a different central position is chosen, the symbol A is erased, while B or C cannot be erased in the future and the derivation is blocked. There is the same situation, if one of rules (vi) or (vii) is used instead. Notice, no rule erases B or C. Then, the derivation continues by using rules (ii) and (iii) and eventually rule (vi) rewriting B to A and erasing B. Otherwise, A is erased and the symbol \$ cannot be erased any more. G continues by using rule (ii) and finally finishes the derivation with rule (vii). Subsequently,

$$L(G, {}_7\Rightarrow) = \{x \in \Delta^* \mid x = a^{2m_1} b^{n_1} a^{2m_2} b^{n_1} c^l b^{n_2} a^{2m_3} b^{n_2} c^l, \\ m_1, m_2, m_3, n_1, n_2, l \geq 0\}$$

Then, the string $aabaabccbaabcc$ is generated by G in the following way:

$$S \,{}_7\Rightarrow ABC\$ \,{}_7\Rightarrow aAaBC\$ \,{}_7\Rightarrow aAabBbC\$ \,{}_7\Rightarrow aAabBbcCc\$ \\ {}_7\Rightarrow aAabBbccCcc\$ \,{}_7\Rightarrow aabAbccBcc\$ \,{}_7\Rightarrow aabaAabccBcc\$ \,{}_7\Rightarrow \\ aabaAabccbBbcc\$ \\ {}_7\Rightarrow aabaabccbAbcc\$ \,{}_7\Rightarrow aabaabccbaAabcc\$ \,{}_7\Rightarrow aabaabccbaabcc$$

Theorem 6.7 $\mathbf{JSC}_{{}_7\Rightarrow} = \mathbf{RE}$.

Proof Clearly, $\mathbf{JSC}_{{}_7\Rightarrow} \subseteq \mathbf{RE}$. We prove $\mathbf{RE} \subseteq \mathbf{JSC}_{{}_7\Rightarrow}$.

Let $G = (\Sigma, \Delta, P, S)$ be the SCG constructed in the proof of Theorem 6.1. Next, we modify G to a new SCG G' so $L(G, {}_1\Rightarrow) = L(G', {}_7\Rightarrow)$.

Construction. Introduce four new symbols—E,F,H, and $|$. Set $N = \{E,F,H,|\}$. Let $G' = (\Sigma', \Delta, P', S)$ be SCG, with $\Sigma' = \Sigma \cup N$ and P' containing the rules:

(1) $(S) \to (FHS_1 11\$|\$11S_2)$;
(2) $(A) \to (C_i(w))$ for $A \to w \in P_i$, where $i = 1, 2$;
(3) $(F) \to (FF)$;
(4) $(a, \$, \$, a) \to (\varepsilon, E, E, \varepsilon)$, for $a = 0, 1$;
(5) $(F, H, E, |, E) \to (H, \$, |, \$, \varepsilon)$;
(6) $(\$) \to (\varepsilon)$, $(H) \to (\varepsilon)$, $(|) \to (\varepsilon)$.

Claim A $L(G, {}_1\Rightarrow) = L(G', {}_7\Rightarrow)$. □

Proof (Claim A) The behavior of context-free rules remains unchanged under ${}_7\Rightarrow$. Since the rules of G' simulating the derivations of G_1, G_2, respectively, are identical to the ones of G simulating both grammars, for every derivation of G

$$S \ {}_1\Rightarrow^* \ \$w_1 1111 w_2\$ = w$$

where w is generated only by using rule (1) and rules from (2) constructed in G and symbols$(w) \cap (N_1 \cup N_2) = \emptyset$, there is

$$S \ {}_7\Rightarrow^* \ FHw_1 11\$|\$11w_2 = w'$$

in G', generated by the corresponding rule (1) and rules from (2) produced in G', and vice versa. Without any loss of generality, we can consider such a sentential form in every successful derivation. Additionally, in G

$$w \ {}_1\Rightarrow^* \ v, v \in \Delta^*$$

if and only if $t'(w_1) = \text{reversal}(w_2)$; then $v = t(w)$. Therefore, we have to prove

$$w' \ {}_4\Rightarrow^* \ v', v' \in \Delta^*$$

if and only if $t'(w_1) = \text{reversal}(w_2)$. Then, obviously $v' = v$ and we can complete the proof by the following claim.

Claim B In G', for some $i \geq 1$,

$$S \ {}_7\Rightarrow^* \ w = F^i H w_1 \$|\$ w_2 E$$

where w is generated only by using rules from (1) through (3) and symbols$(w) \cap (N_1 \cup N_2) = \emptyset$. Then,

$$w \ {}_7\Rightarrow^* \ w'$$

where $w' \in \Delta^*$ if and only if $t'(w_1) = \text{reversal}(w_2)$. □

The new rule (3) may potentially arbitrarily multiply the number of Fs to the left. Then, Fs are erasing by using rule (5). Thus, without any loss of generality, suppose i equals the number of the future usages of rule (5).

For the sake of readability, in the next proof we omit all symbols in w_1 from Δ—we consider only nonterminal symbols, which are to be erased.

Proof (Claim B) *If.* Suppose $w_1 = \text{reversal}(w_2)$, then $w \ {}_7\Rightarrow^* \ \varepsilon$. We prove this by the induction on the length of w_1, w_2, where $|w_1| = |w_2| = k$. Then, obviously $i = k$. By the construction of G', the least k equals 2, but we prove the claim for all $k \geq 0$.

Basis. Let $k = 0$. Then,

$$w = H\$|\$$$

By the rules from (6)

$$H\$|\$ \ {}_7\Rightarrow^* \ \varepsilon$$

and the basis holds.

Induction Hypothesis. Suppose there exists $k \geq 0$ such that the claim holds for all m, where

$$w = F^m H w_1 \$|\$ w_2, |w_1| = |w_2| = m, 0 \le m \le k$$

Induction Step. Consider G' generates w, where

$$w = F^{k+1} H w_1 \$|\$ w_2, |w_1| = |w_2| = k+1$$

Since $w_1 = \text{reversal}(w_2)$ and $|w_1| = |w_2| = k+1$, $w_1 = w'_1 a$, $w_2 = a w'_2$. The symbols a can be erased by application of rules from (4) and rule (5) under several conditions. First, when a rule from (4) is applied, the center for interchanging right-hand-side strings must be chosen between the two \$s; otherwise, both Es appear on the same side of the symbol | and rule (5) is not applicable. Next, no 0 or 1 may be skipped, while proceeding in the direction from the center to the edges. Finally, when rule (5) is applied, a center must be chosen to the left of F; otherwise, H is erased and the future application of this rule is excluded.

$$F^{k+1} H w'_1 a \$|\$ a w'_2 \;{}_7\!\Rightarrow\; F^{k+1} H w'_1 D | D w'_2 \;{}_7\!\Rightarrow\; F^k H w'_1 \$|\$ w'_2 = w'$$

By the induction hypothesis, $w' \;{}_7\!\Rightarrow^* \varepsilon$, which completes the proof.

Only if. Suppose $w_1 \ne \text{reversal}(w_2)$, then, there is no w', where $w \;{}_7\!\Rightarrow^* w'$ and $w' = \varepsilon$.

Since $w_1 \ne \text{reversal}(w_2)$, $w_1 = uav$, $w_2 = va'u'$, and $a \ne a'$. Suppose both vs are correctly erased, and no symbol is skipped producing the sentential form

$$F^i H u a \$|\$ a' u'$$

Next, the rules from (4) can be applied to erase innermost 0s or 1s. However, since $a \ne a'$, even if the center is chosen properly between the two \$s, there is 0 or 1 between inserted Es and, thus, unable to be erased, which completes the proof.

We showed that G' can generate the terminal string from the sentential form w if and only if $t'(w_1) = \text{reversal}(w_2)$, and the claim holds. □

We proved $S \;{}_1\!\Rightarrow^* w$, $w \in \Delta^*$, in G if and only if $S \;{}_7\!\Rightarrow^* w$ in G', hence $L(G, {}_1\!\Rightarrow) = L(G', {}_7\!\Rightarrow)$ and the claim holds. □

Since $L(G, {}_1\!\Rightarrow) = L(G', {}_7\!\Rightarrow)$ and $L(G, {}_1\!\Rightarrow) = L$, the proof of Theorem 6.7 is completed. □

Jumping Derivation Mode 8

Definition 6.12 Let $G = (\Sigma, \Delta, P, S)$ be an SCG. Let $u = u_0 A_1 u_1 \ldots A_n u_n \in \Sigma^*$ and $(A_1, A_2, \ldots, A_n) \to (x_1, x_2, \ldots, x_n) \in P$, for $n \ge 1$. Then,

$$u_0 A_1 u_1 A_2 u_2 \ldots A_n u_n \;{}_8\!\Rightarrow\; v_0 x_1 v_1 x_2 v_2 \ldots x_n v_n$$

where $u_0 z_1 = v_0$, $z_2 u_n = v_n$, $|u_0 u_1 \dots u_{j-1}| \leq |v_0 v_1 \dots v_j|$, $|u_{j+1} \dots u_n| \leq |v_j v_{j+1} \dots v_n|$, $0 < j < n$, and $z_1, z_2 \in \Sigma^*$.

Informally, G obtains $v_0 x_1 v_1 x_2 v_2 \dots x_n v_n$ from $u_0 A_1 u_1 A_2 u_2 \dots A_n u_n$ by using $(A_1, A_2, \dots, A_n) \rightarrow (x_1, x_2, \dots, x_n) \in P$ in $_8\Rightarrow$ as follows:

(1) $A_1, A_2, \dots, A_n$ are deleted;
(2) x_1 and x_n are inserted into u_1 and u_{n-1}, respectively;
(3) x_i is inserted into $u_{i-1}u_i$, for all $1 < i < n$, to the right of x_{i-1} and to the left of x_{i+1}.

Example 6.9 Let $G = (\Sigma, \Delta, P, S)$, where $\Sigma = \{S, \overline{S}, A, B, C, a, b, c\}$, $\Delta = \{a, b, c\}$, be an SCG with P containing the following rules:

(i) $(S) \rightarrow (AS)$	(iv) $(\overline{S}) \rightarrow (B)$
(ii) $(S) \rightarrow (\overline{S})$	(v) $(B) \rightarrow (BB)$
(iii) $(\overline{S}) \rightarrow (b\overline{S}cC)$	(vi) $(A, B, C) \rightarrow (a, \varepsilon, \varepsilon)$

Consider G uses $_8\Rightarrow$. $_8\Rightarrow$ acts in a similar way as $_2\Rightarrow$ does. When a rule is to be applied, there is a nondeterministically chosen center between the affected nonterminals and rule right-hand-side strings can be shifted in the direction to this center, but not farther than the neighboring affected nonterminal was.

Rules (i) through (v) are context-free. Without any loss of generality, we suppose these rules are used only before the first application of rule (vi) producing the string

$$A^m b^n B^l (cC)^n$$

The derivation finishes with the sequence of applications of rule (vi). For As, Bs, and Cs are being rewritten together, $m = n = l$. Moreover, inserted a is always between the rewritten A and B. Subsequently,

$$L(G, {}_8\Rightarrow) = \{x \in \Delta^* \mid x = wc^n, w \in \{a, b\}^*, \\ \text{occur}(w, a) = \text{occur}(w, b) = n, n \geq 1\}$$

For example, the string $baabbaccc$ is generated by G in the following way:

$$S \;{}_8\Rightarrow AS \;{}_8\Rightarrow AAS \;{}_8\Rightarrow AAAS \;{}_8\Rightarrow AAA\overline{S} \;{}_8\Rightarrow AAAb\overline{S}cC \;{}_8\Rightarrow AAAbb\overline{S}cCcC \\ {}_8\Rightarrow AAAbbb\overline{S}cCcCcC \;{}_8\Rightarrow AAAbbbBcCcCcC \;{}_8\Rightarrow AAAbbbBBcCcCcC \\ {}_8\Rightarrow AAAbbbBBBcCcCcC \;{}_8\Rightarrow AAbbbaBBccCcC \;{}_8\Rightarrow AbabbaBcccC \;{}_8\Rightarrow \\ baabbaccc$$

Theorem 6.8 $\mathbf{JSC}_{_8\Rightarrow} = \mathbf{RE}$.

Proof Prove this theorem by analogy with the proof of Theorem 6.2. □

Jumping Derivation Mode 9

Definition 6.13 Let $G = (\Sigma, \Delta, P, S)$ be an SCG. Let $u = u_0A_1u_1 \dots A_nu_n \in \Sigma^*$ and $(A_1,A_2,\dots,A_n) \rightarrow (x_1,x_2,\dots,x_n) \in P$, for $n \geq 1$. Then,

$$u_0A_1u_1A_2u_2 \dots A_nu_n \;{}_9\!\!\Rightarrow v_0x_1v_1x_2v_2 \dots x_nv_n$$

where $u_0 = v_0z_1$, $u_n = z_2v_n$, $|u_0u_1 \dots u_{j-1}| \leq |v_0v_1 \dots v_j|$, $|u_{j+1} \dots u_n| \leq |v_jv_{j+1} \dots v_n|$, $0 < j < n$, and $z_1, z_2 \in \Sigma^*$.

Informally, G obtains $v_0x_1v_1x_2v_2 \dots x_nv_n$ from $u_0A_1u_1A_2u_2 \dots A_nu_n$ by using $(A_1,A_2,\dots,A_n) \rightarrow (x_1,x_2,\dots,x_n) \in P$ in ${}_9\!\!\Rightarrow$ as follows:

(1) $A_1, A_2, \dots, A_n$ are deleted;
(2) x_1 and x_n are inserted into u_0 and u_n, respectively;
(3) x_i is inserted into $u_{i-1}u_i$, for all $1 < i < n$, to the right of x_{i-1} and to the left of x_{i+1}.

Example 6.10 Let $G = (\Sigma, \Delta, P, S)$, where $\Sigma = \{S, \overline{S}, A, B, C, \$, a, b, c\}$, $\Delta = \{a, b, c\}$, be an SCG with P containing the following rules:

(i) $(S) \rightarrow (aSa)$	(v) $(C) \rightarrow (cBC\$)$
(ii) $(S) \rightarrow (A)$	(vi) $(C) \rightarrow (\varepsilon)$
(iii) $(A) \rightarrow (\$A)$	(vii) $(\$, B, \$) \rightarrow (\varepsilon, b, \varepsilon)$
(iv) $(A) \rightarrow (C)$	

Consider G uses ${}_9\!\!\Rightarrow$. ${}_9\!\!\Rightarrow$ acts similarly to ${}_3\!\!\Rightarrow$ with respect to the direction of shift of the rule right-hand sides, but with limitation as in ${}_8\!\!\Rightarrow$. When a rule is to be applied, there is a nondeterministically chosen center between the affected nonterminals and rule right-hand-side strings can be shifted in the direction from this center, but not farther than the neighboring affected nonterminal was.

Rules (i) through (vi) are context-free. Without any loss of generality, we can suppose these rules are used only before the first application of rule (vii), which produce the sentential form

$$a^m\$^n(cB)^l\$^la^m$$

The derivation finishes with the sequence of applications of rule (vii). The symbols \$ and Bs are being rewritten together, thus $n = l$ must hold. Additionally, ${}_9\!\!\Rightarrow$ ensures, b is always inserted between the rewritten \$s. Subsequently,

$$L(G, {}_9\!\!\Rightarrow) = \{x \in \Delta^* \mid x = a^mwa^m, w \in \{b,c\}^*, \text{occur}(w,b) = \text{occur}(w,c), m \geq 0\}$$

For example, the string $aabcbcaa$ is generated by G in the following way:

$$\begin{aligned} S \;{}_9\!\!\Rightarrow aSa \;{}_9\!\!\Rightarrow aaSaa \;{}_9\!\!\Rightarrow aaAaa \;{}_9\!\!\Rightarrow aa\$Aaa \;{}_9\!\!\Rightarrow aa\$\$Aaa \\ {}_9\!\!\Rightarrow aa\$\$Caa \;{}_9\!\!\Rightarrow aa\$\$cBC\$aa \;{}_9\!\!\Rightarrow aa\$\$cBcBC\$\$aa \\ {}_9\!\!\Rightarrow aa\$\$cBcB\$\$aa \;{}_9\!\!\Rightarrow aa\$bccB\$aa \;{}_9\!\!\Rightarrow aabcbcaa \end{aligned}$$

Theorem 6.9 $\mathbf{JSC}_{9\Rightarrow} = \mathbf{RE}$.

Proof Prove this theorem by analogy with the proof of Theorem 6.3. □

Open Problem Areas

Finally, let us suggest some open problem areas concerning the subject of this section.

Open Problem Return to derivation modes (1) through (9) in Section 6.3. Introduce and study further modes. For instance, in a more general way, discuss a jumping derivation mode, in which the only restriction is to preserve a mutual order of the inserted right-hand-side strings, which can be nondeterministicaly spread across the whole sentential form regardless of the positions of the rewritten nonterminals. In a more restrictive way, study a jumping derivation mode over strings satisfying some prescribed requirements, such as a membership in a regular language. □

Open Problem Consider propagating versions of jumping scattered context grammars. In other words, rule out erasing rules in them. Reconsider the investigation of the present section in its terms. □

Open Problem The present section has often demonstrated that some jumping derivation modes work just like ordinary derivation modes in scattered context grammars. State general combinatorial properties that guarantee this behavior. □

Open Problem Establish normal forms of scattered context grammars working in jumping ways. □

Admittedly, apart from scattered context grammars, the language theory is literally overflown with a broad variety of parallel grammars, many of which are underlain by context-free grammars, such as E0L systems (see Rozenberg and Salomaa [1980, 1986]), Indian grammars (see Siromoney and Krithivasan [1974]), k-parallel context-free grammars (see Skyum [1974]), Russian grammars (see Levitina [1972]), and parallel versions of selective substitution grammars (see Kleijn [1987]). To a large extent, an exploration of their jumping versions remains an open investigation area of the language theory in the future. Nevertheless, later on, this book discusses some more jumping versions of parallel grammars, including pure grammars working under jumping parallel mode covered in the next chapter.

Chapter 7
Pure Jumping Grammars

This chapter studies jumping computation based upon the notion of a pure grammar G. Section 7.1 gives an introduction into its subject. Section 7.2 recalls all the terminology needed in this chapter and introduces a variety of jumping pure grammars, illustrated by an example. Finally, Section 7.3 presents fundamental results and concludes by summing up ten open problems.

7.1 Introduction

Jumping versions of language-defining rewriting systems, such as grammars and automata, represent a brand new trend in formal language theory. In essence, they act just like classical rewriting systems except that they work on strings discontinuously. That is, they apply a production rule so they erase an occurrence of its left-hand side in the rewritten string while placing the right-hand side anywhere in the string, so the position of the insertion may occur far away from the position of the erasure. The present chapter contributes to this trend by investigating the generative power of jumping versions of pure grammars, whose original versions were introduced in Gabrielian [1970], and their properties are still intensively investigated in language theory (see Bordihn et al. [2002]; Novotný [2002]). Recently, regulated versions of these grammars have been discussed, too (see Chapter 5 in Dassow and Păun [1989] and Langer and Kelemenová [2012]; Křivka et al. [2014]).

The notion of a pure grammar G represents a language-generating rewriting system based upon an alphabet of symbols and a finite set of production rules (as opposed to the notion of an unrestricted grammar, its alphabet of symbols is not divided into the alphabet of terminals and the alphabet of nonterminals). Each rule represents a pair of the form (x, y), where x and y are strings over the alphabet of G. Customarily, (x, y) is written as $x \rightarrow y$, where x and y are referred to as the left-hand side and the right-hand side of $x \rightarrow y$, respectively. Starting from a special start string, G repeatedly rewrites strings according to its rules, and the set of all strings obtained in this way represents the language generated by G. In a greater detail, G

rewrites a string z according to $x \rightarrow y$ so it (i) selects an occurrence of x in z, (ii) erases it, and (iii) inserts y precisely at the position of this erasure. More formally, let $z = uxv$, where u and v are strings. By using $x \rightarrow y$, G rewrites uxv as uyv.

The notion of a *jumping pure grammar*—that is, the key notion (see Křivka et al. [2018]) introduced in this chapter—is conceptualized just like that of a classical pure grammar; however, it rewrites strings in a slightly different way. Let G, z, and $x \rightarrow y$ have the same meaning as above. G rewrites a string z according to $x \rightarrow y$, so it performs (i) and (ii) as described above, but during (iii), G can jump over a portion of the rewritten string in either direction and inserts y there. More formally, by using $x \rightarrow y$, G rewrites ucv as udv, where u, v, w, c, d are strings such that either (a) $c = xw$ and $d = wy$ or (b) $c = wx$ and $d = yw$. Otherwise, G works as described above.

The present chapter compares the generative power of classical and jumping versions of pure grammars. It distinguishes between these grammars with and without erasing rules. Apart from these sequential versions of pure grammars, it also considers parallel versions of classical and jumping pure grammars represented by 0L grammars (see Rozenberg and Doucet [1971]). As a result, the chapter studies the mutual relationships between eight language families corresponding to the following derivations modes (see Definition 7.1) performed by pure grammars both with and without erasing rules:

- *classical sequential mode* (${}_s\Rightarrow$);
- *jumping sequential mode* (${}_j\Rightarrow$);
- *classical parallel mode* (${}_p\Rightarrow$);
- *jumping parallel mode* (${}_{jp}\Rightarrow$).

In essence, the chapter demonstrates that any version of these grammars with erasing rules is stronger than the same version without them. Furthermore, it shows that almost all of the eight language families under considerations are pairwise incomparable—that is, any two families are not subfamilies of each other, but not disjoint.

7.2 Definitions

Let $I \subset {}_0\mathbb{N}$ be a finite nonempty set. Then, max I denotes the maximum of I. Now, we recall the most important notions for this chapter. For a (binary) relation ϱ over X, ϱ^i, ϱ^+, and ϱ^* denote the ith power of ϱ, for all $i \geq 0$, the transitive closure of ϱ, and the reflexive and transitive closure of ϱ, respectively. For $x, y \in X$, instead of $(x, y) \in \varrho$, we write $x\varrho y$ throughout. Set domain$(\varrho) = \{x \mid x\varrho y\}$.

Let $n \geq 0$. A set $J \subseteq {}_0\mathbb{N}^n$ is said to be *linear* if there exist $\alpha, \beta_1, \beta_2, \ldots, \beta_m \in {}_0\mathbb{N}^n$, $m \geq 0$ such that

$$J = \{x \mid x = \alpha + k_1\beta_1 + k_2\beta_2 + \cdots + k_m\beta_m, \\ k_i \in {}_0\mathbb{N}, 1 \leq i \leq m\}.$$

If J is the union of a finite number of linear sets, we say that J is *semilinear*. If $\Sigma = \{a_1, a_2, \ldots, a_n\}$ is an alphabet, then for $w \in \Sigma^*$,

$$\psi_\Sigma(w) = (\text{occur}(w, a_1), \text{occur}(w, a_2), \ldots, \text{occur}(w, a_n))$$

denote the *commutative (Parikh) image of* w. For $L \subseteq \Sigma^*$, $\psi_\Sigma(L) = \{\psi_\Sigma(w) \mid w \in L\}$ denote the *commutative (Parikh) map of* L. We say that L is a *semilinear language* if and only if $\psi_\Sigma(L)$ is a semilinear set.

Let S be a finite set. Define a permutation of S in the terms of bijective mappings as follows: Let $I = \{1, 2, \ldots, \text{card}(S)\}$ be a set of indices. The set of all permutations of elements of S, setperm(S), is the set of all bijections from I to S.

An *unrestricted grammar* is a quadruple $G = (V, \Sigma, P, \sigma)$, where V is a total alphabet, $\Sigma \subseteq V$ is an alphabet of terminal symbols, $P \subseteq V^+ \times V^*$ is a finite relation, and $\sigma \in V^+$ is the start string of G, called *axiom*. Members of P are called *production rules* or *rules*. Instead of $(x, y) \in P$, we write $x \rightarrow y$ throughout. For brevity, we sometimes denote a rule $x \rightarrow y$ with a unique label r as $r: x \rightarrow y$, and instead of $x \rightarrow y \in P$, we simply write $r \in P$. We say that $x \rightarrow y$ is a *unit rule* if $x, y \in V$. A relation of direct derivation in G, denoted $\Rightarrow$, is defined as follows: If $u, v, x, y \in V^*$ and $x \rightarrow y \in P$, then $uxv \Rightarrow uyv$. The language generated by G, denoted $L(G)$, is defined as $L(G) = \{w \mid \sigma \Rightarrow^* w, w \in \Sigma^*\}$. G is said to be context-free iff for every production rule $x \rightarrow y \in P$, $|x| = 1$. Furthermore, G is said to be context-sensitive iff every $x \rightarrow y \in P$ satisfies $|x| \leq |y|$. A language is context-free iff it is generated by some context-free grammar, and a language is context-sensitive iff it is generated by some context-sensitive grammar. By **CF** and **CS**, we denote the families of context-free and context-sensitive languages, respectively.

Next, we give the formal definition of *pure grammars* (see Maurer et al. [1980]; Dassow and Păun [1989]), together with six modes of derivations.

Definition 7.1 Let $G = (\Sigma, \Delta, P, \sigma)$ be an unrestricted grammar. G is a *pure grammar* (PG), if $\Sigma = \Delta$. For brevity, we simplify $G = (\Sigma, \Delta, P, \sigma)$ to $G = (\Sigma, P, \sigma)$. We say that G is *propagating* or *without erasing rules* iff for every rule $x \rightarrow y \in P$, $y \neq \varepsilon$.

Next, we introduce six modes of *direct derivation steps* as derivation relations over Σ^*. Let $u, v \in \Sigma^*$. The six derivation relations are defined as follows:

(i) $u \;{}_s\!\!\Rightarrow v$ in G iff there exists $x \rightarrow y \in P$ and $w, z \in \Sigma^*$ such that $u = wxz$ and $v = wyz$;

(ii) $u \;{}_{lj}\!\!\Rightarrow v$ in G iff there exists $x \rightarrow y \in P$ and $w, t, z \in \Sigma^*$ such that $u = wtxz$ and $v = wytz$;

(iii) $u \;{}_{rj}\!\!\Rightarrow v$ in G iff there exists $x \rightarrow y \in P$ and $w, t, z \in \Sigma^*$ such that $u = wxtz$ and $v = wtyz$;

(iv) $u \;{}_j\!\!\Rightarrow v$ in G iff $u \;{}_{lj}\!\!\Rightarrow v$ or $u \;{}_{rj}\!\!\Rightarrow v$ in G;

(v) $u \;{}_p\!\!\Rightarrow v$ in G iff there exist $x_1 \rightarrow y_1, x_2 \rightarrow y_2, \ldots, x_n \rightarrow y_n \in P$ such that $u = x_1 x_2 \ldots x_n$ and $v = y_1 y_2 \ldots y_n$, where $n \geq 0$;

(vi) $u \;{}_{jp}\!\!\Rightarrow v$ in G iff there exist $x_1 \rightarrow y_1, x_2 \rightarrow y_2, \ldots, x_n \rightarrow y_n \in P$ such that $u = x_1 x_2 \ldots x_n$ and $v = y_{p(1)} y_{p(2)} \ldots y_{p(n)}$, where $p \in \text{setperm}(\{1, 2, \ldots, n\})$, $n \geq 0$.

Let ${}_h\Rightarrow$ be one of the six derivation relations (i) through (vi) over Σ^*. To express that G applies production rule r during $u\ {}_h\Rightarrow v$, we write $u\ {}_h\Rightarrow v\ [r]$, where $r \in P$. By $u\ {}_h\Rightarrow^* v\ [\pi]$, where π is a sequence of rules from P, we express that G makes $u\ {}_h\Rightarrow^* v$ by using π.

The *language that G generates by using* ${}_h\Rightarrow$, $L(G, {}_h\Rightarrow)$, is defined as

$$L(G, {}_h\Rightarrow) = \{x \mid \sigma\ {}_h\Rightarrow^* x, x \in \Sigma^*\}.$$

The set of all PGs and the set of all PGs without erasing rules are denoted Γ_{PG} and $\Gamma_{\mathrm{PG}^{-\varepsilon}}$, respectively.

Let $G = (\Sigma, P, \sigma)$ be a PG. G is said to be a *pure context-free grammar* (PCFG) if every $x \rightarrow y \in P$ satisfies $x \in \Sigma$. The set of all PCFGs and the set of all PCFGs without erasing rules are denoted Γ_{PCFG} and $\Gamma_{\mathrm{PCFG}^{-\varepsilon}}$, respectively.

Remark 7.1 The inclusions $\Gamma_{\mathrm{PCFG}} \subsetneq \Gamma_{\mathrm{PG}}$, $\Gamma_{\mathrm{PCFG}^{-\varepsilon}} \subsetneq \Gamma_{\mathrm{PCFG}}$, and $\Gamma_{\mathrm{PG}^{-\varepsilon}} \subsetneq \Gamma_{\mathrm{PG}}$ are obvious.

Definition 7.2 Set

(1) $\mathbf{SP} = \{L(G, {}_s\Rightarrow) \mid G \in \Gamma_{\mathrm{PG}}\}$;
(2) $\mathbf{SP}^{-\varepsilon} = \{L(G, {}_s\Rightarrow) \mid G \in \Gamma_{\mathrm{PG}^{-\varepsilon}}\}$;
(3) $\mathbf{JSP} = \{L(G, {}_j\Rightarrow) \mid G \in \Gamma_{\mathrm{PG}}\}$;
(4) $\mathbf{JSP}^{-\varepsilon} = \{L(G, {}_j\Rightarrow) \mid G \in \Gamma_{\mathrm{PG}^{-\varepsilon}}\}$;
(5) $\mathbf{PP} = \{L(G, {}_p\Rightarrow) \mid G \in \Gamma_{\mathrm{PG}}\}$;
(6) $\mathbf{PP}^{-\varepsilon} = \{L(G, {}_p\Rightarrow) \mid G \in \Gamma_{\mathrm{PG}^{-\varepsilon}}\}$;
(7) $\mathbf{JPP} = \{L(G, {}_{jp}\Rightarrow) \mid G \in \Gamma_{\mathrm{PG}}\}$;
(8) $\mathbf{JPP}^{-\varepsilon} = \{L(G, {}_{jp}\Rightarrow) \mid G \in \Gamma_{\mathrm{PG}^{-\varepsilon}}\}$;
(9) $\mathbf{SPCF} = \{L(G, {}_s\Rightarrow) \mid G \in \Gamma_{\mathrm{PCFG}}\}$;
(10) $\mathbf{SPCF}^{-\varepsilon} = \{L(G, {}_s\Rightarrow) \mid G \in \Gamma_{\mathrm{PCFG}^{-\varepsilon}}\}$;
(11) $\mathbf{JSPCF} = \{L(G, {}_j\Rightarrow) \mid G \in \Gamma_{\mathrm{PCFG}}\}$;
(12) $\mathbf{JSPCF}^{-\varepsilon} = \{L(G, {}_j\Rightarrow) \mid G \in \Gamma_{\mathrm{PCFG}^{-\varepsilon}}\}$;
(13) $\mathbf{PPCF} = \{L(G, {}_p\Rightarrow) \mid G \in \Gamma_{\mathrm{PCFG}}\}$;
(14) $\mathbf{PPCF}^{-\varepsilon} = \{L(G, {}_p\Rightarrow) \mid G \in \Gamma_{\mathrm{PCFG}^{-\varepsilon}}\}$;
(15) $\mathbf{0L} = \{L(G, {}_p\Rightarrow) \mid G \in \Gamma_{\mathrm{PCFG}}, G = (\Sigma, P, \sigma), \mathrm{dom}(P) = \Sigma\}$ (see Rozenberg and Doucet [1971]);
(16) $\mathbf{0L}^{-\varepsilon} = \{L(G, {}_p\Rightarrow) \mid G \in \Gamma_{\mathrm{PCFG}^{-\varepsilon}}, G = (\Sigma, P, \sigma), \mathrm{dom}(P) = \Sigma\}$ (see Rozenberg and Doucet [1971], where $\mathbf{0L}^{-\varepsilon}$ is denoted by **P0L**);
(17) $\mathbf{JPPCF} = \{L(G, {}_{jp}\Rightarrow) \mid G \in \Gamma_{\mathrm{PCFG}}\}$;
(18) $\mathbf{JPPCF}^{-\varepsilon} = \{L(G, {}_{jp}\Rightarrow) \mid G \in \Gamma_{\mathrm{PCFG}^{-\varepsilon}}\}$.

Example 7.1 Consider the following PCFG

$$G = (\Sigma = \{a, b, c, d\}, P, a)$$

where $P = \{a \rightarrow abcd, a \rightarrow a, b \rightarrow b, c \rightarrow c, d \rightarrow d\}$. Observe that $L(G, {}_s\Rightarrow) = L(G, {}_p\Rightarrow) = \{a\}\{bcd\}^*$ is a regular language, but $L(G, {}_j\Rightarrow) = L(G, {}_{jp}\Rightarrow) =$

$\{w \mid \text{occur}(w, a) = 1, \text{occur}(w, b) = \text{occur}(w, c) = \text{occur}(w, d), w \in \Sigma^+\}$ is a non-context-free language.

To illustrate variants of derivation relations, we show how we can generate $abcdbcdbcd$ by using ${}_s\Rightarrow$ and ${}_p\Rightarrow$:

$$a \;{}_s\Rightarrow abcd \;{}_s\Rightarrow abcdbcd \;{}_s\Rightarrow abcdbcdbcd$$

$$a \;{}_p\Rightarrow abcd \;{}_p\Rightarrow abcdbcd \;{}_p\Rightarrow abcdbcdbcd$$

On the other hand, by ${}_j\Rightarrow$ and ${}_{jp}\Rightarrow$, we generate, for instance, $dcabcdb$ as follows:

$$a \;{}_j\Rightarrow abcd \;{}_j\Rightarrow dabc \;{}_j\Rightarrow dabcdbc \;{}_j\Rightarrow dcabcdb$$

$$a \;{}_{jp}\Rightarrow abcd \;{}_{jp}\Rightarrow dcabcdb$$

7.3 Results

In this section, we first give an overview about several elementary properties of pure grammars. Second, we investigate the mutual relationships of **SPCF**, **JSPCF**, **PPCF**, **JPPCF**, **CF**, and **CS** and summarize the results by Euler diagram in Figure 7.1. Finally, we study the former without erasing rules and sum up the investigated relations in Table 7.1.

A \ B	**SPCF**	**SPCF**$^{-\varepsilon}$	**JSPCF**	**JSPCF**$^{-\varepsilon}$	**PPCF**	**PPCF**$^{-\varepsilon}$	**JPPCF**	**JPPCF**$^{-\varepsilon}$	**0L**	**0L**$^{-\varepsilon}$
SPCF	$=$	$\supset$	$\parallel$	$\parallel$	$\subset$	$\parallel$	$\parallel$	$\parallel$	$\subset$	$\parallel$
SPCF$^{-\varepsilon}$	$\subset$	$=$	$\parallel$	$\parallel$	$\subset$	$\subset$	$\parallel$	$\parallel$	$\subset$	$\subset$
JSPCF	$\parallel$	$\parallel$	$=$	$\supset$	$\parallel$	$\parallel$	$\parallel$	$\parallel$	$\parallel$	$\parallel$
JSPCF$^{-\varepsilon}$	$\parallel$	$\parallel$	$\subset$	$=$	$\parallel$	$\parallel$	?	?	$\parallel$	$\parallel$
PPCF	$\supset$	$\supset$	$\parallel$	$\parallel$	$=$	$\supset$	$\parallel$	$\parallel$	$\supset$	$\supset$
PPCF$^{-\varepsilon}$	$\parallel$	$\supset$	$\parallel$	$\parallel$	$\subset$	$=$	$\parallel$	$\parallel$	$\parallel$	$\supset$
JPPCF	$\parallel$	$\parallel$	$\parallel$	?	$\parallel$	$\parallel$	$=$	$\supset$	$\parallel$	$\parallel$
JPPCF$^{-\varepsilon}$	$\parallel$	$\parallel$	$\parallel$	?	$\parallel$	$\parallel$	$\subset$	$=$	$\parallel$	$\parallel$
0L	$\supset$	$\supset$	$\parallel$	$\parallel$	$\subset$	$\parallel$	$\parallel$	$\parallel$	$=$	$\supset$
0L$^{-\varepsilon}$	$\parallel$	$\supset$	$\parallel$	$\parallel$	$\subset$	$\subset$	$\parallel$	$\parallel$	$\subset$	$=$

Table 7.1 Mutual relationships between investigated language families. A denotes the language family from the first column, B the language family from the table header. If the relation in the cell given by A and B is $\star$, then $A \star B$. $A \| B$ means that A and B are incomparable, ? stands for an open problem, and the meaning of $\subset$, $=$, and $\supset$ is as usual.

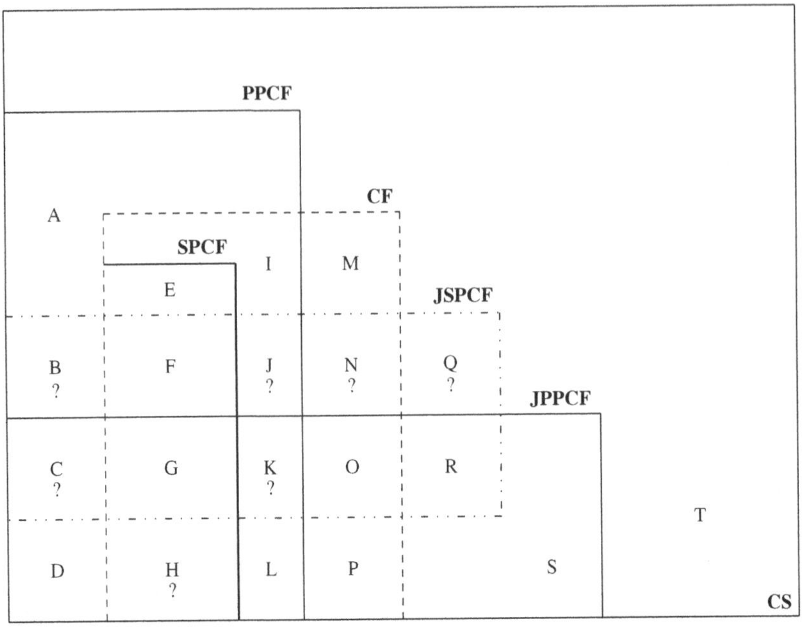

$\{a^{2^n}b^{2^n} \mid n \geq 0\} \in$ A

$\{a^{2^n} \mid n \geq 0\} \in$ D

$\{a^n c b^n \mid n \geq 0\} \in$ E

$\{aa, aab, aac, aabc\} \in$ F

$\{a\}^+ \in$ G

$\{aabb, ccdd\} \in$ I

$\{ab, cd, dc\} \in$ L

$\{a^n b^n \mid n \geq 1\} \in$ M

$\{aabb, abab, abba, baab, baba, bbaa\} \in$ O

$\{aabb, ccdd, cdcd, cddc, dccd, dcdc, ddcc\} \in$ P

$\left\{ w \,\middle|\, \begin{array}{l} \mathrm{occur}(w, a) - 1 = \mathrm{occur}(w, b) = \mathrm{occur}(w, c), \\ w \in \{a, b, c\}^+ \end{array} \right\} \in$ R

$\{\hat{a}\hat{b}\hat{c}\} \cup \left\{ w \,\middle|\, \begin{array}{l} \mathrm{occur}(w, a) - 1 = \mathrm{occur}(w, b) = \mathrm{occur}(w, c), \\ w \in \{a, b, c\}^+ \end{array} \right\} \in$ S

$\{a^p \mid p \text{ is a prime}\} \in$ T

The question whether B, C, H, J, K, N, or Q is empty remains open.

Fig. 7.1 Relationships between **CF**, **CS**, and language families defined by pure grammars.

Elementary Properties

Many properties about pure grammars can be found in Rozenberg and Salomaa [1997a]; Maurer et al. [1980]. Recall that[1] **SPCF** $\subset$ **CF** (see Rozenberg and Salomaa [1997a]; Maurer et al. [1980]). As follows from (13) and (15) in Definition 7.2, **0L** $\subseteq$ **PPCF**. Furthermore, there exist languages that can be generated by parallel PCFG but cannot be generated by any 0L system (such a language is, for example, $\{a, aab\}$). Thus, **0L** $\subset$ **PPCF**.

[1] According to its definition, **SPCF** in this paper coincides with PCF in Maurer et al. [1980].

Lemma 7.1 *Let* $X \in \{$**SP**, **JSP**, **PP**, **JPP**, **SPCF**, **JSPCF**, **PPCF**, **JPPCF**, **0L**$\}$. *Then,* $X^{-\varepsilon} \subseteq X$.

Proof Obvious. □

Theorem 7.1 SPCF *and* **JSPCF** *are semilinear.*

Proof Since **SPCF** ⊂ **CF** and **CF** is semilinear (see Parikh [1966]), **SPCF** must be also semilinear. Consider any PCFG $G = (\Sigma, P, \sigma)$. From the definitions of ${}_s\Rightarrow$ and ${}_j\Rightarrow$ it follows that $\psi_\Sigma(L(G, {}_s\Rightarrow)) = \psi_\Sigma(L(G, {}_j\Rightarrow))$. Thus, **JSPCF** is semilinear as well. □

Theorem 7.2 SPCF ⊂ PPCF.

Proof First, we prove the inclusion **SPCF** ⊆ **PPCF**. The proof is based on the proof from [Rozenberg and Doucet, 1971, Theorem 4.2]. Let Σ be an alphabet. We claim that for every PCFG $G = (\Sigma, P, \sigma)$, there is a PCFG $G' = (\Sigma, P', \sigma')$ such that $L(G', {}_p\Rightarrow) = L(G, {}_s\Rightarrow)$. Set

$$P' = P \cup \{a \to a \mid a \in \Sigma\} \quad \text{and} \quad \sigma' = \sigma$$

Now, we prove the following two claims by induction on $m \geq 0$. Since both proofs are straightforward, we show only their induction steps. As the common hypothesis, assume that the claims hold for all $0 \leq m \leq k$, where $k \geq 0$.

Claim A Let $\sigma\ {}_s\Rightarrow^m w$ in G, where $w \in \Sigma^*$. Then $\sigma'\ {}_p\Rightarrow^* w$ in G'. □

Proof (Claim A) Let $\sigma\ {}_s\Rightarrow^{k+1} w$ in G, where $w \in \Sigma^*$. Express $\sigma\ {}_s\Rightarrow^{k+1} w$ as $\sigma\ {}_s\Rightarrow^k uav\ {}_s\Rightarrow uxv$, where $u, v, x \in \Sigma^*$, $a \in \Sigma$, $a \to x \in P$, and $uxv = w$. By the induction hypothesis, there exists a derivation $\sigma'\ {}_p\Rightarrow^* uav$ in G'. Since $P \subseteq P'$ and there are also unit rules $b \to b \in P'$, for every $b \in \Sigma$, clearly $uav\ {}_p\Rightarrow uxv$ in G', which completes the induction step. □

Claim B Let $\sigma'\ {}_p\Rightarrow^m w$ in G', where $w \in \Sigma^*$. Then $\sigma\ {}_s\Rightarrow^* w$ in G. □

Proof (Claim B) Let $\sigma'\ {}_p\Rightarrow^{k+1} w$ in G', where $w \in \Sigma^*$. Express $\sigma'\ {}_p\Rightarrow^{k+1} w$ as $\sigma'\ {}_p\Rightarrow^k x\ {}_p\Rightarrow w$, where $x \in \Sigma^*$. Set $n = |x|$. Express x and w as $x = a_1a_2 \dots a_n$ and $w = y_1y_2 \dots y_n$, respectively, where $a_i \in \Sigma$, $y_i \in \Sigma^*$, and $a_i \to y_i \in P'$, $1 \leq i \leq n$. Observe that $a_i \to y_i \in P'$ and $a_i \neq y_i$ implies $a_i \to y_i \in P$, for all $1 \leq i \leq n$. Thus, $x\ {}_s\Rightarrow^* w$ in G. By the induction hypothesis, we have that $\sigma\ {}_s\Rightarrow^* x$ in G, which completes the induction step. □

By Claim A and Claim B, $\sigma\ {}_s\Rightarrow^* w$ in G iff $\sigma'\ {}_p\Rightarrow^* w$ in G', that is $L(G, {}_s\Rightarrow) = L(G', {}_p\Rightarrow)$, so **SPCF** ⊆ **PPCF**. By [Rozenberg and Doucet, 1971, Theorem 4.7], **0L** ⊈ **CF**. Clearly, **0L** ⊈ **SPCF**. Since **0L** ⊂ **PPCF**, **PPCF** ⊈ **SPCF** and hence **SPCF** ⊂ **PPCF**. □

Corollary 7.1 SPCF ⊂ 0L.

Proof Observe that G' from the proof of Theorem 7.2 is a correctly defined 0L system according to page 304 in Rozenberg and Doucet [1971]. □

Theorem 7.3 SPCF ⊂ CF ∩ PPCF.

Proof **SPCF** ⊆ **CF**∩**PPCF** is a consequence of recalled inclusion **SPCF** ⊂ **CF** and Theorem 7.2. Let $\Sigma = \{a, b, c, d\}$ be an alphabet and $L = \{ab, ccdd\}$ be a language over Σ. Clearly, $L \in$ **CF** and also $L \in$ **PPCF** since there is a PCFG

$$G = (\Sigma, \{a \to cc, b \to dd, c \to c, d \to d\}, ab)$$

such that $L = L(G, {}_p\Rightarrow)$. We show by contradiction that there is no PCFG $G' = (\Sigma, P', \sigma)$ such that $L(G', {}_s\Rightarrow) = L$. Clearly, σ must be either ab or $ccdd$. If we take $ccdd$ as the axiom, there must be $c \to \varepsilon$ or $d \to \varepsilon$ in P' and hence cdd or ccd are contained in L, which is a contradiction. On the other hand, if we take ab, there is no possible way to directly derive $ccdd$ from ab by using ${}_s\Rightarrow$. Hence, $L \notin$ **SPCF**, which completes the proof. □

Corollary 7.2 SPCF ⊂ CF ∩ 0L.

Theorem 7.4 *For a unary alphabet,* **0L = PPCF = JPPCF**.

Proof It follows directly from the definition of ${}_p\Rightarrow$ and ${}_{jp}\Rightarrow$ and from the definition of $\Rightarrow$ in 0L systems (see Rozenberg and Doucet [1971]). □

Theorem 7.5 *For a unary alphabet,* **SPCF = JSPCF**.

Proof It follows directly from the definition of ${}_s\Rightarrow$ and ${}_j\Rightarrow$. □

Now, we recall the following lemma from Rozenberg and Doucet [1971].

Lemma 7.2 ([Rozenberg and Doucet, 1971, Lemma 4.8 on page 313]) *Let G be a 0L system. Then there exists a number k such that for every string w in $L(G)$ there exists a derivation such that $|u| \leq k|w|$ for every string u in that derivation.*

By analogy with the proof of Lemma 7.2, it is easy to prove the following lemma because PCFGs do not differ from 0L systems when only the longest sentential forms are considered during the derivation of any sentence w.

Lemma 7.3 *Let G be a PCFG. Let $h \in \{s, j, p, jp\}$. Then there exists a number k such that for every string w in $L(G, {}_h\Rightarrow)$ there exists a derivation such that $|u| \leq k|w|$ for every string u in that derivation.*

Lemma 7.4 CS − JPPCF ≠ ∅.

Proof The language $X = \{a^p \mid p \text{ is a prime}\}$ over a unary alphabet $\{a\}$ is a well-known context-sensitive non-context-free language (see Hopcroft et al. [2006]). By contradiction, we show that $X \notin$ **JPPCF**. Assume that there is a PCFG $G = (\{a\}, P, \sigma)$ such that $L(G, {}_{jp}\Rightarrow) = X$. Obviously $a \to \varepsilon \notin P$ and $\sigma = a^2$ since 2 is the smallest prime. As 3 is also prime, $a^2 \; {}_{jp}\Rightarrow^* a^3$ and we have $a \to a \in P$ and $a \to a^2 \in P$. Thus, $a^2 \; {}_{jp}\Rightarrow^* a^4$. Since 4 is not a prime, we have a contradiction. □

Corollary 7.3 CS − JSPCF ≠ ∅.

Proof From Lemma 7.4, we have that $X = \{a^p \mid p \text{ is a prime}\}$ is not contained in **JPPCF**. Since X is a unary language and for unary languages holds **JSPCF** = **SPCF** ⊂ **PPCF** = **JPPCF** (see Theorems 7.2, 7.4, and 7.5), we have that $X \notin$ **JSPCF**. □

Theorem 7.6 JPPCF ⊂ CS.

Proof Let $G = (\Sigma, P, \sigma)$ be a PCFG. As is obvious, there is an unrestricted grammar $H = (V, \Sigma, P', S)$ such that $L(H) = L(G, {}_{jp}\Rightarrow)$. More precisely, we are able to construct H in the way that H simulates G. In this case, Lemma 7.3 also holds for H. Observe that Lemma 7.3 is the workspace theorem, and every language from **JPPCF** must be then context-sensitive.

As **CS** − **JPPCF** ≠ ∅ by Lemma 7.4, we have **JPPCF** ⊂ **CS**. □

Theorem 7.7 JSPCF ⊂ CS.

Proof **JSPCF** ⊆ **CS** can be proved analogously as **JPPCF** ⊆ **CS** from Theorem 7.6. Together with Corollary 7.3, we have **JSPCF** ⊂ **CS**. □

Mutual Relationships of SPCF, JSPCF, PPCF, JPPCF, CF, and CS

Now, we investigate all the mutual relationships between **SPCF**, **JSPCF**, **PPCF**, **JPPCF**, **CF**, and **CS**. We refer to them as language subfamilies A through T in Figure 7.1, which presents them by using an Euler diagram. More precisely, in this diagram, **JSPCF**, **PPCF**, **JPPCF**, **CF** form Venn diagram with 16 subfamilies contained in **CS**; in addition, four more subfamilies are pictured by placing **SPCF** as a subset of **CF** ∩ **PPCF** (see Theorem 7.3). Hereafter, we study 20 subfamilies in the following 13 theorems and seven open problems (Theorems and Open Problems 7.8 through 7.20).

Theorem 7.8 (Subfamily A)

$$\mathbf{PPCF} - (\mathbf{CF} \cup \mathbf{JSPCF} \cup \mathbf{JPPCF}) \neq \emptyset$$

Proof Let $\Sigma = \{a, b\}$ be an alphabet. Let $X = \{a^{2^n} b^{2^n} \mid n \geq 0\}$ be a language over Σ. Clearly, $X \in$ **PPCF**, since there exists a PCFG, $G = (\Sigma, \{a \rightarrow aa, b \rightarrow bb\}, ab)$, such that $L(G, {}_p\Rightarrow) = X$. $X \notin$ **CF** and $X \notin$ **JSPCF** is satisfied since X is not semilinear. By contradiction, we show that $X \notin$ **JPPCF**.

Consider that there is a PCFG, $G' = (\Sigma, P', \sigma')$, such that $L(G', {}_{jp}\Rightarrow) = X$. Observe that $ab \in L(G', {}_{jp}\Rightarrow)$. Let $a \rightarrow x$, $b \rightarrow y$ be production rules from P', $x, y \in \Sigma^*$. Then, there exist two derivations, $ab \; {}_{jp}\Rightarrow xy$ and $ab \; {}_{jp}\Rightarrow yx$, in G'. Now, consider the following cases:

- $x = \varepsilon$ ($y = \varepsilon$). If $y \in X$ ($x \in X$), then either ab is the only string derivable in G' using ${}_{jp}\Rightarrow$ or there is a derivation $y \;{}_{jp}\Rightarrow^* z$ ($x \;{}_{jp}\Rightarrow^* z$) in G' such that $ba \in \text{substrings}(z)$, which is a contradiction. If $y \notin X$, such as $y \in \{\varepsilon, a, b\}$ ($x \notin X$, such as $x \in \{\varepsilon, a, b\}$), then $ab \;{}_{jp}\Rightarrow y$ ($ab \;{}_{jp}\Rightarrow x$), so $y \in X$ ($x \in X$), which is a contradiction as well. In the following, we assume that $x \neq \varepsilon$ and $y \neq \varepsilon$.
- $x = bx'$ or $y = by'$, where $x', y' \in \Sigma^*$. Then, there is a derivation $ab \;{}_{jp}\Rightarrow bz$ in G', where $z \in \Sigma^*$, and thus $bz \in X$, which is a contradiction.
- $x = x'a$ or $y = y'a$, where $x', y' \in \Sigma^*$. Then, there is a derivation $ab \;{}_{jp}\Rightarrow za$ in G', where $z \in \Sigma^*$, and thus $za \in X$, which is a contradiction.
- $x = ax'b$ and $y = ay'b$, where $x', y' \in \Sigma^*$. Then, there is a derivation $ab \;{}_{jp}\Rightarrow z$ in G' such that $ba \in \text{substrings}(z)$, which is a contradiction.

If $a \to x$ or $b \to y$ is missing in P', then X is finite—a contradiction. No other cases are possible, which completes the proof. □

Several intersections of some language families are hard to investigate. Such an intersection is **PPCF** ∩ **JSPCF**. At this moment, we are not able to prove whether **PPCF** ∩ **JSPCF** ⊆ **CF** or not. For this reason, we leave the subfamilies B and C as open problems.

Open Problem (Subfamily B) Is it true that

$$(\mathbf{PPCF} \cap \mathbf{JSPCF}) - (\mathbf{CF} \cup \mathbf{JPPCF}) \neq \emptyset?$$

Open Problem (Subfamily C) Is it true that

$$(\mathbf{PPCF} \cap \mathbf{JSPCF} \cap \mathbf{JPPCF}) - \mathbf{CF} \neq \emptyset?$$

Theorem 7.9 (Subfamily D)

$$(\mathbf{PPCF} \cap \mathbf{JPPCF}) - (\mathbf{CF} \cup \mathbf{JSPCF}) \neq \emptyset$$

Proof For unary alphabet, **0L** = **PPCF** = **JPPCF** (Theorem 7.4). Since **CF** and **JSPCF** are both semilinear, it is sufficient to find any non-semilinear language over unary alphabet which is also contained in **PPCF**. Such a language is indisputably $\{a^{2^n} \mid n \geq 0\}$. □

Theorem 7.10 (Subfamily E)

$$\mathbf{SPCF} - (\mathbf{JSPCF} \cup \mathbf{JPPCF}) \neq \emptyset$$

Proof Let $\Sigma = \{a, b, c\}$ be an alphabet. Let $X = \{a^n c b^n \mid n \geq 0\}$ be a language over Σ. Clearly, there exists a PCFG $G = (\Sigma, \{c \to acb\}, c)$ such that $L(G, {}_s\Rightarrow) = X$ and hence $X \in \mathbf{SPCF}$. We prove by contradiction that X is neither jumping sequential pure context-free nor jumping parallel pure context-free language.

$X \notin \mathbf{JSPCF}$. Assume that there is a PCFG $G' = (\Sigma, P', \sigma')$ such that

$$L(G', {}_j\Rightarrow) = X.$$

Clearly, $\sigma' = c$ must be the axiom since there must be no erasing rules in P' (observe that $ab, ac, cb \notin X$). Because $acb \in X$, we have that $c \to acb \in P'$. But $acb \ {}_j\Rightarrow abacb$ and $abacb \notin X$, which is a contradiction.

$X \notin$ **JPPCF**. Assume that there is a PCFG $H = (\Sigma, R, \omega)$ such that $L(H, {}_{jp}\Rightarrow) = X$. First, let $k \geq 1$ and assume that $\omega = a^k cb^k$ is an axiom. Since $\omega \ {}_{jp}\Rightarrow^* c$, there must be rules $a \to \varepsilon$, $b \to \varepsilon$, and $c \to c$ contained in R. Now, assume that

- $\hat{d} \to dx \in R, \hat{d} \in \{a, b\}, d \in \Sigma, x \in \Sigma^*$; then, $\omega \ {}_{jp}\Rightarrow^* udxcv$ and $\omega \ {}_{jp}\Rightarrow^* ucdxv$ and obviously for $d = a$ holds $ucdxv \notin X$ and for $d = b$ holds $udxcv \notin X$, $u, v \in \Sigma^*$; $d = c$ is obvious;
- $\hat{d} \to xd \in R, \hat{d} \in \{a, b\}, d \in \Sigma, x \in \Sigma^*$; then, $\omega \ {}_{jp}\Rightarrow^* uxdcv$ and $\omega \ {}_{jp}\Rightarrow^* ucxdv$ and obviously for $d = a$ holds $ucxdv \notin X$ and for $d = b$ holds $uxdcv \notin X$, $u, v \in \Sigma^*$; $d = c$ is obvious.

Therefore, $a \to x, b \to y \in R$ implies $x = y = \varepsilon$. Hence, only rules of the form $c \to z$, where $z \in X$, can be considered. But the finiteness of R implies the finiteness of X, which is a contradiction.

Clearly, the axiom must be $\omega = c$, which implies that R contains rules of the form $c \to z$, where $z \in X$. Obviously, there must be also rules $a \to x, b \to y \in R$, $x, y \in \Sigma^*$. If $x = y = \varepsilon$, X must be finite. Thus, assume that $x \neq \varepsilon$ or $y \neq \varepsilon$. Then, like before, we can derive a string which is not contained in X—a contradiction. □

Theorem 7.11 (Subfamily F)

$$(\textbf{SPCF} \cap \textbf{JSPCF}) - \textbf{JPPCF} \neq \emptyset$$

Proof Let $\Sigma = \{a, b, c\}$ be an alphabet and let $X = \{aa, aab, aac, aabc\}$ be a language over Σ. Consider a PCFG

$$G = (\Sigma, \{b \to \varepsilon, c \to \varepsilon\}, aabc).$$

Clearly, $L(G, {}_s\Rightarrow) = L(G, {}_j\Rightarrow) = X$ and hence $X \in$ **SPCF** $\cap$ **JSPCF**.

To show that $X \notin$ **JPPCF**, we use a contradiction. Assume that there exists a PCFG $G' = (\Sigma, P', \sigma)$ such that $L(G', {}_{jp}\Rightarrow) = X$. Since $\sigma \in X$ and $X \subseteq \{aa\}\{b\}^*\{c\}^*$, there must be a rule $a \to x$ in P' with $x \in \Sigma^*$. But this implies that there must be a derivation $\sigma \ {}_{jp}\Rightarrow^* aa \ {}_{jp}\Rightarrow xx$ in G'. The only string from X that has a form xx is aa so $a \to a$ is the only rule with a on its left-hand side so $a \to a \in P'$.

Next, we choose σ. Clearly, $\sigma \neq aa$. Furthermore, $\sigma \notin \{aab, aac\}$ since $\sigma \ {}_{jp}\Rightarrow aabc$ implies that $\sigma \ {}_{jp}\Rightarrow^* abca$, and $abca \notin X$. Thus, the only possibility is to choose $\sigma = aabc$. But $aabc \ {}_{jp}\Rightarrow aab$ means that $\{b \to b, c \to \varepsilon\} \subseteq P'$ or $\{b \to \varepsilon, c \to b\} \subseteq P'$. In both cases, $aabc \ {}_{jp}\Rightarrow aba$. As $aba \notin X$, there is no PCFG G' such that $L(G', {}_{jp}\Rightarrow) = X$, which is a contradiction. □

Theorem 7.12 (Subfamily G)

$$\textbf{SPCF} \cap \textbf{JSPCF} \cap \textbf{JPPCF} \neq \emptyset$$

Proof Let $G = (\{a\}, \{a \to a, a \to aa\}, a)$ be a PCFG. It is easy to see that

$$L(G, {}_s\Rightarrow) = L(G, {}_j\Rightarrow) = L(G, {}_{jp}\Rightarrow) = \{a\}^+.$$

Open Problem (Subfamily H) Is it true that

$$(\mathbf{SPCF} \cap \mathbf{JPPCF}) - \mathbf{JSPCF} \neq \emptyset?$$

Theorem 7.13 (Subfamily I)

$$(\mathbf{PPCF} \cap \mathbf{CF}) - (\mathbf{SPCF} \cup \mathbf{JSPCF} \cup \mathbf{JPPCF}) \neq \emptyset$$

Proof Let $X = \{aabb, ccdd\}$ be a language over an alphabet $\Sigma = \{a, b, c, d\}$. Clearly, $X \in \mathbf{CF}$. Since there exists a PCFG $G = (\Sigma, \{a \to c, b \to d\}, aabb)$ such that $L(G, {}_p\Rightarrow) = X$, $X \in \mathbf{PPCF}$. Furthermore, observe that derivations $aabb\ {}_s\Rightarrow ccdd$ ($aabb\ {}_j\Rightarrow ccdd$) or $ccdd\ {}_s\Rightarrow aabb$ ($ccdd\ {}_j\Rightarrow aabb$) cannot be performed due to the definition of ${}_s\Rightarrow$ (${}_j\Rightarrow$), and hence there is no PCFG G' such that $L(G', {}_s\Rightarrow) = X$ ($L(G', {}_j\Rightarrow) = X$). Thus, $X \notin \mathbf{SPCF}$ and $X \notin \mathbf{JSPCF}$.

Now, suppose that there is a PCFG $H = (\Sigma, P, \sigma)$ such that $L(H, {}_{jp}\Rightarrow) = X$. For $\sigma = aabb$, we have $aabb\ {}_{jp}\Rightarrow ccdd$. If $a \to \varepsilon \in P$ or $b \to \varepsilon \in P$, then $aabb\ {}_{jp}\Rightarrow x$, where $x \notin X$. Thus, $a \to y$ and $b \to z$, where $y, z \in \{c, d\}$, are only possible production rules in P. But $aabb\ {}_{jp}\Rightarrow cdcd$ and since $cdcd \notin X$, there is no PCFG H such that $L(H, {}_{jp}\Rightarrow) = X$. Analogously for $\sigma = ccdd$. We have a contradiction and therefore $X \notin \mathbf{JPPCF}$. □

Open Problem (Subfamily J) Is it true that

$$(\mathbf{PPCF} \cap \mathbf{CF} \cap \mathbf{JSPCF}) - (\mathbf{SPCF} \cup \mathbf{JPPCF}) \neq \emptyset?$$

Open Problem (Subfamily K) Is it true that

$$(\mathbf{PPCF} \cap \mathbf{CF} \cap \mathbf{JSPCF} \cap \mathbf{JPPCF}) - \mathbf{SPCF} \neq \emptyset?$$

Theorem 7.14 (Subfamily L)

$$(\mathbf{PPCF} \cap \mathbf{CF} \cap \mathbf{JPPCF}) - (\mathbf{SPCF} \cup \mathbf{JSPCF}) \neq \emptyset$$

Proof Consider a language $X = \{ab, cd, dc\}$ over an alphabet $\Sigma = \{a, b, c, d\}$. Clearly, X is neither classical sequential pure context-free nor jumping sequential pure context-free language, since at some point during a derivation, we must rewrite two symbols simultaneously.

As X is a finite language, $X \in \mathbf{CF}$. As there exists a PCFG

$$G = (\Sigma, \{a \to c, b \to d, c \to d, d \to c\}, ab)$$

such that $L(G, {}_p\Rightarrow) = L(G, {}_{jp}\Rightarrow) = X$, $X \in \mathbf{PPCF} \cap \mathbf{JPPCF}$. □

Theorem 7.15 (Subfamily M)

$$\mathbf{CF} - (\mathbf{PPCF} \cup \mathbf{JSPCF} \cup \mathbf{JPPCF}) \neq \emptyset$$

Proof Let $\Sigma = \{a, b\}$ and let $X = \{a^n b^n \mid n \geq 1\}$ be a language over Σ. Indisputably, X is a well-known context-free language. According to Rozenberg and Doucet [1971], $X \notin \mathbf{0L}$. Observe that every language Y that belongs to $(\mathbf{PPCF} - \mathbf{0L})$ can be generated by PCFG $G = (\Sigma, P, \sigma)$ such that there exists $c \in \Sigma$ such that for every $x \in \Sigma^*$, $c \to x \notin P$. Thus, if $X \in (\mathbf{PPCF} - \mathbf{0L})$, then X must be a finite language (since either a or b blocks deriving of any string from axiom), which is a contradiction. Therefore, $X \notin (\mathbf{PPCF} - \mathbf{0L})$ and clearly $X \notin \mathbf{PPCF}$. Next, we demonstrate that $X \notin \mathbf{JSPCF}$ and $X \notin \mathbf{JPPCF}$.

$X \notin \mathbf{JSPCF}$. Suppose that $X \in \mathbf{JSPCF}$, so there exists a PCFG $G' = (\Sigma, P', \sigma')$ such that $L(G', {}_j\Rightarrow) = X$. As $a, b \notin X$, there are no erasing rules in P' and thus $\sigma' = ab$ must be the axiom. Now consider a derivation $ab \ {}_j\Rightarrow aabb$. There are exactly two possibilities how to get a string $aabb$ directly from the axiom ab—either expand a to aab ($a \to aab \in P'$) or expand b to abb ($b \to abb \in P'$). Due to the definition of ${}_j\Rightarrow$, $ab \ {}_j\Rightarrow baab$ in the first case, and $ab \ {}_j\Rightarrow abba$ in the second case. Since neither $baab$ nor $abba$ belongs to X, $X \notin \mathbf{JSPCF}$, which is a contradiction.

$X \notin \mathbf{JPPCF}$. Suppose that $X \in \mathbf{JPPCF}$, so there exists a PCFG $H = (\Sigma, R, \omega)$ such that $L(H, {}_{jp}\Rightarrow) = X$. As for all $i \geq 0$, $a^i, b^i \notin X$, there are no erasing rules in R and thus $\omega = ab$ must be the axiom. Clearly, $ab \ {}_{jp}\Rightarrow aabb$. There are exactly three ways to get $aabb$ from ab:

- $a \to a \in R, b \to abb \in R$. In this case, $ab \ {}_{jp}\Rightarrow aabb$ implies that $ab \ {}_{jp}\Rightarrow abba$, but $abba \notin X$.
- $a \to aa \in R, b \to bb \in R$. In this case, $ab \ {}_{jp}\Rightarrow aabb$ implies that $ab \ {}_{jp}\Rightarrow bbaa$, but $bbaa \notin X$.
- $a \to aab \in R, b \to b \in R$. In this case, $ab \ {}_{jp}\Rightarrow aabb$ implies that $ab \ {}_{jp}\Rightarrow baab$, but $baab \notin X$.

Thus, $X \notin \mathbf{JPPCF}$, which is a contradiction. □

Open Problem (Subfamily N) Is it true that

$$(\mathbf{CF} \cap \mathbf{JSPCF}) - (\mathbf{PPCF} \cup \mathbf{JPPCF}) \neq \emptyset?$$

Theorem 7.16 (Subfamily O)

$$(\mathbf{CF} \cap \mathbf{JSPCF} \cap \mathbf{JPPCF}) - \mathbf{PPCF} \neq \emptyset$$

Proof Let $\Sigma = \{a, b\}$ be an alphabet and let

$$X = \{aabb, abab, abba, baab, baba, bbaa\}$$

be a language over Σ. Since X is finite, X is context-free. Given a PCFG

$$G = (\Sigma, \{a \to a, b \to b\}, aabb).$$

Clearly, $L(G, {}_j\Rightarrow) = L(G, {}_{jp}\Rightarrow) = X$. Hence, $X \in$ **CF** $\cap$ **JSPCF** $\cap$ **JPPCF**.

By contradiction, we show that $X \notin$ **PPCF**. Assume that there is a PCFG $H = (\Sigma, P, \sigma)$ such that $L(H, {}_p\Rightarrow) = X$. First, we show that P contains no erasing rules:

- If $a \to \varepsilon \in P$ and $b \to \varepsilon \in P$, we have $\varepsilon \in X$, which is a contradiction.
- If $a \to \varepsilon \in P$, then $b \to x \in P$ implies that $x \in \{aa, bb, ab, ba\}$ because for every $w \in X$, $|w| = 4$. Clearly, if $b \to aa \in P$, then $aaaa \in X$, and if $b \to bb \in P$, then $bbbb \in X$. As is obvious, both cases represent a contradiction. On the other hand, if there are no rules in P starting from b apart from $b \to ab$ and/or $b \to ba$, then $aabb \notin X$, which is a contradiction. Similarly for $b \to \varepsilon \in P$.

Since all strings in X have the same length and there are no erasing rules in P, only unit rules can be contained in P. Because $aaaa \notin X$ and $bbbb \notin X$, either $P = \{a \to a, b \to b\}$ or $P = \{a \to b, b \to a\}$. In both cases, we never get X. Thus, there is no PCFG H such that $L(H, {}_p\Rightarrow) = X$, and hence $X \notin$ **PPCF**. □

Theorem 7.17 (Subfamily P)

$$(\mathbf{CF} \cap \mathbf{JPPCF}) - (\mathbf{PPCF} \cup \mathbf{JSPCF}) \neq \emptyset$$

Proof Consider a language $Y = \{aabb, ccdd, cdcd, cddc, dccd, dcdc, ddcc\}$ over an alphabet $\Sigma = \{a, b, c, d\}$. Clearly, $Y \in$ **CF** and also $Y \in$ **JPPCF** because there is a PCFG

$$G = (\Sigma, \{a \to c, b \to d, c \to c, d \to d\}, aabb)$$

such that $L(G, {}_{jp}\Rightarrow) = Y$. The proof that $Y \notin$ **PPCF** is almost identical to the proof that $X \notin$ **PPCF** from Theorem 7.16, so it is omitted. Because it is not possible to rewrite two or more symbols simultaneously during the direct derivation step by using ${}_j\Rightarrow$, we have $Y \notin$ **JSPCF**. □

Open Problem (Subfamily Q) Is it true that

$$\mathbf{JSPCF} - (\mathbf{CF} \cup \mathbf{PPCF} \cup \mathbf{JPPCF}) \neq \emptyset?$$

Theorem 7.18 (Subfamily R)

$$(\mathbf{JSPCF} \cap \mathbf{JPPCF}) - (\mathbf{CF} \cup \mathbf{PPCF}) \neq \emptyset$$

Proof Let $\Sigma = \{a, b, c\}$ be an alphabet and let $X = \{w \mid \mathrm{occur}(w, a) - 1 = \mathrm{occur}(w, b) = \mathrm{occur}(w, c), w \in \Sigma^+\}$ be a language over Σ. $X \in$ **JSPCF** $\cap$ **JPPCF** since there is a PCFG

$$G = (\Sigma, \{a \to abca, a \to a, b \to b, c \to c\}, a)$$

such that $L(G, {}_j\Rightarrow) = L(G, {}_{jp}\Rightarrow) = X$. By pumping lemma for context-free languages, $X \notin$ **CF**.

By contradiction, we show that $X \notin$ **PPCF**. Assume that there is a PCFG $H = (\Sigma, P, \sigma)$ such that $L(H, {}_p\Rightarrow) = X$. First, we show that $\sigma = a$. Assume that $\sigma \neq a$. Then, $\sigma\ {}_p\Rightarrow^* a$ implies that $a \to \varepsilon \in P$ and we have that $\varepsilon \in X$, which is a contradiction. Thus, a must be the axiom, and $a \to x \in P$ implies that $x \in X$.

Let $l = 3\max\{|\beta| \mid \alpha \to \beta \in P\}$. The smallest possible value of l is 3. Let $\omega = a^{l+1}b^l c^l$. Clearly, $\omega \in X$. Then there is a direct derivation step $\theta\ {}_p\Rightarrow \omega$, where $\theta \in X$. Next, we make the following observations about θ and P:

(1) $\theta \neq a$, since $a \to \omega \notin P$. The choice of l excludes such situation.
(2) θ contains all three symbols a, b, and c.
(3) $a \to a \in P$ is the only production rule with a on its left-hand side that is used during $\theta\ {}_p\Rightarrow \omega$. Observe that if $a \to x \in P$ is chosen to rewrite a during $\theta\ {}_p\Rightarrow \omega$, then $x \in X$ and x must be a substring of ω. Only $x = a$ meets these requirements.
(4) θ can be expressed as $a^+\theta'$, where $\theta' \in \{b, c\}^*$. This follows from the form of ω and the third observation.
(5) During $\theta\ {}_p\Rightarrow \omega$ are used production rules $b \to y, c \to y' \in P$ such that each of y, y' do not contain at least one symbol from Σ. This is secured by the choice of l.
(6) Every rule with b on its left-hand side in P has the same Parikh (commutative) image of its right-hand side, and every rule with c on its left-hand side in P has the same Parikh (commutative) image of its right-hand side. To not break a number of occurrences of symbols a, b, and c in ω during $\theta\ {}_p\Rightarrow \omega$, when $b \to y \in P$ is used, then the corresponding $c \to y' \in P$ must be also used simultaneously with it. To preserve the proper number of occurrences of a, b, and c in ω, we have $\mathrm{card}(\{\psi_\Sigma(\beta) \mid b \to \beta \in P\}) = 1$ and $\mathrm{card}(\{\psi_\Sigma(\gamma) \mid c \to \gamma \in P\}) = 1$.

Now, we inspect the ways $a^+\theta'\ {}_p\Rightarrow \omega$ could be made. Suppose that the first symbol of θ' is b:

- $b \to \varepsilon \in P$ was used. Then, $c \to bc \in P$ must be used ($c \to cb$ is excluded since c is not before b in ω). As there are at least two cs in θ', applying $c \to bc$ brings c before b which is in a contradiction with the form of ω.
- Let $i \geq 1$ and let $b \to a^i \in P$. Then, $c \to b^{i+1}c^{i+1} \in P$. Since $|b^{i+1}c^{i+1}|$ is at most $\frac{l}{3}$, there are at least two occurrences of c in θ', and then we obtain c before b in ω.
- Let $i \geq 1$ and let j be a non-negative integer such that $j \leq i+1$. Let $b \to a^i b^j \in P$. Then $c \to b^k c^m \in P$, where $j + k = m = i + 1$. As in the previous case, when these rules are used during $\theta\ {}_p\Rightarrow \omega$, we get b before a or c before b in ω.
- No as were added during $\theta\ {}_p\Rightarrow \omega$. In this case, the only rules with b and c on their left-hand sides in P can be either $b \to bc$ and $c \to \varepsilon$, or $b \to b$ and $c \to c$, or $b \to c$ and $c \to b$. This implies that the only way to get θ from a is to use $a \to \theta$ rule that is clearly not in P.

For the case that c is the first symbol of θ', we can proceed analogously. Therefore, $\omega \notin L(H, {}_p\Rightarrow)$, which implies that $X \notin$ **PPCF**. □

Theorem 7.19 (Subfamily S)

$$\mathbf{JPPCF} - (\mathbf{CF} \cup \mathbf{PPCF} \cup \mathbf{JSPCF}) \neq \emptyset$$

Proof Let $\Sigma = \{a, b, c, \hat{a}, \hat{b}, \hat{c}\}$ be an alphabet and let

$$X = \{\hat{a}\hat{b}\hat{c}\} \cup \{x \mid \text{occur}(x, a) - 1 = \text{occur}(x, b) = \text{occur}(x, c), \\ x \in \{a, b, c\}^+\}$$

be a language over Σ. Following the pumping lemma for context-free languages, $X \notin \mathbf{CF}$. Since there is a PCFG $G = (\Sigma, \{\hat{a} \rightarrow a, \hat{b} \rightarrow \varepsilon, \hat{c} \rightarrow \varepsilon, a \rightarrow abca, a \rightarrow a, b \rightarrow b, c \rightarrow c\}, \hat{a}\hat{b}\hat{c})$ such that $L(G, {}_{jp}\!\Rightarrow) = X$, $X \in \mathbf{JPPCF}$. By contradiction, we show that $X \notin \mathbf{JSPCF}$ and $X \notin \mathbf{PPCF}$.

Suppose that $X \in \mathbf{JSPCF}$. Then, there is a PCFG $H = (\Sigma, P, \sigma)$ such that $L(H, {}_j\!\Rightarrow) = X$. First, we choose σ. From the definition of X, $a \in X$ and for every string $x \in X - \{a\}$ holds $|x| \geq 3$. Since we are able to erase only one symbol during direct derivation step by ${}_j\!\Rightarrow$ and there is no string of length 2 contained in X, we must choose $\sigma = a$ as the axiom. Because $abca \in X$ and $\hat{a}\hat{b}\hat{c} \in X$, there must be two derivations, $a\ {}_j\!\Rightarrow^* abca$ and $a\ {}_j\!\Rightarrow^* \hat{a}\hat{b}\hat{c}$, and this implies that there exists also a derivation $a\ {}_j\!\Rightarrow^* \hat{a}\hat{b}\hat{c}bca$. Since $\hat{a}\hat{b}\hat{c}bca \notin X$, we have a contradiction.

Next, suppose that $X \in \mathbf{PPCF}$, so there exists a PCFG $H' = (\Sigma, P', \sigma')$ such that $L(H', {}_p\!\Rightarrow) = X$. In this case, we must choose $\sigma' = \hat{a}\hat{b}\hat{c}$ as the axiom. If we choose a, then $a\ {}_p\!\Rightarrow^* abca$ and $a\ {}_p\!\Rightarrow^* \hat{a}\hat{b}\hat{c}$ implies that $a\ {}_p\!\Rightarrow^* u_1 a u_2 \hat{a} u_3$, $u_1, u_2, u_3 \in \Sigma^*$, and $u_1 a u_2 \hat{a} u_3 \notin X$. If we choose $abca$ or similar, then $abca\ {}_p\!\Rightarrow^* a$ implies that $a\ {}_p\!\Rightarrow^* \varepsilon$, and $\varepsilon \notin X$. Without loss of generality, assume that for every $\alpha \rightarrow \beta \in P'$, $\beta \in \{a, b, c\}^*$ (this can be assumed since $\hat{a}\hat{b}\hat{c}$ is the only string over $\{\hat{a}, \hat{b}, \hat{c}\}$ in X). As $a \in X$, $a \rightarrow \varepsilon$, $a \rightarrow b$, and $a \rightarrow c$ are not contained in P'. The observations (1) to (3) from the proof of Theorem 7.18 hold also for H'. The rest of the proof is similar to the proof of Theorem 7.18. □

Theorem 7.20 (Subfamily T)

$$\mathbf{CS} - (\mathbf{CF} \cup \mathbf{JSPCF} \cup \mathbf{PPCF} \cup \mathbf{JPPCF}) \neq \emptyset$$

Proof Let $X = \{a^p \mid p \text{ is a prime}\}$ be a language over unary alphabet $\{a\}$. $X \in \mathbf{CS}$ and $X \notin \mathbf{CF}$ are well-known containments (see Hopcroft et al. [2006]). By Lemma 7.4 and Corollary 7.3, $X \notin \mathbf{JPPCF}$ and $X \notin \mathbf{JSPCF}$. As for unary languages $\mathbf{PPCF} = \mathbf{JPPCF}$, $X \notin \mathbf{PPCF}$. □

The summary of Theorems 7.8 through 7.20 is visualized in Figure 7.1.

Absence of Erasing Rules

As stated in Lemma 7.1, it is natural that the family of languages generated by pure grammars without erasing rules is included in the family of languages generated by pure grammars in which the presence of erasing rules is allowed. As we show further, for PCFG, the inclusions stated in Lemma 7.1 are proper. The PG case is left as an open problem.

Theorem 7.21 *Let*

$$X \in \{\mathbf{SPCF}, \mathbf{JSPCF}, \mathbf{PPCF}, \mathbf{JPPCF}, \mathbf{0L}\}.$$

Then, $X^{-\varepsilon} \subset X$.

Proof Let $K = \{a, ab\}$ and $Y = \{aa, aab\}$ be two languages over $\Sigma = \{a, b\}$. Furthermore, let $G = (\Sigma, \{a \to a, b \to \varepsilon\}, ab)$ and $G' = (\Sigma, \{a \to a, b \to \varepsilon\}, aab)$ be two PCFGs.

(a) $\mathbf{SPCF}^{-\varepsilon} \subset \mathbf{SPCF}$. Since $K = L(G, {}_s\Rightarrow)$, $K \in \mathbf{SPCF}$. Assume that $K \in \mathbf{SPCF}^{-\varepsilon}$; then, there is a PCFG $H = (\Sigma, P, \sigma)$ with no erasing rules in P such that $L(H, {}_s\Rightarrow) = K$. Obviously, $\sigma = a$, so $a \to ab \in P$. We have $a \;{}_s\Rightarrow^* abb$ and since $abb \notin K$, $K \notin \mathbf{SPCF}^{-\varepsilon}$.
(b) $\mathbf{JSPCF}^{-\varepsilon} \subset \mathbf{JSPCF}$. $K \in \mathbf{JSPCF}$ and $K \notin \mathbf{JSPCF}^{-\varepsilon}$ are proved analogously as in (a).
(c) $\mathbf{PPCF}^{-\varepsilon} \subset \mathbf{PPCF}$. Since $Y = L(G', {}_p\Rightarrow)$, $Y \in \mathbf{PPCF}$. Assume that $Y \in \mathbf{PPCF}^{-\varepsilon}$, so there is a PCFG $H = (\Sigma, P, \sigma)$ with no erasing rules in P such that $L(H, {}_p\Rightarrow) = Y$. Obviously, $\sigma = aa$ and then $a \to ab \in P$. We have $aa \;{}_p\Rightarrow^* abab$ and since $abab \notin Y$, $Y \notin \mathbf{PPCF}^{-\varepsilon}$.
(d) $\mathbf{JPPCF}^{-\varepsilon} \subset \mathbf{JPPCF}$. $Y \in \mathbf{JPPCF}$ and $Y \notin \mathbf{JPPCF}^{-\varepsilon}$ are proved analogously as in (c).
(e) $\mathbf{0L}^{-\varepsilon} \subset \mathbf{0L}$ (see [Herman and Rozenberg, 1975, Theorem 2.8]). □

Open Problem Let $X \in \{\mathbf{SP}, \mathbf{JSP}, \mathbf{PP}, \mathbf{JPP}\}$. Is the inclusion $X^{-\varepsilon} \subseteq X$, in fact, proper? □

From Figure 7.1 and from mentioned theorems, we are able to find out the most of relationships between investigated language families (even for those which are generated by PCFGs without erasing rules—the most of languages used in Figure 7.1 have this property), but not all. Following theorems fill this gap.

Theorem 7.22 SPCF *and* $\mathbf{PPCF}^{-\varepsilon}$ *are incomparable.*

Proof Let $X = \{aa, aab\}$ be a language over alphabet $\Sigma = \{a, b\}$. Obviously, there is a PCFG $G = (\Sigma, \{a \to a, b \to \varepsilon\}, aab)$ such that $L(G, {}_s\Rightarrow) = X$, so $X \in \mathbf{SPCF}$. By Theorem 7.21, $X \notin \mathbf{PPCF}^{-\varepsilon}$. Conversely, there is a language $Y = \{a^{2^n} \mid n \geq 0\}$ over $\{a\}$ such that $Y \notin \mathbf{SPCF}$ and $Y \in \mathbf{PPCF}^{-\varepsilon}$ (see D in Figure 7.1 and observe that to get Y we need no erasing rules). Finally, $\{a\}^+ \in \mathbf{SPCF} \cap \mathbf{PPCF}^{-\varepsilon}$. □

Theorem 7.23 SPCF *and* $\mathbf{0L}^{-\varepsilon}$ *are incomparable.*

Proof Analogous to the proof of Theorem 7.22. □

The mutual relation between $\mathbf{JSPCF}^{-\varepsilon}$ and $\mathbf{JPPCF}^{-\varepsilon}$ is either incomparability or $\mathbf{JSPCF}^{-\varepsilon} \subset \mathbf{JPPCF}^{-\varepsilon}$, but we do not know the answer now. We also do not know either if $\mathbf{JSPCF}^{-\varepsilon}$ and $\mathbf{JPPCF}$ are incomparable or $\mathbf{JSPCF}^{-\varepsilon} \subset \mathbf{JPPCF}$.

Open Problem What is the relation between $\mathbf{JSPCF}^{-\varepsilon}$ and $\mathbf{JPPCF}^{-\varepsilon}$? □

Open Problem What is the relation between $\mathbf{JSPCF}^{-\varepsilon}$ and **JPPCF**? □

Theorem 7.24 $\mathbf{PPCF}^{-\varepsilon}$ *and* **0L** *are incomparable.*

Proof Let $X = \{aa, aab\}$ and $Y = \{a, aab\}$ be two languages over $\{a, b\}$. $X \notin \mathbf{PPCF}^{-\varepsilon}$, $X \in \mathbf{0L}$, $Y \in \mathbf{PPCF}^{-\varepsilon}$, and $Y \notin \mathbf{0L}$ proves the incomparability, while $\{a\}^+ \in \mathbf{PPCF}^{-\varepsilon} \cap \mathbf{0L}$ proves the disjointness. □

Remark on Unary Alphabets

We close this section by showing how the mutual relations between investigated language families change if we consider only alphabets containing only one symbol. From Theorem 7.2, Theorem 7.4, and Theorem 7.5, we can conclude that for every unary alphabet

$$\mathbf{SPCF} = \mathbf{JSPCF} \subset \mathbf{PPCF} = \mathbf{JPPCF} = \mathbf{0L}.$$

Trivially,

$$\mathbf{SPCF}^{-\varepsilon} = \mathbf{JSPCF}^{-\varepsilon} \subset \mathbf{PPCF}^{-\varepsilon} = \mathbf{JPPCF}^{-\varepsilon} = \mathbf{0L}^{-\varepsilon}.$$

As the following theorem demonstrates that $\mathbf{PPCF}^{-\varepsilon}$ and **SPCF** are incomparable, we can summarize the results for the unary alphabet by Figure 7.2.

Theorem 7.25 *In the case of unary alphabets,* **SPCF** *and* $\mathbf{PPCF}^{-\varepsilon}$ *are incomparable.*

Proof Clearly, the language $\{a\}^+$ is contained in both **SPCF** and $\mathbf{PPCF}^{-\varepsilon}$. Since the language $\{\varepsilon, a, aa\}$ from **SPCF** is not contained in $\mathbf{PPCF}^{-\varepsilon}$, $\mathbf{SPCF} \not\subseteq \mathbf{PPCF}^{-\varepsilon}$. Conversely, $\mathbf{PPCF}^{-\varepsilon} \not\subseteq \mathbf{SPCF}$ since $\mathbf{PPCF}^{-\varepsilon}$ is not semilinear. □

Open Problems

Consider **SPCF**, **JSPCF**, **PPCF**, **JPPCF**, **0L**, $\mathbf{SPCF}^{-\varepsilon}$, $\mathbf{JSPCF}^{-\varepsilon}$, $\mathbf{PPCF}^{-\varepsilon}$, $\mathbf{JPPCF}^{-\varepsilon}$, and $\mathbf{0L}^{-\varepsilon}$ (see Section 7.2). The present chapter has investigated mutual relations between these language families, which are summarized in Table 7.1 and Figure 7.1. As a special case, it has also performed an analogical study in terms of unary alphabets (see Figure 7.2).

Although we have already pointed out several open problems earlier in this chapter (see Open Problems), we repeat the questions of a particular significance next.

- Is it true that $(\mathbf{PPCF} \cap \mathbf{JSPCF}) - (\mathbf{CF} \cup \mathbf{JPPCF}) \neq \emptyset$ (Open Problem)?

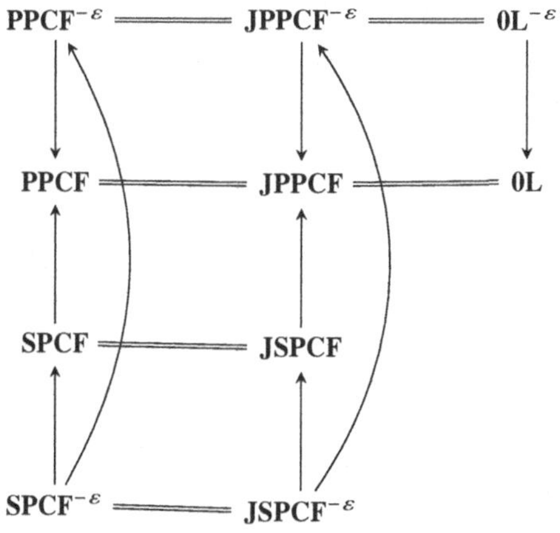

Fig. 7.2 Relationships between unary-language families defined by pure grammars.

- Is it true that $(\mathbf{PPCF} \cap \mathbf{JSPCF} \cap \mathbf{JPPCF}) - \mathbf{CF} \neq \emptyset$ (Open Problem)?
- Is it true that $(\mathbf{SPCF} \cap \mathbf{JPPCF}) - \mathbf{JSPCF} \neq \emptyset$ (Open Problem)?
- Is it true that $(\mathbf{PPCF} \cap \mathbf{CF} \cap \mathbf{JSPCF}) - (\mathbf{SPCF} \cup \mathbf{JPPCF}) \neq \emptyset$ (Open Problem)?
- Is it true that $(\mathbf{PPCF} \cap \mathbf{CF} \cap \mathbf{JSPCF} \cap \mathbf{JPPCF}) - \mathbf{SPCF} \neq \emptyset$ (Open Problem)?
- Is it true that $(\mathbf{CF} \cap \mathbf{JSPCF}) - (\mathbf{PPCF} \cup \mathbf{JPPCF}) \neq \emptyset$ (Open Problem)?
- Is it true that $\mathbf{JSPCF} - (\mathbf{CF} \cup \mathbf{PPCF} \cup \mathbf{JPPCF}) \neq \emptyset$ (Open Problem)?
- Let $X \in \{\mathbf{SP}, \mathbf{JSP}, \mathbf{PP}, \mathbf{JPP}\}$. Is the inclusion $X^{-\varepsilon} \subseteq X$, in fact, proper (Open Problem)?
- What is the relation between $\mathbf{JSPCF}^{-\varepsilon}$ and $\mathbf{JPPCF}^{-\varepsilon}$ (Open Problem)?
- What is the relation between $\mathbf{JSPCF}^{-\varepsilon}$ and **JPPCF** (Open Problem)?

Recall that the present study has only considered pure grammars based upon context-free production rules. Of course, from a broader perspective, we might reconsider all the study in terms of grammars that allow non-context-free production rules as well.

Part IV
Conclusion

This concluding part consists of three chapters. Chapter 8 outlines other important approaches to discontinuous computation and its formalizations. Chapter 9 sketches applications of jumping automata and grammars. In addition, it suggests its future possibilities. Chapter 10 summarizes the book as a whole. It places all its material into a historical and bibliographical context. Also, it recommends further crucially important reading to the serious reader who finds jumping automata and grammars interesting.

Chapter 8
Other Models of Discontinuous Computation

We have been careful not to say that the jumping formal models given in this book are the only formalizations of discontinuous computation. In fact, formal language theory has introduced numerous other alternatives for this purpose. Out of these, the present chapter highlights a few that appear to be of a great interest.

Section 8.1 discusses deep pushdown automata, which represent modified versions of ordinary pushdown automata. Specifically, these modified versions can rewrite non-input symbols deeper than on the very top of their pushdown lists. Section 8.2 formalizes discontinuous computation by grammars and automata working with unordered strings. Section 8.3 continues with the discussion of models that define unodered strings. It covers permutation grammars, which are based upon classical grammars that generate unordered strings.

8.1 Deep Pushdown Automata

Finite automata are strictly finitary and memoryless models, so their jumping versions can only jump over their input tapes (see Chapter 3). Pushdown automata, however, represent finite automata extended by potentially infinite stacks. As is obvious, this extention allows them to perform jumps over their stacks as explored in the present section.

Pushdown automata discussed in this section represent language-accepting models based upon slightly generalized stack structures, which can be modified deeper than on their tops. As opposed to the ordinary versions of pushdown automata, which can only expand the stack tops, these generalized versions can jump deeper into their stacks or, speaking in terms of automata theory, pushdown lists and make expansions therein, hence their name—deep pushdown automata.

To give a more precise insight into the concept of deep pushdown automata, consider the well-known conversion of any context-free grammar to an equivalent pushdown automaton M, frequently referred to as the general top-down parser for the converted grammar (see, for instance, [Meduna, 2000, page 444]). Recall that during every move, M either pops or expands its pushdown depending on the symbol occurring on the pushdown top. If an input symbol a occurs on the pushdown top, M compares the pushdown top symbol with the current input symbol, and if they coincide, M pops the topmost symbol from the pushdown and proceeds to the next input symbol on the input tape. If a nonterminal occurs on the pushdown top, the parser expands its pushdown by replacing the top nonterminal with a string. M accepts an input string x if it makes a sequence of moves during which it completely reads x, empties its pushdown, and enters a final state; the latter requirement of entering a final state is dropped in some books (see, for instance, [Meduna, 2000, Algorithm 5.3.1.1.1]). In essence, a deep pushdown automaton D represents a slight generalization of M. Indeed, D works exactly as M except that it can make expansions of depth m, meaning that D replaces the mth topmost pushdown symbol with a string, for some positive integer m.

This chapter proves that deep pushdown automata are stronger than ordinary pushdown automata but less powerful than linear-bounded automata. More precisely, we demonstrate that the deep pushdown automata that make expansions of depth m or less, where $m \geq 1$, accept a proper language subfamily of the language family accepted by deep pushdown automata that make expansions of depth $m + 1$ or less. They give rise to an infinite hierarchy of language families occurring between the family of context-free languages and that of context-sensitive languages.

Basic Model

The concept of deep pushdown automata is inspired by the well-known transformation of a context-free grammar to an equivalent pushdown automaton M, referred to as the general top-down parser for the grammar (see [Rozenberg and Salomaa, 1997a, page 176]). During every move, M either pops or expands its pushdown. More precisely, if an input symbol occurs on the pushdown top, M compares the pushdown top symbol with the current input symbol, and if they coincide, M pops the topmost symbol from the pushdown and proceeds to the next input symbol on the input tape. If a nonterminal occurs on the pushdown top, the parser expands its pushdown so it replaces the top nonterminal with a string. M accepts an input string if it makes a sequence of moves so it completely reads the string, empties its pushdown, and enters a final state.

Compared to M, a deep pushdown automaton $_{deep}M$ works in a slightly generalized way. Indeed, $_{deep}M$ functions exactly as M except that it may make expansions of depth m so $_{deep}M$ replaces the mth topmost pushdown symbol with a string, for some $m \geq 1$. We demonstrate that the deep pushdown automata that make expansions of depth m or less, where $m \geq 1$, are equivalent to m-limited state grammars (see Definition 8.2), so these automata accept a proper language subfamily of the language family accepted by deep pushdown automata that make expansions of depth $m + 1$ or less. The resulting infinite hierarchy of language families obtained in this way occurs between the families of context-free and context-sensitive languages. For every positive integer n, however, there exist some context-sensitive languages that cannot be accepted by any deep pushdown automata that make expansions of depth n or less.

Definitions and Examples

Next, we define the notion of a deep pushdown automaton, after which we illustrate it by an example. Recall that by Convention 1.2, $\mathbb{N}$ denotes the set of all positive integers without 0.

Definition 8.1 A *deep pushdown automaton* (DPDA) is a septuple

$$M = (Q, \Delta, \Gamma, R, s, S, F)$$

where

- Q is a finite set of *states*;
- Δ is an *input alphabet*;
- Γ is a *pushdown alphabet*, $\mathbb{N}$, Q, and Γ are pairwise disjoint, $\Delta \subseteq \Gamma$, and $\Gamma - \Delta$ contains a special *bottom symbol*, denoted by #;
- $R \subseteq (\mathbb{N} \times Q \times (\Gamma - (\Delta \cup \{\#\})) \times Q \times (\Gamma - \{\#\})^{+})$
  $\cup (\mathbb{N} \times Q \times \{\#\} \times Q \times (\Gamma - \{\#\})^{*}\{\#\})$ is a finite relation;
- $s \in Q$ is the *start state*;
- $S \in \Gamma$ is the *start pushdown symbol*;
- $F \subseteq Q$ is the set of *final states*.

Instead of $(m, q, A, p, v) \in R$, we write $mqA \rightarrow pv \in R$ and call $mqA \rightarrow pv$ a *rule*; accordingly, R is referred to as the *set of rules* of M. A *configuration* of M is a triple in $Q \times \Delta^{*} \times (\Gamma - \{\#\})^{*}\{\#\}$. Let χ denote the set of all configurations of M. Let $x, y \in \chi$ be two configurations. M *pops* its pushdown from x to y, symbolically written as

$$x \ {}_{p}\vdash y$$

if $x = (q, au, az)$, $y = (q, u, z)$, where $a \in \Delta$, $u \in \Delta^{*}$, $z \in \Gamma^{*}$. M *expands* its pushdown from x to y, symbolically written as

$$x \ {}_{e}\vdash y$$

if $x = (q, w, uAz)$, $y = (p, w, uvz)$, $mqA \rightarrow pv \in R$, where $q, p \in Q$, $w \in \Delta^{*}$, $A \in \Gamma$, $u, v, z \in \Gamma^{*}$, and $\text{occur}(u, \Gamma - \Delta) = m - 1$. To express that M makes $x \ {}_{e}\vdash y$ according to $mqA \rightarrow pv$, we write

$$x \ {}_{e}\vdash y \ [mqA \rightarrow pv]$$

We say that $mqA \rightarrow pv$ is a *rule of depth* m; accordingly, $x \ {}_{e}\vdash y \ [mqA \rightarrow pv]$ is an *expansion of depth* m. M makes a *move* from x to y, symbolically written as

$$x \vdash y$$

if M makes either $x\ {}_e\!\vdash\ y$ or $x\ {}_p\!\vdash\ y$. If $n \in \mathbb{N}$ is the minimal positive integer such that each rule of M is of depth n or less, we say that M *is of depth* n, symbolically written as ${}_nM$. In the standard manner, we extend ${}_p\!\vdash$, ${}_e\!\vdash$, and $\vdash$ to ${}_p\!\vdash^m$, ${}_e\!\vdash^m$, and $\vdash^m$, respectively, for $m \geq 0$; then, based on ${}_p\!\vdash^m$, ${}_e\!\vdash^m$, and $\vdash^m$, we define ${}_p\!\vdash^+$, ${}_p\!\vdash^*$, ${}_e\!\vdash^+$, ${}_e\!\vdash^*$, $\vdash^+$, and $\vdash^*$.

Let M be of depth n, for some $n \in \mathbb{N}$. We define the *language accepted by* ${}_nM$, $L({}_nM)$, as

$$L({}_nM) = \left\{w \in \Delta^* \mid (s, w, S\#) \vdash^* (f, \varepsilon, \#) \text{ in } {}_nM \text{ with } f \in F\right\}$$

In addition, we define the *language that* ${}_nM$ *accepts by empty pushdown*, $E({}_nM)$, as

$$E({}_nM) = \left\{w \in \Delta^* \mid (s, w, S\#) \vdash^* (q, \varepsilon, \#) \text{ in } {}_nM \text{ with } q \in Q\right\}$$

For every $k \geq 1$, $\mathbf{DPDA}_k$ denotes the family of languages defined by DPDAs of depth i, where $1 \leq i \leq k$. Analogously, $\mathbf{DEPDA}_k$ denotes the family of languages defined by DPDAs of depth i by empty pushdown, where $1 \leq i \leq k$.

The following example gives a DPDA accepting a language from

$$\left(\mathbf{DPDA}_2 \cap \mathbf{DEPDA}_2 \cap \mathbf{CS}\right) - \mathbf{CF}$$

Example 8.1 Consider the DPDA

$${}_2M = \left(\{s, q, p\}, \{a, b, c\}, \{A, S, \#\}, R, s, S, \{f\}\right)$$

with R containing the following five rules

$$\begin{array}{lll} 1sS \rightarrow qAA & 1qA \rightarrow fab & 1fA \rightarrow fc \\ 1qA \rightarrow paAb & 2pA \rightarrow qAc & \end{array}$$

On $aabbcc$, M makes

$$\begin{array}{rll}
(s, aabbcc, S\#) & {}_e\!\vdash\ (q, aabbcc, AA\#) & [1sS \rightarrow qAA] \\
& {}_e\!\vdash\ (p, aabbcc, aAbA\#) & [1qA \rightarrow paAb] \\
& {}_p\!\vdash\ (p, abbcc, AbA\#) & \\
& {}_e\!\vdash\ (q, abbcc, AbAc\#) & [2pA \rightarrow qAc] \\
& {}_e\!\vdash\ (q, abbcc, abbAc\#) & [1qA \rightarrow fab] \\
& {}_p\!\vdash\ (f, bcc, bAc\#) & \\
& {}_p\!\vdash\ (f, cc, Ac\#) & \\
& {}_e\!\vdash\ (f, cc, Ac\#) & [1fA \rightarrow fc] \\
& {}_p\!\vdash\ (f, cc, cc\#) & \\
& {}_p\!\vdash\ (f, c, c\#) & \\
& {}_p\!\vdash\ (f, \varepsilon, \#) &
\end{array}$$

In brief, $(s, aabbcc, S\#) \vdash^* (f, \varepsilon, \#)$. Observe that $L({}_2M) = E({}_2M) = \{a^n b^n c^n | n \geq 1\}$, which belongs to **CS** – **CF**.

State Grammars

To establish key results about DPDAs concerning their power and an infinite language family hierarchy underlain by these automata (Corollaries 8.1 through 8.3), we first recall the definition of state grammars as well as some results about these grammars, needed to prove these key results.

A *state grammar* G is a context-free grammar extended by an additional state mechanism that strongly resembles a finite-state control of finite automata. During every derivation step, G rewrites the leftmost occurrence of a nonterminal that can be rewritten under the current state; in addition, it moves from a state to another state, which influences the choice of the rule to be applied in the next step. If the application of a rule always takes place within the first n occurrences of nonterminals, G is referred to as *n-limited*.

First, the state grammars are defined, and then we illustrate them by examples and describe their generative power.

Definition 8.2 A *state grammar* (see Kasai [1970]) is a quintuple

$$G = (\Sigma, W, \Delta, R, S)$$

where

- Σ is a *total alphabet*;
- W is a finite set of *states*;
- $\Delta \subset \Sigma$ is an alphabet of *terminals*;
- $S \in \Sigma - \Delta$ is the *start symbol*;
- $R \subseteq (W \times (\Sigma - \Delta)) \times (W \times \Sigma^+)$ is a finite relation.

Instead of $(q, A, p, v) \in R$, we write $(q, A) \to (p, v) \in R$. If $(q, A) \to (p, v) \in R$, $x, y \in \Sigma^*$, and for each $B \in \text{symbols}(x)$, R contains no rule with (q, B) on its left-hand side, then G makes a *derivation step* from (q, xAy) to (p, xvy), symbolically written as

$$(q, xAy) \Rightarrow (p, xvy)\ [(q, A) \to (p, v)]$$

In addition, if n is a positive integer satisfying that $\text{occur}(xA, \Sigma - \Delta) \leq n$, we say that $(q, xAy) \Rightarrow (p, xvy)\ [(q, A) \to (p, v)]$ is *n-limited*, symbolically written as

$$(q, xAy) \to_n (p, xvy)\ [(q, A) \to (p, v)]$$

Whenever there is no danger of confusion, we simplify $(q, xAy) \Rightarrow (p, xvy)\ [(q, A) \to (p, v)]$ and $(q, xAy) \Rightarrow_n (p, xvy)\ [(q, A) \to (p, v)]$ to

$$(q, xAy) \Rightarrow (p, xvy)$$

and

$$(q, xAy) \Rightarrow_n (p, xvy),$$

respectively. In the standard manner, we extend $\Rightarrow$ to $\Rightarrow^m$, where $m \geq 0$; then, based on $\Rightarrow^m$, we define $\Rightarrow^+$ and $\Rightarrow^*$.

Let n be a positive integer, and let $\nu, \omega \in W \times \Sigma^+$. To express that every derivation step in $\nu \Rightarrow^m \omega$, $\nu \Rightarrow^+ \omega$, and $\nu \Rightarrow^* \omega$ is n-limited, we write $\nu \; {}_n{\Rightarrow}^m \; \omega$, $\nu \; {}_n{\Rightarrow}^+ \; \omega$, and $\nu \; {}_n{\Rightarrow}^* \; \omega$ instead of $\nu \Rightarrow^m \omega$, $\nu \Rightarrow^+ \omega$, and $\nu \Rightarrow^* \omega$, respectively.

By strings$(\nu \; {}_n{\Rightarrow}^* \; \omega)$, we denote the set of all strings occurring in the derivation $\nu \; {}_n{\Rightarrow}^* \; \omega$. The *language* of G, denoted by $L(G)$, is defined as

$$L(G) = \{w \in \Delta^* \mid (q, S) \Rightarrow^* (p, w), q, p \in W\}$$

Furthermore, for every $n \geq 1$, define

$$L(G, n) = \{w \in \Delta^* \mid (q, S) \; {}_n{\Rightarrow}^* \; (p, w), q, p \in W\}$$

A derivation of the form $(q, S) \; {}_n{\Rightarrow}^* \; (p, w)$, where $q, p \in W$ and $w \in \Delta^*$, represents a *successful n-limited generation* of w in G.

Next, we illustrate the previous definition by an example.

Example 8.2 Consider the state grammar

$$G = (\{S, X, Y, a, b\}, \{p_0, p_1, p_2, p_3, p_4\}, \{a, b\}, R, S)$$

with the following nine rules in R

$$\begin{array}{ll}
(p_0, S) \rightarrow (p_0, XY) & (p_0, X) \rightarrow (p_3, a) \\
(p_0, X) \rightarrow (p_1, aX) & (p_3, Y) \rightarrow (p_0, a) \\
(p_1, Y) \rightarrow (p_0, aY) & (p_0, X) \rightarrow (p_4, b) \\
(p_0, X) \rightarrow (p_2, bX) & (p_4, Y) \rightarrow (p_0, b) \\
(p_2, Y) \rightarrow (p_0, bY) &
\end{array}$$

Observe that G generates the non-context-free language

$$L(G) = \{ww \mid w \in \{a, b\}^+\}$$

Indeed, first, S is rewritten to XY. Then, by using its states, G ensures that whenever X is rewritten to aX, the current state is changed to force the rewrite of Y to aY. Similarly, whenever X is rewritten to bX, the current state is changed to force the rewrite of Y to bY. Every successful derivation is finished by rewriting X to a or b and then Y to a or b, respectively.

For example, $abab$ is produced by the following derivation

$$
\begin{aligned}
(p_0, S) &\Rightarrow (p_0, XY) & [(p_0, S) \rightarrow (p_0, XY)] \\
&\Rightarrow (p_1, aXY) & [(p_0, X) \rightarrow (p_1, aX)] \\
&\Rightarrow (p_0, aXaY) & [(p_1, Y) \rightarrow (p_0, aY)] \\
&\Rightarrow (p_4, abaY) & [(p_0, X) \rightarrow (p_4, b)] \\
&\Rightarrow (p_0, abab) & [(p_4, Y) \rightarrow (p_0, b)]
\end{aligned}
$$

By **ST**, we denote the family of languages generated by state grammars. For every $n \geq 1$, $\mathbf{ST}_n$ denotes the family of languages generated by n-limited state grammars. Set

$$\mathbf{ST}_\infty = \bigcup_{n \geq 1} \mathbf{ST}_n$$

In the conclusion of this section, we give the key result concerning state grammars, originally established in Kasai [1970].

Theorem 8.1 $\mathbf{CF} = \mathbf{ST}_1 \subset \mathbf{ST}_2 \subset \cdots \subset \mathbf{ST}_\infty \subset \mathbf{ST} = \mathbf{CS}$

Accepting Power

In the present section, we establish the main results of this chapter. That is, we demonstrate that DPDAs that make expansions of depth m or less, where $m \geq 1$, are equivalent to m-limited state grammars, so these automata accept a proper subfamily of the language family accepted by DPDAs that make expansions of depth $m + 1$ or less. Then, we point out that the resulting infinite hierarchy of language families obtained in this way occurs between the families of context-free and context-sensitive languages. However, we also show that there always exist some context-sensitive languages that cannot be accepted by any DPDAs that make expansions of depth n or less, for every positive integer n.

To rephrase these results briefly and formally, in Meduna [2006], it is demonstrated that

$$\mathbf{DPDA}_1 = \mathbf{DEPDA}_1 = \mathbf{CF}$$

and for every $n \geq 1$,

$$\mathbf{DEPDA}_n = \mathbf{DPDA}_n \subset \mathbf{DEPDA}_{n+1} = \mathbf{DPDA}_{n+1} \subset \mathbf{CS}$$

After giving basic ideas and constructive parts of the proofs of all these results, we recall several open problem areas, including some suggestions concerning new deterministic and generalized versions of DPDAs.

Lemma 8.1 (see Lemma 1 in Meduna [2006]) *For every state grammar G and for every $n \geq 1$, there exists a DPDA of depth n, ${}_nM$, such that $L(G, n) = L({}_nM)$.*

Proof Let $G = (\Sigma, W, \Delta, R, S)$ be a state grammar and let $n \geq 1$. Set $N = \Sigma - \Delta$. Define the homomorphism f over $(\{\#\} \cup \Sigma)^*$ as $f(A) = A$, for every $A \in \{\#\} \cup N$, and $f(a) = \varepsilon$, for every $a \in \Delta$. Introduce the DPDA of depth n

$$_nM = \left(Q, \Delta, \{\#\} \cup \Sigma, R, s, S, \{\$\}\right)$$

where

$$Q = \left\{S, \$\right\} \cup \left\{\langle p, u\rangle \mid p \in W, u \in N^*\{\#\}^n, |u| \leq n\right\}$$

and R is constructed by performing the following four steps:

1. for each $(p, S) \rightarrow (q, x) \in R$, $p, q \in W$, $x \in \Sigma^+$, add

   $$1sS \rightarrow \langle p, S\rangle S \text{ to } R;$$

2. if $(p, A) \rightarrow (q, x) \in R$, $\langle p, uAv\rangle \in Q$, $p, q \in W$, $A \in N$, $x \in \Sigma^+$, $u \in N^*$, $v \in N^*\{\#\}^*$, $|uAv| = n$, $p \notin {}_G states(u)$, add

   $$|uA|\langle p, uAv\rangle A \rightarrow \langle q, \text{prefix}(uf(x)v, n,)\rangle x \text{ to } R;$$

3. if $A \in N$, $p \in W$, $u \in N^*$, $v \in \{\#\}^*$, $|uv| \leq n - 1$, $p \notin {}_G states(u)$, add

   $$|uA|\langle p, uv\rangle A \rightarrow \langle p, uAv\rangle A \text{ and}$$
   $$|uA|\langle p, uv\rangle\# \rightarrow \langle p, uv\#\rangle\# \text{ to } R;$$

4. for each $q \in W$, add

   $$1\langle q, \#^n\rangle\# \rightarrow \$\# \text{ to } R.$$

$_nM$ simulates n-limited derivations of G so it always records the first n nonterminals occurring in the current sentential form in its state (if there appear fewer than n nonterminals in the sentential form, it completes them to n in the state by #s from behind). $_nM$ simulates a derivation step in the pushdown and, simultaneously, records the newly generated nonterminals in the state. When G successfully completes the generation of a terminal string, $_nM$ completes reading the string, empties its pushdown, and enters the final state $.

We refer to Meduna [2006], to see that $L(G, n) = L({}_nM)$ rigorously.

Consider the previous claim for $b = y = \varepsilon$ to see that

$$(\langle p, S\#^{n-1}\rangle, c, S\#) \vdash^* (\langle q, \text{prefix}(f(\#), n,)\rangle, \varepsilon, \#^n) \text{ in } {}_nM$$

implies that $(p, S)\ {}_n{\Rightarrow}^*\ (q, c)$ in G. Let $c \in L({}_nM)$. Then,

$$(s, c, S\#) \vdash^* (\$, \varepsilon, \#) \text{ in } {}_nM$$

Examine the construction of $_nM$ to see that $(s, c, S) \vdash^* (\$, \varepsilon, \#)$ starts by using a rule introduced in (1), so $(s, c, S) \vdash^* (\langle p, S\#^{n-1}\rangle, c, S\#)$. Furthermore, notice that this sequence of moves ends $(s, c, S) \vdash^* (\$, \varepsilon, \varepsilon)$ by using a rule introduced in step (4). Thus, we can express

$$(s, c, \#) \vdash^* (\$, \varepsilon, \#)$$

as

$$\begin{aligned}(s, c, \#) &\vdash^* (\langle p, S\#^{n-1}\rangle, c, S\#)\\ &\vdash^* (\langle q, \text{prefix}(f(\#^n), n,)\rangle, \varepsilon, \#)\\ &\vdash (\$, \varepsilon, \#) \text{ in } {}_nM\end{aligned}$$

Therefore, $c \in L({}_nM)$ implies that $c \in L(G, n)$, so $L({}_nM) \subseteq L(G, n)$.

As $L({}_nM) \subseteq L(G, n)$ and $L(G, n) \subseteq L({}_nM)$, $L(G, n) = L({}_nM)$. Thus, Lemma 8.1 holds. □

Lemma 8.2 ([Meduna, 2006, Lemma 2]) *For every $n \geq 1$ and every DPDA ${}_nM$, there exists a state grammar G such that $L(G, n) = L({}_nM)$.*

Proof Let $n \geq 1$ and ${}_nM = (Q, \Delta, \Sigma, R, s, S, F)$ be a DPDA. Let Z and \$ be two new symbols that occur in no component of ${}_nM$. Set $N = \Sigma - \Delta$. Introduce sets

$$C = \{\langle q, i, \triangleright\rangle \mid q \in Q, 1 \leq i \leq n - 1\}$$

and

$$D = \{\langle q, i, \triangleleft\rangle \mid q \in Q, 0 \leq i \leq n - 1\}$$

Moreover, introduce an alphabet W such that $\text{card}(\Sigma) = \text{card}(W)$, and for all i, $1 \leq i \leq n$, an alphabet U_i such that $\text{card}(U_i) = \text{card}(N)$. Without any loss of generality, assume that Σ, Q, and all these newly introduced sets and alphabets are pairwise disjoint. Set $U = \bigcup_{i=1}^{n} U_i$. For each i, $1 \leq i \leq n - 1$, set $C_i = \{\langle q, i, \triangleright\rangle \mid q \in Q\}$ and for each i, $0 \leq i \leq n - 1$, set $D_i = \{\langle q, i, \triangleleft\rangle \mid q \in Q\}$. Introduce a bijection h from Σ to W. For each i, $1 \leq i \leq n$, introduce a bijection ${}_ig$ from N to U_i. Define the state grammar

$$G = \big(\Sigma \cup W \cup U \cup \{Z\}, Q \cup C \cup D \cup \{\$\}, \Delta, R, Z\big)$$

where R is constructed by performing the following steps:

1. add $(s, Z) \to (\langle s, 1, \triangleright\rangle, h(S))$ to R;
2. for each $q \in Q$, $A \in N$, $1 \leq i \leq n - 1$, $x \in \Sigma^+$, add
   a. $(\langle q, i, \triangleright\rangle, A) \to (\langle q, i + 1, \triangleright\rangle, {}_ig(A))$ and
   b. $(\langle q, i, \triangleleft\rangle, {}_ig(A)) \to (\langle p, i - 1, \triangleleft\rangle, A)$ to R;
3. if $ipA \to qxY \in R$, for some $p, q \in Q$, $A \in N$, $x \in \Sigma^*$, $Y \in \Sigma$, $i = 1, \ldots, n$, add

   $(\langle p, i, \triangleright\rangle, A) \to (\langle q, i - 1, \triangleleft\rangle, xY)$ and
   $(\langle p, i, \triangleright\rangle, h(A)) \to (\langle q, i - 1, \triangleleft\rangle, xh(Y))$ to R;
4. for each $q \in Q$, $A \in N$, add

   $(\langle q, 0, \triangleleft\rangle, A) \to (\langle q, 1, \triangleright\rangle, A)$ and
   $(\langle q, 0, \triangleleft\rangle, h(Y)) \to (\langle q, 1, \triangleright\rangle, h(Y))$ to R;
5. for each $q \in F$, $a \in \Delta$, add

   $(\langle q, 0, \triangleleft\rangle, h(a)) \to (\$, a)$ to R.

G simulates the application of $ipA \to qy \in R$ so it makes a left-to-right scan of the sentential form, counting the occurrences of nonterminals until it reaches the ith occurrence of a nonterminal. If this occurrence equals A, it replaces this A with y and returns to the beginning of the sentential form in order to analogously simulate a move from q. Throughout the simulation of moves of ${}_nM$ by G, the rightmost symbol of every sentential form is from W. G completes the simulation of an acceptance of a string x by ${}_nM$ so it uses a rule introduced in step (5) of the construction of R to change the rightmost symbol of x, $h(a)$, to a and, thereby, to generate x.

We next establish $L(G, n) = L({}_nM)$. To keep the rest of the proof as readable as possible, we omit some details in what follows. The reader can easily fill them in.

As $L({}_nM) \subseteq L(G, n)$ and $L(G, n) \subseteq L({}_nM)$, we have $L(G, n) = L({}_nM)$, so this lemma holds true. □

Theorem 8.2 *For every $n \geq 1$ and for every language L, $L = L(G, n)$ for a state grammar G if and only if $L = L({}_nM)$ for a DPDA ${}_nM$.*

Proof This theorem follows from Lemmas 8.1 and 8.2. □

By analogy with the demonstration of Theorem 8.2, we can establish the next theorem.

Theorem 8.3 *For every $n \geq 1$ and for every language L, $L = L(G, n)$ for a state grammar G if and only if $L = E({}_nM)$ for a DPDA ${}_nM$.*

The main result of this chapter follows next.

Corollary 8.1 *For every $n \geq 1$,*

$$\mathbf{DEPDA}_n = \mathbf{DPDA}_n \subset \mathbf{DPDA}_{n+1} = \mathbf{DEPDA}_{n+1}$$

Proof This corollary follows from Theorems 8.2 and 8.3 above and from Theorem 8.1, which says that the m-limited state grammars generate a proper subfamily of the family generated by $(m + 1)$-limited state grammars, for every $m \geq 1$. □

Finally, we state two results concerning **CF** and **CS**.

Corollary 8.2 $\mathbf{DPDA}_1 = \mathbf{DEPDA}_1 = \mathbf{CF}$

Proof This corollary follows from Lemmas 8.1 and 8.2 for $n = 1$, and from Theorem 8.1, which says that one-limited state grammars characterize **CF**. □

Corollary 8.3 *For every $n \geq 1$,* $\mathbf{DPDA}_n = \mathbf{DEPDA}_n \subset \mathbf{CS}$.

Proof This corollary follows from Lemmas 8.1 and 8.2, Theorems 8.2 and 8.3, and from Theorem 8.1, which says that $\mathbf{ST}_m$, for every $m \geq 1$, is properly included in **CS**. □

Open Problems

Finally, we suggest two open problem areas concerning DPDAs.

Determinism

This chapter has discussed a general version of DPDAs, which work nondeterministically. Undoubtedly, the future investigation of these automata should pay a special attention to their deterministic versions, which fulfill a crucial role in practice. In fact, we can introduce a variety of deterministic versions, including the following two types. First, we consider the fundamental strict form of determinism.

Definition 8.3 Let $M = (Q, \Delta, \Gamma, R, s, S, F)$ be a DPDA. We say that M is *deterministic* if for every $mqA \rightarrow pv \in R$,

$$\text{card}(\{mqA \rightarrow ow \mid mqA \rightarrow ow \in R, o \in Q, w \in \Gamma^+\} - \{mqA \rightarrow pv\}) = 0$$

As a weaker form of determinism, we obtain the following definition.

Definition 8.4 Let $M = (Q, \Delta, \Gamma, R, s, S, F)$ be a deep pushdown automaton. We say that M is *deterministic with respect to the depth of its expansions* if for every $q \in Q$

$$\text{card}(\{m \mid mqA \rightarrow pv \in R, A \in \Gamma, p \in Q, v \in \Gamma^+\}) \leq 1$$

because at this point from the same state, all expansions that M can make are of the same depth.

To illustrate, consider, for instance, the DPDA $_2M$ from Example 8.1. This automaton is deterministic with respect to the depth of its expansions; however, it does not satisfy the strict determinism. Notice that $_nM$ constructed in the proof of Lemma 8.1 is deterministic with respect to the depth of its expansions, so we obtain this corollary.

Corollary 8.4 *For every state grammar G and for every $n \geq 1$, there exists a DPDA $_nM$ such that $L(G, n) = L(_nM)$ and $_nM$ is deterministic with respect to the depth of its expansions.*

Open Problem Can an analogical statement to Corollary 8.4 be established in terms of the strict determinism? □

Generalization

Let us note that throughout this chapter, we have considered only true pushdown expansions in the sense that the pushdown symbol is replaced with a nonempty string rather than with the empty string; at this point, no pushdown expansion can result in shortening the pushdown length. Nevertheless, the discussion of moves that allow DPDAs to replace a pushdown symbol with ε and, thereby, shorten its pushdown represent a natural generalization of DPDAs discussed in this chapter.

Open Problem What is the language family defined by DPDAs generalized in this way? □

Restricted Versions

In essence, DPDAs represent language-accepting models based upon a generalized concept of classical stacks. Apart from the standard topmost modification, this generalized concept allows stacks to be modified under their top. As a result, these automata can make expansions deeper in their pushdown lists as opposed to ordinary pushdown automata, which can expand only the very pushdown top.

The present section narrows its attention to n-expandable deep pushdown automata, where n is a positive integer. In essence, during any computation, their pushdown lists contain #, which always appears as the pushdown bottom, and no more than $n - 1$ occurrences of other non-input symbols. This section demonstrates how to reduce the number of their non-input pushdown symbols different from # to one symbol, denoted by \$, without affecting the power of these automata. Based on this main result, we establish an infinite hierarchy of language families resulting from these reduced versions of n-expandable deep pushdown automata. More precisely, consider n-expandable deep pushdown automata with pushdown alphabets containing #, \$, and input symbols. This section shows that $(n + 1)$-expandable versions of these automata are stronger than their n-expandable versions, for every positive integer n. In addition, it points out that these automata with # as their only non-input symbol characterize the family of regular languages. In its conclusion, this section formulates several open problem areas related to the subject for the future study.

Preliminaries and Definitions

As usual, let $\mathbb{N}$ denote the set of all positive integers. For an alphabet Γ, Γ^* represents the free monoid generated by Γ under the operation of concatenation. The identity of Γ^* is denoted by ϵ. For $w \in \Gamma^*$, $|w|$ denotes the length of w.

Definition 8.5 Let M be a deep pushdown automaton (see Definition 8.1) and $n \in \mathbb{N}$. If during any $\alpha \vdash^* \beta$ in M, $\alpha, \beta \in \Xi$, M has no more than n occurrences of symbols form $\Gamma - \Delta$ in its pushdown, then M is an *n-expandable deep pushdown automaton.*

Let $n, r \in \mathbb{N}$. ${}_n$**DPDA** denotes the language family accepted by n-expandable deep pushdown automata. ${}_n$**DPDA**$_r$ denotes the language family accepted by n-expandable deep pushdown automata with # and no more than $(r - 1)$ non-input pushdown symbols.

A *right-linear grammar* is a quadruple $G = (N, \Delta, R, S)$, where N is an alphabet of nonterminals, Δ is an alphabet of terminals such that $N \cap \Delta = \emptyset$, R is a finite subset of $N \times \Delta^*(N \cup \{\epsilon\})$, and $S \in N$. R is called the *set of rules* in G; instead of $(A, x) \in R$, we write $A \to x$. Define the language of G, $L(G)$, as usual (see Meduna [2000]).

REG denotes the regular language family. Recall that **REG** is characterized by right-linear grammars (see Theorem 7.2.2. in Meduna [2000]).

Results

Next, we establish Lemma 8.3, which implies the main result of this section.

Lemma 8.3 *Let $n \in \mathbb{N}$. For every n-expandable deep pushdown automaton M, there exists an n-expendable deep pushdown automaton M_R such that $L(M) = L(M_R)$ and M_R contains only two non-input pushdown symbols—\$ and #.*

Proof *Construction.* Let $n \in \mathbb{N}$. Let

$$M = (Q, \Delta, \Gamma, R, s, S, F)$$

be an n-expandable deep pushdown automaton. Recall that rules in R are of the form $mqA \rightarrow pv$, where $m \in \mathbb{N}$, $q, p \in Q$, either $A \in N$ and $v \in (\Gamma - \{\#\})^+$ or $A = \#$ and $v \in (\Gamma - \{\#\})^*\{\#\}$, where # denotes the pushdown bottom.

Let \$ be a new symbol, $\$ \notin Q \cup \Gamma$, and let homomorphisms f and g over Γ^* be defined as $f(A) = A$ and $g(A) = \$$, for every $A \in N$, and $f(a) = \epsilon$ and $g(a) = a$, for every $a \in (\Delta \cup \{\#\})$. Next, we construct an n-expandable deep pushdown automaton

$$M_R = (Q_R, \Delta, \Delta \cup \{\$, \#\}, R_R, s_R, \$, F_R)$$

by performing (i) through (iv), given next:

1. Add $m\langle q; uAz\rangle\$ \rightarrow \langle p; uf(v)z\rangle g(v)$ to R_R and add $\langle q; uAz\rangle$, $\langle p; uf(v)z\rangle$ to Q_R if $mqA \rightarrow pv \in R$, $u, z \in N^*$, $|u| = m - 1$, $|z| \leq n - m - 1$, $|uf(v)z| < n$, $m \in \mathbb{N}$, $q, p \in Q$, $A \in N$, and $v \in (\Gamma - \{\#\})^+$;
2. Add $m\langle q; u\rangle\# \rightarrow \langle p; uf(v)\rangle g(v)\#$ to R_R and add $\langle q; u\rangle$, $\langle p; uf(v)\rangle$ to Q_R if $mq\# \rightarrow pv\# \in R$, $u \in N^*$, $|u| = m - 1$, $|uf(v)| < n$, $m \in \mathbb{N}$, $q, p \in Q$, and $v \in (\Gamma - \{\#\})^*$;
3. Set $s_R = \langle s; S\rangle$;
4. Add all $\langle p; u\rangle$ to F_R, where $p \in F$, $u \in N^*$, $u < n$. □

Later in this proof, we demonstrate that $L(M) = L(M_R)$.
Basic Idea. States in Q_R include not only the states corresponding to the states in Q but also strings of non-input symbols. Whenever M pushes a non-input symbol onto the pushdown, M_R records this information within its current state and pushes \$ onto the pushdown instead.

By [Leupold and Meduna, 2010, Lemma 3.1], any n-expandable deep pushdown automaton M can accept every $w \in L(M)$ so all expansions precede all pops during the accepting process. Without any loss of generality, we assume that M and M_R work in this way in what follows, too.

To establish $L(M) = L(M_R)$, see the proof of in [Meduna, 2006, Claims 1 and 2].

The next example illustrates the construction described in the previous proof.
Example. Take this three-expandable DPDA

$$M = (\{s, q, p\}, \{a, b, c\}, \{a, b, c, A, S, \#\}, R, s, S, \{f\}),$$

with the set of rules defined as

$$\begin{aligned} R = \{&1sS \to qAA, \\ &1qA \to fab, \\ &1fA \to fc, \\ &1qA \to paAb, \\ &2pA \to qAc\} \end{aligned}$$

By the construction given in the proof of Lemma 8.3, we construct $M_R = (Q_R, \{a, b, c\}, \{a, b, c, \$, \#\}, R_R, \langle s; S\rangle, \$, \{\langle f; A\rangle, \langle f; \epsilon\rangle\})$, where $Q_R = \{\langle s; S\rangle, \langle q; AA\rangle, \langle f; A\rangle, \langle f; \epsilon\rangle, \langle p; AA\rangle\}$ and

$$\begin{aligned} R_R = \{&1\langle s; S\rangle\$ \to \langle q; AA\rangle\$\$, \\ &1\langle q; AA\rangle\$ \to \langle f; A\rangle ab, \\ &1\langle f; A\rangle\$ \to \langle f; \epsilon\rangle c, \\ &1\langle q; AA\rangle\$ \to \langle p; AA\rangle a\$b, \\ &2\langle p; AA\rangle\$ \to \langle q; AA\rangle\$c\} \end{aligned}$$

For instance, M_R makes

$$\begin{aligned} (\langle s; S\rangle, aabbcc, \$\#) \ {}_e\vdash\ & (\langle q; AA\rangle, aabbcc, \$\$\#) && [1\langle s; S\rangle\$ \to \langle q; AA\rangle\$\$] \\ {}_e\vdash\ & (\langle p; AA\rangle, aabbcc, a\$b\$\#) && [1\langle q; AA\rangle\$ \to \langle p; AA\rangle a\$b] \\ {}_p\vdash\ & (\langle p; AA\rangle, abbcc, \$b\$\#) && \\ {}_e\vdash\ & (\langle q; AA\rangle, abbcc, \$b\$c\#) && [2\langle p; AA\rangle\$ \to \langle q; AA\rangle\$c] \\ {}_e\vdash\ & (\langle f; A\rangle, abbcc, abb\$c\#) && [1\langle q; AA\rangle\$ \to \langle f; A\rangle ab] \\ {}_p\vdash\ & (\langle f; A\rangle, cc, \$c\#) && \\ {}_e\vdash\ & (\langle f; \epsilon\rangle, cc, cc\#) && [1\langle f; A\rangle\$ \to \langle f; \epsilon\rangle c] \\ {}_p\vdash\ & (\langle f; \epsilon\rangle, \epsilon, \#) && \end{aligned}$$

Theorem 8.4 *For all* $n \geq 1$, ${}_n\mathbf{DPDA} = {}_n\mathbf{DPDA}_2$.

Proof This theorem follows from Lemma 8.3. □

Corollary 8.5 *For all* $n \geq 1$, ${}_n\mathbf{DPDA}_2 \subset {}_{n+1}\mathbf{DPDA}_2$.

Proof This corollary follows from Theorem 8.4 in this section and from [Leupold and Meduna, 2010, Corollary 3.1]. □

Can we reformulate Theorem 8.4 and Corollary 8.5 in terms of ${}_n\mathbf{DPDA}_1$? The answer is no as we show next.

Lemma 8.4 *Let* $M = (Q, \Delta, \Gamma, R, s, S, F)$ *be a DPDA with* $\Gamma - \Delta = \{\#\}$. *Then, there is a right-linear grammar G such that* $L(G) = L(M)$.

Proof Let $M = (Q, \Delta, \Gamma, R, s, S, F)$ with $\Gamma - \Delta = \{\#\}$. Thus, every rule in R is of the form $1q\# \rightarrow px\#$, where $q, p \in Q$, $x \in \Delta^*$. Next, we construct a right-linear grammar $G = (Q, \Delta, R, s)$ so $L(M) = L(G)$. We construct R as follows:

1. For every $1q\# \rightarrow px\# \in R$, where $p, q \in Q$, $x \in \Delta^*$, add $q \rightarrow xp$ to R;
2. For every $f \in F$, add $f \rightarrow \epsilon$ to R.

A rigorous proof that $L(M) = L(G)$ is left to the reader. □

Theorem 8.5 $\mathbf{REG} = {}_1\mathbf{DPDA}_1 = {}_n\mathbf{DPDA}_1$, *for any* $n \geq 1$.

Proof Let $n \geq 1$. $\mathbf{REG} \subseteq {}_1\mathbf{DPDA}_1 = {}_n\mathbf{DPDA}_1$ is clear. Recall that right-linear grammars characterize **REG**, so ${}_n\mathbf{DPDA}_1 \subseteq \mathbf{REG}$ follows from Lemma 8.4. Thus, $\mathbf{REG} = {}_n\mathbf{DPDA}_1$. □

Corollary 8.6 $\mathbf{REG} = {}_1\mathbf{DPDA}_1 = {}_n\mathbf{DPDA}_1 \subset {}_n\mathbf{DPDA}_2$, *for all* $n \geq 2$.

Proof Let $n \geq 1$. As is obvious, ${}_1\mathbf{DPDA}_1 = {}_n\mathbf{DPDA}_1 \subseteq {}_n\mathbf{DPDA}_2$. Observe that

$$\{a^n b^n \mid n \geq 1\} \in {}_n\mathbf{DPDA}_2 - {}_n\mathbf{DPDA}_1$$

Therefore, Corollary 8.6 holds. □

Open Problems

In the present section, we have reduced finitely expandable deep pushdown automata with respect to the number of non-input pushdown symbols. Before closing this section, we suggest some open problem areas related to this subject for the future investigation.

1. Can we reduce these automata with respect to the number of states?
2. Can we simultaneously reduce them with respect to the number of both states and non-input pushdown symbols?
3. Can we achieve the reductions described above in terms of general deep pushdown automata, which are not finitely expandable? In fact, Lemma 8.4 holds for these automata, so it can be considered as a preliminary result related to this investigation area.

8.2 Computation over Unordered Strings

The order of symbols in a string is a fundamental part of the string's identity—*ab* and *ba* are not the same string despite containing exactly the same symbols exactly the same number of times. This is of course desirable, as a lot of information can be encoded using this aspect of strings, and it is an important consideration for most computational models. However, a somewhat relaxed approach to the order of symbols, at least on a non-local level, is at the very core of what jumping models are, and some of them can even be said to ignore it completely.

As an example, consider a jumping finite automaton M (see Definition 3.2) such that its input alphabet contains both symbols a, b. No matter what its rules are, M is unable to distinguish between ab and ba—either it accepts both of them, or neither of them. In fact, given any string w over the input alphabet of M, M accepts w if and only if M accepts all permutations of w (see Theorem 3.6). This suggests an interesting mathematical possibility—instead of adding an extra jumping mechanic to traditional computational models designed to work with strings and thus also with their order, we can look for some other mathematical concept to serve as *unordered strings* as a basis for an entirely new type of computational model.

Bags

To start our search for a formalization of *unordered strings*, let us consider what remains of strings when we abstract away their order. Under this formalization, any two strings, x and y, are considered as equivalent if x represents a symbol permutation of y. For example, the strings abb, bab and bba are all permutations of one another and could all denote the same *unordered string*, consisting of one a and two b's in no particular order. As this example suggests, we can fully identify strings up to symbol reordering by specifying exactly how many instances of which symbols they contain. This means that *unordered strings* can be thought of as *finite multisets* of symbols.

Informally, *multisets* (also called *bags*) are a modification of sets which can contain multiple instances of the same element. One way to put this is that each element of a multiset is paired with a positive integer[1], called its *multiplicity*. A multiset is finite if it only contains a finite number of distinct elements, each with a finite multiplicity. Assuming an universal alphabet as introduced in Section 1.2, denoted by Δ, we can formalize multisets as total functions from Δ to ${}_0\mathbb{N}$. Alternatively, because most symbols in Δ will usually be assigned 0, we can think of them as partial functions which only assign values to symbols with nonzero multiplicities. In either case, we are successfully avoiding representing the same bag over different alphabets as a different object. Note, however, that either of these two representations is easily convertible to the other. Let us now define this notion of *unordered strings* formally under the name *bag*.

Let Δ denote the *universal alphabet*, that is, a possibly infinite alphabet containing all possible symbols, and let $\Sigma \subseteq \Delta$ be a finite subalphabet. A *bag over* Σ is a function $\sigma : \Delta \to {}_0\mathbb{N}$ such that the set $\{a \in \Delta \mid \sigma(a) > 0\}$, called the *underlying set* of σ and denoted by $\text{underlying}(\sigma)$, is a subset of Σ. For convenience, we may also think of them as functions from $\text{underlying}(\sigma)$ to $\mathbb{N}$—the infinitely many pairs $(a, 0)$ for all

[1] Some definitions also allow infinite multiplicities.

$a \in \Delta$ not appearing in σ are the only difference between the two definitions and we sometimes want to avoid them, such as when explicitly enumerating the members of the bag. This can be thought of as the bag assigning the number of occurences to each symbol of Σ it contains, and assigning nothing to the remaining symbols. For example, $\tau = \{(a, 2), (b, 1)\}$ is a bag over the alphabet $\{a, b, c\}$ which contains a twice, b once, and other than that contains no other symbols.

We can represent τ as a string by enumerating its symbols in any order—so aab, aba and baa all describe the same bag, τ. For clarity and standardization, we choose to use alphabetically ordered strings—given some linear order on the alphabet, no symbol in the string may be followed by a symbol that precedes it in said order. Furthermore, repeated occurences of the same symbol may be replaced using the power notation. Thus, τ would be represented as a^2b. Evidently, the concept of a bag corresponds to the concept of an *unordered string* we set out to find.

We denote the empty bag by ε, just like the empty string. This is the unique bag with the property that $\varepsilon(a) = 0$ for all symbols a. Given an alphabet Σ, we denote by ${}^*\Sigma$ and ${}^+\Sigma$ the set of all bags over Σ and the set of all nonempty bags over Σ, respectively. Let $\sigma \in {}^*\Sigma$ be a bag. The *cardinality* of σ (also called its *weight* or *norm*) is denoted by $|\sigma|$ and is defined as the sum of $\sigma(a)$ over all symbols a in its alphabet:

$$|\sigma| = \sum_{a \in \Sigma} \sigma(a).$$

For any two bags $\sigma, \tau \in {}^*\Sigma$, we say that σ *is included in* τ, denoted by $\sigma \subseteq \tau$, if and only if $\sigma(a) \leq \tau(a)$ holds for all $a \in \Sigma$. We can also define the *sum*, *difference*, *union* and *intersection* of σ and τ, denoted by $\sigma + \tau$, $\sigma - \tau$, $\sigma \cup \tau$ and $\sigma \cap \tau$, respectively, as operations on bags such that the following equalities hold for all $a \in \Sigma$ (note, however, that $\sigma - \tau$ is defined only if $\sigma \subseteq \tau$):

$$\begin{aligned}
(\sigma + \tau)(a) &= \sigma(a) + \tau(a) \\
(\sigma - \tau)(a) &= \sigma(a) - \tau(a) \\
(\sigma \cup \tau)(a) &= \max\{\sigma(a), \tau(a)\} \\
(\sigma \cap \tau)(a) &= \min\{\sigma(a), \tau(a)\}
\end{aligned}$$

The sum is also called the *concatenation* in some contexts, denoted by $\sigma\tau$ rather than $\sigma + \tau$. We will, however, avoid this notation, as it can lead to confusion between bags and strings in some contexts. This operation also serves as a basis for the *ith power* of a bag for any $i \in {}_0\mathbb{N}$, defined for $\sigma \in {}^*\Sigma$ recursively as $\sigma^0 = \varepsilon$ for $i = 0$ and $\sigma^i = \sigma + \sigma^{i-1}$ otherwise.

To give some examples, $a^2b + abc^2 = a^3b^2c^2$, $a^2b \cup abc^2 = a^2b^2c$, $a^2b \cap abc^2 = ab$, and $a^2b - abc^2$ is undefined, as is $abc^2 - a^2b$, because these two bags are incomparable with respect to multiset inclusion. However, $a^2b - ab = a$. Finally, $(a^2b)^3 = a^2b + a^2b + a^2b = a^6b^3$. It is left as an exercise to the reader to prove that if $\sigma, \tau \in {}^*\Sigma$, then also $\sigma + \tau, \sigma \cup \tau, \sigma \cap \tau \in {}^*\Sigma$, and furthermore, if also $\sigma \subseteq \tau$, then also $\sigma - \tau \in {}^*\Sigma$.

Because we are mainly talking about bags in relation to and in contrast with strings, it is useful to introduce some precise notions to connect these two worlds. Let Σ be an alphabet. We can define a function $\Psi_\Sigma : \Sigma^* \to {}^*\Sigma$ such that for each $w \in \Sigma^*$, $\Psi_\Sigma(w)$ is the bag containing each symbol of Σ exactly the same number of times as w; in other words, $\Psi_\Sigma(w)(a) = \text{occur}(w, a)$. The function Ψ_Σ is called the *Parikh mapping*, and $\Psi_\Sigma(w)$ is the *Parikh vector* of w. Due to how we defined bags to be independent of their alphabet, we can drop the subscript and think of Ψ as a more general function such that $\Psi(w) = \Psi_\Sigma(w)$ for any alphabet Σ and any $w \in \Sigma^*$.

Parikh vectors were not originally defined as bags, but rather as k-tuples of integers corresponding to the numbers of occurences of each symbol in the original string. The choice to define them as bags might seem like a big departure from the original spirit of Parikh vectors, but this is in fact not the case—bags over a particular alphabet Σ of cardinality $k \in \mathbb{N}$ can also be represented as k-tuples of natural numbers, also called *vectors*, each number representing the multiplicity of its corresponding symbol. Note that this representation is dependent not only on Σ, but also on how we pair up symbols of Σ with components of the vector. This pairing up corresponds to specifying a linear ordering of the alphabet. Thus, given $\Sigma = \{a_1, \ldots, a_k\}$, we can define a function $h_\Sigma : {}^*\Sigma \to {}_0\mathbb{N}^k$ as follows for each $\sigma \in {}^*\Sigma$:

$$h_\Sigma(\sigma) = (\sigma(a_1), \ldots, \sigma(a_k)).$$

It is easy to see that h_Σ is a bijection, supporting the claim about the representability of bags as vectors of integers. Note that by composing this function with the Parikh mapping, we can also use it to directly map strings to vectors of numbers of occurences of each symbol. Such an object is then closer to the original notion of a Parikh vector:

$$h_\Sigma(\Psi_\Sigma(w)) = (\text{occur}(w, a_1), \ldots, \text{occur}(w, a_k)).$$

The mapping Ψ is surjective and non-injective, pointing to the rather obvious fact that in general, multiple strings are mapped to the same bag. Therefore, when viewing the structures of Σ^* and ${}^*\Sigma$ through the lens of this mapping, it appears as if bags are in some sense less numerous than strings. More precisely, assuming $k = \text{card}(\Sigma)$ and given a size limit $n \in {}_0\mathbb{N}$, there will be more strings of length n over Σ than there will be bags of cardinality n over Σ, as long as $k \geq 2$ and $n \geq 2$ (and in the instances that $k = 1$ or $n \leq 1$, the number of strings and bags of given size over Σ is equal). To give precise figures, there are k^n different strings of length n over an alphabet with k distinct symbols, whereas the number of bags of cardinality n over said alphabet is given by the *multiset coefficient* $\left(\!\binom{k}{n}\!\right)$, read "$k$ multichoose n", defined as follows based on the binomial coefficient:

$$\left(\!\!\binom{k}{n}\!\!\right) = \binom{n+k-1}{n} = \frac{(n+k-1)!}{n!(k-1)!}.$$

Note that arriving at this number corresponds to the combinatorial problem of counting so-called n-combinations with repetition from a set of k elements. In such contexts, the symbols n and k are usually interchanged.

It would be a mistake, however, to concede that bags are somewhat inferior to strings, that they somehow hold less information. Even though we arrived at bags while searching for some notion of unordered strings, they are nevertheless a fundamentally different way of using symbols to represent data. Thus, comparing strings and bags "of the same size" is not a fair comparison, because the length of a string and the cardinality of a bag are simply not the same thing—pragmatically, we can in general encode bags of cardinality n much more efficiently than strings of length n due to fundamental differences in their nature. Furthermore, due to both Σ^* and $^*\Sigma$ being countably infinite (assuming a finite, nonempty Σ), bags can, at least in principle, encode information just as well as strings can.

An interesting interpretation of bags arises if you consider their representation as k-tuples of natural numbers—in this sense, a bag over an alphabet can be thought of as a fixed-length string over $_0\mathbb{N}$. Thus, analogously to how strings over a given alphabet can have arbitrary length but select their symbols from a limited, finite set, bags over the same alphabet can be thought of as strings of limited length which select from arbitrarily many possible symbols to put at each position.

Let us now define more complex notions built on bags with the ultimate goal of exploring multiset computation.

Macrosets

Just how languages are sets of strings, we define a corresponding notion of sets of bags. Let Σ be an alphabet. A *macroset* is any subset of $^*\Sigma$. In particular, $^*\Sigma$ is the *universal macroset* over Σ, whereas $\emptyset$ is the *empty macroset* (over any alphabet). For example, let $\Sigma = \{a, b, c\}$. An example of a macroset over Σ is the macroset $M_1 = \{\sigma \in {}^*\Sigma \mid \sigma(a) = \sigma(b) = \sigma(c)\}$, containing all the bags of the form $a^i b^i c^i$ for some $i \in {}_0\mathbb{N}$.

Even though, as discussed previously, strings and bags are fundamentally different objects, we are still interested in comparing languages with macrosets, and once we define some models of computation based on bags, we will be interested in comparing their power with the power of string-based models of computation. Perhaps the most obvious and natural connection between the worlds of strings and bags comes in the form of the Parikh mapping (see Section 1.2), generalized to sets of strings. That is, for a language $L \subseteq \Sigma^*$, reformulate the notion of Parikh image so that $\Psi(L) = \{\Psi(w) \mid w \in L\}$ denotes the macroset of Parikh vectors of all strings in L (this reformulation is straightforward and left to the reader). We call $\Psi(L)$ the *Parikh image* of L. Given any macroset $M \subseteq {}^*\Sigma$, if $\Psi(L) = M$, we say that L and M are *Ψ-equivalent*.

To better illustrate these notions, consider the languages $L_1 = \{a^i b^i c^i \mid i \geq 0\}$ and $L_2 = \{w \in \{a, b, c\}^* \mid \text{occur}(w, a) = \text{occur}(w, b) = \text{occur}(w, c)\}$. Any string

$w \in L_1 \cup L_2$ from either one of these languages contains each symbol from $\{a, b, c\}$ exactly the same number of times, and for any given number $n \in {}_0\mathbb{N}$, there is exactly one $w \in L_1$ and at least one $w' \in L_2$ with exactly n occurences of each symbol. From these observations we can establish that $\Psi(L_1) = \Psi(L_2) = M_1$, where M_1 is the macroset defined earlier in this section.

These examples also demonstrate that Ψ, when understood as a mapping from power(Σ^*) to power($^*\Sigma$), is not injective—two different languages can map to the same macroset, as a direct consequence of the original Parikh mapping from Σ^* to $^*\Sigma$ being non-injective. Note, however, that this does not hold for unary languages. Indeed, two unary languages L_1 and L_2 will have the same Parikh image if and only if they are the same. Formally, $\Psi(L_1) = \Psi(L_2)$ if and only if $L_1 = L_2$ for all unary languages L_1, L_2.

Similarly to families of languages, we can define *families of macrosets* simply as sets whose members are macrosets. Even though we have not yet established any models for multiset computation, we can derive macroset families from language families using Parikh mapping. Let $\mathcal{L}$ denote a family of languages. Then $p\mathcal{L}$ denotes the family of Parikh images of languages in the original family of languages. Formally, $p\mathcal{L} = \{\Psi(L) \mid L \in \mathcal{L}\}$. For example, $p\mathbf{REG}$, $p\mathbf{LIN}$, $p\mathbf{CF}$, $p\mathbf{CS}$, and $p\mathbf{RE}$ denote the families of Parikh images for all regular, linear, context-free, context-sensitive and recursively enumerable languages, respectively. It follows immediately from the Chomsky hierarchy that

$$p\mathbf{REG} \subseteq p\mathbf{LIN} \subseteq p\mathbf{CF} \subseteq p\mathbf{CS} \subseteq p\mathbf{RE},$$

however, it turns out that only the last two of these inclusions are proper, meaning that the first three families of macrosets are identical. Before formalizing this in a theorem, let us introduce another useful term for this purpose—another family of macrosets that also turns out to be equivalent to these families. A macroset of the form $\{\sigma_0 + \sigma_1^{i_1} + \cdots + \sigma_m^{i_m} \mid i_1, \ldots, i_m \in {}_0\mathbb{N}\}$ for some $m \in {}_0\mathbb{N}$ and bags $\sigma_0, \ldots, \sigma_m \in {}^*\Sigma$ is a *linear* macroset. The family of linear macrosets is denoted by **Lin**. A union of finitely many linear macrosets is a *semilinear* macroset. The family of semilinear macrosets is denoted by **SLin**.

Theorem 8.6 *Parikh's Theorem*

$$p\mathbf{CF} = p\mathbf{REG} = \mathbf{SLin}.$$

Proof For a proof of $p\mathbf{CF} = \mathbf{SLin}$, see [Rozenberg and Salomaa, 1997a, Chapter 9]. The inclusion $p\mathbf{REG} \subseteq p\mathbf{CF}$ follows immediately from the definitions of these two families of macrosets. It is a simple exercise to prove the converse inclusion, $\mathbf{SLin} \subseteq p\mathbf{REG}$. We will first briefly describe how to transform an arbitrary linear macroset M' into a right-linear grammar G' such that $\Psi(L(G')) = M'$, demonstrating the inclusion $\mathbf{Lin} \subseteq p\mathbf{REG}$. The inclusion $\mathbf{SLin} \subseteq p\mathbf{REG}$ then follows easily as a consequence of the class of regular languages being closed under union.

Let Δ be an alphabet and $\sigma_0, \ldots, \sigma_m \in {}^*\Delta$ for some $m \in {}_0\mathbb{N}$ be the basis bags which describe the macroset $M' = \{\sigma_0 + \sigma_1^{i_1} + \cdots + \sigma_m^{i_m} \mid i_1, \ldots, i_m \in {}_0\mathbb{N}\}$. Let

$s_0, \ldots, s_m \in \Delta^*$ be strings such that $\Psi(s_i) = \sigma_i$ for $1 \leq i \leq m$. Also, let $S' \notin \Delta$ be a new symbol. Define a new set of right-linear production rules, P', as follows:

$$P' = \{S' \to s_0\} \cup \{S' \to s_i S' \mid 1 \leq i \leq m\}.$$

Let $G' = (\Delta \cup \{S'\}, \Delta, P', S')$. Obviously, $\Psi(L(G')) = M'$, proving that **Lin** $\subseteq$ p**REG**.

Now, let $M = \bigcup_{i=1}^{n} M_i$ be an arbitrary semilinear macroset formed as the union of n linear macrosets $M_1, \ldots, M_n$ for some $n \geq 1$, and $G_1, \ldots, G_n$ be right-linear grammars such that $\Psi(L(G_i)) = M_i$ for each $1 \leq i \leq n$. A grammar $G = (\Sigma = N \cup \Delta, \Delta, P, S)$ such that $\Psi(L(G)) = M$ can be constructed from these grammars as follows.

Let $G_i = (\Sigma_i = N_i \cup \Delta_i, \Delta_i, P_i, S_i)$ for all $1 \leq i \leq n$. Assume (without loss of generality) that the sets $N_1, \ldots, N_n$ are pairwise disjoint, and let S be a new symbol such that $S \notin N_i$ for any $1 \leq i \leq n$. Let $N = \{S\} \cup \bigcup_{i=1}^{n} N_i$, $\Delta = \bigcup_{i=1}^{n} \Delta_i$ and $P = \{S \to S_i \mid 1 \leq i \leq n\} \cup \bigcup_{i=1}^{n} P_i$. The grammar G generates the union of the languages $L(G_1), \ldots, L(G_n)$, and, therefore, $\Psi(L(G)) = M$. This construction can be repeated for an arbitrary semilinear macroset, proving that **SLin** $\subseteq$ p**REG**.

Putting all this information together, we get **SLin** $\subseteq$ p**REG** $\subseteq$ p**CF** $=$ **SLin**, meaning that all three of these families are equivalent. □

Theorem 8.6 shows that a part of the Chomsky hierarchy for macrosets collapses into a single family. However, we have yet to show that the rest of the hierarchy does not collapse. We demonstrate this using unary languages in the proof of the following theorem.

Theorem 8.7 p**CF** $\subset$ p**CS** $\subset$ p**RE**.

Proof The improper version of the above statement, p**CF** $\subseteq$ p**CS** $\subseteq$ p**RE**, follows directly from the definitions of these macroset families and the original models. It remains to show that each of these two inclusions is proper.

To show that p**CS** $-$ p**CF** is not empty, consider the unary language $L = \{a^{2^k} \mid k \geq 0\}$ and its Parikh image, the macroset $M = \Psi(L)$ (which can also be described using set builder notation in exactly the same way as L). It is a well-known fact that $L \in$ **CS** $-$ **CF**, and, seeing as L is unary, no other language has the same Parikh image, thus proving that $M \notin$ p**CF**, and, consequently, p**CF** $\subset$ p**CS**.

The statement p**CS** $\subset$ p**RE** follows analogously from the existence of unary recursively enumerable languages that are not context-sensitive, such as a unary encoding of the halting problem. □

Multiset Grammars

We have now laid a sufficient foundation to explore macroset theory, but as far as computational models go, we only know how to describe macrosets indirectly as Parikh images of languages generated by traditional string-based models. Let us now finally dive into the world of multiset computation by introducing some bag-based computational models. The first such model will be *multiset grammars* (also called *commutative grammars*), which are essentially traditional phrase-structure grammars modified to work with bags instead of strings.

Definition 8.6 A *multiset grammar* (also called a *commutative grammar*) is a quadruple $G = (\Sigma, \Delta, R, A)$, where

- Σ is a nonempty total alphabet called the *total alphabet*;
- $\Delta \subseteq \Sigma$ is the set of *terminals*;
- $R \subseteq ({}^*\Sigma - {}^*\Delta) \times {}^*\Sigma$ is a finite set of *multiset rewriting rules*;
- $A \subseteq {}^*\Sigma$ is a finite macroset called the *start macroset*; elements of A are called *axioms*.

Rewriting rules $(\mu_1, \mu_2) \in R$ are written as $\mu_1 \to \mu_2$. Let $\sigma, \tau \in {}^*\Sigma$ and let $\mu_1 \to \mu_2 \in R$. We say that σ directly derives τ in G using $\mu_1 \to \mu_2$, written as

$$\sigma \Rightarrow_G \tau \; [\mu_1 \to \mu_2]$$

if and only if $\mu_1 \subseteq \sigma$ and $\tau = \sigma - \mu_1 + \mu_2$. The subscript G is omitted whenever not necessary, meaning that we usually always write $\Rightarrow$ instead of $\Rightarrow_G$. We also define $\Rightarrow^k$ for every non-negative integer k, $\Rightarrow^*$ and $\Rightarrow^+$ similarly as for traditional grammars. The *macroset generated by* G is denoted by $M(G)$ and defined as

$$M(G) = \{\sigma \in {}^*\Delta \mid \alpha \Rightarrow^* \sigma \text{ for some } \alpha \in A\}.$$

By applying additional constraints on the shape of the rewriting rules, we can establish a hierarchy of multiset grammars and their corresponding macroset families. A multiset grammar $G = (\Sigma, \Delta, R, A)$ is said to be

- *phrase-structure* regardless of the shapes of its rewriting rules;
- *monotone* if $|\mu_1| \leq |\mu_2|$ for all $\mu_1 \to \mu_2 \in R$;
- *context-free* if $|\mu_1| = 1$ for all $\mu_1 \to \mu_2 \in R$;
- *linear* if $|\mu_1| = 1$ and $\mu_2(N) \leq 1$ for all $\mu_1 \to \mu_2 \in R$;
- *regular* if $|\mu_1| = 1$, $|\mu_2| \leq 2$ and $\mu_2(N) \leq 1$ for all $\mu_1 \to \mu_2 \in R$.

We will denote the families of macrosets generated by regular, linear, context-free, monotone, and phrase-structure multiset grammars by m**REG**, m**LIN**, m**CF**, m**MON**, and m**PS**, respectively.

As an example, consider the grammar $G_1 = (\{S, a, b, c\}, \{a, b, c\}, \{S \to Sabc, S \to \varepsilon\}, \{S\})$. Clearly, any derivation of a terminal bag in this grammar will consist of zero or more applications of the rule $S \to Sabc$, followed by a single application of the rule $S \to \varepsilon$. It is therefore easy to see that G_1 generates exactly those bags over $\{a, b, c\}$ in which all three symbols have the same multiplicity, comprising the macroset M_1 from the previous section. Written explicitly, the macroset generated by G_1 is $M(G_1) = \{a^i + b^i + c^i \mid i \in {}_0\mathbb{N}\} = M_1$. Notice that G_1 is a linear multiset grammar, meaning that $M_1 \in m$**LIN**. To demonstrate how G_1 works, let us demonstrate the derivation of $a^3b^3c^3$:

$$S \Rightarrow Sabc \Rightarrow Sa^2b^2c^2 \Rightarrow Sa^3b^3c^3 \Rightarrow a^3b^3c^3$$

One striking difference between Definition 8.6 and Definition 2.8 is that phrase-structure grammars have a single start symbol S, whereas multiset grammars have an entire set $A = \{\alpha_1, \ldots, \alpha_k\}$ of axioms (where $k = \mathrm{card}(A)$). However, it turns out that a grammar of any of the types of multiset grammars described above can be transformed to an equivalent multiset grammar of the same type such that its start macroset consists only of a single bag of cardinality 1 (that is, $A = \{S\}$). This is easily shown for phrase-structure, monotone and context-free multiset grammars, simply by introducing a new start symbol S and rules $S \rightarrow \alpha_1, \ldots, S \rightarrow \alpha_k$. Demonstrating this for linear and regular grammars requires a more intricate construction, such as replacing the set of nonterminals N in the original grammar with the set of strings over N of length up to $\max\{\mathrm{occur}(\alpha, N) \mid \alpha \in A\}$ (see Kudlek et al. [2000] for details of this construction).

In the previous sections, we used the Greek letter Ψ for connections between the world of strings and the world of macrosets—to denote the Parikh mapping, as well as its generalization to sets. To avoid confusion, we will now select a different symbol, Φ, to map traditional grammars to their multiset counterparts. Given any phrase-structure grammar, G, we define $\Phi(G)$ to be the multiset grammar constructed from G by simply replacing all the strings in its production rules and its axioms by corresponding multisets. Thanks to the convention of writing multisets as strings, this means that we can describe a phrase-structure grammar and a multiset grammar in exactly the same way with the only difference coming from context—we understand a particular model to be either string-based or multiset-based.

One might expect that when we construct a multiset grammar in this way, the macroset it generates is simply the macroset of Parikh vectors of strings generated by the original grammar, that is, given an arbitrary phrase-structure grammar G, $M(\Phi(G)) = \Psi(L(G))$ holds, and that, consequently, the class of Parikh images of languages generated by a particular class of grammars corresponds to the class of macroset generated by their multiset counterparts. For context-free grammars, this is indeed the case—the left-hand side of every rule is a single non-terminal, so the application of a rule only requires that this nonterminal be contained in the current sentential form, and this is easily simulated by a context-free multiset grammar, meaning that $M(\Phi(G)) = \Psi(L(G))$ always holds for context-free grammars G, which combined with Theorem 8.6 gives the consequence that $m\mathbf{CF} = m\mathbf{LIN} = m\mathbf{REG} = \mathbf{SLin}$.

However, as we will show in the remainder of this section, neither $M(\Phi(G)) = \Psi(L(G))$ nor $m\mathcal{L} = p\mathcal{L}$ holds in the general case. For example, consider the grammar $G = (\{S, B, C\}, \{a\}, \{S \rightarrow BaC, BC \rightarrow a\}, S)$. It is easy to see that $L(G) = \emptyset$. However, in $\Phi(G)$, the derivation $S \Rightarrow aBC \Rightarrow aa$ becomes possible, meaning that $M(\Phi(G)) = \{aa\} \neq \Psi(L(G)) = \emptyset$. This alone, however, is not enough to prove that $m\mathbf{MON} \neq p\mathbf{MON} = p\mathbf{CS}$ or $m\mathbf{PS} \neq p\mathbf{PS}$, or indeed to show where these macroset classes fit within the hierarchy shown in the previous section. For this, we need to introduce yet another class of multiset grammars—*matrix multiset grammars*.

Definition 8.7 A *matrix multiset grammar with appearance checking* is a pair $H = (G, M, W)$, where

- $G = (\Sigma, \Delta, R, A)$ is a context-free multiset grammar called the *core grammar*,
- $M \subseteq R^+$ is a finite language over R called the set of *matrices*,
- $W \subseteq \Sigma - \Delta$ is the *appearance checking set*.

If $W = \emptyset$, H is simply called a *matrix multiset grammar* (without appearance checking). Furthermore, H is *propagating* if none of its production rules has ε as its right-hand side. Let $\sigma, \tau \in {}^*\Sigma$ and let $m \in M$. Note that $m = r_1 \cdots r_k$ for some $k \geq 1$ and $r_i \in R$ for $1 \leq i \leq k$. We say that σ directly derives τ in H using m, written as

$$\sigma \Rightarrow_H \tau\,[m]$$

if and only if there exist bags $\chi_0, \ldots, \chi_k \in {}^*\Sigma$ such that $\chi_0 = \sigma$, $\chi_k = \tau$, and for each $1 \leq i \leq k$ one of the following holds:

(a) $\chi_{i-1} \Rightarrow_G \chi_i\,[r_i]$,
(b) $\chi_{i-1}(A) = 0$, $A \in W$ and $\chi_{i-1} = \chi_i$, where A is the left-hand side of r_i.

Again, we omit the subscript H unless necessary. We also define $\Rightarrow^k$ for every non-negative integer k, $\Rightarrow^*$ and $\Rightarrow^+$ similarly as for traditional grammars. The *macroset generated by* H is denoted by $M(H)$ and defined as

$$M(G) = \{\sigma \in {}^*\Delta \mid \alpha \Rightarrow_H^* \sigma \text{ for some } \alpha \in A\}.$$

These grammars are introduced as multiset counterparts of matrix grammars, a well-established regulated language model, the strongest of which achieve Turing power. Unlike traditional Chomsky types of grammars, however, they have the property that given any matrix grammar G, it is the case that $\Psi(L(G)) = M(\Phi(G))$. This is easily demonstrated by analyzing how these models work—all individual rewritings are context-free, and the control mechanisms beyond remain unchanged between the string-based and the multiset-based models.

The families of languages generated by (propagating) matrix multiset grammars and (propagating) matrix multiset grammars with appearance checking are denoted by $m\mathbf{M}^{-\varepsilon}$, $m\mathbf{M}$, $m\mathbf{M}_{ac}^{-\varepsilon}$, and $m\mathbf{M}_{ac}$, respectively.

The main reason we are interested in matrix multiset grammars in this section is their relation to monotone and phrase-structure multiset grammars. These have the same generative power as the propagating and non-propagating variant of matrix multiset grammars without appearance checking, respectively, as formalized in the following two theorems.

Theorem 8.8 $m\mathbf{M}^{-\varepsilon} = m\mathbf{MON}$,

Proof We will show that any monotone multiset grammar can be transformed into an equivalent propagating matrix multiset grammar and vice versa. Both constructions sketched here are taken from Kudlek et al. [2000].

Let $G = (\Sigma, \Delta, R, A)$ be a monotone multiset grammar. Note that every rule in R is of the form

$$X_1 \cdots X_k \to Y_1 \cdots Y_l$$

for some k, l such that $k \leq l$. For each $X \in \Sigma$, we introduce new nonterminals X', X''. We can then simulate each production rule $X_1 \cdots X_k \to Y_1 \cdots Y_l$ with a matrix consisting of the following rules in order:

- Rules $X_i' \to Y_i''$ for each $1 \leq i < k$,
- A single rule $X_k' \to Y_k'' \cdots Y_l''$,
- Rules $Y_i'' \to Y_i'$ for each $1 \leq i < k$.

Both single-primed and double-primed symbols are used to prevent the rewriting of symbols that should not be rewritten—if $X_j = Y_i$ for some $1 \leq i < j \leq k$, a matrix constructed as above but without primed symbols would allow the Y_i generated by the i-th rule of the matrix to be rewritten as X_j by the j-th rule, which would not be possible by the original rule in G. Having constructed these matrices, only a few technical details remain (such as creating a new set of axioms containing primed variants of the multisets in A, or adding rules to convert primed terminals to their non-primed variants) to construct a propagating matrix multiset grammar (without appearance checking) equivalent to G. Consequently, $m\mathbf{MON} \subseteq m\mathbf{M}^{-\varepsilon}$.

Conversely, let $H' = (G', M', \emptyset)$ be a propagating matrix multiset grammar corresponding to a string matrix grammar in binary normal form. To simulate a matrix of the form $(A \to x, X \to Y)$ (where A, X, Y are nonterminals and x is an arbitrary string over the total alphabet of G'), simply create a monotone rule $AX \to xX$. Thanks to H' being in binary normal form, $X \notin \text{symbols}(x)$, so the resulting monotone rule will be applicable to exactly the same sentential forms as the original matrix. This can be utilized to construct a monotone multiset grammar equivalent to H', proving that also $m\mathbf{M}^{-\varepsilon} \subseteq m\mathbf{MON}$. □

Theorem 8.9 $m\mathbf{M} = m\mathbf{PS}$.

Proof To demonstrate this theorem, modify the proof of Theorem 8.8 so it works with non-propagating rules. □

Figure 8.1 shows how the macroset families generated by different types of multiset matrix grammars compare to the macroset variant of Chomsky hierarchy established in the previous section. The improper inclusions in the diagram easily follow from what we have already discussed and the well-known hierarchy of language families generated by matrix grammars (see Dassow and Păun [1989]). However, we are yet to justify the properness of these inclusions, which we will do in the remainder of this section.

To show that $\mathbf{SLin} \subset m\mathbf{MON}$, simply consider the monotone multiset grammar $G_2 = (\{X, Y, A, a, b\}, \{a, b\}, P_2, \{Xa\})$ where $P_2 = \{Xa \to XAA, X \to Y, X \to$

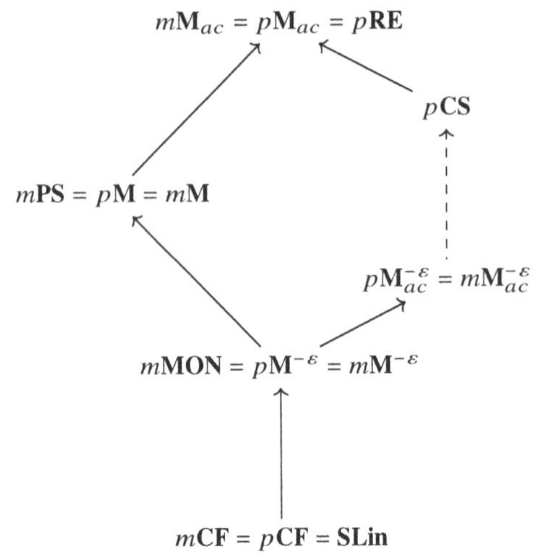

Fig. 8.1 Language families resulting from multiset grammars.

$b, YA \to Ya, Y \to Xb\}$. The macroset generated by this grammar is $M(G_2) = \{\mu \in {}^*\{a,b\} \mid 1 \leq \mu(a) \leq 2^{\mu(b)-1}\}$, which is not a semilinear set.

The inclusion $m\mathbf{MON} \subset m\mathbf{PS}$ can be proven using complexity arguments—it follows easily from the facts that $m\mathbf{MON} \subseteq \mathbf{PSPACE} \subset \mathbf{EXPSPACE}$ and that the uniform word problem for $m\mathbf{PS}$ is **EXPSPACE**-hard, where **EXPSPACE** is the set of all decision problems solvable by a deterministic Turing machine in exponential space (see Sipser [2006]).

We will prove the remaining proper inclusions using the following theorem, which we include without proof (which can be found in Hauschildt and Jantzen [1994]). Let the language family generated by classical matrix grammars be denoted by **M**.

Theorem 8.10 *All unary languages in* **M** *are regular.*

Notice that the language $L = \{a^{2^n} | n \geq 0\}$ is not context-free and its corresponding macroset $M = \Psi(L)$ is not semilinear. It thus follows from the previous theorem that $L \notin \mathbf{M}$. Furthermore, as L is unary, there is no other language L' such that $\Psi(L') = M$ and $L' \neq L$. As a consequence, $M \notin p\mathbf{M} = m\mathbf{PS}$. However, because L can be generated by a propagating matrix grammar with appearance checking, it is also the case that $M \in p\mathbf{M}_{ac}^{-\varepsilon} = m\mathbf{M}_{ac}^{-\varepsilon}$, thus proving the final two proper inclusions, $m\mathbf{MON} \subset m\mathbf{M}_{ac}^{-\varepsilon}$ and $m\mathbf{PS} \subset m\mathbf{M}_{ac} = p\mathbf{RE}$.

Corollary 8.7 *The inclusions shown in Figure 8.1 hold.*

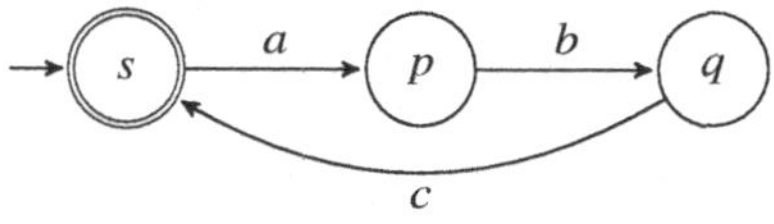

Fig. 8.2 A_1.

Multiset Automata

In the previous section we examined multiset-based counterparts of traditional, string-based grammars. It is a natural next step to do the same for traditional automata. Therefore, let us introduce the first of these models.

Definition 8.8 A *multiset finite automaton* (MFA) is a quintuple $A = (Q, \Delta, f, s, F)$, where

- Q is a finite *set of states*,
- Δ is the *input alphabet*,
- $f : Q \times \Delta \to \text{power}(Q)$ is the *transition mapping*,
- $s \in Q$ is the *initial state*, and
- $F \subseteq Q$ is the *set of final states*.

A *configuration* of A is a pair $(q, \tau) \in Q \times {}^*\Delta$, and we define the relation $\vdash_A$ on the set of all configurations as follows. For any $p, q \in Q$ and $\tau, \rho \in {}^*\Delta$,

$$(p, \tau) \vdash_A (q, \rho)$$

if and only if there is a symbol $a \in \Delta$ such that $\tau(a) \geq 1$, $q \in f(p, a)$ and $\rho = \tau - a$. We also define $\vdash_A^k$ for every non-negative integer k, $\vdash_A^*$ and $\vdash_A^+$ similarly as for traditional automata, and we omit the subscript whenever it is not necessary. The macroset accepted by A is denoted by $M(A)$ and defined as

$$M(A) = \{\tau \in {}^*\Delta \mid (s, \tau) \vdash_M^* (f, \varepsilon) \text{ for some } f \in F\}.$$

Looking over the definition, it is clear that this model is very closely related to finite automata. Indeed, essentially the only difference is that while finite automata work with strings, multiset finite automata work with multisets. In light of Theorem 3.6, a very close relation to jumping finite automata can also be seen—the way a JFA ignores the order of symbols in its input string corresponds closely to the non-existence of order in the input of a MFA. So while a MFA may accept or reject a particular multiset μ, a JFA may accept or reject all permutation of a string w such that $\Psi(w) = \mu$.

As a simple example, consider MFA $A_1 = (\{s, p, q\}, \{a, b, c\}, f, s, \{s\})$ where $f(s, a) = \{p\}$, $f(p, b) = \{q\}$, $f(q, c) = \{s\}$, and $f(x, y) = \emptyset$ for all other pairs $(x, y) \in \{s, p, q\} \times \{a, b, c\}$. The diagram of this automaton can be seen in Figure 8.2. It is not hard to see that this MFA accepts the macroset M_1 from the section about macrosets, that is, $M(A_1) = M_1 = \{a^i + b^i + c^i \mid i \geq 0\}$.

While a traditional finite automaton, working with ordered strings, decides upon its next step based on the first symbol of the unprocessed input, an MFA, working with bags, has no such limitations—it has more of a global view of its input, performing a transition if a particular symbol is present in its input, regardless of its position; in fact, it does not even make sense to talk about the position of a symbol within a bag. In this light, it makes sense to consider a modification to this model which would allow it to decide on a particular computational step based on whether a particular symbol is not present in its input bag. This modification is presented formally in the following definition.

Definition 8.9 A *multiset finite automaton with detection* (MFAD) is a quintuple $A = (Q, \Delta, f, s, F)$, where

- Q, Δ, s and F are defined exactly as in Definition 8.8,
- $\bar{\Delta} = \{\bar{a} \mid a \in \Delta\}$ is a new alphabet consisting of barred copies of symbols of Δ, $\Delta \cap \bar{\Delta} = \emptyset$,
- $f : Q \times (\Delta \cup \bar{\Delta}) \to \text{power}(Q)$ is the *transition mapping*.

For convenience, barring a barred symbol turns it into its unbarred version, that is, $\bar{\bar{a}} = a$. For any $p, q \in Q$ and $\tau, \rho \in {}^*\Delta$,

$$(p, \tau) \vdash_A (q, \rho)$$

if and only if one of the following conditions holds:

(a) there is a symbol $a \in \Delta$ such that $q \in f(p, a)$ and $\rho = \tau - a$,
(b) there is a symbol $a \in \Delta$ such that $q \in f(p, \bar{a})$, $\tau(a) = 0$ and $\rho = \tau$.

For MFAs, this modification does not actually provide an increase in accepting power; however, they do increase the accepting power of their deterministic variants, as well as some stronger models which we will discuss later in this section. An MFA $A = (Q, \Delta, f, s, F)$ is *deterministic* (DMFA) if and only if the following two conditions hold:

1. For all $q \in Q$ and for all $a \in \Delta$, $\text{card}(f(q, a)) \leq 1$;
2. For all $q \in Q$ and for all $a \in \Delta$, $\text{card}(f(q, a)) > 0$ implies $f(q, b) = \emptyset$ for all $b \in \Delta - \{a\}$.

Notice that MFA A_1 in Figure 8.2 is deterministic. Similarly, but rather more complexly, a MFAD $A = (Q, \Delta, f, s, F)$ is *deterministic* (DMFAD) if and only if the following two conditions hold:

1. For all $q \in Q$ and for all $a \in \Delta \cup \bar{\Delta}$, $\text{card}(f(q, a)) \leq 1$;
2. For all $q \in Q$ and for all $a \in \Delta \cup \bar{\Delta}$, $\text{card}(f(q, a)) > 0$ implies $f(q, b) = \emptyset$ for all $b \in \Delta \cup \bar{\Delta} - \{a, \bar{a}\}$.

MFA, **MFAD**, **DMFA**, and **DMFAD** denote the classes of macrosets generated by MFAs, MFADs, DMFAs, and DMFADs, respectively. By definition, it must be the case that **DMFA** $\subseteq$ **MFA** $\subseteq$ **MFAD** and **DMFA** $\subseteq$ **DMFAD** $\subseteq$ **MFAD**. From the close relation of MFA to finite automata, it is easy to see that **MFA** $=$ *p***REG** $=$ **SLin**.

In Csuhaj-Varjú et al. [2001], it is also proven that **MFAD** = **MFA**. However, the deterministic variants are both strictly weaker. DMFA cannot even deal with some finite macrosets, such as $\{a, b\}$—if there is any transition from the start state reading a, there can be no such transition reading b, and vice versa. DMFAD on the other hand can accept all finite macrosets, but are unable to accept certain linear macrosets, such as $\{a^{k+2l} + b^{2k+l} \mid k, l \in {}_0\mathbb{N}\}$, which is proven in Csuhaj-Varjú et al. [2001] as well. The relative accepting powers of these automata can thus be summarized as follows:

$$\mathbf{DMFA} \subset \mathbf{DMFAD} \subset \mathbf{MFAD} = \mathbf{MFA} = \mathbf{SLin},$$

with the extra note that **DMFAD** and **DMFA** are both incomparable with **Lin** and **DMFA** is incomparable with the class of finite macrosets, while **DMFAD** contains the class of finite macrosets.

A reader familiar with traditional automata theory might now expect a multiset analog of pushdown automata; however, no such model will be introduced in this section, for at least two reasons. First, the last in, first out nature of the pushdown cannot be meaningfully simulated only using bags, as there is no notion of order or position. Second, as we have seen in the section on multiset grammars, the distinctions between regular, context-free and semilinear are blurred in the world of multiset computation, evidenced by the fact that **REG** = p**CF** = **SLin**. Therefore, we will skip directly to a multiset analog of linear bounded automata.

Definition 8.10 A *multiset linear bounded automaton* (MLBA) is a sextuple $N = (Q, \Delta, U, f, s, F)$, where

- Q is a finite *set of states*,
- Δ is the *input alphabet*,
- U is the *bag alphabet*, $\Delta \subseteq U$,
- $f : Q \times U \to \text{power}(Q \times (U \cup \{\varepsilon\}))$ is the *transition mapping*,
- $s \in Q$ is the *initial state*, and
- $F \subseteq Q$ is the *set of final states*.

A *configuration* of N is a pair $(q, \tau) \in Q \times {}^*U$, and we define the relation $\vdash_N$ on the set of all configurations as follows. For any $p, q \in Q$ and $\tau, \rho \in {}^*U$,

$$(p, \tau) \vdash_N (q, \rho)$$

if and only if there are $a \in U$, $b \in U \cup \{\varepsilon\}$ such that $\tau(a) \geq 1$, $(q, b) \in f(p, a)$ and $\rho = \tau - a + b$. We also define $\vdash_N^k$ for every non-negative integer k, $\vdash_N^*$ and $\vdash_N^+$ similarly as for traditional automata, and we omit the subscript whenever it is not necessary. The macroset accepted by N is denoted by $M(N)$ and defined as

$$M(N) = \{\tau \in {}^*\Delta \mid (s, \tau) \vdash_N^* (f, \varepsilon) \text{ for some } f \in F\}.$$

Whereas a MFA can only read its input bag symbol by symbol, a MLBA can also output symbols to its bag. This, combined with the unordered nature of bags, would give rise to an analog of the Turing Machine in the general case; however, the linear boundedness is enforced by not allowing the automaton to write more than it reads in a single step.

Analogously to MFA, we can extend this definition to allow the automaton to detect the non-presence of a particular symbol, with the caveat that this time we introduce barred symbols for the entire bag alphabet, U. More precisely, in a *multiset linear bounded automaton with detection* (MLBAD), $N = (Q, \Delta, U, f, s, F)$, all of Q, Δ, U, s, F retain the same meaning as in a MLBA, but we introduce a barred alphabet $\bar{U} = \{\bar{a} \mid a \in U\}$ of new symbols, and modify the definition of the transition mapping as a function $f : Q \times (U \cup \bar{U}) \to \text{power}(Q \times (U \cup \{\varepsilon\}))$, and for any $p, q \in Q, \tau, \rho \in {}^*U$,

$$(p, \tau) \vdash_N (q, \rho)$$

if and only if one of the following holds for some $a \in U$, $b \in U \cup \{\varepsilon\}$:

(a) $(q, b) \in f(p, a)$ and $\rho = \tau - a + b$,
(b) $(q, b) \in f(p, \bar{a})$, $\tau(a) = 0$ and $\rho = \tau + b$.

Both of these models also have deterministic variants, defined the same way as for MFA—no more than one transition should be possible from any state while reading any particular symbol, and for deterministic MLBAD, no particular state can combine transitions with barred and unbarred symbols, unless it has exactly one transition for an unbarred symbol, exactly one transition for its barred variant, and no other transitions other than these two. These variants can be referred to, predictably, by the acronyms DMLBA and DMLBAD.

As an example, consider the MLBAD

$$N_1 = (\{q_0, q_1, q_r, p_0, p_1, p_r, q_e, q_f\}, \{a\}, \{a, b\}, f_{N_1}, q_0, \{q_f\})$$

where the transition mapping, f_{N_1}, is described in Figure 8.2—an arrow from p to q labeled "x/y" means that $(q, y) \in f_{N_1}(p, x)$, and f_{N_1} is fully described by these arrows. The automaton starts its computation with some number of as in its bag, and, moving between the pair of states q_0 and q_1, rewrites it to half as many bs, passing control to the pair of states p_0 and p_1, where it rewrites these bs to half as many as, and so on, until an odd number of symbols is detected by transitioning into one of the states q_r, p_r. The automaton then decides whether or not to accept the input by determining whether the odd number that has just been detected was 1 or not (based on whether some new symbols of the other kind had been generated before determining the number to be odd). It is therefore not hard to see that the macroset accepted by this automaton is $M(N_1) = \{a^{2^n} \mid n \geq 0\}$. Notice also that N_1 is deterministic (and thus a DMLBAD).

By **MLBA**, **MLBAD**, **DMLBA**, and **DMLBAD**, we denote the classes of macrosets generated by MLBAs, MLBADs, DMLBAs, and DMLBADs, respectively. Just like with MFA, it again follows from definition that **DMLBA** $\subseteq$ **MLBA** $\subseteq$ **MLBAD** and **DMLBA** $\subseteq$ **DMLBAD** $\subseteq$ **MLBAD**. However, this time, detection actually increases the accepting power of the model. Indeed, it is proven in Csuhaj-Varjú et al. [2001] that **MLBA** $=$ m**MON**, and thus by Theorem 8.10 and m**MON** $\subseteq$ m**M**, all unary languages in **MLBA** are semilinear. However, the MLBAD N_1 described

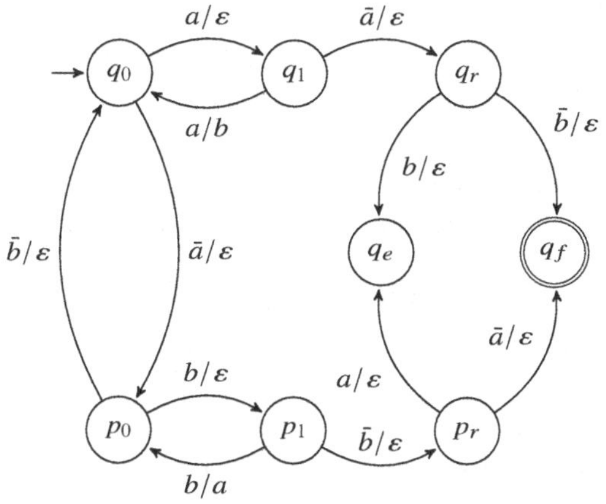

Fig. 8.3 N_1.

earlier in this section accepts the non-semilinear macroset $\{a^{2^n} \mid n \geq 0\}$, thus proving that **MLBA** $\subset$ **MLBAD**. DMLBA are unable to accept even simple macrosets like $\{a, b\}$ due to limitations similar to DMFA. As such, **DMLBA** $\subset$ **MLBA**, which contrasts with the original, string-based variants, where the relationship between the language classes accepted by deterministic and nondeterministic LBA is still an open problem. This also serves to show that **DLMBA** $\subset$ **DMLBAD**. Based on this information, we can refine the hierarchies above to

$$\mathbf{DMLBA} \subset \mathbf{MLBA} = m\mathbf{MON} \subset \mathbf{MLBAD}$$

and

$$\mathbf{DMLBA} \subset \mathbf{DMLBAD} \subseteq \mathbf{MLBAD}.$$

The relationship between **MLBAD** and other established superclasses of **MLBA**, such as p**MON** and m**PS**, is unclear; however, it is shown in Csuhaj-Varjú et al. [2001] to contain all macroset generated by multiset random context grammars limited to non-erasing rules.

Our final stop on this tour of multiset automata will be, unsurprisingly, the multiset counterpart of Turing machines—a variant of Turing machines the tape of which behaves like a bag rather than a string. The version defined in Csuhaj-Varjú et al. [2001] differs from MLBA in that it is always allowed to read a special symbol which is in unlimited supply in the bag. We will introduce a slightly modified but equivalent version, which is instead allowed to not read anything in a computational move.

Definition 8.11 A *multiset Turing machine* (MTM) is a sextuple $N = (Q, \Delta, U, f, s, F)$, where

- Q is a finite *set of states*,
- Δ is the *input alphabet*,

- U is the *bag alphabet*, $\Delta \subseteq U$,
- $f : Q \times (U \cup \{\varepsilon\}) \to \text{power}(Q \times (U \cup \{\varepsilon\}))$ is the *transition mapping*,
- $s \in Q$ is the *initial state*, and
- $F \subseteq Q$ is the *set of final states*.

A *configuration* of N is a pair $(q, \tau) \in Q \times {}^*U$, and we define the relation $\vdash_N$ on the set of all configurations as follows. For any $p, q \in Q$ and $\tau, \rho \in {}^*U$,

$$(p, \tau) \vdash_N (q, \rho)$$

if and only if there are $a, b \in U \cup \{\varepsilon\}$ such that $(q, b) \in f(p, a)$ and $\rho = \tau - a + b$. We also define $\vdash_N^k$ for every non-negative integer k, $\vdash_N^*$ and $\vdash_N^+$ similarly as for traditional automata, and we omit the subscript whenever it is not necessary. The macroset accepted by N is denoted by $M(N)$ and defined as

$$M(N) = \{\tau \in {}^*\Delta \mid (s, \tau) \vdash_N^* (f, \varepsilon) \text{ for some } f \in F\}.$$

A MTM (or a MTMD) is *deterministic* (a DMTM or a DMTMD) if no more than a single move is possible from any given configuration.

MTM, **MTMD**, **DMTM**, and **DMTMD** denote the classes of macrosets generated by MTMs, MTMDs, DMTMs, and DMTMDs, respectively. Analogously to MLBA, it can be proven that **MTM** = m**PS**, and DMTM are, again, unable to accept simple macrosets such as $\{a, b\}$. MTMDs are again more powerful than MTMs. In fact, as a MTMD is essentially a register machine, it is a Turing-complete model, meaning that **MTMD** = p**PS**. DMTMDs are clearly strictly more powerful than DMTMs, but their relationship with the other two variants is unclear. The relationships of the other three models can be summarized as follows:

$$\mathbf{DMTM} \subset \mathbf{MTM} = m\mathbf{PS} \subset \mathbf{MTMD} = p\mathbf{PS}.$$

This concludes our discussion of multiset-based grammars and automata, and we will shift our attention to *Petri nets* which are very closely related to multiset computation despite being based on different principles.

Petri Nets

At the core of Petri nets is the concept of a *net*, which consists of *places*, *transitions*, and *arcs* between them. Essentially, a net is a bipartite directed graph, meaning its vertices are divided into two disjoint subsets (places and transitions) such that every edge (arc) of the graph connects a vertex in one subset with one in the other. In a diagram, places are usually represented by circles, transitions are represented by rectangles or squares, and arcs are represented as directed arrows between them.

While the exact semantics of a particular class of Petri nets depends on its exact definition, generally, the places of a Petri net are intended to contain *tokens*, which can be removed or added by *firing* transitions. Arcs represent the connections between

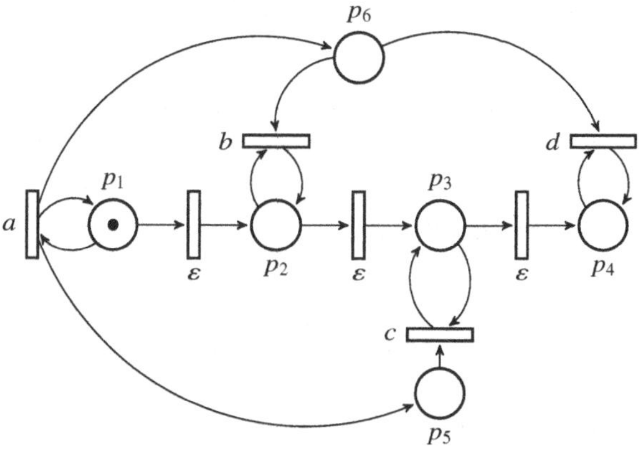

Fig. 8.4 A Petri net.

places and transitions—from the perspective of a transition, incoming arrows specify the places it receives tokens from, and outgoing arrows specify the places it sends tokens to.

Definition 8.12 A *net* is a triple $N = (P, T, F)$, where

- P and T are finite disjoint sets of *places* and *transitions*,
- $F \subseteq (P \times T) \cup (T \times P)$ is the *flow* relation.

Let $x \in (P \cup T)$. The set $\{y \mid yFx\}$, denoted by ${}^\bullet x$, is the *preset* of x, and the set $\{y \mid xFy\}$, denoted by $x^\bullet$, is the *postset* of x.

This definition provides the underlying structure of a Petri net, but it says nothing about its behavior. Thus, many different types of Petri nets can be built on top of Definition 8.12; however, we will focus our attention on the type most closely resembling multiset computation—*Place/Transition Petri nets*, more commonly referred to simply as *P/T Petri nets*.

Throughout this section, starting with the following definition, we will be using the symbol ω alongside natural numbers to represent an unlimited amount. To specify its semantics in various arithmetic expressions, we require ω to satisfy the following three rules:

1. $n < \omega$ for all $n \in \mathbb{N}$,
2. $m + \omega = m + \omega = \omega - m = \omega$ for all $m \in \mathbb{N} \cup \{\omega\}$,
3. $\sup(A) = \omega$ for any infinitely large set $A \subseteq \mathbb{N}$.

Definition 8.13 A *P/T Petri net* is a sextuple $N = (P, T, F, W, K, M_0)$, where

- (P, T, F) is a net,
- $W : F \to \mathbb{N}$ is a function specifying the *weight* of each arc,
- $K : P \to {}_0\mathbb{N} \cup \{\omega\}$ is a function specifying the *capacity* of each place, with ω representing an unlimited capacity,

- $M_0 : P \to {}_0\mathbb{N} \cup \{\omega\}$ is the *initial marking* of N, which must satisfy $M_0(p) \leq K(p)$ for all $p \in P$.

A *marking* of N is any function $M : P \to {}_0\mathbb{N} \cup \{\omega\}$ which satisfies $M(p) \leq K(p)$ for all $p \in P$.

A transition $t \in T$ is *enabled in M* (or M-enabled) if:

- $M(p) \geq W(p, t)$ for all $p \in {}^\bullet t$, and
- $M(p) + W(t, p) \geq K(p)$ for all $p \in t^\bullet$.

Let $W' : (P \times T) \cup (T \times P) \to {}_0\mathbb{N}$ be a total function defined as $W'(a, b) = W(a, b)$ for $(a, b) \in F$, and $W'(a, b) = 0$, otherwise.

In marking M, any M-enabled transition t can be fired, resulting in a new marking, M', defined as $M'(p) = M(p) - W'(p, t) + W'(t, p)$ for all places $p \in P$. We denote this relation between the markings and the transition as $M[t\rangle M'$.

We are now ready to start drawing parallels between Petri nets and multiset computation. The marking of a Petri net can be thought of as a multiset of its places, with the caveat that a place can be assigned the marking ω, representing infinite multiplicity. Transitions then behave exactly as production rules in a multiset grammar—the incoming arcs and their weights represent the left-hand side of the rule, while the right-hand side is represented by the outgoing arcs and their weights.

Following these observations, we can simulate derivations of multiset grammars using Petri nets, but it is worth noting that there are some aspects of the semantics of Petri nets that we do not need for this simulation, such as the capacities of places, or the possibility of a place being marked with infinitely many tokens.

Observe that languages accepted by variants of jumping automata are semilinear, so it is worth to consider their relation to Petri nets, because their reachability sets are semilinear as well (see Yen [2016]).

8.3 Permutation Grammars

This section modifies phrase-structure grammars by adding extra non-context-free rules, referred to as permutation rules, which can permutate substrings of sentential forms.

Definition 8.14 A phrase-structure grammar $G = (\Sigma, \Delta, P, S)$ is a *permutation grammar*, if for every $r \in P$ one of the following holds:

1. Either r is a non-erasing[2] context-free rule $r : A \to \gamma$, $A \in N$, $\gamma \in \Sigma^+$ with $N = \Sigma \cup \Delta$,
2. or r is a *permutation rule* $r : \alpha \to \beta$ where $\psi_\Sigma(\alpha) = \psi_\Sigma(\beta)$, $\alpha \neq \beta$.

[2] An exception can be made for a single rule of the form $S \to \varepsilon$, in which case S may not appear on the right-hand side of any rule in G.

The language generated by G, $L(G)$, is a *permutation language*. The family of all permutation languages is denoted by **Perm**.

Let $L = L(G)$ and let $P' \subseteq P$ denote the set of all context-free rules in P. Then, $G' = (\Sigma, \Delta, P', S)$ is a context-free grammar, and the language $L^B = L(G')$ is the *basis language* of L with regard to G.

For convenience, if there are two mutually inverse rules $\alpha \to \beta$ and $\beta \to \alpha$ in a grammar, we denote them both by $\alpha \leftrightarrow \beta$.

Lemma 8.5 CF ⊆ Perm ⊆ CS.

Proof Follows directly from the definition—clearly, any context-free grammar is also a permutation grammar (with no permutation rules), and as the production rules of a permutation grammar are all non-contracting, they cannot exceed context-sensitive grammars in power. □

In fact, it can quite easily be shown that the above inclusions are proper, by examining two example languages—a permutation language which is not context-free, and a context-sensitive language which is not a permutation language.

Example 8.3 Let $G_1 = (\{S, X, A, B, C\}, \{a, b, c\}, P_1, S)$, where P_1 contains the following rules:

- $S \to \varepsilon$, $S \to X$,
- $X \to ABCX$, $X \to ABC$,
- $A \to a$,
- $B \to b$,
- $C \to c$,
- $AB \leftrightarrow BA$,
- $AC \leftrightarrow CA$,
- $BC \leftrightarrow CB$.

This grammar generates the language $L_1 = L(G_1) = \{w \in \{a, b, c\}^* \mid \text{occur}(w, a) = \text{occur}(w, b) = \text{occur}(w, c)\}$.

L_1 is a well-known example of a non-context-free language, but as it is generated by a permutation grammar, it is a permutation language. An example of a basis language for this language is $L_1^B = \{abc\}^*$.

Example 8.4 Conversely, let us consider a counter-example of a permutation language. Let $L_2 = \{a^n b^n c^n \mid n \geq 1\}$. This is a well-known example of a context-sensitive language; however, it is not a permutation language, following from the fact that despite being infinite, it contains no infinite context-free subsets, which means that there is no possible basis language for L_2. Any permutation grammar capable of generating all the strings of L_2 will necessarily generate some strings not in L_2.

Theorem 8.11 **CF** $\subset$ **Perm** $\subset$ **CS**.

Proof Follows directly from Lemma 8.5 and the languages from Examples 8.3 and 8.4 satisfying $L_1 \in$ **Perm** – **CF** and $L_2 \in$ **CS** – **Perm**, respectively. □

Theorem 8.11 shows the position of permutation languages in the Chomsky hierarchy, between context-free languages and context-sensitive languages.

Definition 8.15 Let n be a positive integer. A permutation rule $\alpha \rightarrow \beta$ is of length n if $|\alpha| = |\beta| = n$. A permutation grammar containing permutation rules of length at most n is a *permutation grammar of order n*, and the language it generates is a *permutation language of order n*. The class of all such languages is denoted by $\mathbf{Perm}_n$.

The case for $n = 1$ in the above definition is not very interesting, as permutation rules of length 1 are context-free and offer no increase in generative power, meaning that $\mathbf{Perm}_1 = \mathbf{CF}$. However, Example 8.3 alone is enough to show that $\mathbf{CF} \subset \mathbf{Perm}_n$ for all $n \geq 2$. Furthermore, it follows immediately from Definition 8.15 that for any $n \geq 1$, $\mathbf{Perm}_n \subseteq \mathbf{Perm}$ and $\mathbf{Perm}_n \subseteq \mathbf{Perm}_{n+1}$. The following theorem shows that infinitely many of these inclusions are proper, leading to an infinite hierarchy of language classes contained strictly between context-free and context-sensitive languages.

Theorem 8.12 *For* $n \geq 1$, $\mathbf{Perm}_{4n-2} \subset \mathbf{Perm}_{4n-1}$.

Proof See Madejski [2014]. □

Chapter 9
Remarks on Applications and Their Perspectives

Principally and primarily, the objective of this book consists in building up a strictly mathematical body of knowledge concerning jumping automata and grammars. That is also why Parts II and III, which represent the heart of this book, have concentrated their attention solely on theoretical aspects of jumping formal models while refraining from their applications. The present three-section chapter somewhat relaxes this purely mathematical approach by briefly sketching some of these applications in order to demonstrate the use of these models in practice of the current and, perhaps even more significantly, future computer science. Specifically, Section 9.1 considers jumping automata as language-defining devices. Once again, it compares their behavior against classical sequential automata, and based upon this comparison, it demonstrates circumstances under which the use of the jumping versions has their obvious advantages over that of their sequential counterparts. Then, in a more specific and realistic way, Section 9.2 describes the use of jumping grammars as DNA-computational models in bioinformatics. Section 9.3 returns to theoretical computer scince, but it concetrates its attention on the applications of some of previously achieved results in this field. More specifically, it demonstrates how Lemma 4.28 gives rise to a brand new proof technique applicable to a variety of automata, which is shortly shown for classical finite automata.

9.1 Jumping Automata Used as Language-Defining Devices

First, let us start with the discussion on the reading behavior of jumping finite automata and the types of languages that these models accept. As we have stated in the introduction of this book (see Preface and Chapter 3), the main initial motivation behind the jumping concept was the fact that in modern computation methods we often process information in a discontinuous way, but classical formal models usually work in a strictly continuous way. Consequently, the description of modern computation methods with classical formal models can be in many cases inadequately complicated. Nonetheless, this does not mean that the proposed jumping finite automata can or should properly cover all needs of discontinuous information processing. Indeed, there are many formal models that try to adequately capture different parts of this phenomenon (see the introduction of Chapter 3). This diversity stems from the fact that, with these new models, we are trying to move some complex parts of the behavior of the computation methods into the core structure of the models. As a result, these new models are then more suited for specific tasks rather than for general purpose computing.

Let us take a closer look at the original jumping finite automata (JFA; see Chapter 3). Generally, these models can very easily compare quantities of input symbols. Observe the increasing complexity of crossed agreements on the number of symbols in the languages like:

- $\{w \in \{a, b\}^* \mid \text{occur}(w, a) = \text{occur}(w, b)\}$,
- $\{w \in \{a, b, c\}^* \mid \text{occur}(w, a) = \text{occur}(w, b) = \text{occur}(w, c)\}$, and
- $\{w \in \{a, b, c, d\}^* \mid \text{occur}(w, a) = \text{occur}(w, b) = \text{occur}(w, c) = \text{occur}(w, d)\}$.

Since classical formal models need to handle all symbols in the precise order, we quickly get out of the capabilities of even pushdown automata. On the other hand, there is almost no increase in the complexity of the model when we accept these languages with jumping finite automata. For instance, in Obare et al. [2019], JFAs are built to evaluate the counts of the occurrences of keywords in order to implement basic comprehension of tweets. Nonetheless, the discontinuous nature of jumping finite automata has its severe drawbacks when we try to accept languages that actually do require some precise reading order. We can see that JFAs cannot accept even the trivial language $\{ab\}$. This can be partially overcome with GJFAs for finite strings. However, there is no GJFA that could accept the simple regular language $\{a\}^*\{b\}^*$. Moreover, we pay a significant price for this partial reading order with the increased expected parsing complexity. According to Fernau et al. [2015, 2017] and using the standard complexity classes from computational complexity theory, we know that the parsing of JFAs falls into **NL**, whereas the parsing of GJFAs falls into **NP** and there exists a GJFA for which the parsing is **NP**-complete.

In this regard, we can see the behavior of original jumping finite automata mainly as a purely discontinuous reading.

If we take a look at the automata introduced in Chapter 4, we can say that these parallel versions of jumping finite automata explore controlled discontinuous reading behaviors.

n-Parallel Jumping Finite Automata

Considering models from Section 4.2, we can see that they precisely fit the description of parallelism (P.1) that increases the power of the model (see page 62). Moreover, the parallel mechanism integrated into the jumping finite automaton model can also partially control the reading order of the input sting. Indeed, we can use the initial splitting of the input string to establish some required fixed order between the separated parts.

Due to Theorems 4.29 and 4.30, we know that, with any number of reading heads, we can accept all languages accepted by the original jumping finite automata. Now, consider the following languages that cannot be accepted with the original jumping finite automata:

(1) $\{a\}^*\{b\}^*$, $\{a\}^*\{b\}^*\{c\}^*$, $\{a\}^*\{b\}^*\{c\}^*\{d\}^*$,
(2) $\{a^n b^n \mid n \geq 0\}$, $\{a^n b^n c^n \mid n \geq 0\}$, and $\{a^n b^n c^n d^n \mid n \geq 0\}$.

In group (1), the languages are clearly all regular. By contrast, in group (2), the languages get again quickly out of the capabilities of even push automata. It is possible to easily accept all these languages with n-PGJFAs; even if we restrict these automata so that the rules can contain only a single symbol. Nonetheless, each distinct section in the input string that occupies a specific position between other sections of the input string requires an additional reading head (see Lemma 4.16). Therefore, we can see that this technique of controlling the order of symbols has its limitations. For example, with a finite number of reading heads, we are not able to cover all regular languages.

As we have shown, there is a possibility to use the right n-jumping relation and thus extend the basic behavior of classical finite automata rather than jumping finite automata. In this case, we decrease the capabilities of the discontinuous reading but increase the capabilities of the continuous reading. In this mode, n-PGJFAs are still able to accept all languages introduced in the previous paragraph and also all regular languages, but they are no longer able to accept the previous languages like $\{w \in \{a, b, c\}^* \mid \text{occur}(w, a) = \text{occur}(w, b) = \text{occur}(w, c)\}$.

It should be a relatively simple task to simulate the parallel behavior of these automata. The model conveniently splits the input into several almost independent parts at the start, and then we need to synchronize only the number of performed steps by the reading heads. The synchronization behavior in this model is also easily reconfigurable, and thus it can be further fine-tuned for the specific needs of the given task. After such a reconfiguration, the changes in the power of the model should be also relatively easy to predict because many different versions of these types of synchronizations were already thoroughly studied in formal grammars (see Martín-Vide and Mitrana [2000]; Csuhaj-Varjú et al. [2000]; Martín-Vide et al. [2002]; Vollweiler and Otto [2014]).

Double-Jumping Finite Automata

Even though the previous n-PGJFAs are already able to partially control the discontinuous reading, we can see that they can ensure only a relatively simple reading order and that it can potentially require many additional reading heads. Therefore, let us take a look at the advanced reading modes with two reading heads from Section 4.1. We can see that the behavior of the jumping finite automaton model in these modes differs from n-PGJFAs: (1) the input string is not split into separate parts at the start; however, the heads cannot cross each other; (2) each head has its own reading direction; and (3) both heads always follow the same rule in a single step. These changes have a large impact on the jumping behavior and the families of accepted languages, but they help us to better control the discontinuous reading and combine it with the continuous reading. Indeed, we could make these modes more general if we removed (3), but the main focus of our research was to study the core behavior of these modes.

From our initial study, the unrestricted 2-jumping relation does not seem to be particularly interesting for further research. It offers a somewhat similar effect as n-PGJFAs, but the impact of rules on the accepted language is less clear because there is no clear point on the input tape which the heads cannot cross. Consequently, we were not able to link this mode to some specific behavior used in modern computation methods.

Considering the right-left and left-right 2-jumping relations, we see that the model loses almost all its jumping capabilities. Indeed, the reading heads can reposition themselves only during the initialization phase. However, this gives us a great control over the reading behavior since the model can still read from two distinct places at once and the position of the heads is always well predictable. Of course, the reduction of jumping capabilities has its drawbacks, and the model can now accept only a subfamily of linear languages. Nonetheless, these 2-jumping relations draw a nice connection to $5' \rightarrow 3'$ Watson–Crick finite automata, where this concept can be expanded and studied further.

Lastly, let us take a look at the right-right and left-left 2-jumping relations. On the first glance, their behavior may seem hard to grasp, but under a closer inspection we see here some similarities with methods that ensure data consistency or with other similar types of tasks. In computer science, there are many tasks where several processes may need to work with the same resources together in parallel and where we need to guarantee data consistency. To demonstrate our idea, let us consider database transactions. Typically, in a transaction, we load data from a database, we modify some values, and we save the data back to the database. These three operations together are not atomic, and the database may need to handle other requests at the same time. Thus, when we consider a stream of operations performed by the database, the load and store operations may not follow precisely after each other, but there cannot be a different operation between them that modifies the same data. If we consider the right-right 2-jumping relation, we see that it can accept input strings where the data (symbols) are not in some precise order but where two sequences read by the heads are interlined according to the rule that the first head cannot ever cross the second head. Of course, the model would need to be further appropriately tweaked to precisely match the needs of a real-world task.

Jumping $5' \rightarrow 3'$ Watson–Crick Finite Automata

Compared to the previous models, jumping $5' \rightarrow 3'$ Watson–Crick finite automata are already constructed with more specific types of tasks in mind. Furthermore, they offer a significant control of their reading behavior that can be adjusted with the rules in the model. We can explore languages accepted by these automata from two points of view.

First, from a purely theoretical point of view, we can observe how the rules of the model affects the reading behavior. Considering Lemma 4.26 and Theorem 4.42, we can see that if we use only certain types of rules, we can almost completely disable the jumping behavior of the model. Observe that the meeting point of the heads splits the input string into two parts in which different rules are used. The heads are able to jump in the given part only in cases in which both heads can read some symbols in this part according to the rules of the model. Thus, we can force the heads to read some parts of the input completely continuously. This allows us to accept all regular and even all linear languages. Furthermore, the model is also able to accept some of the more complicated languages with balanced quantities of symbols. Nonetheless, the model is not able to work in a completely discontinuous way, and thus there are more severe restrictions on the form of these languages compared to the original jumping finite automata.

Second, from a more practical point of view, let us consider the biology inspired nature of this model. As we have mentioned in Section 2.2.3, Watson–Crick finite automata work with double-stranded strings, each strand of the string has $5'$ end and $3'$ end, and the strands are combined together from opposite directions. Therefore, if we want both heads to read each strand from $5'$ end to $3'$ end, one head must read from left to right, and the other head must read from right to left. Since this is not a typical behavior of finite automata, it is useful to have special models for these tasks. There are already (full-reading) sensing $5' \rightarrow 3'$ Watson–Crick finite automata that work in this way, but their heads can read the input only in a continuous way. Our jumping version of $5' \rightarrow 3'$ Watson–Crick finite automata can cover situations where we want to search for sequences in DNA that are not necessarily continuous but rather interlined together from both directions. Of course, one of the imminent follow-up questions is the complexity of a parsing algorithm that would be based on this model. We do not have an answer yet, but we hope that the controlled nature of this discontinuous reading will help us find shortcuts for the parsing process.

9.2 Jumping Grammars Used as Models of DNA Computation

This section presents two biologically oriented case studies. First, Section 9.2.1 describes a simple case study that suggests how to make use of jumping scattered context derivation in DNA processing. Then, within the framework of genetic algorithms, Section 9.2.2 sketches an application of pure jumping grammars.

9.2.1 DNA Processing with Jumping Scattered Context Derivations

In this section, we add some remarks concerning application-related perspectives of jumping scattered context grammars (see Chapter 6) in terms of molecular biology—namely, DNA processing.

As already sketched, jumping grammars serve as grammatical models that allow us to explore information processing performed in a discontinuous way adequately and rigorously. Taking into account the way these grammars are conceptualized, we see that they are particularly useful and applicable under the circumstances that primarily concern the number of occurrences of various symbols or substrings rather than their mutual context.

Recall that a DNA is a molecule encoding genetic information by a repetition of four basic units called nucleotides—namely, guanine, adenine, thymine, and cytosine, denoted by letters G, A, T, and C, respectively. In terms of formal language theory, a DNA is described as a string over $\{G, A, T, C\}$; for instance,

$$GGGGAGTGGGATTGGGAGAGGGGTTTGCCCCGCTCCC$$

Suppose that a DNA-computing-related investigation needs to study all the strings that contain the same number of As and Cs so all As precede Cs; for instance, $AGGAATCGCGTC$ is a proper string, but $CGCACCGGTA$ is not. Consider the jumping scattered context grammar

$$G = (\{1, 2, 3, 4, G, A, T, C\}, \{G, A, T, C\}, P, 1)$$

with P containing rules

$$\begin{array}{cc}
(1) \rightarrow (23) & (3) \rightarrow (G3) \\
(3) \rightarrow (T3) & (3) \rightarrow (4) \\
(2, 4) \rightarrow (A2, 4C) & (2)|(4) \rightarrow (\varepsilon)
\end{array}$$

Assume that the grammar works under ${}_2\Rightarrow$. It first generates an arbitrary string of Gs and Ts, in which there are no restrictions, by classical regular rules, since ${}_2\Rightarrow$ does not change the behavior of context-free rules. However, then it comes the essential phase generating As and Cs. Indeed, the only context-sensitive rule under ${}_2\Rightarrow$ generates the equal number of As and Cs randomly scattered through the resulting sentence, but always with As preceding Cs. For instance, previously mentioned string $AGGAATCGCGTC$ can be generated by the following derivation.

$$
\begin{array}{llll}
1 & {}_2\!\Rightarrow 23 & & {}_2\!\Rightarrow 2G3 \\
 & {}_2\!\Rightarrow 2GG3 & & {}_2\!\Rightarrow 2GGT3 \\
 & {}_2\!\Rightarrow 2GGTG3 & & {}_2\!\Rightarrow 2GGTGG3 \\
 & {}_2\!\Rightarrow 2GGTGGT3 & & {}_2\!\Rightarrow 2GGTGGT4 \\
 & {}_2\!\Rightarrow A2GGTGGT4C & & {}_2\!\Rightarrow AGGA2TG4CGTC \\
 & {}_2\!\Rightarrow AGGAA2T4CGCGTC & & {}_2\!\Rightarrow^2 AGGAATCGCGTC
\end{array}
$$

As is obvious, under ${}_2\!\Rightarrow$, the grammar generates the language consisting of all the strings satisfying the above-stated requirements. Therefore, as we can see, jumping grammars may fulfill a useful role in studies related to DNA computing.

9.2.2 Genetic Algorithms Supported by Pure Jumping Grammars

While Chapter 7 discusses pure jumping grammars from a theoretical viewpoint, the present section deals with them from a more practical standpoint. Specifically, it sketches their use within the framework of genetic algorithms, into which a brief insight is given next.

Genetic algorithms (see Koza [1992]) are inspired by natural evolution, and they are customarily used to find an approximate solution of NP-hard problems. In a genetic algorithm, a solution of a problem is represented by a *chromosome*. A chromosome is a sequence of *genes*, where any gene can represent a property or a parameter, depending on what kind of a problem is to be solved. A set of chromosomes is called a *population*. An important part of a genetic algorithm is a *fitness function*. Its purpose is to map a chromosome to its *fitness value*, while its definition depends on the given problem. Based on its fitness value, it is decided whether an individual's chromosome survives or not.

Any genetic algorithm works as follows. In the beginning, an initial population is generated. Then, individuals with the best fitness values are selected. These individuals become *parents* of a new population. Two parental chromosomes, uv and xy, are combined to make a new pair of chromosomes, xv and uy, called an *offspring*. This process is called a *crossover*. Offsprings are then included into the new population. At times, some offspring genes may be randomly changed. This process is called *mutation*, and it introduces a diversity element. The new population is then used in the next iteration of the algorithm. The algorithm terminates when there are no notable differences between the new and old population.

In terms of the formal language theory, genes can be represented by symbols, chromosomes by strings, and population by finite languages. Suppose that chromosomes of individuals consist of genes a, b, and c, whereas only individuals with chromosomes with the number of as equal to the number of bs can survive. This can be expressed by the language

$$L_{ab} = \{w \in \{a, b, c\}^+ \mid \text{occur}(w, a) = \text{occur}(w, b)\}$$

generated by the sequential context-free pure jumping grammar

$$G_{ab} = (\{a, b, c\}, \{c \to cc, c \to ab, a \to a, b \to b\}, \{c\})$$

Of course, L_{ab} can be also generated by the unrestricted grammar

$$H_{ab} = (\{S, A, B, a, b, c\}, \{a, b, c\}, P, S)$$

with P containing rules

$$\begin{array}{ccc} S \to SS, & S \to AB, & S \to c, \\ SA \to AS, & SB \to BS, & AS \to SA, \\ AB \to BA, & BS \to SB, & BA \to AB, \\ A \to a, & B \to b & \end{array}$$

However, G_{ab} contains only four rules and, therefore, describes L_{ab} in a more economical way than H_{ab} does.

9.3 Theoretically Oriented Applications

Next, we explore how to use one of the presented proof techniques in a broader context. From the content of Sections 4.1, 4.2, and 4.4, it is clear that the parallel jumping finite automaton models require different approaches in proofs than classical finite automata that process the input in a continuous way. In Sections 4.1 and 4.2, it was still possible to cleverly adapt the more or less classical proof techniques for the new conditions. However, we can see that the proofs in Section 4.4 sometimes require a significantly different approach. More specifically, let us recall one of the crucial lemmas:

Lemma 4.28 (see page 112) *Let L be a language, and let $M = (Q, \Delta, \delta, q_0, F)$ be a jumping $5' \to 3'$ WKFA. If $L(M) = L$, there exists a constant k for M such that M accepts all $w \in L$ using only configurations that have their debt bounded by k.*

For convenience, we name it the *debt lemma*. Traditionally, when we want to show that a language is not accepted by the model in question, we use some form of a pumping lemma (see Rozenberg and Salomaa [1997a]). Nonetheless, pumping lemmas usually reason about the resulting language families and not about the actual models. This can become limiting in situations where we do not know how the resulting language family precisely looks like, but where we otherwise know a lot about the model that defines it. This situation seems to be quite common for jumping models because the details of the jumping behavior have a large impact on the resulting language family. If we look at other approaches, it is common in finite automata to say that the model has a finite state control and thus it cannot remember an infinite amount of information. This is, however, only an informal reasoning that is not used in formal proofs. We are not aware of any proof technique that would try to capture such an approach in a formal way. Therefore, we have developed the debt lemma that allows us to take into consideration both the language and also the model.

Even though the debt lemma was designed for the parallel jumping finite automaton model, it is not limited only for these types of models. We believe that it can be easily adapted for any finite automaton model that does not use an infinite storage and that reads the input at least semi-continuously. To demonstrate this in detail, we show how to adapt the debt lemma for classical finite automata.

First, we adapt the supporting definitions and lemmas for the new model:

Definition 4.11 (see page 111) Let $M = (Q, \Delta, \delta, q_0, F)$ be a jumping $5' \rightarrow 3'$ WKFA. Assuming some states $q, q' \in Q$ and a mutual position of heads $s \in \{\oplus, \ominus\}$, we say that q' is *reachable* from q and s if there exists a configuration (q, s, w_1, w_2, w_3) such that $(q, s, w_1, w_2, w_3) \curvearrowright^* (q', s', w_1', w_2', w_3')$ in M, $s' \in \{\oplus, \ominus\}$, $w_1, w_2, w_3, w_1', w_2', w_3' \in (\Delta \cup \{\#\})^*$.

Definition 9.1 Let $M = (Q, \Delta, \delta, q_0, F)$ be a finite automaton. Assuming some states $q, q' \in Q$, we say that q' is *reachable* from q if there exists a configuration qw such that $qw \Rightarrow^* q'$ in M, $w \in \Delta^*$.

Lemma 4.27 (see page 111) *For each jumping $5' \rightarrow 3'$ WKFA $M = (Q, \Delta, \delta, q_0, F)$ there exists a constant k such that the following holds. Let $q \in Q$ and $s \in \{\oplus, \ominus\}$ such that $f \in F$ is reachable from q and s. For every computation C that takes M from $(q_0, \oplus, \varepsilon, w, \varepsilon)$ to (q, s, w_1, w_2, w_3), $w \in \Delta^*$, $w_1, w_2, w_3 \in (\Delta \cup \{\#\})^*$, there exists $w' \in L(M)$ such that M starting with w' can reach q and $s' \in \{\oplus, \ominus\}$ by using the same sequence of $\oplus$/$\ominus$-reading steps as in C and the rest of w' can be processed with a limited number of additional steps bounded by k.*

Lemma 9.1 *For each finite automaton $M = (Q, \Delta, \delta, q_0, F)$ there exists a constant k such that the following holds. Let $q \in Q$ such that $f \in F$ is reachable from q. For every computation C that takes M from $q_0w_1w_2$ to qw_2, $w_1, w_2 \in \Delta^*$, there exists $w' \in L(M)$ such that M starting with w' can reach q by using the same sequence of steps as in C and the rest of w' can be processed with a limited number of additional steps bounded by k.*

Proof The proof is trivial. If f is reachable from q, there has to exist some sequence of state transitions from q to f that does not repeat states; this sequence is finite, and its maximum length is bounded by $k' = \text{card}(Q)$. Assume that the sequence reads $w_3 \in \Delta^*$. Set $w' = w_1w_3$. Clearly, $q_0w_1w_3 \Rightarrow^* qw_3 \Rightarrow^* f$ in M. Thus, $w' \in L(M)$ and there exists $k \leq k'$ for M that bounds the number of additional steps. □

Definition 4.12 (see page 112) Let $M = (Q, \Delta, \delta, q_0, F)$ be a jumping $5' \rightarrow 3'$ WKFA, where $\Delta = \{a_1, \dots, a_n\}$, and let $w \in \Delta^*$. We define the Parikh vector $o = (o_1, \dots, o_n)$ of processed (read) symbols from w in a configuration $\gamma = (q, s, w_1, w_2, w_3)$ of M reached from an initial configuration $(q_0, \oplus, \varepsilon, w, \varepsilon)$ of M as $o = \psi_\Delta(w) - \psi_\Delta(w_1w_2w_3)$, $q \in Q$, $s \in \{\oplus, \ominus\}$, $w_1, w_2, w_3 \in (\Delta \cup \{\#\})^*$. Using the Parikh mapping of $L(M)$, we define $\Delta(o) = \{\sum_{i=1}^{n}(m_i - o_i) \mid (m_1, \ldots, m_n) \in \psi_\Delta(L(M)),\ m_i \geq o_i,\ 1 \leq i \leq n\} \cup \{\infty\}$. Finally, we define the *debt* of the configuration γ of M as $\min \Delta(o)$.

Definition 9.2 Let $M = (Q, \Delta, \delta, q_0, F)$ be a finite automaton, where $\Delta = \{a_1, \ldots, a_n\}$, and let $w \in \Delta^*$. We define the Parikh vector $o = (o_1, \ldots, o_n)$ of processed (read) symbols from w in a configuration $\gamma = qw'$ of M reached from an initial configuration q_0w of M as $o = \psi_\Delta(w) - \psi_\Delta(w')$, $q \in Q$, $w' \in \Delta^*$. Using the Parikh mapping of $L(M)$, we define $\Delta(o) = \{\sum_{i=1}^{n}(m_i - o_i) \mid (m_1, \ldots, m_n) \in \psi_\Delta(L(M)),\ m_i \geq o_i,\ 1 \leq i \leq n\} \cup \{\infty\}$. Finally, we define the *debt* of the configuration γ of M as $\min \Delta(o)$.

Now, we can adapt the main debt lemma:

Lemma 9.2 *Let L be a language, and let $M = (Q, \Delta, \delta, q_0, F)$ be a finite automaton. If $L(M) = L$, there exists a constant k for M such that M accepts all $w \in L$ using only configurations that have their debt bounded by k.*

Proof By contradiction. Assume that there is no constant k for M such that M accepts all $w \in L$ using only configurations that have their debt bounded by k. Then, M can accept some $w \in L$ over a configuration for which the debt cannot be bounded by any k. Let $\Delta = \{a_1, \ldots, a_n\}$. Consider any configuration γ of M reached from an initial configuration q_0w of M. Let $o = (o_1, \ldots, o_n)$ be the Parikh vector of processed symbols from w in γ. First, assume that γ contains a state $q \in Q$ from which a final state $f \in F$ is reachable. Then, due to Lemma 9.1, there is $w' \in L(M)$ such that $\psi_\Delta(w') = (m_1, \ldots, m_n)$, $m_i \geq o_i$, $1 \leq i \leq n$, and $|w'| \leq \sum_{i=1}^{n}(o_i) + k'$, where k' is some constant for M. According to Definition 9.2, $w' \in L(M)$ implies $\min \Delta(o) \leq k'$. Second, assume that γ contains a state q from which no final state f is reachable. Then, by Definition 9.1, there is no computation that takes M from γ to a final accepting configuration. Thus, when M accepts w, it must be done over configurations with the debt $\leq k'$. However, that is a contradiction with the assumption that M can accept some $w \in L$ over a configuration for which the debt cannot be bounded by any k. □

Finally, we show how the adapted debt lemma can be used in the proof that finite automata cannot define the context-free language $L = \{a^n b^n \mid n \geq 0\}$.

Theorem 9.1 *There is no finite automaton M such that $L(M) = \{a^n b^n \mid n \geq 0\}$.*

Proof By contradiction. Let $L = \{a^n b^n \mid n \geq 0\}$, and let M be a finite automaton such that $L(M) = L$. Due to Lemma 9.2, there must exist a constant k for M such that M accepts all $w \in L$ using only configurations that have their debt bounded by k. Consider any $k \geq 0$. Let $w = a^{k+1}b^{k+1}$. Clearly, after reading a^k, the debt of the configuration is k, and no further reading is possible. Thus, we can see that M is not able to accept $w = a^{k+1}b^{k+1}$ when the debt of configurations of M is bounded by k. Since, for any k, $w \in L$, there is no constant k for M such that M accepts all $w \in L$ using only configurations that have their debt bounded by k. But that is a contradiction with the assumption that there is a finite automaton M such that $L(M) = \{a^n b^n \mid n \geq 0\}$. □

Of course, since pumping lemmas for regular languages are well known, it is not necessary to adapt the debt lemma for classical finite automata. However, we can see that the adaptation process is straightforward, and the resulting proof technique is simple to use.

Chapter 10
Summary and Bibliographical Remarks

The present book has been written for one reason and one reason only: a necessary update of the fundamental formal models used in the theory of computation for discontinuous information processing, which belongs to the most common ways of computation on today's mutually heavily cooperating multi-processor computers. In the previous century, most classical computer science methods were developed for continuous information processing; accordingly, their models work on the input string-represented information in a strictly continuous way from the left side to the right side of the string. Today's methods, however, often process information in an utterly discontinuous way so that they *jump* over large portions of the input information between individual computational steps. An adequate formalization of this modern computation, referred to as *jumping computation* in this book, necessitates an update of the original models so that the resulting updated models reflect jumping computation properly.

By no means, however, does this update intend, metaphorically speaking, to throw the baby out with the bathwater. That is, as almost always in the theory of computation, the models under update are categorizable into the two well-known categories—automata and grammars, whose updated versions are hence referred to as *jumping automata and grammars*, respectively. In fact, the *theory of jumping computation* usually selects and turns the most common types of the original models, such as finite automata and context-free grammars, to their jumping versions. Also, just like the classical theory of computation often simultaneously uses automata and grammars to formalize the same kind of computation, so does this new theory. In other words, the theory of jumping computation often formalizes the same kind of discontinuous computation by both jumping automata and jumping grammars, which represent, in essence, nothing but two different, but literary inseparable mathematical approaches to the same computational phenomenon. In the present book, any formalization like this is preceded by an explanation why its introduction is needed in order to cope with a particular type of real computational discontinuity occurring in computer science at present.

Primarily, from a theoretical standpoint, this book gives an account of crucially important concepts and results concerning jumping automata and grammars, whose investigation represents a vivid trend in the theory of computation as a whole. It pays a special attention to the power of these jumping models because it significantly differs from that of the classical models. To rephrase this difference in terms of the language families resulting from the jumping versions of automata and grammars, these families usually intersect the well-known language families of the Chomsky hierarchy. Apart from this topic, the book also discusses most other common themes of the language theory, such as closure properties and decidability. The principal goal of all this investigation consists in obtaining a systematized body of mathematically established knowledge concerning methods underlain by discontinuously working computation.

Secondarily, from a more practical standpoint, the text constantly struggles to maintain a balance between the theory of jumping models and the practice of discontinuous computation formalized by them. In fact, the text quite realistically illustrates the applicability of these models by several computer-science engineering techniques, such as the use of jumping automata as language-defining devices or the use of jumping grammars in bioinformatics.

The entire text of the present book is divided into the following four parts.

Part I, consisting of Chapters 1 and 2, gives an introduction to this book. Chapter 1 reviews basic mathematical notions used throughout the book. Chapter 2, in a greater detail, gives the essentials of formal language theory, including automata and grammars.

Part II consists of Chapters 3 and 4. Chapter 3 is solely devoted to one-head jumping finite automata as the very basic model of discontinuous computation. Chapter 4 explores jumping finite automata that have more than one head.

Part III, consisting of Chapters 5 through 7, covers jumping grammars as crucially important grammatical counterparts to jumping automata. Chapter 5 studies the jumping generation of language by classical grammars, which work in a strictly sequential way. Then, Chapter 6 discusses the same topic in terms of parallel grammars represented by scattered context grammars. Finally, Chapter 7 explores the jumping generation of language by pure sequential and parallel grammars, which use only one kind of symbols, namely, terminals.

Part IV is the present three-chapter part. Chapter 8 gives an outline of other important approaches to discontinuous computation and its formalizations. Chapter 9 sketches current applications of jumping automata and grammars and sketches its perspectives. Chapter 10 summarizes the book as a whole.

We close this chapter and, in fact, the entire book by placing jumping automata and grammars into a historical and bibliographical context. Numerous papers on these models have been published since their introduction. Rather than attempt to be encyclopedic, we recommend only those that appear to be of the greatest interest to the serious reader who finds this subject worth studying in the future.

Bibliographical History

We close this chapter and, in fact, the entire book by placing jumping automata and grammars into a historical and bibliographical context. Despite its short, about-ten-year-old development, a great number of papers about these models have been published. Rather than attempt to be encyclopedic, we next mention only the papers, which seem to fulfill the most important role during this brief development.

Historically, Meduna and Zemek [2012] opened the subject of this book by introducing the basic versions of jumping finite automata, and to a large extent, Chapter 3 is based upon this pioneer paper. This paper carefully explains how their introduction results from a real need of coping with discontinuous computation today, and it established their fundamental properties. Indeed, it covers all the major topics in the theory of automata and computation in terms of jumping finite automata.

Following the principal idea of models working in a jumping way described in Meduna and Zemek (2012), many more related studies have been published on this subject since. More specifically, up until now, the authors are aware of over 30 studies concerning jumping automata and grammars. Most of these models define the language families that intersect some of the well-known families of the Chomsky hierarchy, which is probably the fundamental reason for investigating them so intensively: an incomparability like this represents, in general, a rather unusual phenomenon in the language theory as a whole. Out of all these studies, we next bring the reader's attention to several papers, which arguably fulfill the most important role in this new vivid trend.

Immanuel and Thomas [2016b] modify jumping finite automata for accepting two-dimensional languages. It compares the family of languages accepted by these automata with other two-dimensional language families, such as the family of Siromoney matrix languages and that of picture languages. It also proves some of closure and decidability properties. Many additional variants and properties of two-dimensional JFAs are investigated by Immanuel and Thomas [2016a], Immanuel and Thomas [2017], and Madejski and Szepietowski [2017].

Wang and Li [2018] introduce new variants of restarting automata, where the move-right operation is replaced by a jump operation. The paper proves that the jumping restarting automata with auxiliary symbols can accept all growing context-sensitive languages, and for some special cases they are even more expressive. Next, the deterministic and monotone versions of the jumping restarting automata with auxiliary symbols have the same expressive power as the corresponding types of general restarting automata. Finally, it is demonstrated that for the types without auxiliary symbols, the general restarting automata are strictly more powerful than jumping restarting automata.

Kuperberg et al. [2019] introduce alternative versions of multi-head finite automata, which differs from the multi-head finite automata discussed in Chapter 4 of this book. In the alternative versions, tape heads can jump according to a prescribed set of rules, and they actually combine both categories of parallelisms (PA.1) and (PA.2) described in Chapter 4. Perhaps most importantly, from a general viewpoint, this paper demonstrates a close relation between the theory of jumping automata, logic, and algebra. More specifically, the paper expresses a fragment of a cyclic sequent proof system for Kleene algebra, which is viewed as a computational device for recognizing languages. The starting proof system is linear, and it defines precisely the regular languages. When adding the standard contraction rule, the expressivity raises and characterizes precisely the family of languages accepted by the alternative multi-head finite automata.

Fazekas et al. [2021] define and investigate two-way finite automata as modified versions of ordinary deterministic finite automata that can jump to the nearest letter they can read in either direction. The paper shows that these automata are more powerful than one-way jumping finite automata. It also proves several non-closure properties of the language family defined by these automata.

Mishra et al. [2021b] (non-reviewed on-line publication) introduce generalized linear one-way jumping finite automata, which make a jump after deleting an input substring, and after this deletion, they change the current state. Furthermore, they make a sequence of jumps only in one direction—either from left to right or from right to left. The paper shows that these automata are more powerful than one-way jumping finite automata defined in Chigahara et al. [2016]. The paper studies several special cases, such as generalized right linear one-way jumping finite automata and generalized left linear one-way jumping finite automata. Several closure properties of the language families defined by all these variants are established.

Mishra et al. [2021a] (non-reviewed on-line publication) study generalized linear one-way jumping finite automata, which strongly resemble the automata studied in Mishra et al. [2021b], except that they work on the input in a circular way. The paper shows that these automata are more powerful than one-way jumping finite automata. It considers several special versions of these automata and studies their power. Many closure properties of the language relationships resulting from these versions are demonstrated.

Fazekas et al. [2022] continue the discussion of one-way jumping finite automata that skip over letters for which they do not have any rules to apply instead of halting and rejecting the input. These automata are strictly more powerful than classical finite automata. The paper restricts these automata asymptotically similarly to the way computational complexity classes are bounded. It points out a gap between the resulting constant and linear jumping complexity classes. The paper demonstrates the existence of automata with logarithmic jumping complexity. It introduces a measure called sweep complexity in order to characterize the regular language family by one-way jumping machines with limited resources.

Beier and Holzer [2022] continue the discussion opened in Chigahara et al. [2016] by investigating nondeterministic one-way jumping finite automata. The paper considers a great number of versions of these machines with multiple initial states and various transition functions, such as spontaneous functions or λ-based functions. It achieves many results concerning the relationships of the associated language families defined by all these versions. These relationships are also established with respect to the Chomsky hierarchy.

Fazekas et al. [2022] study a variety of modified versions of jumping automata. In many respects, these modifications resemble common computational mechanisms used in classical automata, such as finite-state, pushdown or linear bounded automata. The paper concentrates on determining the language families resulting from these modified jumping automata. It establishes several new results, such as pumping lemmas, closure properties as well as non-closure properties. Based on these results, the paper develops methods to decide whether or not a given language belongs to some of these families. In addition, this paper establishes basic relationships, such as inclusion or incomparability, between these families.

Bibliography

This bibliographical list contains all the publications referenced in the text. In addition, it includes some more useful references concerning the theory of languages and computation, many of which were published prior to the introduction of jumping automata and grammars. These publications discuss formal models, such as finite automata or context-free grammars, which underlie their jumping versions. Therefore, the reader without a solid background in these areas can treat them as useful references for a comfortable explanation of the necessary terminology, outlined in Chapter 1 extremely succinctly.

Beier, S. and M. Holzer (2018a). Decidability of right one-way jumping finite automata. In *Developments in Language Theory, DLT 2018*, Volume 11088 of *LNCS*, pp. 109–120. Springer International Publishing.

Beier, S. and M. Holzer (2018b). Properties of right one-way jumping finite automata. In *Descriptional Complexity of Formal Systems, DCFS 2018*, Volume 10952 of *LNCS*, pp. 11–23. Springer International Publishing.

Beier, S. and M. Holzer (2019). Properties of right one-way jumping finite automata. *Theoretical Computer Science 798*, 78–94.

Beier, S. and M. Holzer (2022). Nondeterministic right one-way jumping finite automata. *Information and Computation 284*, 104687. Selected Papers from DCFS 2019, the 21st International Conference on Descriptional Complexity of Formal Systems.

Beier, S., M. Holzer, and M. Kutrib (2017). Operational state complexity and decidability of jumping finite automata. In *Developments in Language Theory, DLT 2017*, Volume 10396 of *LNCS*, pp. 96–108.

Beier, S., M. Holzer, and M. Kutrib (2019). Operational state complexity and decidability of jumping finite automata. *International Journal of Foundations of Computer Science 30*(1), 5–27.

Bordihn, H., H. Fernau, and M. Holzer (2002). Accepting pure grammars. *Publ. Math. 60*, 483–510.

Chatterjee, K. and K. S. Ray (2017). Watson–Crick pushdown automata. *Kybernetika 53*(5), 868–876.

Chigahara, H., S. Z. Fazekas, and A. Yamamura (2015). One-way jumping finite automata. In *The 77th Nat. Convention of IPSJ*.

Chigahara, H., S. Z. Fazekas, and A. Yamamura (2016). One-way jumping finite automata. *International Journal of Foundations of Computer Science 27*(03), 391–405.

Chomsky, N. (1959). On certain formal properties of grammars. *Information and Control 2*, 137–167.

Csuhaj-Varju, E., J. Dassow, J. Kelemen, and G. Păun (1994). *Grammar Systems: A Grammatical Approach to Distribution and Cooperation*. Gordon and Breach, Yverdon.

Csuhaj-Varjú, E., C. Martín-Vide, and V. Mitrana (2001). Multiset automata. In C. S. C. S. Calude, G. Păun, G. Rozenberg, and A. Salomaa (Eds.), *Multiset Processing*, Volume 2235 of *LNCS*, pp. 69–83. Springer Berlin Heidelberg.

Csuhaj-Varjú, E., C. Martín-Vide, V. Mitrana, and G. Vaszil (2000). Parallel communicating pushdown automata systems. *International Journal of Foundations of Computer Science 11*(4), 631–650.

Csuhaj-Varjú, E. and G. Vaszil (2010). Scattered context grammars generate any recursively enumerable language with two nonterminals. *Information Processing Letters 110*, 902–907.

Czeizler, E. and E. Czeizler (2006). A short survey on Watson–Crick automata. *Bull. EATCS 88*, 104–119.

Dassow, J. and G. Păun (1989). *Regulated Rewriting in Formal Language Theory*. Springer, Berlin.

Eğecioğlu, O., L. Hegedüs, and B. Nagy (2010). Stateless multicounter $5' \rightarrow 3'$ Watson–Crick automata. In *Fifth IEEE International Conference on Bio-Inspired Computing: Theories and Applications, BIC-TA 2010*, pp. 1599–1606.

Fazekas, S. Z., K. Hoshi, and A. Yamamura (2019). Enhancement of automata with jumping modes. In *AUTOMATA 2019*, Volume 11525 of *LNCS*, pp. 62–76.

Fazekas, S. Z., K. Hoshi, and A. Yamamura (2021). Two-way deterministic automata with jumping mode. *Theoretical Computer Science 864*, 92–102.

Fazekas, S. Z., K. Hoshi, and A. Yamamura (2022). The effect of jumping modes on various automata models. *Nat. Comput. 21*(1), 17–30.

Fazekas, S. Z., R. Mercaş, and O. Wu (2022). Complexities for jumps and sweeps. *Journal of Automata, Languages and Combinatorics 27*(1–3), 131–149.

Fazekas, S. Z. and A. Yamamura (2016). On regular languages accepted by one-way jumping finite automata. In *Eighth Workshop on Non-Classical Models of Automata and Applications (NCMA 2016) Short papers*, pp. 7–14.

Fernau, H. and A. Meduna (2003). A simultaneous reduction of several measures of descriptional complexity in scattered context grammars. *Information Processing Letters 86*(5), 235–240.

Fernau, H., M. Paramasivan, and M. L. Schmid (2015). Jumping finite automata: Characterizations and complexity. In F. Drewes (Ed.), *CIAA 2015*, Volume 9223 of *LNCS*, pp. 89–101. Springer.

Fernau, H., M. Paramasivan, M. L. Schmid, and V. Vorel (2017). Characterization and complexity results on jumping finite automata. *Theoretical Computer Science 679*, 31–52.

Freund, R., G. Paun, G. Rozenberg, and A. Salomaa (1997). Watson–Crick finite automata. In H. Rubin and D. H. Wood (Eds.), *DNA Based Computers, Proceedings of a DIMACS Workshop, Philadelphia, Pennsylvania, USA, June 23-25, 1997*, Volume 48 of *DIMACS Series in Discrete Mathematics and Theoretical Computer Science*, pp. 297–328. DIMACS/AMS.

Gabrielian, A. (1970). Pure grammars and pure languages. Technical Report Rep. C.S.R.R. 2027, Department of Computer Research, University of Waterloo, Waterloo, Ontario, Canada.

Ginsburg, S., S. A. Greibach, and M. Harrison (1967). One-way stack automata. *Journal of the ACM 14*(2), 389–418.

Greibach, S. A. and J. E. Hopcroft (1969). Scattered context grammars. *Journal of Computer and System Sciences 3*(3), 233–247.

Grune, D. and C. J. Jacobs (2008). *Parsing Techniques: A Practical Guide* (2nd ed.). Springer.

Hammer, J. and Z. Křivka (2022). Practical aspects of membership problem of Watson–Crick context-free grammars. In *Proceedings 12th International Workshop on Non-Classical Models of Automata and Applications*, Number 367, pp. 88–111. School of Computer Science and Engineering, University of New South Wales.

Harrison, M. A. (1978). *Introduction to Formal Language Theory*. Addison-Wesley, Boston.

Hauschildt, D. and M. Jantzen (1994). Petri net algorithms in the theory of matrix grammars. *Acta Informatica 31*, 719–728.

Hegedüs, L., B. Nagy, and O. Eğecioğlu (2012). Stateless multicounter $5' \longrightarrow 3'$ Watson–Crick automata: The deterministic case. *Natural Computing 11*(3), 361–368.

Herman, G. T. and G. Rozenberg (1975). *Developmental Systems and Languages*. Amsterdam: North-Holland Publishing Company.

Holzer, M., M. Kutrib, and A. Malcher (2009). Multi-head finite automata: Characterizations, concepts and open problems. In *The Complexity of Simple Programs 2008*, EPTCS, pp. 93–107.

Hopcroft, J. E., R. Motwani, and J. D. Ullman (2006). *Introduction to Automata Theory, Languages, and Computation* (3rd ed.). Addison-Wesley, Boston.

Hopcroft, J. E. and J. D. Ullman (1979). *Introduction to Automata Theory, Languages, and Computation*. Addison-Wesley, Boston.

Ibarra, O. H. (1970). Simple matrix languages. *Information and Control 17*, 359–394.

Immanuel, S. J. and D. G. Thomas (2016a). New results on two-dimensional jumping finite automata. *International Journal of Pure and Applied Mathematics 109*(5), 101–108.

Immanuel, S. J. and D. G. Thomas (2016b). Two-dimensional jumping finite automata. *Mathematics for Applications 5*(2), 105–122.

Immanuel, S. J. and D. G. Thomas (2017). Two-dimensional double jumping finite automata. *International Journal of Artificial Intelligence and Soft Computing 6*(3), 250–264.

Inoue, K., I. Takanami, A. Nakamura, and T. Ae (1979). One-way simple multihead finite automata. *Theoretical Computer Science 9*(3), 311–328.

Kasai, T. (1970). A hierarchy between context-free and context-sensitive languages. *Journal of Computer and System Sciences 4*, 492–508.

Kleijn, H. C. M. (1983). *Selective Substitution Grammars Based on Context-Free Productions*. Ph. D. thesis, Leiden University, Netherlands.

Kleijn, H. C. M. (1987). Basic ideas of selective substitution grammars. In A. Kelemenová and J. Kelemen (Eds.), *Trends, Techniques, and Problems in Theoretical Computer Science*, Volume 281 of *Lecture Notes in Computer Science*, pp. 75–95. Springer.

Kocman, R., Z. Křivka, and A. Meduna (2018). On double-jumping finite automata and their closure properties. *RAIRO-Theor. Inf. Appl. 52*(2-3-4), 185–199.

Kocman, R., Z. Křivka, A. Meduna, and B. Nagy (2022). A jumping $5' \rightarrow 3'$ Watson–Crick finite automata model. *Acta Informatica 59*(5), 557–584.

Kocman, R., Z. Křivka, and A. Meduna (2016). On double-jumping finite automata. In *Eighth Workshop on Non-Classical Models of Automata and Applications (NCMA 2016)*, Volume 321 of *OCG*, pp. 195–210.

Kocman, R. and A. Meduna (2016). On parallel versions of jumping finite automata. In *Proc. of the 2015 Federated Conf. on Softw. Dev. and Object Technol. (SDOT 2015)*, Volume 511 of *Adv. Intell. Syst. Comput.*, pp. 142–149. Springer.

Koza, J. R. (1992). *Genetic Programming: On the Programming of Computers by Means of Natural Selection*. The MIT Press, Cambridge, Massachusetts.

Kudlek, M., C. Martín-Vide, and G. Păun (2000). Toward FMT (formal macroset theory). In *Pre-proceedings of the Workshop on Multiset Processing*, pp. 149–158. Curtea de Arges.

Kuperberg, D., L. Pinault, and D. Pous (2019). Cyclic proofs and jumping automata. In *Foundations of Software Technology and Theoretical Computer Science 2019*.

Kuske, D. and P. Weigel (2004). The role of the complementarity relation in Watson–Crick automata and sticker systems. In *Developments in Language Theory*, Volume 3340 of *Lecture Notes in Computer Science*, pp. 272–283. Springer Berlin Heidelberg.

Křivka, Z., J. Kučera, and A. Meduna (2018). Jumping pure grammars. *The Computer Journal 62*(1), 30–41.

Křivka, Z., C. Martín-Vide, A. Meduna, and K. G. Subramanian (2014, May 28-30). A variant of pure two-dimensional context-free grammars generating picture languages. In *Proceedings of 16th International Workshop on Combinatorial Image Analysis (IWCIA 2014)*, Brno, Czech Republic, pp. 123–133. Springer.

Křivka, Z. and A. Meduna (2015). Jumping grammars. *International Journal of Foundations of Computer Science 26*(6), 709–731.

Křivka, Z. and A. Meduna (2021). Scattered context grammars with one non-context-free production are computationally complete. *Fundamenta Informaticae 179*(4), 361–384.

Křoustek, J., S. Židek, D. Kolář, and A. Meduna (2011). Scattered context grammars with priority. *International Journal of Advanced Research in Computer Science 2*(4), 1–6.

Langer, M. and A. Kelemenová (2012). Positioned agents in eco-grammar systems with border markers and pure regulated grammars. *Kybernetika 48*(3), 502–517.

Leupold, P. and A. Meduna (2010). Finitely expandable deep PDAs. In *Automata, Formal Languages and Algebraic Systems: Proceedings of AFLAS 2008*, pp. 113–123. Hong Kong University of Scinece and Technology.

Levitina, M. (1972). On some grammars with global productions. *Akad. Nauk SSSR Nauchno-Tekhn. Inform. Ser. 2*(3), 32–36.

Loos, R. and B. Nagy (2011). On the concepts of parallelism in biomolecular computing. *Triangle 6 (Languages: Bioinspired Approaches)*, 109–118.

Madejski, G. (2014). Infinite hierarchy of permutation languages. *Fundamenta Informaticae 130*, 263–274.

Madejski, G. (2016). Jumping and pumping lemmas and their applications. In *Proceedings of NCMA 2016 - 8th Workshop on Non-Classical Models of Automata and Applications*, pp. 25–34.

Madejski, G. and A. Szepietowski (2017). Membership problem for two-dimensional jumping finite automata. In *Ninth Workshop on Non-Classical Models of Automata and Applications, NCMA 2017 (Short Papers)*, pp. 33–40.

Mahalingam, K., U. K. Mishra, and R. Raghavan (2020). Watson–Crick jumping finite automata. *International Journal of Foundations of Computer Science 31*(07), 891–913.

Mahalingam, K., R. Raghavan, and U. K. Mishra (2019). Watson–Crick jumping finite automata. In *Theory and Applications of Models of Computation, TAMC 2019*, Volume 11436 of *LNCS*, pp. 467–480. Springer International Publishing.

Martín-Vide, C., A. Mateescu, and V. Mitrana (2002). Parallel finite automata systems communicating by states. *International Journal of Foundations of Computer Science 13*(05), 733–749.

Martín-Vide, C. and V. Mitrana (2000). Parallel communicating automata systems — a survey. *Korean Journal of Applied Mathematics and Computing 7*(2), 237–257.

Martín-Vide, C. and G. Păun (2000). *The Complete Linguist: A Collection of Papers in Honour of Alexis Manaster Ramer*, Chapter Normal forms for Watson–Crick finite automata, pp. 281–296. Lincom Europa.

Masopust, T. and A. Meduna (2009). Descriptional complexity of three-nonterminal scattered context grammars: An improvement. In *Proceedings of 11th International Workshop on Descriptional Complexity of Formal Systems*, pp. 235–245. Otto-von-Guericke-Universität Magdeburg.

Maurer, H. A., A. Salomaa, and D. Wood (1980). Pure grammars. *Information and Control 44*(1), 47–72.

Mayer, O. (1972). Some restrictive devices for context-free grammars. *Information and Control 20*, 69–92.

Meduna, A. (2000). *Automata and Languages: Theory and Applications*. Springer, London.

Meduna, A. (2006). Deep pushdown automata. *Acta Informatica 2006*(98), 114–124.

Meduna, A. (2007). *Elements of Compiler Design*. Auerbach Publications, Boston.

Meduna, A. (2014). *Formal Languages and Computation: Models and Their Applications*. Taylor & Francis, New York.

Meduna, A. and T. Masopust (2007). Self-regulating finite automata. *Acta Cybernetica 18*(1), 135–153.

Meduna, A. and O. Soukup (2017a). Jumping scattered context grammars. *Fundam. Inf. 152*(1), 51–86.

Meduna, A. and O. Soukup (2017b). *Modern Language Models and Computation: Theory with Applications*. Springer.

Meduna, A. and J. Techet (2010). *Scattered Context Grammars and their Applications*. WIT Press, Southampton.

Meduna, A. and M. Švec (2005). *Grammars with Context Conditions and Their Applications*. Wiley, New Jersey.

Meduna, A. and P. Zemek (2012). Jumping finite automata. *International Journal of Foundations of Computer Science 23*(7), 1555–1578.

Meduna, A. and P. Zemek (2014). *Regulated Grammars and Automata*. Springer US.

Mishra, U. K., K. Mahalingam, and R. Raghavan (2021a). Generalized circular one-way jumping finite automata. *CoRR abs/2106.03852*.

Mishra, U. K., K. Mahalingam, and R. Raghavan (2021b). Generalized linear one-way jumping finite automata. *CoRR abs/2106.02937*.

Mishra, U. K., K. Mahalingam, and R. Raghavan (2021c). Watson–Crick jumping finite automata: Combination, comparison and closure. *The Computer Journal*. bxaa166.

Mohamad Zulkufli, N. L., S. Turaev, M. I. Mohd Tamrin, and A. Messikh (2016). Generative power and closure properties of Watson–Crick grammars. *Applied Computational Intelligence and Soft Computing 2016*, 1–12.

Mohamad Zulkufli, N. L., S. Turaev, M. I. Mohd Tamrin, and A. Messikh (2018). Watson–Crick context-free grammars: Grammar simplifications and a parsing algorithm. *The Computer Journal 61*(9), 1361–1373.

Mohamad Zulkufli, N. L., S. Turaev, M. I. M. Tamrin, and A. Messikh (2017). The computational power of Watson–Crick grammars: Revisited. In *Bio-inspired Computing – Theories and*

Applications, Volume 681 of *Communications in Computer and Information Science*, Singapore, pp. 215–225. Springer Singapore.

Nagy, B. (2008). On $5' \rightarrow 3'$ sensing Watson–Crick finite automata. In M. H. Garzon and H. Yan (Eds.), *DNA Computing, 13th International Meeting on DNA Computing, DNA13, Memphis, TN, USA, June 4-8, 2007, Revised Selected Papers*, Volume 4848 of *Lecture Notes in Computer Science*, pp. 256–262. Springer.

Nagy, B. (2009). On a hierarchy of $5' \rightarrow 3'$ sensing WK finite automata languages. In *Computability in Europe 2009: Mathematical Theory and Computational Practice, CiE 2009*, pp. 266–275.

Nagy, B. (2010). $5' \rightarrow 3'$ sensing Watson–Crick finite automata. In G. Fung (Ed.), *Sequence and Genome Analysis II – Methods and Applications*, pp. 39–56. iConcept Press.

Nagy, B. (2012). A class of 2-head finite automata for linear languages. *Triangle (Languages: Mathematical Approaches) 8*, 89–99.

Nagy, B. (2013). On a hierarchy of $5' \rightarrow 3'$ sensing Watson–Crick finite automata languages. *J. Log. Comput. 23*(4), 855–872.

Nagy, B. (2020). $5' \rightarrow 3'$ Watson–Crick pushdown automata. *Information Sciences 537*, 452–466.

Nagy, B., L. Hegedüs, and O. Eğecioğlu (2011). Hierarchy results on stateless multicounter $5' \rightarrow 3'$ Watson–Crick automata. In *Advances in Computational Intelligence: 11th International Work-Conference on Artificial Neural Networks, IWANN 2011*, Volume 6691 of *LNCS*, pp. 465–472. Springer.

Nagy, B. and Z. Kovács (2019). On simple $5' \rightarrow 3'$ sensing Watson–Crick finite-state transducers. In *Eleventh Workshop on Non-Classical Models of Automata and Applications (NCMA 2019)*, pp. 155–170.

Nagy, B. and F. Otto (2019). Two-head finite-state acceptors with translucent letters. In *SOFSEM 2019*, Volume 11376 of *LNCS*, pp. 406–418.

Nagy, B. and F. Otto (2020). Linear automata with translucent letters and linear context-free trace languages. *RAIRO-Theor. Inf. Appl. 54*(3), 23.

Nagy, B. and S. Parchami (2020). On deterministic sensing $5' \rightarrow 3'$ Watson–Crick finite automata: a full hierarchy in 2detLIN. *Acta Informatica 58*(3), 153–175.

Nagy, B., S. Parchami, and H. Mir-Mohammad-Sadeghi (2017). A new sensing $5' \rightarrow 3'$ Watson–Crick automata concept. In *AFL 2017*, Volume 252 of *EPTCS*, pp. 195–204.

Novotný, M. (2002). Construction of pure grammars. *Fundam. Inform. 52*(4), 345–360.

Obare, S., A. Ade-Ibijola, and G. Okeyo (2019). Jumping finite automata for tweet comprehension. In *International Multidisciplinary Information Technology and Engineering Conference (IMITEC)*, pp. 7. IEEE.

Parchami, S. and B. Nagy (2018). Deterministic sensing $5' \rightarrow 3'$ Watson–Crick automata without sensing parameter. In *UCNC 2018*, Volume 10876 of *LNCS*, pp. 173–187.

Parikh, R. J. (1966). On context-free languages. *J. ACM 13*(4), 570–581.

Păun, G., G. Rozenberg, and A. Salomaa (1998). *DNA Computing: New Computing Paradigms*, Chapter Watson–Crick Automata, pp. 151–186. Springer Berlin Heidelberg.

Rosebrugh, R. D. and D. Wood (1973). A characterization theorem for n-parallel right linear languages. *Journal of Computer and System Sciences 7*, 579–582.

Rosebrugh, R. D. and D. Wood (1974). Image theorem for simple matrix languages and n-parallel languages. *Mathematical Systems Theory 8*(2), 150–155.

Rosebrugh, R. D. and D. Wood (1975). Restricted parallelism and right linear grammars. *Utilitas Mathematica 7*, 151–186.

Rosenberg, A. L. (1965). On multi-head finite automata. In *6th Annual Symposium on Switching Circuit Theory and Logical Design, SWCT 1965*, pp. 221–228.

Rozenberg, G. and P. G. Doucet (1971). On 0L-languages. *Information and Control 19*(4), 302–318.

Rozenberg, G. and A. Salomaa (1980). *Mathematical Theory of L Systems*. Academic Press, Orlando.

Rozenberg, G. and A. Salomaa (1986). *The Book of L*. Springer-Verlag, New York.

Rozenberg, G. and A. Salomaa (Eds.) (1997a). *Handbook of Formal Languages, Vol. 1: Word, Language, Grammar*. Springer, New York.

Rozenberg, G. and A. Salomaa (Eds.) (1997b). *Handbook of Formal Languages, Vol. 2: Linear Modeling: Background and Application*. Springer, New York.

Russell, S. and P. Norvig (2002). *Artificial Intelligence: A Modern Approach* (2nd ed.). Prentice-Hall, New Jersey.

Salomaa, A. (1973). *Formal Languages*. Academic Press, London.

Shaull, A. and Y. Omer (2023). Jumping automata over infinite words. In F. Drewes and M. Volkov (Eds.), *Developments in Language Theory - 27th International Conference, DLT 2023, Umeå, Sweden, June 12-16, 2023, Proceedings*, Volume 13911 of *Lecture Notes in Computer Science*, pp. 9–22. Springer.

Sipser, M. (2006). *Introduction to the Theory of Computation* (2nd ed.). PWS Publishing Company, Boston.

Siromoney, R. (1971). Finite-turn checking automata. *Journal of Computer and System Sciences 5*, 549–559.

Siromoney, R. and K. Krithivasan (1974). Parallel context-free languages. *Information and Control 24*(2), 155–162.

Skyum, S. (1974). Parallel context-free languages. *Information and Control 26*(3), 280–285.

Subramanian, K., S. Hemalatha, and I. Venkat (2012). On Watson–Crick automata. In *Proceedings of the Second International Conference on Computational Science, Engineering and Information Technology*, CCSEIT '12, New York, NY, USA, pp. 151–156. Association for Computing Machinery.

Ďuriš, P. and J. Hromkovič (1983). One-way simple multihead finite automata are not closed under concatenation. *Theoretical Computer Science 27*(1), 121–125.

Vollweiler, M. and F. Otto (2014). Systems of parallel communicating restarting automata. *RAIRO - Theoretical Informatics and Applications - Informatique Théorique et Applications 48*(1), 3–22.

Vorel, V. (2016). Two results on discontinuous input processing. In *Descriptional Complex. of Form. Syst. (DCFS 2016)*, Volume 9777 of *LNCS*, pp. 205–216. Springer.

Vorel, V. (2017). Two results on discontinuous input processing. *Journal of Automata, Languages and Combinatorics 22*(1–3), 189–203.

Vorel, V. (2018). On basic properties of jumping finite automata. *International Journal of Foundations of Computer Science 29*(1), 1–15.

Wang, Q. and Y. Li (2018). Jumping restarting automata. In *Tenth Workshop on Non-Classical Models of Automata and Applications, NCMA 2018*, Volume 332 of *books@ocg.at*, pp. 181–196. Osterreichische Computer Gesellschaft.

Wood, D. (1973). Properties of n-parallel finite state languages. *Utilitas Mathematica 4*, 103–113.

Wood, D. (1975). m-parallel n-right linear simple matrix languages. *Utilitas Mathematica 8*, 3–28.

Wood, D. (1977). n-linear simple matrix languages and n-parallel linear languages. *Rev. Roum. de Math. Pures et Appl.*, 408–412.

Wood, D. (1987). *Theory of Computation: A Primer*. Addison-Wesley, Boston.

Yen, H.-C. (2016). Petri nets and semilinear sets (extended abstract). In A. Sampaio and F. Wang (Eds.), *Theoretical Aspects of Computing – ICTAC 2016*, Cham, pp. 25–29. Springer International Publishing.

Indices

The rest of this book contains two indices to help the reader with a quick orientation in the text. First, it gives the index to major language families together with their symbolic denotation. This index is followed by the subject index, which closes the entire text.

Index to Key Language Families

This index includes the basic versions of all key language families used in the book while excluding their special versions, which are to be found (nearly or exactly) on the same page as the basic versions and which are usually distinguished by subscripts appended to the basic version denotation. For instance, the index includes **JFA**, which denotes the family accepted by JFAs defined on page 39, but it excludes $\mathbf{JFA}^{-\varepsilon}$, which denotes the family accepted by JFAs without ε-rules defined on page 39.

Subject Index

Printed in the United States
by Baker & Taylor Publisher Services